FOUR
OF A
KIND

Also by Erma Bombeck

At Wit's End

"Just Wait Till You Have Children
of Your Own!"

I Lost Everything
in the Post-Natal Depression

But the need to hold a book in my arms was strong, and in 1983, *Motherhood—The Second Oldest Profession* came along. I love it best.

It was the culmination of twenty years of writing about the women I admire and respect the most in this world—Mothers. But other dimensions were added to the laughter. There were women who had feelings of pain, loneliness, joy, emptiness, pride, fulfillment, anger, gratitude, and wonderment.

They are all here in this hernia edition of *Four of a Kind*.

Nearly a decade of family humor.

It seems I have sat in a million bookstores personalizing my "children" and sending them out into homes. And that has been the rewarding part. The teen-ager in Richmond with tears streaming down her face who said her mother had cancer and my books were the only thing that made her laugh. The Yuppie mother in Denver who picked a pacifier off the floor, jammed it into her son's mouth, and said tiredly, "And I thought you wrote fiction!"

And the two elderly women who stood in line in New Jersey and observed, "Erma Bombeck writes for men and women." "I know," said one of them, "She's probably one of the few bisexual writers in the country today."

My agent and my editor said to me the other day, "Don't you miss the sound of pages turning on a new book?"

Animals! I just got my shape back.

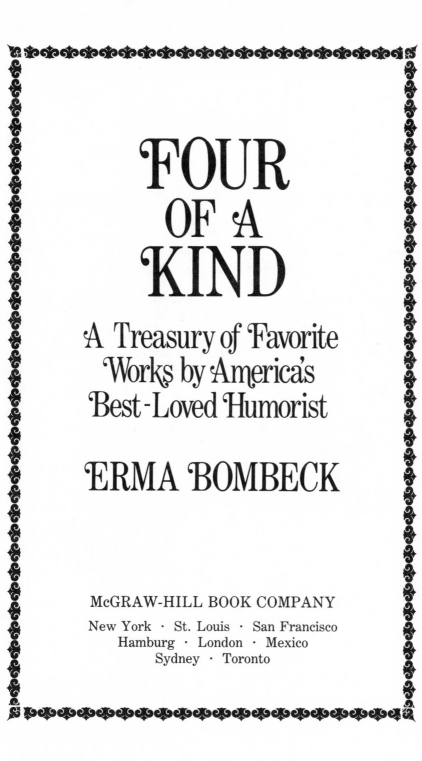

FOUR
OF A
KIND

A Treasury of Favorite
Works by America's
Best-Loved Humorist

ERMA BOMBECK

McGRAW-HILL BOOK COMPANY

New York · St. Louis · San Francisco
Hamburg · London · Mexico
Sydney · Toronto

Published by The Reader's Digest Association, Inc., 1991,
by permission of McGraw-Hill Publishing Co.

1 2 3 4 5 6 7 8 9 HAL HAL 8 7 6 5

LIBRARY OF CONGRESS CATALOGING IN PUBLICATION DATA

Bombeck, Erma.
  Four of a kind.

  I. Title.
PS3552.059A6 1985   814'.54   85-11390
ISBN 0-07-006456-3

BOOK DESIGN BY KATHRYN PARISE

Contents ❧❧❧

Foreword ❧❧❧

Between the years of 1976 and 1983, I gave birth to four healthy, planned volumes of humor. They ranged in size from 175 to 203 pages.

The offspring were divinely conceived. My agent, Aaron Priest, and my editor at McGraw-Hill, Gladys Carr, assisted at the delivery.

If I speak of these volumes as "children," it is because there are a lot of similarities. They're something you always put off until you're sure your marriage is stable. When you discover you are "with book," there is ecstasy at first, heightened by a lot of attention and an advance check. By the third set of rewrites, when you have seen none of your friends in months and the "baby" has reached epic proportions, you bargain with God, "If you deliver me a healthy book, I promise, I will clean my oven."

By the time the name is picked out, the cover approved, and Donahue has been invited to the birth, you are ready to see what you've been carrying around for nine months. You gently peek under the cover.

Is it a hit or a remainder?

Mothers love all of their children. You know that. But I must tell you, I loved *The Grass Is Always Greener Over the Septic Tank* best.

It represented for me the best part of my life. The time when I was living in the suburbs of Centerville, Ohio, between Helen and Charmaine, with Marianna, Lil, Mary Ellen, and Annie only a Primal Scream away.

"Grass" was born kicking and screaming in 1976 with a lusty voice that was heard by every man who had ever lusted for a car that outlasted the payments, every mother who suffered from the car-pool crouch, and every family who endured a vacation where the oldest blew on the hairs in Daddy's ears, the youngest announced she had spots on her stomach, and the dog threw up in the picnic basket.

Before its birth, I referred to it as "Confessions of a Girl Scout Cookie Captain." However, when I saw it, I called my agent and said, "Its name is 'The Grass Is Always Greener Over the Septic Tank.'" He said, "Cute, but is that true?" I said, "Trust me. Haven't you enjoyed the salad at our house?"

"Grass" was two years old when *If Life Is a Bowl of Cherries —What Am I Doing in the Pits?* was born. I must tell you, I loved "Cherries" the best. It was a story of survival and allowed me to dump all my frustrations into one volume. Why did the washer return one sock out of every pair? What was the real story behind oversexed coat hangers? Was I the only woman in North America with a phantom child living with her called "I dunno"?

I got a little careless with the success of "Cherries" and became "with book" almost immediately. One year later, *Aunt Erma's Cope Book* arrived on the literary scene. It was to become my absolute favorite book. I was drowning in self-help tomes telling me there was a draft in my open marriage and that guilt was the only gift that keeps giving. "Cope" gave me an opportunity to stand back, take a long look at them, and put them in some perspective.

I needed a rest. Juggling three siblings had taken its toll on me. I read, played a little tennis, took a vacation, and listened to Jane Fonda cassettes.

The Grass Is Always Greener Over The Septic Tank

For
Marianna, Helen, Charmaine,
Marie, Lil, Mary Ellen, and Annie,
who when I was drowning in a car pool
threw me a line . . . always a funny one

Contents ෴

Foreword ❧❧

Soon after the West was settled, Americans became restless and began to look for new frontiers.

Bored with the conveniences of running water, electricity, central heating, rapid communication, and public transportation, they turned to a new challenge . . . the suburbs.

The suburbs were discovered quite by accident one day in the early 1940's by a Welcome-Wagon lady who was lost. As she stood in a mushy marshland, her sturdy Red Cross shoes sinking into the mire, she looked down, and exclaimed, "It's a septic tank. I've discovered the suburbs!"

News of the discovery of a septic tank spread and within weeks thirty million city dwellers readied their station wagons and began the long journey to the edge of town in search of a bath and a half and a tree.

It wasn't easy for the first settlers. They planted trees and crabgrass came up. They planted schools and taxes came up. Surveyors planted stakes and they disintegrated.

The first winter, more than half of the original settlers perished. Some lost their way in cul-de-sacs and winding streets with the same name trying to find their way home.

Other poor devils died of old age trying to merge onto the freeway to the city. One was attacked by a fast-growing evergreen that the builder planted near his front door. (They named a high school after him.)

There wasn't a day that went by that they weren't threatened by forces from the city: salesmen of storm doors, Tupperware and Avon ladies, traffic lights, encyclopedia salesmen, Girl Scout cookie pushers, and Golden Arches everywhere.

The survival by at least one family of PTA's, garage sales, car pools, horse privileges, Sunday drivers, Little Leagues, and lights from the shopping center is what this book is all about.

It traces the migration of the Bombeck family from their modest—but pathetic—apartment in the heart of the city to a plat house (one original and 216 carbons) just outside the city limits.

They made the trip with a son who has spoken four words in five years ("I get the window"), their daughter who sleeps with a baton, and a toddler who has never known anything but apartment living and consequently does not own a pair of hard shoes.

It took a week to load their station wagon and after the good-byes they settled back to enjoy their new adventure.

"Look, honey, sit down on the seat. Daddy cannot drive with scissors in his ear. No, I don't know how long it has been since I cut the hairs in my ears! Erma, for God's sake, find something for him to do."

"Are we there yet?"

"It's my window and I say when it goes down and when it goes up. Mom! Isn't it *my* window?"

"You did not see a cow and if you mark it down I'm going to mark down a chariot on my list. A chariot gives me fifty points."

"I'm hungry."

"Start the motor. They'll be better when we get moving."

"Erma, do you smell something? Check the dog."

"The dog checks out."

"Check the feet of the kids."

"They all check."

"Check your own."

"You check yours first."

"Mom! I'm gonna be sick."

"You are not going to be sick and that's my final word!"

"Boys! Get your hands in this car or they'll blow off."

"How many kids had their hands blown off last year?"

"Too many to count."

"Did you ever see a hand that blew off on your windshield, Dad?"

"Erma, for God's sake find something for the kids to do."

"Mom! Andy took a bite out of a cookie and put it back. I'm telling."

"You tell about the cookies and I'm telling about your chicken bone collection."

"Stop the car! That's what we smell."

"Dad, when you get mad the veins in your nose swell up."

"I thought you were going to give them a sedative. How much farther?"

"We've got a hairpin, a thumbnail and a breathmint to go, according to this map."

"Can't you interpret a simple road map?"

"Don't shout at me, Bill, I can't handle shouting today."

"I'm not shouting, I'm just suggesting that you are a high-school graduate and are capable of interpreting a simple scale on a map."

"Hey, Dad, I just saw a hand fly by."

"What day is it?" I asked. "I don't know how much longer I can stand the driving, the confinement, the loneliness. Not being able to talk to anyone. Bill, maybe we shouldn't have come."

"It won't be long now!" he said.

The Bombecks made it to the suburbs in their station wagon on June 9th. It was the longest fifty-five-minute drive any of them had ever endured.

1 〰〰

Station Wagons . . . Ho!

Staking Out a Claim

It was either Thomas Jefferson—or maybe it was John Wayne—who once said, "Your foot will never get well as long as there is a horse standing on it."

It was logic like this that attracted thirty million settlers to the suburbs following World War II.

The suburbs were a wilderness with nothing to offer but wide, open spaces, virgin forests, and a cool breeze at night that made you breathe deep, close your eyes and sigh, "My God! Who's fertilizing with sheep dip?"

My husband held out against migration for as long as he could. Then one day we heard from our good friends, Marge and Ralph, who, together with their two children, set out in one of the first station wagons to a housing development thirty miles south of the city.

As Marge wrote, "We reached the suburbs on the 14th. There was no water and no electricity in our house so we had to hole up in a Holiday Motel for three days. The pool wasn't even heated.

"The yard is barren and there are no sidewalks. Mud is everywhere. There is no garbage pickup, our old stove won't fit in the new hole, and the general store has never heard of oregano.

"We have aluminum foil at the windows to keep the sun from fading the children. I feel like a turkey. We have to claim our mail at the post office a mile and a half away. There is no super. We have our own washer and dryer which don't require quarters. I understand, however, that at the end of the month, there is something called a utility bill that is presented to us.

"There are some bright spots. We have a bath and a half. It is wonderful not to have to take numbers any more. Tomorrow, we are going to visit our first tree. It is situated on the only 'wooded' lot in the subdivision and is owned by the builder's daughter. Pray for us. . . . Affectionately, Marge."

"Doesn't that sound exciting?" I said, jumping to my feet.

"You say the same thing when your soup is hot."

"Where's your adventurous spirit?" I asked. "It's a new world out there—full of challenges. We're young yet. We could survive."

He put down his paper and swept his arms around to encompass the entire apartment. "What! Move and give up all of this?"

I looked around. I had to iron in the playpen. The kids were stacked in a triple bunk at night like they were awaiting burial at sea. If the phone rang, I had to stand on my husband's face to answer it. The dog slept under the oven, next to the crackers. And one day I yawned, stretched my arms and someone stored the complete works of Dr. Seuss and a pot of African violets on them.

"You'd never survive," he predicted. "It's a raw frontier—no schools, no churches, and only three registered Republicans. Frankly, I don't think you have the stamina or the threshold of pain for it."

"Stamina!" I shouted. "Are you telling me I have no stamina? A woman who has lived on the fourth floor of this apartment building for five years with the stairs out of order has no stamina? I have legs like a discus thrower. As for pain, I have been known to go without support stockings for as long as two hours."

"Do you honestly think you could move to a land where your mother is a 35-cent toll charge for the first three minutes?"

I hesitated, then squared my shoulders and said, "Yes!"

It was probably my imagination, but I thought I heard a whip crack and a voice shout, "Station Wagons . . . Ho!"

The selling of the suburbs made the coronation of Queen Elizabeth look like an impulse.

On a Sunday afternoon you could tour Cinderella's Red Coach Farms, Mortgage Mañana, Saul Lieberman's Bonsai Gardens, or Bonaparte's Retreat ("Live the Rest of Your Life Like a Weak King").

Every development had its gimmick: flags flying, billboards, free rain bonnets, balloons for the kiddies, and pom pom girls that spelled out LOW INTEREST RATES in script.

My husband spread out the newspaper and together we went over the plats we had visited.

"What did you think of Tahitian Village?" he asked.

"Cute," I said, "but a little overdone. I mean dropping the kids into a volcano to play each morning just . . ."

"What about Chateau on Waldren's Pond?"

"Call it a woman's intuition, but I've never trusted a lake that had a sudsing problem on Monday mornings."

"Wanta check out Sherwood Forest?"

"Why not?"

The sales office of Sherwood Forest was a tree stump surrounded by five or six salesmen dressed in tunics. Nearby was a plastic campfire that held a plastic pig on a spit and beyond that were 800 plastic houses.

"Welcome to Sherwood Forest," said a salesman schlepping

along in a brown frock, a rope, and a pair of sandals. "I'm Friar Tuck and if you have any questions, feel free to ask them."

"If this is Sherwood Forest," I asked, "where are the trees?"

"You're standing over it," he said, staring at my knees.

My husband picked up the price list.

"You'll find that it is in keeping with the Robin Hood philosophy," he smiled.

We bolted toward the car, pursued by six Merry Men.

The adventure of moving to the suburbs had nearly worn off when we stumbled into Suburbian Gems.

"How much are the houses?" asked my husband.

"We have one standard price in Suburbian Gems," said the salesman. "$15,000."

We couldn't believe it. "Could we see the tracts?" we asked. He pulled down a giant map behind him solid with blocks representing houses. "I'm afraid we're pretty well sold out," he said. "The Diamond section went before we even advertised. Jade went fast. So did Ruby. And Pearl. I see even Zircon is blocked off."

"What's left?" we asked.

"Frankly Fake," he said. "Climb in the car and I'll drive you over to the sites so you can get the feel of the development."

When we pulled up in front of the house, I couldn't believe it. I got out of the car and ran through the two-story iron gates, up the half mile of driveway to the veranda porch, touched the massive white pillars and ran my fingers over the large carved door. "It's Tara!" I said, my eyes misting, "I've come home to Tara."

"You understand, this is only the model home," said the salesman.

I buried my face in the wisteria that crept along the windows. "We understand. Could we see the rest of it?"

The double doors opened and our voices echoed our pleasure in the house, from the huge foyer to the curved stairway leading to the second floor.

Then, inside the living room, I saw it—the fireplace. A warmth came over me. I could see my husband standing against it in a sports coat with leather patches on the elbows holding a brandy and a copy of Emerson's essays.

I visualized me hanging a della Robbia wreath over it at Christmas and laughing children basking in its reflection after a snow. "We'll take it," I said suddenly.

As my husband lifted his hand to touch my face in a gesture of love, he was amazed to find a pen in it.

"If you will just sign the purchase agreement," said the salesman, "we can get on with the details of your new home in Frankly Fake."

I squeezed my husband's arm as he signed the agreement.

"We've never had a fireplace before."

"Oh, then you want the model with the fireplace?" asked the salesman.

We nodded.

"Well, now, is there anything else about the Williamsburg model that you like?"

"We like everything," I said.

"Oh, then you want the second floor, the extra baths, the tiled foyer, the stairway, the veranda porch, the larger lot . . . ?"

"Are you saying all those things are extra?"

"The Williamsburg is our best home," he said stiffly. "Our basic $15,000 is much the same only on a smaller scale."

"How small?" asked my husband.

"Let's see," he said, checking his price list. "The Pee Wee has three bedrooms and a one-car garage, spouting to protect your porch from the sun, full landscaping, and 850 luxurious square feet."

"Does it have a family room?"

"Two of them—both in white fixtures."

"But the Pee Wee does have the pillars and the porch . . ." I asked anxiously.

"I told you, it has everything except a second story, stairway, entranceway, and extra lot. Now, that covers about everything except what you want to do about the garage."

"What about the garage?" asked my husband.

"Do you plan on putting your car in it?"

"It crossed our minds."

"I see. I only mention it because a lot of people like to have a driveway leading to it. You don't have to, you understand, but it does get a little muddy and it's worth the extra cost to some people to have it filled in."

"But everything else is included in the original price?" asked my husband.

"Absolutely. All you have to do is make some decisions regarding the quality of materials. For example, all wiring is borderline standard unless you want to pay extra and have it pass inspection. (We nodded.) I think that's wise. Now, about your tub. Do you want it hooked up under your shower?"

We nodded numbly.

"I assumed you did because you already said you wanted to put a car in your garage and that's where we usually store the tub until the owner tells us otherwise. Speaking of storage, you are aware that without the second story, there is a crawl space over your entire house for storage?"

We smiled happily.

"Do you have some way of getting up there or do you want us to install a pull-down stairway as an extra? Let's see—apart from the paint, floor covering, spouting, storm windows, kitchen hardware, countertops, lighting fixtures, and keys, which are all extra, I think that does it."

His fingers fairly raced across the keys of the tabulator as the extras mounted. Finally, he smiled and said, "The final tab is $29,500. Welcome to Frankly Fake!"

As my husband handed back the pen, he smiled, waved it aside, and said, "Keep it. As a token of our mutual faith in one another."

Out of the corner of my eye, I saw him add, "Pen @ 59 cents," bringing the total to $29,500.59.

Lot No. 15436 . . .
Where Are You?

We must have driven two and a half hours before we found our house.

"Are you sure this is it?" asked my husband.

"I'm sure," I said tiredly. "This is the eighth house from the corner and the builder always staggers his styles so they won't all look alike. I counted them. There were the Williamsburg, the Richmond, the Shenandoah, and the Pee Wee, a Williamsburg, a Richmond, a Shenandoah, and this is our Pee Wee."

"I thought it was supposed to look like Mt. Vernon," whined our daughter, "with the big pillars."

"But it does have pillars," I said, pointing toward the four supports that looked like filter-tip cigarettes.

"Will they grow?" asked our son.

"Children, please!" said my husband. Then, turning to me he asked, "Happy?"

I looked at the packing boxes stacked at the curb, the mail box on the ground, chunks of plaster embedded in the mud, windows dusty and spackled with paint and said, "I wish I could tell you— in front of the children."

"Well, let's go in and get settled," he said, "And take your muddy boots on the porch inside."

"What muddy boots?" I said. "Aren't they yours?"

"They're mine," said a woman coming out of one of the bedrooms.

"Who are you?" asked my husband.

"I live here," she said.

"Isn't this 5425 Ho Hum Lane?" he asked.

"Yes, but it's 5425 Ho Hum Lane Northeast. It used to be 18 Bluebird of Happiness Drive, but then the other street came through and changed it. When we bought it, it was 157 Squirrel Road, but Ho Hum Lane is on a circle and the even numbers change to the odd numbers at the house where the door is on backwards. You know the one?"

"Right. That's two down from the chuckhole in the road where your car falls through."

"That's the one. Besides, 5425 isn't going to be your permanent number. That's a lot number and will change when the post office assigns you your new one."

"Oh? Where's the post office? We haven't been able to find it."

"No one is quite sure yet. You notice how everything blends with the surroundings out here?"

"I've noticed. We went to a furniture store today and there was a bread card in the window. We almost passed it by."

"I know," she said. "The gas station on the corner blends in so well, I feel guilty if I pull in after dinner when he's cutting the grass. It was the council who decided they didn't want commercial businesses to look like commercial businesses. We had enough of that in the city. They wanted them to have that residential feeling."

"That makes a lot of sense," I said.

"I suppose so," she said, "but the other night it was embarrassing. My husband and I went out to dinner and there was a huge line so Russell (my husband) slipped the maître d' $2 and said, 'I think if you'll check your reservations, you'll find we're next. You came personally recommended.'

'By whom?' asked the man in the black suit. 'This is a funeral home.' "

As we continued the search for our new home, I expressed some concern that every time we left the house we'd have to leave a kid on the front porch for a landmark.

"Things will be different," said my husband, "when the builder puts in the shrubbery."

"How much landscaping comes with the house?" I asked.

He tilted his head and recited from memory. "Let's see, we're down for five maples, eight taxus, six evergreens, two ash, four locust, 109 living rose hedge plants, two flowering mother-in-law tongues, and a grove of fifteen assorted, colorful fruit trees."

"Hey, I think this is it," I said, as he pulled into a driveway. "We are officially home!"

We turned the key in the door. My husband and I raced through the house to the backyard to get a glimpse of the flatbed truck and the lift that would turn our barren patch of mud into a jungle. The yard was empty.

"Where's the shrubbery?" asked my husband.

One of the children called from the house, "Mommy! Daddy! The shrubbery is here!"

"Where?" asked my husband.

"On the dining room table with the mail." We stood around the table. No one spoke as we viewed the envelope holding five maples, eight taxus, six evergreens, two ash, four locust, 109 living rose hedge plants, two flowering mother-in-law tongues, and a grove of fifteen assorted, colorful fruit trees.

My son had more foliage than that growing under his bed.

"Gather it up," said my husband, "and put it in the garage and for God's sake watch the dog. He has eight assorted fruit trees stuck in his tail."

By noon the next day we had planted the entire package.

"Whatya think?" asked my husband.

"It looks like a missile site," I grumbled.

"I think everything will survive the transplanting with the exception of the maple tree. The dog . . ."

"He didn't."

"Yep. His tail brushed against it and the trunk snapped in half."

"I'm worried about the flowering mother-in-law tongues."

"Why?"

"They just spoke to me. They said, 'Help.' "

The Original Settlers

The triumph of man over the suburbs was made possible by the sheer guts of a band of original settlers.

Later, other fringe businesses would sprout up: a water supply, hospitals, grocery stores, post offices and schools; scouting programs and Good Humor trucks, but at the beginning, these scouts welcomed the newcomers from the city with hands outstretched—and palms upward.

The Telephone Representative

"Do you want a phone?" asked the lady at the door.

"What kind of a joke is that?" I asked irritably. "Does John Wayne salute the flag? Does Dean Martin drink? Does the Pope work Sundays? Of course I want a phone," I said, literally dragging her into the living room. "Where do I sign?"

"My goodness," she smiled. "Not so fast. We have some decisions to make. First, let me introduce myself. I am Miss Turtletaub, your telephone representative, and I'll be handling your application. Now, to begin with, what type of service do you want?"

"The one where the phone is in the house."

"You're teasing," she said. "Do you want the party line that is quaint, but a drag, the two-party line where you share your phone with an informer, or the popular private service?"

"Private. Now when . . ."

"I assume you want more than one phone in a house of this size. Where is your family room?"

"Down the hall, first door to the left and lock it or the kids will bust in on you."

"Oh. Then what about a phone in your bedroom? After all, there is nothing more frightening than the insistent ring of the phone after midnight when your loved ones need you the most and you are busy breaking your leg in a dark hallway."

"The bedroom sounds great. Could you . . ."

"Three phones. That's smart. Now, what about a jack? After all, basking out of doors is the reason you moved to this cornfield in the first place. Just say you are standing out in the backyard talking to your neighbors. Without a phone nearby, you'll never know when some disc jockey is trying to give away $10,000. Look at it this way—a jackpot like that would pay for the jack in one phone call's time."

"Terrific. One jack. Now could we talk about . . ."

"Color? I knew you were discerning the moment I walked in. I brought along some color chips and I think you'll find coordinated phones for every room in your house. There's God's green, barnyard brown, brothel red, and of course boring black."

"One barnyard, one God's, and one boring."

"Wise choice. Now, have you thought about which model you prefer? We have a great one that hangs from the wall for the kitchen that doesn't take up valuable counter space. Then we have the cradle type with the traditional dial, and we have the collector's gallery: the conversation-piece types in the French provincial, the Early American ones shaped like a pump, and here's a cutesie shaped like an ear trumpet."

"Ah . . . traditional is fine," I said, fidgeting, "now, would you be able to tell me . . ."

"You have to live with it. Now about the listing. I know you have youngsters in the family and most of our sophisticated clientele such as yourself want their children listed so they might reap the entire benefits of a phone."

"That's fine," I said.

"Now, unless you have any questions, I think that does it," she said, smiling and snapping her book shut.

"Just one," I said excitedly. "When can you install the phones?"

She shuffled through her papers and came out with a schedule. Then, tracing down with her fingernail, she paused and said, "A year and a half."

"*A year and a half!*"

"You sound shocked," she smiled. "Have you any idea how much money is involved in cables and poles and electronics to bring phone service all the way out to Suburban Gems? Why it takes an Act of Congress just to clear the land. We can't perform miracles, can we? Excuse me," she said, "I must dash. There's a couple moving in today down the street. What would they think if the phone company wasn't there to offer their services?"

The Insurance Salesman

Biff Rah said, "You look familiar. Didn't we go to school together?"

It was a funny thing for a man to say over the telephone.

But that's the way neighborhood insurance men in the suburbs were. They clutched at any straw to establish some common basis for your trust and your signature on an endowment. "Listen," he said, "I know you are busy getting settled. Don't I know it? I'm ten years—and I'm still unpacking, right?"

"The children are a little . . ."

"Hey, kids. Do I know kids?" he said. "Got five of them myself so I understand your problem. All I want to do is to come over and review what you've got in the way of protection, and leave, okay?"

We agreed.

Biff grabbed my hand at the door, pumped it and said, "You look familiar. Didn't we go to school together?"

"Not unless you wore a plaid jumper and knee socks. It was an all-girls' school."

"I was the one with the knobby knees who never shaved!" he grinned, punching me in the arm and knocking me into the bookcases. "But seriously folks," he said, whipping open his briefcase. "I didn't come here to make jokes. I simply dropped by to spell out a few facts of life. You've just moved into a new house, your kids are in their jammies watching TV, you're employed (nodding to my husband), you've got a car, and you (nodding at me) stay home and bake bread. You gotta be like this family here in the picture, right?"

We looked down to a page in his notebook at a picture depicting what had to be the All-American family with straight teeth, healthy gums, yellow hair, tennis sweaters, and a house behind them that looked like the Williamsburg.

"Now, what if this happened?" he asked dramatically and with a small brush that took no longer than fifteen seconds removed my husband from the picture.

"How did you do that?" I asked.

"You're missing the point," he said irritably. "Now what happens to that happy little family if Daddy is gone. They're repossessing the car. They're taking the house away. They're taking the furniture away. The children are crying. Mommy doesn't know which way to turn. Now, do you know what that means?"

"It means I get custody of the kids," I snapped.

"It means Daddy didn't make plans."

"It wouldn't be the first time," I snapped.

"Lucky," interrupted Biff, "it's not too late. There is still time to protect your loved ones with this twenty-year-pay life. While you are young, the premiums aren't too bad, but in a few years when you develop those heart problems, circulatory disorders, high blood pressure, and an aneurysm, it may not be available to you at any price."

My husband signed the agreement in mid-air. As I squeezed his hand in appreciation, Biff leaned down and addressed himself to our children. "I can tell by looking at you that Mommy has done a wonderful job. And you're not to blame her when she leaves and you are left alone to shift for yourselves."

"Where am I going?" I asked.

"Face it. It's inevitable that someday you'll be going to the big utility room in the sky. May I ask you something? How much insurance do you carry on yourself?"

"I don't know," I stammered, "my husband takes care of that."

"I don't like to make trouble," he said, "but usually a man will cover his wife with a policy which he considers to be her value to him."

"How much am I covered for?" I asked.

"You have the basic $96-no-frill-no-fault-burial-policy," he mumbled.

Ninety-six bucks! That wouldn't bury a bird in a shoebox!"

"That's right," said Biff. "Basically what this means is that when you go, they prop you up in a Christian Science reading room, play a record of Perry Como singing 'Don't Fence Me In,' put you on a public bus, and God knows what happens to you."

We signed another policy.

As Biff got up to go he said, "You're such bright people I'm almost embarrassed to ask, but I have a responsibility to you. You are putting aside $50 a week for each child's education aren't you? Don't bother to answer. Of course you are."

"As a matter of fact," said my husband, "we aren't."

Biff shrugged, "Forget I mentioned it. I mean the chances are they'll never need it. Depressed and disappointed at the lack of opportunity, they will drop out of high school, pick up with another dropout who pumps gas, marry, and live in one room until the baby comes . . ."

"*Stop!*" I shouted. "Tell us what to do."

"Well, there are endowments. They're expensive, but it all depends on what your children are worth to you."

"They're worth everything we own."

"That'll about cover it," he smiled. "Well, you are wonderful people and a great little family and if, by some act of God, the house should burn to the ground, don't fail to call me and I'll try to work something out—contributions from neighbors, a phone call to an agency . . ."

"You mean we're not covered?"

"It's so simple to be covered, it's hardly worth mentioning, but if you'll sign here, it's done." My husband scribbled his signature.

"Listen," said Biff, "I've overstayed my visit. I must be running along. And don't worry about the coverage on your car. Parents are great for pitching in when bad luck strikes. According to statistics, two out of every three cars will be involved in an accident this year, but who knows, you could be the lucky one. Anyway, welcome to Suburbian Gems—and don't you feel better now?"

The Antique Dealer

Some say the antique syndrome surfaced to offset the newness of the land, the homes, and the settlers.

Some say the interest was initiated by a desire to return to the roots of yesterday.

I contend the entire movement to acquire antiques was born out of sheer respect for things that lasted longer than fifteen minutes.

Whatever the reason, in Suburbian Gems, there was an Eagle over every sofa, a slop jar of geraniums in every bathroom, and a deacon's bench in every hallway.

The weekends found every husband in the neighborhood sanding, sawing, staining, restoring, or stalking every antique dealer and show in the area.

My husband became an antique nut. I never saw a man become so possessed. He brought home white SuppHose, reputedly worn by Thomas Jefferson, a moose's head that had personally witnessed the Battle of Appomattox, and a primitive machine for storing water during the cattle drives west. (I didn't have the heart to tell him he bought the water cooler in the church hallway where they were holding the sale.)

It's hard to single out any one antique dealer for this documentary. They all had a different "style." Some were "story tellers." My husband loved the "story tellers." They were the ones who if you bought a button would relate how this button was from the uniform of a Confederate soldier who had scratched the name JAY on the back. His brother, who had been visiting north, joined the Union forces and he too had their family name, Jay, scratched on the back of one of his buttons. The two buttons would bring a price of $150. Unfortunately, he had only one, but if we would leave our phone number, when he came across the other one, he would give a call. In less than a week (isn't that unbelievable!) he called to say the other button had been found and was available.

There were the scavenger dealers who were like ambulance chasers. They watched the death notices and anyone over the age of forty-three got a visit from them to appraise and buy goodies from the estate. Scavenger dealers knew only one phrase, "Do you have any idea what we could have gotten for this pitcher/glass/bowl/tumbler/plate/mirror/etc., had it not been cracked?" My husband loved the "scavenger dealers." He always felt he was getting a real buy under the table from them.

There were also the "hustlers in bib overalls." These were the little farmers who feigned surprise that someone would want to buy boards from a barn that was ready to fall down.

My husband loved the "barnyard hustlers." He would stop the car, introduce himself, chew on a piece of hay, and talk about how the rains or drought had affected the crops. Then he would venture, "Hey, how much would you want for a couple of those old two-by-fours over there on your barn?"

The farmers would give a little crooked smile and say, "You kiddin' me, mister? You mean those old faded, weathered boards, wormy with termites on that barn that a good wind would knock over?"

"Those are the ones," said my husband.

"Oh, I suppose $50 would put 'em in your trunk."

We were dealing with pros.

If I had to name one original settler who was known by everyone, it would have to be Miss Emma. Miss Emma was a sweet, little, old lady whose farmhouse in the suburbs stuck out like a birth-control clinic in a retirement community.

There was no quaint sign flapping from her lamppost proclaiming, "ANTIQUES." She never advertised. Never brought her wares to a show at the church. The word just got around that if Miss Emma answered the door on that particular day and was in a good mood, she "might" sell you some of her precious heirlooms right out from under her.

In truth, Miss Emma should have been voted by the Academy of Arts and Sciences as the year's Best Actress of any year.

Responding to your knock, she would open the door a crack and say, "Today isn't a good day. Come back—say tomorrow?" which only made you more determined to somehow smuggle a checkbook into that house and cart away half of its furnishings.

Once inside, if you expressed an interest in, say a desk, she would throw her body in front of it protectively and say, "Oh no, this is the one thing I couldn't possibly sell. Martin (her late husband) would come right out of his grave. You see, it belonged to his great-grandmother who got it from a General Washburn."

"Are you sure it was Washburn? Could it have been Washington?"

"Could be. Great-grandma Tucker was a little hard of hearing."

Five minutes later, the desk would be in the back of someone's trunk and on its way to a place of prominence to be treated as a member of the family.

My husband and I begged her to let us come in one Saturday. "Only if you don't stay too long," she agreed. Then my husband spotted it. One of the most enormous wooden bowls we had ever seen. "How much would you sell this bowl for, Miss Emma?" asked my husband.

She jumped between the bowl and my husband. "This bowl is not for sale. You may buy anything in this house, but not this bowl."

At that moment I knew if I didn't have that bowl, I would not continue breathing. "Please, Miss Emma, we'd give it a good home and cherish it as you have cherished it."

"It's been in our family for generations," she said sadly. "I can remember my grandmother bathing the babies in it (my throat hurt and I wanted to cry). My mother used to bake bread in it—

ten loaves at a time—and I just keep it around to store apples in it for the little children who visit."

"I know," I sobbed, "I know and I will do likewise."

A few minutes and a substantial check later, we were headed home with the bowl. "Do you know what I'm going to do with that bowl?" asked my husband. "I'm going to sand it down and then varnish it with a clear varnish and keep it in a natural state. We can put it on our divider and keep bright, shiny apples in it all the time."

He must have put in 184 man hours on that bowl. Every night in the garage I heard him sanding away. Then one night he came into the bedroom from the garage and said, "I don't believe it. I sanded all the way down through the stain and do you know what I found? (I shook my head.) MADE IN JAPAN. That can only mean one thing."

"What?" I asked excitedly.

"That Great-grandmother Tucker was Japanese. We've got an oriental antique on our hands."

We were elated, of course, and spared no time in telling our antique enthusiasts about our "find."

"Is it a huge wooden bowl with a crack down the middle?" asked the Martins.

"Yes! You've heard of it!"

"Heard of it? We've got one too," said the Martins. "So have the Palmers and the Judsons."

"You're kidding! Where did they get theirs?"

"Miss Emma's."

During the next few years Miss Emma's family heirlooms became as standard in Suburban Gems as doorknobs.

It's funny. In the five or six years everyone bought furniture out of Miss Emma's house, the house always was filled and always looked the same. You'd have thought someone would have noticed.

2 〰〰
Major Battles Fought in the Suburbs

Finding the Builder Who
Built the House
(1945–1954)

Edward C. Phlegg, the builder of Suburbian Gems, made Howard Hughes look like an exhibitionist.

No one had ever seen him. His phone number was a candy store that took messages. The billboards bearing his picture showed only the back of his head.

"If it's an emergency," said my husband, "I suppose I could track him down."

"Well, every time I push down the toaster, the garage door goes up. The hot-water heater is hooked up to the garden hose and I am sautéeing the lawn. The sliding glass doors don't slide. The wall heats up when I turn on the porch light. The hall toilet does not accept tissue. Half of our driveway is on our neighbor's property, the grapes on the kitchen wallpaper are growing upside down, and I have a sign on our front door reading, 'OUT OF ORDER! PLEASE USE HOUSE NEXT DOOR.' "

"I think our best bet is to try and pin down the contractors," said my husband. "I'll see what I can do."

Two months later, we had tracked down our plumber. He had defected to a small country behind the iron curtain taking with him the last of the 1/15-inch pipe used in our bathrooms. Delivery was guaranteed in three years.

Our electrician was facing charges of involuntary arson of a large office building where political corruption was suspect. (He contended his bid was the lowest offered—a case of Coors.)

Our building foreman had returned to high school. He explained it had only been a temporary summer job to earn enough for a bicycle.

Our furnace man was living under an assumed name in Yuma, Arizona.

Our painter was drying out in a sanitorium in upper New York State.

And our concrete man was studying contract law at the University of Cincinnati.

"I don't want to panic you," said my husband, "but I think we're stuck with our own repairs."

"Why should I panic? Just because when our water pipes sweat you prescribed an anti-perspirant?"

"Oh c'mon."

"Just because you were too embarrassed to ask for a male or a female plug at the hardware store and I had to write you a note."

"You made your point."

"Just because we have the only toilet in the block reseated with Play Doh . . ."

"Look," he said, "did you marry for love or did you marry to have your toilet fixed?"

When I didn't answer he said, "I'll get my toolbox and we can talk about what has to be done."

He set down a small fishing tackle box that had been originally inscribed "FIRST AID." This had been crossed out and "TOLS" was misspelled across the top in pencil.

Inside was a cork, five feet of pink, plastic clothesline, a small hammer, a flashlight with no batteries, a curler, a poker chip, and a book of rain-soaked matches.

"This is it?"

"This is it. What do you need first?" he asked.

"Storm windows for the entire house."

"Are you crazy?" he gasped. "I'll need a miter box."

"I thought we sprayed for them."

"Couldn't I start with something easy—like a revolving door?"

"As a matter of fact, you could make one of those little doors for the dog that saves you from letting them in and out all the time. You know, the one with the little hinges that flap in and out?"

"Right," he said. "No problem. You just saw a little hole in the door, attach the hinges, and you're in business."

When I left him he was standing the dog against the wall with a tape measure and saying, "Let's see how much you've grown today."

A few hours later I felt a draft in the bedrooms and went to check. You could have slung a herd of buffalo through the little hole in the door.

"Don't worry," he cautioned, "the door on it will eliminate the wind whistling through."

"Now what are you doing?" I asked, as he dropped to his hands and knees.

"Showing the dog how to go through it. Dogs have to be taught, you know. But they're great little mimics." He twisted and groaned until his body was halfway through the door.

"What's wrong?" I asked.

"I'm stuck."

"Which end do you want me to save?"

"Will you knock it off with the jokes? Here I am with half of my body on the front porch and the other half in the hallway and . . ."

"Would you be terribly upset if I opened the door right now?"

"Why?"

"The dog has to go out."

"Well, hurry up. When I'm finished here, I want to start on the storm windows."

The search for Edward C. Phlegg continued for nine years. Someone thought they spotted the back of his head at an Arthur Fiedler concert. Another neighbor heard he was involved in selling beachfront property in Fargo, North Dakota.

Whatever, we never saw the builder of Suburban Gems face to face.

Then one day we opened our newspaper and saw where Edward C. Phlegg had died. His funeral was one of the biggest the city had ever known. Mourners from Suburban Gems alone filled the church. (Contractors who hadn't been paid couldn't even get inside.)

There wasn't a dry eye in the church.

We were saying goodbye to the only man who knew where in Hong Kong our furnace was made. Who alone knew the secret ingredients of our patios that bubbled when the sun hit them. Who would take with him his reasons for slanting the roof toward the center of the house and burying the septic tank under the living room floor.

As we stood in the cemetery mourning our loss, there was a flash of lightning and a rumble of thunder as before our very eyes, the large stone bearing the name Edward C. Phlegg sunk to one side and remained at a 40-degree angle.

There was no doubt in any of our minds. God was trying to tell us that Mr. Phlegg had gone to that big Escrow in the sky.

The Second-Car Ten-Day War

We had talked about the isolation of the suburbs and the expense of a second car before moving there and I thought I had made my position very clear.

I did not want a car. Did not need a car. And would not take a car if it were offered me.

I lied.

"I've got to have wheels," I said to my husband one night after dinner.

"We've talked about this before," he said, "and we agreed that the reason we migrated was to explore all the adventures the suburbs has to offer."

"I've explored both of them. Now I need a car. A car will put me in touch with the outside world. It will be my link with another culture, another civilization, another world of trade."

"Aren't you being a little dramatic?" he suggested.

"Let me lay it on you, Cleavie, the high spot in my day is taking knots out of shoestrings—with my teeth—that a kid has wet on all day long. I'm beginning to have feelings for my shower-massage pik. Yesterday, I etched a dirty word on the leaf of my philodendron."

"And you think a car is going to help you?"

"Of course it will help. I'll be able to go to the store, join a bowling league, have lunch downtown with the girls, volunteer, go to the dentist, take long drives in the country. I want to see the big, outside world from atop a lube rack. I want to whirl dizzily in a cloud of exhaust, rotate my tires with the rest of the girls. Don't you understand? I want to *honk* if I love Jesus!"

For a reason I was soon to understand, *all* of us went to the showroom to pick out *my* car. Within minutes, I saw it. It was a bright, yellow sports number—a one-seater that puts you three inches off the ground and sounds like a volcano when the motor turns over. Near to ecstasy, I closed my eyes and imagined myself at a traffic light, my large sunglasses on top of my head like Marlo Thomas, and as I quickly brushed lip gloss on my lips from a small pot, a dark stranger from the car next to me shouted, "Could we meet and talk?" And I laughed cruelly, "Don't be a fool! I'm a homeroom mother!" and sped off.

The rest of the family was gathered around a four-wheel-drive station wagon with a spare tire on top, space for extra gas cans along the back, and fold-down seats giving you room to transport the Cleveland Symphony and all their instruments.

"Hey, is this a car?" asked my husband, his eyes shining.

"That was *my* next question," I said. "Look, I don't want transportation to a war, I just want a car to take me to the store and back."

"Of course you do," he said, "and this is the no-nonsense car that can get the job done."

Oh, I tried all right to hide my disappointment. I put glasses on top of my head, touched up my lip gloss at traffic lights, and even occasionally ran my tongue over my lips like Jennifer O'Neill, but I never climbed behind the wheel of that orthopedic vehicle without feeling like I was following General Patton into Belgium.

Besides, I was the only woman in the neighborhood with a big wagon. All the others tooled around in small, sleek sports cars that had previously belonged to their husbands.

By the end of the first week, the newness of owning my own car had begun to wear off. I had transported six kids a day to school, a power mower to the repair shop, a porch swing for a garage sale, and the neighbor's dog to the vet who would not fit into a Volkswagen, Nova, Pontiac, Plymouth, Oldsmobile, Tank, or Global Van Lines.

The second week things picked up. I transported thirty-five sleeping bags and supplies for a week at camp, paneling from a lumber yard which wouldn't make delivery until the following week, a missile launch for a science fair, eight baseball bats, four base bags and twelve Little-League players, eight bags of fertilizer for the lawn and six surly homeroom mothers who arrived at a tea smelling like fertilizer.

It was of no comfort to me whatsoever knowing that I would make U-Haul Mother of the Year. I had to unload that car. Things came to a head one afternoon when I stopped for a traffic light and a huge transport truck pulled alongside me. The ones that travel all night to get your bread fresh to you in the morning. While waiting for the light to change, a burly driver looked over and shouted, "Hey, Mac, where's a good place to eat and get some sack time?"

I knew then I had to make my move and trade up—to my husband's car.

"You don't suppose we could switch cars?" I asked that night after dinner.

"Why would we want to do a thing like that?" he asked.

I hesitated dramatically, "I didn't want to tell you but the children get drowsy in the back seat. I think something is leaking in."

"Then, by all means, take it to the garage and have it fixed." (STRIKE ONE.)

"I'm in the garage so often now, I have my own key to the

restroom. What would you say if I told you I only get seven miles to the gallon and I'm costing you $1.50 every time I wait for a light to turn green?"

"We knew the car would be an added expense when we bought it." (STRIKE TWO.)

"It's really a shame for your new, small, compact car to sit out all day in the harsh sun and the rain and the cold when it could sit in a nice, warm garage."

"There's something to that, but how would you transport all those children every day?" (BALL ONE.)

"I just read a survey that a smaller car is safer because the children are packed together and do not have room to swing around and argue about who gets a window."

"That makes sense (BALL TWO) but what would I do with a big car that eats gas and attracts burly truck drivers?" (BALL THREE.)

It was three and two and I wound up for the big one.

"In a way it's a shame you don't have the station wagon. That way you could pick up some paying riders who would love transportation to the city. The extra money would pay for your gas."

HOME RUN!

"It's funny you should mention that," he said. "The Osborn's daughter, Fluffy, asked me just the other day if I had room in my car for her to ride to the city."

"You mean the girl in the next block who always looks like she's wearing a life preserver?"

"What a thing to say. She just has good posture."

"That's inflatable—I mean debatable."

"Then it's settled. We trade cars. You can drive mine and I'll drive the wagon."

I never knew victory could make you feel so rotten.

Getting Sex Out of the Schools and Back into the Gutter Where It Belongs

My son was five years old when his teacher sent home a note informing me he was sexually immature.

I confronted her the next day after school and said, "What is this supposed to mean, Mrs. Kravitz?"

"It means we had a little quiz the other day on reproductive organs and he defined every one of them as an Askyourfather. You are sending a child into the world, Mrs. Bombeck, who thinks Masters and Johnson is a golf tournament and fertilization is something you do in the fall to make the lawns green."

"That's true," I nodded.

"Have you ever discussed sex in your home?" she asked.

"No, but once he caught Barbie and Ken together in a cardboard car in their underwear."

"Have you ever discussed with him the parts of his body?"

"Only those that showed dirt."

"You have to do better than that. This is a new day, Mrs. Bombeck. We don't hide our heads in the sand any more. Suburban schools are taking the lead in informing our young people about sex at an early age. For example, I am expecting a baby and I told the class about it."

"You told them you had something in the oven?" I asked incredulously.

"I told them I was pregnant!" she said.

I bit my finger. "Good Lord, Mrs. Kravitz. I didn't know why my husband gasped every time Lassie cleared the fence until I was twenty-six."

"Then you had better get used to it," she said. "Your son is about to be informed."

The suburbs didn't invent sex—it only gave it a wider distribution. No one could have known the ramifications sex education could have had in the community. Little boys wrote dirty sayings on the sidewalks with chalk as they always did, but adults didn't protest. They didn't understand what they meant.

Parents who tried to deal directly with their children by saying, "Look, Brucie, there seems to be some confusion between sexual and asexual reproduction," only to be interrupted with, "Look, Dad, you should have come to me sooner. What do you need to know?"

Eavesdropping (among young people) dropped off 75 percent but increased 86 percent among adults. And one second-grader confronted his parents one night with, "You little devils, you. And you told me I was conceived without sin."

Things had clearly gotten out of hand and we knew it. So, a meeting was called at the school to discuss the future of sex education.

"Frankly," said the librarian, "I'm worried. Do you realize the new *National Geographic* has been in for three weeks and has not been checked out once by a third-grader?"

We gasped. "The youngsters don't want to play Doctor and Nursie any more," said a distraught father. "My son wants to open up his own office."

"I'm afraid," said Ken Kinsey, "that the impact of sex education goes even deeper. We now have before us the problem of dress code. It seems with the laxity of certain rules and the casualness with which we are regarding the human body, some youngsters are coming to school in various attire. Tonight, we have been asked to consider the outcome of displaying—(he swallowed hard)—the navel."

The librarian sucked in her breath. The co-chairman cleared his throat and I grabbed for my son's sex manual to see if it had a double meaning.

"It seems," continued Ken, "that many of our little girls have been wearing jeans that fit around the hips and shirts that hang just below the rib cage and there is a bare area in between that needs some clarification. Anyone have any ideas?"

"Well, I have always felt if the Good Lord had meant for people to go nude He would never have invented the wicker chair," said one mother.

"That is a good point," said Ken. "Anyone else?"

"Have we established what a navel is?" asked a teacher.

"I think it is safe to assume that most of us are familiar with the navel . . ."

"Wait a minute," said a mother, "there are navels and there are navels. I mean some are 'outies' and some are 'innies.' I personally find the outies disgusting."

"That's strange," said her husband, "I find them sexy."

"You don't know how strange," said his wife. "I have an 'innie' and demand to know where you've seen an 'outie.' "

"Please people. Let's get back to the issue here. Should we permit the navel to be displayed in a classroom atmosphere?"

"Today the navel, tomorrow the buttock," grumbled the math teacher.

"It seems to me," said a parent, "that if lax dress codes are allowed to continue, we may be in for something that only the National Guard can handle."

"I worry," said a mother who had been sitting quietly, "that it will blow the lid off a whole can of emotions. I mean, how do you expect a six-year-old to stay in the lines when he colors if he is distracted by a bared navel sitting at the desk next to his."

"That's a good point, Ethel," said Ken.

"I see nothing wrong with navels," said a militant in the rear. "Why are all of you so hung up over something as normal as a navel?"

"Navels are not on trial here," interrupted Ken. "It's simply we must draw the line somewhere with the relaxing of morals among our young people."

"So, if you're ashamed of your navel," persisted the militant, "I'll put a Band-Aid over it."

"What does the U.S. government say about navels?" asked a businessman.

"To my knowledge, there is no department at the moment that is conducting any sort of findings on the subject," said Ken. "If we could just get back to the subject . . ."

"If you ask me," said a concerned mother, "I think by our condoning navels in a public-school building, we are lowering the age of puberty. Next thing you know, we will permit them to have acne before they are ten and lower their voices at nine. I say they are growing up too fast. Let's save the navels for later when they can handle them and enjoy them like adults."

There was a round of applause and a few in the back stood up and said, "Here, here."

"Should we put it to a vote?" asked Ken. "Okay, all of you in favor of issuing a dress code in which navels must be covered, signify by saying, 'Aye' (a roar). Opposed? (One, 'You bet your sweet umbilical cord!')

"Now, the next thing on the agenda," said Ken nervously, "is Miss Baker, who teaches the third-graders human sexuality, would like to have a lab . . ."

I slipped out the back door. I wanted time to consider the ramifications, the objectives, the impact of bringing such a program within my child's learning processes. Also, to have my six-year-old explain to me what human sexuality is.

Saving the Recession from a Depression

Following World War II, when the nation began its migration to the suburbs, there was fear that the economy would give way to a period of depression.

There entered upon the scene three commodities destined to bring the country to its economic feet again: The Picture Window, the Green-Lawn Syndrome, and two teenage dolls, Barbie and Ken.

No one could have imagined the impact these three items had on the spending habits of the settlers. In retrospect, it was simply a matter of figuring the odds. Thirty-million suburbanites, all supporting and maintaining a picture window, green grass, and two naked dolls—it would have brought any nation out of the darkness of despair and into prosperity once more.

The Picture Window

To build a house in the suburbs without at least one picture window was considered un-American.

I personally knew my heart would stop beating if I did not have one.

As I said to my husband, "Imagine! A window with nine feet of glass that would invite the sunshine in during the day and reflect the stars at night. That would reveal neighbors waving a friendly 'hello.' That would allow the gentle breezes of a summer night to come indoors and hold the snow of winter at bay with its frosty patterns on the glass. Who would need any form of entertainment with nature's panorama changing with the seasons? Who would need rewards in this life other than viewing happy children at play?"

"You got the picture window," he said helplessly.

Two days later, I said, "The man is coming today to cover the picture window. It will cost $500."

"Cover the window!" he gasped. "What about your 'inviting the sunshine in during the day and reflecting the stars at night'?"

"That sun is blinding me. I can't get away from it. And the dog is beginning to tan. As for stars, forget it. The only thing that window attracts at night are window peepers."

A month later I informed my husband, "The furniture has to be covered. It will cost $800."

"But it's always been good enough for us."

"Exactly, but is it good enough for the 'neighbors waving a friendly hello' through our picture window?"

"But I thought we got the windows covered."

"You can't keep the curtains drawn on a picture window all of the time or people will think you have something to hide."

Four months to the day, I casually mentioned the picture window would need storm covering and screen. They would run about $400.

"Wait a minute," he charged, "is this the same woman who said she 'was going to allow the gentle breezes of a summer night to come indoors and hold the snow of winter at bay with its frosty patterns on the glass'?"

"That's before I realized the summer breezes harbor mosquitoes that suck your blood. Besides, I've had it with those 'frosty patterns on the glass.' The window is causing frosty patterns on the children's lungs and our walls look like a waterfall."

We were two weeks into summer when I informed my husband, "We are getting a liner to block out the light of our window so we can watch TV during the daytime. It will cost $150."

His head jerked up sharply, "What happened to 'nature's panorama changing with the seasons before your eyes'?"

"Nature's panorama has deteriorated into a view of old Mr. Hudson framed in his picture window in his underwear scratching his stomach and picking his teeth with a matchbook cover."

One night I met my husband at the door. "We are getting Picture Window insurance. It will cost $28 a year."

"I don't believe this," he said. "When did you become disenchanted with the 'rewards of viewing happy children at play'?"

"When Michael Ormstead's baseball came crashing through our picture window. Meanwhile, we will have to have this one replaced. It will cost $160."

I had never seen my husband bite his necktie in half before.

The Suburban Lawn

Never, in the history of the world, have so many men sacrificed so much, so often, at such a price, for so little.

The green grass is what lured settlers to the wilderness in the first place. They wanted to cultivate a little patch of greenery that would tickle the feet of their barefooted babies, cushion their falls, and cradle them in the bosom of the soil.

It seemed incongruous in the quiet of an evening to hear a father pull his son close to him and say, *"You cut across that lawn one more time, Gilbert, and I'm going to break every bone in your body."*

The suburban lawn not only became an obsession with the suburban husband, it became the very symbol of manhood. Not to have a lawn was like admitting you turned off the Super Bowl to take a nap, used deodorant shields in your T-shirts, or had training wheels on your Harley-Davidson. Every casual greeting opened with: "How's the lawn, Buddy?" "Hey, Frank, see you got your crabgrass on the run." Or, "Set your blade down an inch, Buck. We all did."

Keeping up with a couple of hundred lawn enthusiasts was not only back-breaking, it was downright expensive. No one knew it any better than one poor devil in Suburban Gems who divorced his wife. His name was Lyle Link. The settlement was rumored to be the stiffest decision ever handed down in a court of law.

Lyle's wife received no alimony, no support whatsoever for the children, and she assumed payments on the house, the car, and the furniture.

Lyle got custody of the lawn.

It was like being on parole. He couldn't leave the state. He couldn't afford to remarry and there wasn't time to drink.

There were fertilizers, weed killers, maintenance, and keeping up with his neighbors. Lyle was spending more time at home than he ever did when he was married.

There wasn't a night he was not hauling bags of manure and nitrogen, trimming around walks and trees on his hands and knees, watering, mulching, and clipping.

Lyle started out with a hand mower, but eventually bowed to neighborhood pressure and got a rotary mower. This led to a lawn sweeper to pick up the grass, and an electric lawn trimmer to get close to the walk, and a spreader to evenly distribute new seed and fertilizer.

Every week there was some new gimmick to buy that sent everyone racing to the garden center. One evening as Lyle was tooling around in his riding mower with the reclining bucket seats and the console dashboard—his automatic sprinkler creeping along silently over the green carpet, his hedges topped perfectly with his electric hedge clipper, his trees being fed automatically just the right amounts of iron and nitrogen—his neighbor dropped by and said, "Too bad about your lawn, Lyle."

Lyle shut off his motor and paled slightly. "What do you mean, 'Too bad about my lawn'?"

"The whole neighborhood is talking about it. I thought you knew."

"Knew what? For God's sake tell me."

"Your lawn has root rot nematode."

Lyle's eyes misted. "Are you sure?"

"Didn't you see the little brown spots that never seemed to get better when you watered them?"

"And it's such a young lawn," said Lyle. "How long does it have?"

"With no bicycles, sleds, or kids running over it, I give it about a year."

"Well, we're not going to give up," said Lyle, squaring his shoulders, "they come up with new things every day. We're going to fight!" he said, heading out toward the garden center.

"Hey," yelled his neighbor, "maybe this isn't the time to bring it up, but I heard your wife is getting remarried."

Lyle turned slowly, disgust written plainly on his face. "What kind of an animal are you?" he asked, his voice quavering with emotion. "First you come here and tell me my lawn has root rot nematode and there's nothing anyone can do to save it and at best it only has a year to live, and then you babble on about my wife remarrying. Who cares? Don't you understand? If my lawn dies, I don't want to go on living any more. Leave me alone."

As the neighbor retreated, Lyle got down on his hands and knees and sobbed, "We'll travel. That's what we'll do—just you and me. We'll visit the White House lawn, the grounds at Mt. Vernon, maybe upper New York State where the grass is green most of the time and you can make new friends . . ."

Barbie and Ken

The real lifesaver of the economy was a pair of teenage dolls who appeared ironically one Christmas stacked (excuse the expression) among the baby dolls who burped, ate, cried, wet, walked, and were as sexless as a stick of gum.

My daughter picked Barbie up off the counter and exclaimed, "Look, Mommy, here is a doll that looks just like you."

I checked out the two-and-a-half-inch bust, the three-inch hips, and the legs that looked like two filter tips without tobacco and said, "She looks like she just whipped through puberty in fifteen minutes."

"I want her," my daughter whined.

Barbie cost $5.98 in the buff, so we purchased a little dress, a pair of pumps, a bra, and a pair of briefs that came to $6.95.

"Aren't we going to buy her a girdle?" asked my daughter.

"Let's wait until she eats and see if she needs one," I said.

If any of us believed for a moment that Barbie was going to be happy as a simple housewife, we were in for a surprise. Barbie was a swinger and she needed the wardrobe to do it.

Within a week, she had three lounge outfits ($5.95 each), an entire pool ensemble ($4.95), two formals ($7.95 each), a traveling suit ($6.95), and skating outfit ($5.00).

One afternoon as I was on my hands and knees fishing Barbie's beach ball out of the sweeper bag, my daughter announced, "Barbie's lonely."

"Terrific!" I said. "Why don't you mail her to Camp Pendleton. And send her satin sheets with her."

"I think we ought to buy Ken."

There was something weird about Ken, but I couldn't put my finger on it. He was a taller version of Barbie who came wearing a jock strap and an insincere smile. He cost $5.98. Within a week, his wardrobe consisted of tennis attire ($7.95), jump suit ($4.95), white tuxedo ($10.95), and a terry cloth robe ($3.95), plus a cardboard car ($12.95). As I explained to my husband, "You don't expect them to sit around night after night passing a beach ball back and forth, do you?"

The little freaks were draining our budget, but I bought some of the patterns and was able to satisfy their clothing appetite by sitting at the sewing machine day and night.

Then one day my daughter announced, "Ken and Barbie are getting married."

It seemed reasonable. After all, they were thrown together day after day in a shoe box under the bed and they were only human.

"What exactly does this mean to me?" I asked.

"Barbie has to have a wedding dress ($10.95) and a trousseau ($36.50) and Ken has to have a tuxedo."

"What's wrong with his white one?" I asked.

"That's for dancing—not marrying," she said.

"Anything else?"

"A wedding party."

"A what!"

"We have to buy Midge and some more people so they'll have people at their wedding."

"Can't you invite some of your other dolls?"

"Would you want someone at your wedding with bowed legs and diapers?"

The wedding was the social event of the year. Our gift to them was a cardboard house that looked like the Hilton.

It was months before all the bills were in but I figured the worst was over. Some families on the block were just starting with their first doll. All that was behind us now.

Then one afternoon in the kitchen, my daughter said excitedly,

"Guess what? Barbie's going to have a baby. You're going to be a grandmother."

My eyes welled with self-pity as I ticked off the needs—one naked doctor (who played golf on Wednesdays), two naked nurses (who snorkled on weekends), one ambulance driver in the buff who skied, an unclothed intern who . . .

3 〰〰

The Great Plastic Rush

"You Will Come to My Home Party"

One day, a typical suburban housewife was storing a leftover in a small, plastic bowl. As she pushed down the center of the lid with her thumb, a whooshing sound came out and her neighbor, who was having coffee, said, "Did you just belch?"

"Of course not," she smiled, "I am burping my Suckerware."

"Burping your Suckerware?"

"Right. I find when you force all the air out of your plastic bowl, your cantaloupe will keep for days in your refrigerator."

This was the beginning of the Great Plastic Rush. Within weeks, news had spread throughout the country and the city and women were coming on buses, cars, and bicycles to witness this religious experience.

They did not go home empty-handed. The Home Party was born and there was no stopping its growth.

This is how it worked. A housewife, motivated by the promise of a leftover tote bag, would invite twenty of her dearest friends to a party in her home.

Once inside, a professional pitch man would guide the guests to a dining room table laden with wares, and then oil his way through the group with an order form and a ballpoint pen.

No one was forced to go to a home party.

You went out of pure fellowship, need, and unsolicited fear. Fear that when you were tapped to host a party, no one would show up if you didn't go to theirs.

For an added incentive, you played games like "Dessert Bingo" to see how many words you could make out of the word "Leftover."

The plastics were the first to arrive on the suburban scene, but not for long. They were followed by the discovery of Whatever Cookware, Sarah Covet-Thy-Neighbor Jewelry, One-Size-Fits-All Sportswear, Bow-Wow Cosmetics, and many more.

Probably the most boring party I ever attended was hosted by the Whatever Cookware company. The Burly brothers (two manufacturer's representatives) came to our house early to cook the entire dinner in their pots that locked in flavor and held captive all the natural juices.

The natural juices weren't the only things held captive. As we sat around drinking celery cocktails I turned to my husband and asked, "So, whatya wanta do now?"

"We could check the expiration dates on our driver's licenses."

"I want to go home," I said stubbornly.

"You *are* home," he said. "What time do these birds serve dinner? I don't smell anything cooking."

"Of course you can't smell anything. The food is wallowing in its own juices which are locked in under the flavor-sealed lids."

Finally, one of the Burly brothers announced, "Dinner is served." That was only the beginning of the pitch. The Burleys were everywhere. At our elbows grinning, "Is that the most delicious roast you have ever put into your mouth? You have permission to talk with your mouth full."

"How's it going over here, guy? Here, give me your fork. Do you see how I can press it against this brussels sprout and the juices continue to flow?"

"Don't get up. What do you need? No salt, guy, please. Learn to eat au naturel. The taste buds will adjust to it in time."

"Do you detect just a hint of mint? Ahh, you are discerning."

"Eat the jackets!" he commanded one guest who was scooping out his potatoes. "Look at this folks. He's leaving all the nutrition on his plate."

Following the dinner, we arranged our chairs into rows and watched a double feature: "The Birth of Grease" and "An Enzyme Visits New York."

One Thursday night as I was preparing to go to a home hair-coloring party, I got a call from Dollie Sullivan.

"Guess what?" she said excitedly. "I am giving a plant party. Can you come?"

"What is a plant party?" I asked.

"It's where you bring your sick plants to be healed and to buy new ones. It's really different," she said and hung up.

I figured, why not?

The plant party attracted a group of people I had never seen before. I had been there only five minutes when someone wanted to go halvsies on a 100-pound bag of manure and a perfect stranger showed me her aphids.

"Girls! Girls!" said the plant representative, "I hate to break this up, but we've a lot of ground to cover this evening. No pun intended. First, I want to introduce you to my friends." Gathered around her on little chairs were a half dozen or so potted plants. She began to introduce them one by one. "This is Florence Floribunda, Polly Pothus, Ginny Geranium, Irene Iris, Dorothy Daffodil, and Phyllis Potbound—we'll talk more about Phyllis later. Now, before we get to the sickies, I want each of you to answer roll call with your favorite insecticide.

"Very good," she said when we had finished. "Now you all have an opportunity to find out about how to deal with your sick plants, so if you'll bring them up one at a time, we'll talk about them."

The first was a woman who was near tears.

"What seems to be the problem?" asked the leader.

"They have icky boo boo on the leaves," she sobbed.

"You're not being too scientific, but I know what you mean," she smiled. "Can all of you see the icky boo boo in the back? In Latin, it's called *primus blosis*. Its common name is dust. When a leaf is covered with five or six years of dust, it can't breathe. It suffocates."

"What should I do?" asked the woman.

"Let's do something gutsy," she said. "Let's wash it." (The crowd cheered.)

Next up was a woman whose plant was in the final stages of deterioration. The leaves were ashen and crumpled limply to the floor. The leader studied it carefully. "Do you talk to your plant? Give it encouragement? The will to live? The incentive to grow?"

"I talked to it yesterday," she said, "but I didn't talk very nice to it. I called it something."

"What did you call it?" asked the plant lady.

The owner whispered the word in the leader's ear. She too turned ashen and crumpled limply to the floor.

Toward the end of the evening, we were given the opportunity to buy fresh, new plants to refurbish the ones in our homes. I chose a beautiful split-leaf philodendron with shiny, green leaves in a pot of mulch fluffed up at its feet like a pillow. That night as I paced the floor with the plant over my shoulder I patted it gently and thought, "What the heck. It beats burping Suckerware."

4 ᭤᭤

Hazards of
Suburban Living

The Car Pool Crouch

A lot of my neighbors suffered from the Car Pool Crouch. It
was one of those dreaded diseases you say can never happen to
you.

Then one afternoon when you are attending a tea, someone will
point out that your knees are apart and your right foot is extended
out in an accelerator position. Your elbows are bent slightly and
you are holding your purse in front of you like a steering wheel.
When a woman leans forward next to you, your arm automatically
goes out to catch her when she hits the windshield that isn't there.

You've got it. The Car Pool Crouch.

I have seen perfectly healthy, young, upright women climb into
a car in September. By spring, they walked like Groucho Marx.

Out of the malady came the invention of the drive-in. A lot of
people think the drive-in was born out of convenience. That's not
true. It was born out of desperation of a community of women
who could no longer get in and out of their cars.

52

I once went for an entire week behind the wheel of the car and never missed a beat running my house.

I drove the children to school, idling my motor as they tumbled out of the back seat.

Then it was on to the bank where I pulled in to within inches of the window, slid my check under a bean bag in the drawer, and massaged my legs as I waited.

With money by my side, I next pulled into the cleaners where I left off a bundle and was rewarded with hangers full of clean ones.

At the film service drive-in, I barely had to slow down the car. Just make a hook shot and promise to be back by tomorrow.

At the service station, I sat numbly while he checked my oil, my water, and cleaned off my glasses.

Then it was lunchtime and into a drive-in eatery for a quick bite.

Positioning my wheels on the pulley, I sat in my car while I went through the car wash, feeling just a little uncomfortable with the numbness that was causing shooting back pains.

But there was the post office that had to be driven through and then it was time to pick up the children.

Naturally, we drove to a drive-in for a slushee treat and as dusk was approaching, we hit for a drive-in movie.

On the seventh day, my husband said, "Look, you've been in that car all week. You're pale. You need fresh air. You are also very short. Let's go to that new church everyone is talking about over on Rural Road."

I dressed carefully. And painfully. It had been a long time.

Hesitating, I climbed into the car. It was a drive-in church.

As I sat listening to the voice of the minister on the speaker, I heard him say, "This is the time to pray for any special favors you might wish from God."

I opened my door and with great effort, pushed my legs out.

Steadying myself, I grabbed onto the car with my hands and pulled myself up to my feet. I was standing.

From the other cars, I heard the applause, the voices raised in awe. Some blew their horns. "It's a miracle . . . a miracle!"

The Neighborhood Nomad

My husband put down his paper at breakfast one morning and said, "How many children do we have?"

"Three," I answered quickly.

"Then how come we have four children at breakfast every morning and at dinner each evening?"

I put down the cereal box and studied each one carefully. There was no mistaking the one boy. He had my husband's eyes and the girl definitely had my coloring. But the other two could have been phoned in.

"There's only one way to settle it," said my husband. "Will the real Bombecks please stand up."

They exchanged sheepish glances, a chair scraped, one started to get up, then sat down and finally, three got to their feet.

We all looked at Kenny, who sat there staring at a piece of toast.

"Son of a gun," said my husband, "I didn't know Kenny wasn't ours. And I just apologized to him yesterday for not spending more time with him."

"How do you think I feel?" I snarled. "I just got him toilet trained!"

When we pressed for details, it seems a little over a year ago, Kenny had wandered into our house to use the bathroom, liked it, and sorta hung around.

"How did you know where our bathroom was?" I asked.

"You have the Pee Wee model just like ours—only with a fireplace. I like a fireplace."

"Doesn't your mother worry about you?" I asked.

"She knows where I am."

"I think I met her. We both went to your parent-teacher conference. At the time I thought she was being a little pushy when she wanted to see your attendance record."

I went to the phone and dialed Kenny's mother. "Mrs. Wick," I said, "I am bringing Kenny home."

"Who?" she asked.

"Kenny, your son."

"Has he been acting up?" she asked.

"No, I just feel Kenny has been with us too long."

"Why do you say that?"

"Because my husband and I just realized we postponed our vacation because we couldn't get anyone to sit with Kenny."

"I understand," she said.

Kenny was right. Their house plan was identical to ours with the exception of a driveway lamp (extra) and colored bathroom fixtures (also extra).

I couldn't help but feel a twinge of guilt as I watched Mrs. Wick bustle around with her brood. No wonder she hadn't missed Kenny. The house was crawling with children.

"Joey, you turn off that garden hose this minute. It's making spots on the TV picture tube."

"Leroy did *what* in the swimming pool?"

"Celia! Get your sister off that sofa in that wet diaper."

"Who wanted the peanut butter and catsup sandwich? It's ready."

"Ann, get the phone and tell whoever it is I've run away from home."

"Shut the door!"

"Now you've done it. You've swallowed your space maintainer in your bubble gum."

"When you put meal worms in the refrigerator, Dan, kindly mark them 'meal worms.' Labeling them 'cole slaw' is not funny."

"Roger. I want to talk with you. Sit down. I've had it with you. You tease the younger kids. You hog all the toys. You refuse to take naps. Mr. Wick and I had a talk about you just last night. If you don't shape up, we're going to send you home to live, do you understand?"

I breathed a sigh of relief. "Thank goodness. Do you realize that for a moment, I thought all these children were yours?"

Mrs. Wick looked at me numbly. "None of them are mine. Kenny is an only child. Some of these children are lost, strayed, or just plain bored at home. They wander in and just sorta blend with the surroundings. Kenny just said to me one day, 'I hate crowds' and wandered off to your house."

"How did you know where he was?" I asked.

She shrugged. "Saw him pictured with your family on your Christmas card."

"How do things get so confused?" I mused.

"I don't know," she said tiredly, "you just wake up in the morning and mechanically feed anyone who's at the table and you get so busy with the door opening and shutting and little people wandering in and out and water fights and—excuse me (she leaned over to hear a toddler whisper something in her ear). It seems your son, Bruce, just locked himself in my bathroom. Do you want to talk to him?"

"My son, Bruce? What's he doing here?"

"He's been coming every day since Christmas. It seems Kenny got a fleet of heavy-duty trucks and Bruce is crazy for them. If you want to leave him here, we could use the exemption on our income tax."

"No, I'll take him home," I said.

Later, I lifted the phone to call my husband. "Hey, guess who's coming to dinner? Remember the little kid who looks like your mother?"

The Elusive
Washer Repairman

Every woman in the suburbs had a picture of a washer repairman in her billfold and a telephone number.

If, at any time, she spotted one, she was to report it to a central office where they recorded the sighting and tried to track him down. The fast-talking-elusive-repairman was an endangered species. Only five had been sighted in the suburbs during a five-year period.

We had all heard their voices. They said essentially the same thing, "I have you down for Tuesday." What we didn't know was (a) Who was I? (b) Where is down? and (c) What Tuesday?

But like fools, we waited. Every Tuesday, the streets were barren. Cars stood idle in the driveway. Doors were ajar. Some housewives sat on the curb in anticipation of the arrival of the washer repairman.

My washer had been broken for three weeks when I could stand it no longer. I called the washer repair service and said, "I demand you send me a washer repairman."

"Where do you live?" he asked mechanically.

"In Suburbian Gems."

"Our serviceman is probably lost. The houses all look alike to us. He'll get to you."

"When?"

"Look, lady, some people have been waiting longer than you and are desperate."

"Do you know what desperate is?" I asked evenly. "Desperate

is sending your kids to school in underwear made from broiler foil. Desperate is washing sheets in a double boiler. Don't you understand? I need a repairman."

"I have you down for Tuesday," he said.

On Tuesday, I was talking in the yard with Helen when suddenly, a few streets away I got a glimpse of a black leather bow tie.

"It's him," I shouted excitedly.

"What are you talking about?" asked Helen.

"A washer repairman. I saw my first washer repairman." I ran to the house to get the picture. "That's him all right," I said smugly. "Blue shirt, black leather bow tie, dark trousers, and a cap with a bill on it. You phone it in. I'm going over and collar him."

"I can't believe it," I said. "A real, live washer repairman right here in my kitchen. Would you mind if I called my neighbor, Helen? She's never seen a washer repairman and she wouldn't spread it around, honest."

"What's wrong with the machine?" he asked gruffly.

"It won't work."

"Anything else?"

"That's it."

"And for that you called me?" He removed the front panel and from that moment started to speak in tongues.

"Your rump bump is nad. Can't pft the snock without trickin the snear."

"That's easy for you to say," I said, "but what's wrong with it?"

"I said the roughing won't nit sowse you can't snapf the lig if the ffag won't chort."

"That bad?"

"Bad enough to need a raunch ring sloop."

"Is that why it won't spin?" I asked.

"No, the krincop broke and mital values stoffed to the weil ham made it groin."

I felt like I was talking to Professor Corey with a lip full of Novocain.

"Could you speak a bit more slowly?"

"How old is the zoinc spring?"

"Oh, the machine is three years old."

His eyes rolled back in his head and he shrugged his shoulders, "Whatya smag?"

"Will it live?"

"With a new thircon tube and a blowfest."

"Sir, could you possibly translate all that for me in a simple sentence that I could tell my husband?"

He stood up, wiped grease off his hands and in a voice that would have put Rex Harrison out of work announced, "Seventy-four dollars and thirty-four cents."

"Well, I suppose it will have to be fixed," I shrugged.

"Can't. Your fasack box is a 19689 model."

"Is that bad?"

"It's a discontinued fasack box. Used 'em only two months. When the smlax csble ghotend the galopian tube, it conjested the tubular laxenspiel and the overflowed hose kinked and someone screwed up and FIRE!"

"Let me get this straight. Are you telling me my fasack box catches fire?"

"What's a fasack box?" he asked.

"Whatever my 19689 model is. Are you telling me it's unsafe and I'll have to get a new machine? Well, I won't pay for it."

"Rapf your warranty, lady," he shrugged.

"Where is my warranty?"

"Printed on the bottom side of the washer."

After the washer repairman left, I discovered I had become an instant celebrity. Women all over the neighborhood piled in to ask questions about what a washer repairman looked like.

"I don't see why you didn't just lock the door and keep him here," said Helen.

"Some things are meant to be free," I said.

Trick or Treat . . . Sweetheart

Halloween was my sixteenth favorite holiday.

It rated somewhere between the April 15th Income Tax deadline, and a New Year's eve without a baby sitter.

My husband and I readied for Beggar's Night a full week before. We stored the lawn furniture, brought the garden hose indoors, hid the clothesline and clothes posts, and dragged the Junglegym set into the garage for safe-keeping.

When we lived in the city, Halloween had been a night for little people to dress up as witches and little clowns, knock timidly at your door, and wait to be identified before you dropped a gingersnap into their little bags.

In the suburbs, Halloween wasn't a holiday. It was a full-scale invasion. Car pools transported herds of children from one plat to another (planes and buses deposited children from as far as three counties away). Greed stations were set up where loot could be emptied and they could start out "fresh." And the beggars themselves were so intimidating that if your "treat" wasn't acceptable you could conceivably lose your health through pain.

The small children usually came between 5 and 5:30 P.M., while it was still daylight. After that the beggars got bigger, the costumes less colorful, and the demands more aggressive.

Opening the door, I confronted a lad over six feet tall, wearing a mustache, and carrying a shopping bag.

"My goodness," I cooed, "and what's your name?"

"*¿Qué?*" he shrugged.

"Do I know you?" I asked reaching up to tweak his mustache. The mustache was connected to his face by his own hair.

His partner nudged him. "*¿Cuál es su nombre?*"

"Manuel," he answered hesitantly. (Good grief, these had come all the way across the border for a bag of caramel corn.)

Next at the door was a twenty-seven-year-old or so wearing a dirty T-shirt and a leather band across his forehead and carrying a pillow case filled with ten-cent candy bars.

"Let's see," I mused, "you are too old for my insurance man and too big for King Kong. I give up."

He blew a giant bubble in my face and juggled his bag impatiently, "I'm Tonto."

"All right, Tonto," I said, "Here's a bright, shiny penny for you."

"Cripes, lady," he said, "can you spare this?" (Later, I was to discover Tonto very strong. Tonto bent TV antenna after I gave him his shiny new penny.)

Mentally, I began to draw up a list of rules and regulations that would give Halloween back to the little children. How do you know when you are too old to go "begging"?

1. You're too old to go begging when your mask tickles your mustache.
2. You're too old when you've figured out the only thing a penny will buy is your weight and you're watching it.
3. You're too old when you drive yourself to the subdivisions.
4. You're too old when you say "thank-you" and your voice is changing.
5. You're too old when you are rapping on the doors and Johnny Carson is signing off.

6. You're too old when you reach over to close your bag and your cigarettes fall out of your pocket.
7. You're too old when you have a sign on your bag that reads, "Personal Checks Accepted."
8. You're too old when the lady of the house turns you on more than the candy apple she just gave you.

Around eleven o'clock I refused to answer the door.

"Why?" asked my husband.

"Because we have run out of treats and when I told the last guy all I had left to give was a bruised orange, he moistened his lips and said, 'That's what you think, baby.' "

Seconds later, my husband returned from the door, "Quick! Give me some treats."

"I told you I don't have anything left. The refrigerator is cleaned out. So are the snacks. What do you think they would do if you offered them a raw potato?"

He peeked through the curtain and viewed two motorcycle freaks wearing sleeveless leather vests with no shirt and a helmet with a horn coming out of either side. "I think they would turn my nose inside out."

Crawling into the children's bedroom, we felt around in the darkness until we found their little orange trick or treat bags. We grabbed a few handfuls of taffy to appease the motorcycle gang.

Later, crouched in the hallway, the children's bags between us, my husband looked at his watch. "It's 11:30," he said. "Do we dare turn off the porch light?"

"I don't think so," I said tiredly. "It's too risky. The Mintons turned their lights off early last year and a group stole their garage. How much longer do you think we can hold out?"

"I don't know. How much ammunition do we have left?"

My fingers deftly counted out the bubble gum, the miniature candy bars, an apple with a bite out of it, and a few loose pieces of Halloween corn. "With luck, two or three hours."

We both sat up stiffly as the doorbell rang.

"I love you," I said simply, without emotion.

"I know," he whispered.

The Identity Crisis

You would have thought that with five thousand people living in Suburbian Gems we would have had an identity problem. This was just not true.

As I told my husband, "All you have to do is reach out to people and the warmth is there."

"I don't have time to socialize," he said. "I work. I cut grass. I watch a little TV and I go to bed so I can get up tomorrow and start all over again."

"And you're missing the entire concept of rural living," I said. "That of getting to know one another on a personal basis. Today is Saturday. Why don't you go down and borrow Lawnsweeper no. 1's charcoal starter for the party we are having this evening?"

"Is he the one next to the pot-bellied stove on the porch?"

"That's Lawnsweeper no. 2 and you know it. Besides, the stove was stolen last Halloween. No, Lawnsweeper no. 1 lives next to the faulty muffler."

"Oh *him*."

"I know, but his wife's nice."

"What's her name?"

"She's the size 18½ with five garbage cans."

"Why didn't you say so. Incidentally, did you invite the guy who saves his anti-freeze each year?"

"Had to. I invited the people with the air conditioner in their bedroom window and they live right next door to one another."

"That would be awkward."

"I only hope they get along with the super liberals."

"What super liberals?"

"The ones who live two blocks over next to the kid who sets fires."

"How do you know they are super liberals?"

"You know that little black jockey statue that has a ring in it to hitch a horse to? They painted him white."

"I remember that. The rhubarb grower had a fit."

"I've never trusted anyone who grows rhubarb."

"Before I go, do we have anything we've borrowed from Lawn-sweeper no. 1 and never returned? I'd feel like a fool asking to borrow something that's never been returned."

"You should feel like a fool. He's the one who borrowed our plunger and loaned it to the people with CATS FOR SALE."

"They've had CATS FOR SALE since we lived here. Do you suppose it's the same cat?"

"I feel sorry for the new people who just moved in next door."

"Who are they?"

"The Airstream people. What that little beauty doesn't have in it, they'll never need."

"They must have money."

"Wait until they find out they're wedged in between CATS FOR SALE and the people who let the plastic pool kill their grass."

"I remember him. Met him at a party at the house with the nut who flew the flag on John Wayne's birthday."

"How could you forget them? They own the house with that big Doberman who hides his head in your crotch and you're afraid to move. Speaking of weirdos, got a card from the two-car garage people."

"How did they ever fit a two-car garage on that lot is what I'll never know."

"If you met them personally, you would know. They're pushy."

"I thought so. Where did they go?"

"Went camping with the people with the built-in appliances."

"It figures."

"You'd better get going."

"Hey, I just remembered. You know how you always accuse me of not meeting new people? I met a newcomer last night when I was looking for our newspaper."

"Who is he?"

"Name of Alan Cornwall."

"I'll never remember that. Who is he?"

"The Porsche with the kid who spits on our tires."

"The one who just sprayed for bagworms?"

"That's him."

"Why didn't you say so? I hate name droppers."

5 ♨♨

The Heartbreak of Psuburbaniasis

The Seven-Inch Plague

In 1946, the suburbs suffered its first plague.

It struck with little warning and attacked the weak, the bored, the vulnerable seeking relief from the monotony. Its name was television and by 1966, it would enslave sixty-two million families.

We fell victims just before Christmas when my husband carried it home to us from the city.

The disease looked harmless enough—a seven-inch screen that looked like a hand mirror. We put it on the bookcase in the living room, got a vanity bench from the bedroom, and positioned our eyeballs sixteen inches from the screen where we became mesmerized as a full-grown woman carried on a conversation with two puppets.

Television was a terminal disease that was to spread and worsen, driving people from acute withdrawal to chip-dip attacks.

Because I am basically a strong person, I was able to resist the disease better than most, but my husband's addiction to television grew steadily worse. He became a sports addict who was in a catatonic state twelve months out of every year.

No one would have guessed that his condition would become so hopeless that I would approach a lawyer to have him considered legally dead. The lawyer advised me that due to the legalities this was not an easy thing to do. Just because a man sits in front of a TV set with eyes fixed and no pulse is not enough. He said I would have to keep a log of my husband's behavior over a year's period of time. I began to keep a diary in August.

August

The fifteenth of this month was visiting day for the children. Waiting for a beer commercial, I lined them up and said stiffly, "Children, this is your father." He offered them a pretzel at the same time watching a beer can dancing with a hot dog. When we insisted he stand up, the children gasped. They remembered him as a much shorter man.

September

The set went out today during the Dallas–Los Angeles game. "It could be a tube," I said.

"Shhh . . . get out of the way. The Cowboys are ready to score."

"No one is ready to score," I said. "You don't understand. The tube is black."

"That's ridiculous. Look at that lateral . . . my God, they've fumbled."

"Just relax. It could be only this channel experiencing temporary . . ."

"Lady, you are going to be temporary if you don't get out of this room and let me watch my game in peace."

I left him sitting in front of the black screen screaming and cheering. Maybe I can talk some sense to him when he is watching the commercial that isn't there.

October

Today, our living room was named the first recycling center to be served by a mobile unit. My husband was so engrossed in watching the World Series, he was quite unaware of what was going on.

Television cameras ground away while cub scouts gathered together eight barrels of cans, six barrels of bottles, and 500 pounds of paper.

I pecked my husband on the cheek as I left. He swatted at me and grumbled, "How did that fly get in here?"

November

I am really worried about my husband. On Sunday he sat in front of the TV set from noon until 10:30 P.M. There was no evidence of breathing. I called our doctor, who wheeled in an EKG machine to check the blood supply to his heart.

My husband rallied for a moment when the machine was placed directly in front of him. He bolted upright in his chair, blinked a few times, started fiddling with the knobs, and said, "All right, who's been messing around with the antenna?"

December

We have found it easier to decorate Daddy than to move him away from the television set.

First, we covered his feet with a simple felt skirt dotted with sequins. Then we hung a candy cane from each ear, and a string of lights around his head. Tonight, we are going to string popcorn and tinsel around his chest.

It's wonderful being a family again.

January

I'm terribly concerned about what's-his-name. He has watched more bowls this month than the restroom attendant at Kennedy Airport.

He does not eat well. I poked my head through the door today and said, "Have I got a bowl for you!"

"What is it?" he asked, dipping his spoon into it.

"I call it, 'Instant Replay.' In it are shredded sports pages, a dozen or so flip tops from beer cans, a few cigarette butts, and a lock of Howard Cosell's hair."

His eyes never left the set as he chewed mechanically. "It needs salt."

February

I read somewhere man does not live by Curt Gowdy alone.

Tonight, I slid into a nightgown made of Astro-Turf, and sat on the arm of his chair.

"I have a surprise for you," I said huskily.

"Keep it down. Fess Parker is trying to tree a coon."

"What would you say if I told you I had just bought a water bed?"

At first, I thought he didn't hear me. Then he turned slowly. "Are you serious?"

He bounded from his chair, ran to the bedroom, and a smile crept across his face. "Are you thinking what I'm thinking?" he asked.

"I hope so," I breathed.

"Now I can stock my own trout."

March

All the green things are coming out this month, except my husband. He is alive (if you call this living) and is being fed intravenously on a diet of basketball, baseball, golf, and hockey.

It has become a game with the family trying to think of ways to get Daddy out of his chair. We have tried, "Your sweater is on fire," "Watching hockey can cause bleeding gums," and "I am leaving. You get custody of the kids."

There is something very unnatural about a man who has a niche in the wall and every day puts fresh flowers under a picture of George Blanda.

April

The baseball strike postponed the opening game thirteen days. Through conscientious throat massage and stuffing his mouth with pebbles, we were able to get my husband up to four words a day during this period.

The first day he said, "Wha . . ."

The second day he said, "What."

The third day he was up to, "Whhhat is yyyour naaaame?"

The players settled their differences soon after and he has regressed once more to clearing his throat.

May

We put his mother in knee socks, shin guards, and a hockey face mask and shoved her in front of his chair for Mother's Day.

My husband was watching a ping-pong game and granted her an audience for only a few seconds. Then he punched her playfully on the arm and said, "Hang in there, kid."

June

In an attempt to clean out all the old things we never use any more, I realized that I had inadvertently set my husband at the curb on top of a rusted bicycle.

The driver of the truck led him to the house and said, "It's cute, but what's it for?"

"It does a lot of things," I said. "It eats leftovers, contributes body heat to a room, and can quote more statistics than the *Sports Almanac*. We use him for a doorstop."

"What's he doing with a candy cane over each ear?"

"He looked so great at Christmas, we hated to take him down."

July

"I am leaving you," I said calmly. "I can't stand it any more—the loneliness, the boredom, the roller derbies, the golf tournaments, the snacks. I'm young. I have all my own teeth. I want to see a movie besides the Frazier-Ali fight. I want to dance and drink champagne from a slipper. Do you understand?"

"Shh," he said, "there's a commercial coming up. The one where the beer can dances with the hot dog."

The Suburban Myth

There was a rumor going through the city that the suburban housewife drank her breakfast, accepted obscene phone calls—collect—played musical beds with her neighbors, and rewrote the book on Show and Tell.

The rumor was started by Edward C. Phlegg, the builder of Suburbian Gems, who was smart enough to know that when virtue moves in, there goes the neighborhood. And if anyone could sell the suburbs, sin could.

Everyone who lived there had the feeling that everyone was "swinging" except them. In fact, one evening in the paper there was a story about a "local" young mother who put her children under sedation every afternoon and engaged in an affair.

The idea intrigued us and we devoted our entire coffee klatsch to it. "Okay, who's the little temptress who is spiking the peanut butter with Sominex and carrying on in the daylight?"

We all sat there stunned.

"Marci?"

"What!" she sputtered. "And give up my nap?"

"Helen?"

"If you find my car in the driveway and my front door locked, call the police. I have my head in the oven."

"Linda?"

"Get serious. The last time I was in my bathrobe at noon, I had a baby in the morning and was dressed in time to get dinner that evening."

The plain and simple truth is the suburbs were not conducive to affairs. Bus service was lousy and in the winter you couldn't depend on it at all. The house numbers were all fouled up and it was difficult to find your way through the rows of houses in the plat.

The neighborhood was crawling with pre-schoolers who insisted on coming into their own houses to use the bathroom. The floor plan was clumsy. There were too many traffic areas—too much glass—and besides, there were no alleys for a Plan B alternate exit.

Everything was against us from the beginning, including the domestic rut we had fallen into.

As Marci pointed out, "I think we're fighting a losing battle. We wouldn't recognize a pitch if we heard it. Take me. Please. My vocabulary has been reduced to five sentences which I mumble like a robot every day of my life. They never change.

1. Close the door.
2. Don't talk with food in your mouth.
3. Check out the clothes hamper.
4. I saw you playing with the dog so go wash your hands.
5. You should have gone before you left home.

"The responses never vary—not in ten years of child raising. One night at a party," she related, "I drifted into the kitchen in search of an ice cube when a devastating man leaned over my shoulder and said, 'Hello there, beautiful.'

" 'Close the door,' I said mechanically.

" 'I don't believe we've met,' he progressed. 'My name is Jim and you are ????'

" 'Don't talk with food in your mouth.'

" 'Hey, you're cute. I like a sense of humor. What say we freshen up your drinkypoo and find a nice, quiet spot all to ourselves.'

" 'Check out the clothes hamper,' I said brusquely.

"He hesitated, looking around cautiously, 'Are you putting me on? I mean we aren't on Candid Camera or anything are we?' He slipped his arm around my waist.

" 'I saw you playing with the dog so go wash your hands.'

"His arm dropped and he edged his way to the door. 'Listen, you just stay put,' he said, 'I've got something to attend to.' "

"Tell me you didn't," said Helen.

"I yelled after him, 'You should have gone before you left home.' "

"Did you ever see him again?"

"Never," said Marci sadly.

"Well, someone is having a good time out there," said Linda. "Who could it be?"

"What about that slim blonde in the cul-de-sac, Leslie?"

"What about her?"

"I think she drinks," said Linda.

"What makes you think that?"

"Her curtains are drawn all day, the dog is never out, the car is always there, and she's pale."

We all exchanged glances. "You don't know about Leslie?"

Linda shrugged her shoulders. "She doesn't drink?"

"Not a drop," I said. "She's a Daytime Soap Operaholic."

"You're kidding."

"No, she has a fifteen-serial-a-day habit. Just sits there day in and day out with the curtains drawn and cries."

"Just because you watch a lot of soap operas doesn't mean you're addicted," defended Linda.

"Haven't you seen the literature from SO (Soap Operaholics)? Here, if you have any one of these symptoms, you're in trouble."

Helen handed Linda the SO Handbook.

1. Do you watch a soap opera at seven in the morning just to get you going?

2. Do you watch soap operas alone?
3. Do you hide *TV Guide* so your family won't know how many serials you are watching?
4. Do you lie about how many shows you watch a day?
5. Do you contend you can turn off "As the World Turns" and "Love of Life" any time you want to?
6. When you are "Guiding Light"-ed are you an embarrassment?
7. Do you refuse to admit you're a Soap Operaholic even though you refused to miss "The Secret Storm" to have your baby?

"If that isn't a kick in the head," said Linda. "The Suburban Orgy is a myth!"

Helen clapped her hand over her mouth. "Lower your voice, you fool. What do you think would be the resale value of these houses if that got out?"

Hosting a Famine

Fat just never caught on in the suburbs like I thought it would. I used to sit around and think how this is the year for the Obese Olympics, or the Pillsbury Eatoff or Bert Parks warbling, "There she goes, Miss North, South, and Central Americas," but it never happened.

Fat just never made it big. No one championed thin more than the women in Suburban Gems. Some dedicated their entire lives searching for a lettuce that tasted like lasagne.

They exercised. They counted calories. They attended Diet Seminars. Their entire conversation centered around how wonderful it felt to starve to death.

Ever since the babies came I had noticed a deterioration in my own body. My neck became extended, my waist filled in, the hips ballooned, the stomach crested, and my knees grew together.

One day my husband looked at me and said, "Good heavens. Are you aware that you are shaped like a gourd?"

At that moment, I converted to the suburban religion called Cottage Cheese. I ate so much cottage cheese my teeth curdled.

That wasn't the worst of it. Once you were an ordained cottage cheese disciple, you were committed to total understanding of the entire diet community.

I don't think I will ever forget the first luncheon I gave for my neighbors in Suburbian Gems. They were all on a different diet. It was like hosting a famine.

Helen was on the Stillman diet which means eight glasses of water, lean meat, and a bathroom of her own. (What does it profit a woman to look thin if you have to wear a nose plug for the rest of your life?)

Ceil was on the Atkins diet for which I cooked an egg swimming in butter served on a table in the corner due to her acute bad breath. (No diet is perfect.)

Marge was still on the drinking man's diet. She required a bottle, a little ice, and a clean glass. (Marge hadn't lost a pound, but it didn't seem to make any difference to her.)

Ethel was on the Vinegar-Kelp diet. (She worried us. She kept drifting toward the ocean.)

Wilma was enjoying maintenance on her Weight Watchers program. Before dinner was served, she ate the centerpiece (a candle and a plastic banana) and mumbled, "Bless me Jean Nidetch for I have sinned."

I, of course, had my cottage cheese.

Why do women do it?

You're talking to a pro. There was a time when I derived some comfort out of the knowledge that one out of every three Americans is overweight. But I never saw the one. Everywhere I went I was flanked on either side by the two chart-perfect women.

I was surrounded by women whose pleats never separate when they sit down, who wear suspenders to hold up their underwear, who have concave stomachs and the gall to say to me, "I'm cutting down. Do you want my dessert, honey?"

Every dieter has her moment of truth when she faces up to the fact that she is overweight. Sometimes, it's just a little thing like seeing a $50 bill on the sidewalk and not being able to pick it up, or accusing the car wash of shrinking your seat belt, or having shortness of breath when you chew gum. With me, it was a photograph taken on the beach. You couldn't see the blanket I was sitting on, or the sand, and only a small part of the ocean.

My husband said, "The best diet in the world is to put that picture of yourself on the refrigerator door."

He was right. The picture was delicious and actually contained few calories, but with the picture gone I fell into my old eating habits.

The Fat-Picture-on-the-Door diet is just one of many that have swept the country during the past decade, each one promising you more food than you can eat, instant results, and strangers on the bus coming up and asking you to dance.

There was one diet that wasn't publicized, but I think had great merit. It was called the Tall Rat Experiment X-70, or as it was popularly called, "Grow Up—Not Out."

The program was perfected by a scientist named Bert Briarcuff whose basic philosophy was, "There is no such thing as a fat girl. They're only too short." Of course; why hadn't anyone thought of that! Women weren't overweight. They were undertall.

He gathered together several cages of obese rats and went to work to make them look taller.

The results were astounding. Rats in wedgies looked five pounds thinner than those in loafers. The rats in jump suits with vertical stripes gave the illusion of being thin while those in polka dots looked grossly overweight.

Then he employed the old photographic trick. When a rat was talking with someone in the gutter, the rat placed himself on the curb. If his companion was on the curb, he stood on the steps. If his partner jumped on the steps, he would leap to a spouting above.

Briarcuff found that by teasing the rat's hair, his cheekbones would stand out like Katherine Hepburn's. Women didn't have to starve to death any more. They would just have to learn to create an illusion of tallness.

The Tall Rat Experiment X-70 spread like wildfire in our neighborhood. We shopped at tall girl shops to get the waistlines to hang around our hips. We volunteered to take off our hats at movies. I personally made no new friends over five foot two.

At a dance one night I vowed to dance with no one taller than I. I bet I danced with every ten-year-old boy there.

After six months, however, the Tall Rat Experiment X-70 began to bore me. I was sick of stacking pillows in the car to make me look like my head was coming through the roof.

Besides, I had a new toy. The kids chipped in and bought me a Flab-Control belt. As they explained it to me, there was no dieting. All I had to do was put the adjustable belt, which was equipped with a small electronic buzzer, around my waist. When my stomach muscles became slack, the buzzer would sound. It was a case of chronic flab. The noise drove me crazy. I went back to cottage cheese.

Desperate, I enrolled in one of the Gastric Show and Tell classes offered at the high school in the evenings.

Their program seemed quite revolutionary to me. Foods that I had always considered decorations for the mantel like carrots, cucumbers, squash, and chard were touted as edibles. Following interesting lectures on nutrition and how certain foods were needed for the body, our instructor, Miss Feeney, asked, "Are there any questions?"

"What if I go through all of this and discover the life after this one is all fat people?"

"Don't make trouble," she said softly. "Just try the foods."

By the end of three weeks when I had not dropped an ounce, Miss Feeney took me aside and said, "You promised you would try to stick to our diet. What happened?"

"Miss Feeney," I said, "you have to face up to what you are dealing with. Dieters are basically nice people. I have a snout full of integrity. I don't throw my chewing gum on the sidewalk. I don't put less postage on my letter than I know it takes. And I don't lie about my age. But when it comes to diets, you can't believe a word I say."

"You will live to eat those words," she said.

My face brightened. "Are they fattening?"

Oh, there were others. The denture-adhesive diet where you cement your teeth together and the one-size-fits-all pantyhose worn to the table, but I always came back to cottage cheese.

It's not so bad—a little gravy over it once in awhile, a cottage cheese sandwich between two warm slices of homemade bread, a cottage cheese sundae with a glob of chocolate. . . .

6 ❦

Ya Got Trouble

NEWS ITEM: Plans for a proposed drive-in movie will be submitted to members of the Suburbian Gems Plat Council at Wednesday night's meeting.

The theater, to be known as The Last Roundup, would be erected on the patch of ground between "CLEAN FILL DIRT WANTED. CALL AFTER 5 P.M. at 959–8800" and Ned Stems' Car Wash. Estimated to occupy about thirty acres, it will feature a western motif, 350 speakers, a refreshment stand, and permanent personal facilities. Prof. Harold Swill, vocal band director of Suburbian Gems High School, is heading a group of dissidents opposing The Last Roundup and is expected to speak out against the proposal.

"A drive-in movie!"

"Don't you understand? Friends, either you are closing your eyes to a situation you do not wish to acknowledge or you are not aware of the caliber of disaster indicated by the presence of a drive-in movie in your community.

"Well, ya got trouble, my friends, right here, I say trouble right here in Suburbian Gems. Sure, I'm a lover of the arts and certainly mighty proud, I say mighty proud to say it.

80

"I consider the hours I've spent with Sousa and Romberg are golden, helps you cultivate timing, discipline, a natural ear, and a way to get girls.

"Did you ever take a pocket comb covered with toilet paper on a picnic and improvise with Tiger Rag—hah! I say any boob can fake a few bars of the "Beer Barrel Polka," but I call that tacky— the first big step on the road to the depths of degrada . . . I say first the Rape of Mozart, then a near-beer six-pack.

"And the next thing you know your son is marching with hair right down to his knees, listening to some stoned-out hippie talking about pot.

"Not a shiny cooking pot with Mom's ham and beans, no siree, but a pot where they freak out of their skulls, makes you sick I should say, now friends let me tell you what I mean, you got R (restricted), X (nothing censored) and a GP where Flipper gets a hickey—movies that make the difference between a pervert and a bum with a capital B that rhymes with D that stands for drive-in.

"And all week long your Suburbian Gems youth'll be goofing off—I say your young men will be goofing—goofing away their noontime, suppertime, choretime too, hook the speaker to the car, never mind getting the lawn fertilized, the sand in the litter box, sitting little sister and never bother delivering the Sunday paper till the supervisor calls on a Sunday afternoon and that's trouble, my friend—lots of trouble—I'm thinking of the kids in the back seat, kissing till their braces spark, cold popcorn, melted ice balls and that's trouble, right here in Suburbian Gems with a capital T which rhymes with D which stands for drive-in.

"Now I know all you folks are the right kind of parents. I'm gonna be perfectly frank. Would you like to know what kind of conversation goes on while they're watchin' those outdoor flicks? They'll be talkin' about Gatorade, trying out filter tips, popping in breath mints like pill-popping fiends, and bragging all about how they read *Valley of the Dolls* in one swell evening.

"One fine night as they leave the drive-in, headed for the malt shop, you'll find your son, your daughter in the arms of an over-sexed sophomore, mattress-minded—all systems go, parental guidance . . .

"Friends! The idle motor is the devil's playground!

"Trouble, oh ya got trouble, trouble right here in Suburbian Gems, trouble with a capital T that rhymes with D that stands for drive-in. We surely got trouble—gotta figure out a way to stamp out puberty.

"Trouble—trouble—trouble.

"Mothers of Suburbian Gems. Heed the warnings and the tell-tale signs of corruption before it's too late.

"The minute your son leaves the house, does he stuff his 4-H bylaws in the glove compartment?

"Does he take a blanket on a date and tell you the heater in the car isn't working and it's August?

"Does he have a copy of *Playboy* hidden between the pages of *Boy's Life?*

"Has he ever refused to finish a knock-knock joke in your presence?

"Are certain words creeping into his conversation—words like 'far out' and 'Linda Lovelace' and 'Ma, where's your purse?'

"Well, my friends, you got trouble, trouble with a capital T that rhymes with D that stands for drive-in.

"You surely got trouble, right here in Suburbian Gems, re-member God, Motherhood, Flag—and Paul Harvey.

"Oh, oh you got trouble, terrible, terrible trouble that field of passion under a sky of stars is the flag of sin.

"You got trouble, trouble, trouble, oh great big trouble right here in Suburbian Gems with a T that rhymes with D that stands for drive-in."

*   *   *

NEWS ITEM: Plans for a proposed drive-in movie were approved last night when members of the Suburbian Gems Plat Council reached a compromise.

Originally, council members complained that the speakers might contribute to noise pollution in the area. Approximately 140 students, representing Suburbian Gems High School, volunteered as a group to turn the sound off completely during the showing of movies.

Prof. Harold Swill, band director of Suburbian Gems High School, said, "It is maturity like this that restores my faith in young people."

7 ঙঙ

It Comes with the Territory

Loneliness

No one talked about it a lot, but everyone knew what it was.

It was the day you alphabetized your spices on the spice rack.

Then you dressed all the naked dolls in the house and arranged them on the bed according to size.

You talked to your plants and they fell asleep on you.

It was a condition, and it came with the territory.

I tried to explain it to my neighbor, Helen.

"I'm depressed, Helen," I said, "and I think I know what it is. (Excuse me) *'Lonnie!* I see you sneaking out of the house with my mixer and I know what you are going to do with it. Put it back!' "

"More coffee?" asked Helen.

"Just a half a cup. I've seen this coming for a long time. The symptoms are all there."

"What symptoms?" asked Helen.

84

"Helen, I'm so bored. I went to the food locker yesterday to visit my meat."

"You're kidding."

"No. And the other day I flushed a Twinkie down the toilet just to please Jack La Lanne. (Just a minute) 'Is anyone going to get the phone? Never mind. Hello. Yes. What do you want? I'm in therapy with Helen. You'll be home late and don't wait dinner. Right.' Now, where was I, Helen? Oh yes, my behavior. It's bizarre. Remember when a man came out to clean the septic tank? I dropped everything, ran out, and sat on the edge of the hole and asked, 'So, what's new with you?' "

Helen nodded silently.

"I called my mother long distance the other day just to tell her I found a green stamp in my sweeper bag."

Helen stirred her coffee slowly. "Did you ever put up your hair to answer the door?"

"Yes. Oh yes," I said with relief. "Excuse me, Helen, someone's at the door. (Later) It was Joan. She just dropped off her two and she'll be back for lunch. Where was I? Oh yes, my problem. I find myself doing odd things I've never done before. Remember when Dr. Joyce Brothers was on a local talk show and they invited questions from the audience? I called in, Helen. I really did. And I announced to the entire English-speaking world that I wanted her psychological opinion of a man who insisted on sleeping next to the wall. Did I ever tell you that, Helen? Bill refuses to sleep on the outside of a bed. He's positively paranoid about the inside track. Didn't it ever occur to him that just once I might like to sleep next to the wall?"

"Your phone is ringing again," said Helen.

"It was the school nurse. Wanted permission to give my son an aspirin. What he really needs is an enema. I wonder how many people are wandering the streets today in glasses who only need an enema. More coffee?"

"No, I can't stay long," said Helen.

"I've thought about my problem ever since we moved out here and I think I've finally put my finger on it. Every morning, we see the men driving out of paradise onto the freeway and into the city. Leaving us to what? Did I tell you I spent an hour and a half the other morning putting together a cannon out of balsa wood that I found in the cereal box only to discover one of the kids swallowed the wheel and we couldn't play with it? Wouldn't you know if you had a wheel in your mouth?"

Helen sighed. "You going to the Frisbee recital at the school Friday?"

"I suppose so. Hang on a minute. There goes Nancy and I still wanted to talk with her about Wednesday. 'Hey Nancy! We going to that 1-cent tree sale Friday after the store? Let's go early. It's a mob scene.' Sometimes, Helen, I wonder why we moved to the suburbs. As I told the girls at Trim Gym class last week, I never thought I'd see the day when I'd want my own apartment before the kids did."

"You're just restless," said Helen.

"No! I'm not restless. That's not the word," I said vehemently. "Restless is having lunch with your wigs and having a good time with them. It's a temporary condition that goes away. I'm talking about old, Helen. I'm old. Don't protest. I know what I am. I'm old and fighting for my identity in a young society. Everyone around me is under twenty. My doctor carries a gym bag. Our lawyer is still in braces. And I swear to you my dentist had a string on his mittens last winter. Do you know what it is to go into a confessional and have your priest reeking of Clearasil?"

"It's not your imagination?"

"It's not my imagination. I don't know what is wrong with me. I'm . . . I'm so desperate. I purposely picked a fight with the hamster yesterday. I stood in front of the hall mirror and said, 'So, who did you expect? Snow White?' "

"There's nothing wrong with the way you look," comforted Helen.

"I'm a mental midget, Helen. My husband is growing professionally every hour and I didn't even know penguins got barnacles on their feet until Pearl Bailey missed it on 'Hollywood Squares.' It's hard to talk to a man who has a meaningful relationship with the TV set."

"Well," said Helen, "I've got to be going."

"Say it! I'm boring, aren't I?"

"Of course you're not boring."

"Do you know that if I had continued my night school classes I would have graduated from college this June. That's right. If I had just found my car keys I could have picked up my B.A. and could be one of those women who only wash on Saturdays and freeze their bread."

Helen looked at me squarely. "Do you know what you are?"

For a moment, there was only the silence of a toilet being flushed consecutively, two dogs chasing one another through the living room, a horn honking in the driveway, a telephone ringing insistently, a neighbor calling her children, the theme of "Gilligan's Island" blaring on the TV set, a competing stereo of John Denver, one child at my feet chewing a hole in the brown-sugar bag, and a loud voice from somewhere screaming, "I'm telling."

"I'm lonely," I said softly.

"Tell your husband," said Helen.

Tell my husband.

I once read a poll of what husbands think their wives do all day long.

The results were rather what you would expect.

Thirty-three percent said women spent five hours out of each day putting lint on their husband's socks.

Twenty-seven percent said they spent four hours daily pouring grease down the sink and watching it harden to give their husbands something to do when they got home.

Ten percent swore their wives held the door open all day to make sure all the warm/cool air (depending on the season) got out of the house.

A walloping 58 percent said women divided their time between hiding from the children, watching soap operas, drinking coffee, shrinking shirt collars, discarding one sock from every pair in the drawer, lugging power tools out to the sandbox for the kids to play with, and trying to get the chenille creases out of their faces before their husbands came home.

I was dialing Mrs. Craig's number when my husband came home one night after my conversation with Helen.

"Who are you calling?" he asked.

"Mrs. Craig. I thought she could sit with the children for a few days while I ran into the city to visit Mother."

My husband leaned over and gently replaced the receiver. "Do you honestly believe that I can't handle things around here without you? I'll do double time between here and the office and fill in until you get back."

"You've never been a strong man," I said.

"What kind of a crack is that?"

"I'm only suggesting that any man who has to have a spinal block to trim his toenails doesn't have the greatest threshold of pain in the world."

"And who went to bed for three days when she had her ears pierced?"

"That's not true. Look, I was only trying to spare you. Are you sure you can handle things around here? The kids? The cooking? The laundry? The routine?"

"Does Dean Martin know how to handle a martini?" he grinned. "Of course I can handle this stuff. Don't worry about it. You just go off and do what you have to do and don't give us another thought."

I didn't give them a thought until I let myself into Mother's house in the city. "Call home," she said.

"One quick question," said my husband, "what does 'Bwee, no nah noo' mean?"

"Who said it?"

"Whatya mean who said it? Your baby just said it and looked kinda desperate."

"It means, 'I have to go to the bathroom.' "

"Thanks, that's all I needed to know. Have a good . . ."

"It also means, 'I want a cookie. Where are my coloring books? The dog just crawled into the dryer. There's a policeman at the door. I am floating my $20 orthopedic shoes in the john.' The kid has a limited vocabulary and has to double up."

"I can handle this. It's just that she looks so miserable."

"It also means, 'It's too late for the bathroom.' "

As I readied for bed, the phone rang again.

"What's up?" I asked.

"No problem," he said cheerfully. "It's just that Maxine Miltshire just called and can't drive the car pool tomorrow because she's subbing for Janice Winerob on the bowling team. She can pick up—unless it rains. Her convertible top won't go up. However, if the weather is decent she can pick up and trade with Jo Caldwell who is pregnant and three weeks overdue, but who had a doctor who was weak in math. That means I will drive Thursday unless Jo Caldwell's doctor lucks out. In that case I'll have to call Caroline Seale because I have an early meeting and it might rain. Do you understand any of this?"

"No."

"I'll call you tomorrow night."

The next night I answered the phone. There was a brief silence. Then, "Well, I hope you're happy, Missy. I am now the only thirty-eight-year-old child in my office who has been exposed to roseola. I was late for work because little Buster Smarts was eating chili off the dashboard of my car and spilled it all over the upholstery and my job is in jeopardy."

"Why is your job in jeopardy?" I asked.

"Because *your* son answered the phone this morning while I was putting catsup on sandwiches and I heard him tell Mr. Weems, 'Daddy can't come to the phone now. He's hitting the bottle.' "

"Tomorrow is Saturday. It'll get better," I promised.

The phone rang early Saturday.

"Hello," I giggled. "This is Dial-a-Prayer."

"Oh, you're cute," he snarled, "real cute. Just a couple of questions here. First, where are the wheels off the sweeper?"

"On the back of the bicycle in the garage."

"Check. Where does the washer walk to when it walks?"

"It never gets any farther than the door."

"Check. When was the last time you were in the boys' bedroom?"

"When I was looking for eight place settings of my good china."

I arrived home much later from the city than I intended. Everyone was in bed. My husband staggered to the door.

"I'm home," I announced brightly. "Tell me, why is there an X chalked on the side of our house?"

He rubbed his eyes tiredly.

"A baby sitter put it there. I think we're marked for demolition."

I wandered through the house. The dog was drinking out of an ashtray. There was a pad of blank checks by the phone with messages scribbled on them. The blackboard had a single message on it, "I'm leaving and I'm not coming back." Signed, "Daddy."

"Why is the baby asleep in the bathtub?" I asked.

"She drank four glasses of water just before bedtime."

"There is a crease on your face shaped like a duck."

"I had to separate the boys so I slept in the baby's bed."

I opened up the refrigerator and a leftover reached for me and I slammed the door shut.

"What happened?" I asked, spreading my arms out to make a wide circle.

"Don't start up," he said. "It's all your fault. I had dinner so long in the oven that the bucket caught fire."

"What bucket?"

"The cardboard bucket holding the chicken."

"You're supposed . . ."

"Don't say anything. I mean it. While I was trying to put out the fire, *your* baby chose a rather inopportune time to get a penny stuck up her nose. I've got thirty-five boys in the bathroom watching movies. I tried to make a drink and there are no ice cubes, and besides, Maxine called to tell me I've been named homeroom mother! And all the while you are living it up at your mother's, drinking out of clean glasses."

"You'll feel better after a good night's sleep," I said as he crawled back into the crib.

I was right. The next morning he turned to me brightly and said, "Good-bye, dear. You'll find everything in ship-shape order. Boys, kiss your father good-bye."

The boys turned away and one said flatly, "He murdered our guppies."

"We'll talk about it tonight," he said. Then he whispered, "By the way, could you call and let me know how Lisa makes out on 'As the World Turns'?"

The Pampered Dog

When the dogs in the city talked among themselves, the conversation always drifted to the suburbs.

It was the dream of every canine to someday live out where every dog had his own tree, where bad breath had been conquered, and where fleas had to register at the city limits and carry their I.D.'s at all times.

The suburban dog had it made. Owners pampered them to death with dietary dog food, dental appointments, knitted stoles to take off the evening chill, dog beds shaped like hearts, doggie bar nibbles, and car seats.

I personally felt I could live a fulfilled life without a live-in lawn fertilizer, but my husband convinced me the children would grow up to steal hubcaps without the security and affection of a dog.

In a weak moment, we bought Arlo.

The first day Arlo came home, his feet never touched the floor. In a single day he was fed eight times, burped five, danced on the TV set, slid down the banister, was given a bath, blown dry with my hair dryer, visited twelve homes, rode on a bicycle, and barked long distance on the phone to Grandma. He slept his first night under my dual-control thermal blanket.

On the second day, Arlo continued to reign. It took eight saucepans to warm his dinner, he watched a puppet show staged by the children for his benefit and as he headed for the door, one of the children slapped his brother while the third child leaped for the dog and opened the door . . . first.

On the third day, there were some complaints from the children that Arlo had kept them awake all night with his howling. When I suggested the dog be fed, one son said his brother did it, who vowed his sister did it, who said, "It's not my turn."

On the fourth day, my daughter took Arlo to Show and Tell. He blew it by showing too much and didn't have a finish, and a clean-up committee of one was delegated to do the honors. One of the children said if Arlo followed him to school one more time and he had to bring him home he was going to kick him.

On the fifth day I reminded all of them that the rule of the house was that the first one to spot a puddle, etc., automatically cleaned it up. The entire household fell victim to indoor blindness.

On the sixth day, I said, "Has anyone seen Arlo?"

One of the children yelled back, "Arlo who?"

So much for security and affection.

I began to become suspicious that Arlo was not a registered Irish setter when his roots came in white, his nose was concave, and within six weeks he was eye level to the kitchen table.

This was confirmed as I sat in the vet's office one afternoon. I shifted uncomfortably as a woman read a magazine to a cat with running eyes, a pet raccoon ran around the playpen, and a small terrier mistook my leg for a forest.

Finally, a well-dressed man on my left with a small poodle ventured, "I am intrigued with your breed. What kind of a dog is that?"

"Irish Setter," I said.

He looked astounded. "You have papers?"

"All over the house." I got a firmer grip on the forty feet of pink plastic clothesline around Arlo's neck and ventured, "What's wrong with your dog?"

He looked soulfully at the poodle and patted it gently, "Jessamyn isn't sleeping well."

"Me either," I said.

"She's just been through a rather bad pregnancy."

"Me too," I said excitedly.

"Actually, Jessamyn is too highly bred and tense for motherhood."

"I know what you mean," I commiserated.

"We thought of aborting, but there was so much social pressure brought to bear, we finally consulted a psychiatrist who thought it best to go through with the births and then get them away from

her as soon as possible so she could pull herself and her life together again and then exercise some measure of birth control.
What's wrong with your . . . Setter?"

"Worms."

"How disgusting," he said, wrinkling his nose. "I wonder what's
keeping that vet?" he said. "I have some flowers in the car for
Jessamyn's mother."

"Jessamyn's mother?" I asked, my eyes widening.

"She's (he leaned over and spelled slowly) P-A-S-S-E-D-
O-V-E-R. Jessamyn and I go once a month to visit. They were
very close. She's at the Bow Wow Cemetery. Beautiful grounds.
Incidentally, if you ever go on a vacation and need a reliable shelter
the K-9 Country Club is a marv. Restricted, you know. None of
your tacky clientele. The ones with the new luggage. They have
a chef there you wouldn't believe. Well," he said as he was summoned, "Nice meeting you and good luck to—what's-his-name?"

"Arlo."

"Oh my God," he said, touching his nose with his linen hand-
kerchief and sniffing.

Because I am basically a "swift" person, it didn't take me long
to realize that Arlo and I were to become an "item." Just the two
of us. I fed him, kept his water bowl filled, got him shots, license,
fought fleas, took out ticks, and let him in and out of the house,
2,672 times a day.

My husband came home one evening to view the dishes on the
breakfast table with hardened egg, the unmade beds, the papers
from the night before strewn all over the living room, the laundry
spilling out over the clothes hamper onto the floor, and said, "Fess
up! You've been playing with that dog all day long."

"Did anyone ever tell you you have a future in comedy . . . along
with Jane Fonda and Eric Sevareid?"

"C'mon now," he teased, "look at the way that little dickens is
jumping up and down."

"The little dickens is aiming for your throat. He wants out."

"Don't be ridiculous," he said. "He just came in when I did."

"So now he wants out. I go through this over two thousand times a day. The dog has a Door Wish. He can't go by one without scratching it until it opens. The other day he scratched, barked, and jumped for fifteen minutes. Finally, I opened the door and he ran in and two minutes later started scratching again. He realized he was under the sink."

"Why does he want out so much? Maybe something is wrong with his kidneys?"

"A dog with kidneys the size of a lentil could have better control than he has."

"I got it," said my husband, snapping his finger. "We'll go out when he goes in. That way we'll confuse him into not knowing if he's out or in."

Standing there huddled in the darkness on the cold porch scratching with our paws to get in, I tried to figure out where I went wrong. I think it was when my mother said to me, "You're not getting any younger."

"You are going to think this is a dumb question," I asked, "but why did we get a dog in the first place? I mean, if it was for the kids, forget it. All it has done for them is to keep them from looking down when they walk."

My husband took me by the shoulders and I saw shock written on his face. "Do you mean to tell me you really don't know?" he asked.

"No."

"We did it for you," he said.

"You bought a dog for me?" I asked numbly.

"But of course. For your protection. Maybe you don't realize the dangers of being by yourself out here in this wilderness. There are loonies and crazies running around all over the place."

"True, but we're all on a first-name basis."

"You may be as light about it as you like, but just wait until some day when I am at work in the city, and a wild-eyed stranger knocks at your door and wants to use your phone on some pretense and you'll be mighty thankful Arlo is around."

I looked at Arlo. He was lying on his back in front of the fireplace with all four paws sticking up in the air—passing gas.

The mental picture of a sex pervert at my door and the only thing between us was Arlo sent a shiver down my spine.

It was several weeks later that Arlo was to be put to the test. I answered the door to find two men standing there rubbing Arlo behind the ears.

"Pardon us," said one of the men, "but our truck broke down and we'd like to phone our company for help."

I grabbed Arlo by the collar and jerked him to his feet. "I must apologize for the dog." I said. "I'll try to hold him so he won't tear you to shreds. Down boy!"

The men looked at one another and shrugged as the dog blinked sleepily and slumped to the floor. "He looks pretty friendly to me," said one of them.

I knelt and pushed back Arlo's lip to show his teeth. When I released the lip, it fell back into a ripple as he licked my hand. "You may not believe this but I had to register this dog with the police as a deadly weapon. Just ask anyone around here and they'll tell you about Arlo."

"Arlo?" the men grinned.

"Steady boy!" I said, propping him up to get him off my foot. "Just don't make any sudden moves," I cautioned.

One of the men came inside to use the phone while Arlo and I held the other man at bay at the door.

"Why, one of the kids was just playing around one day," I related nervously, "and inadvertently punched me on the arm. Arlo liked to have made raw meat out of him before we could pull him off."

"Is that right?" asked the stranger.

His friend returned and together they thanked me, playfully pushed Arlo over on his back, scratched his stomach, and left.

As they walked to the car I heard one say, "Boy, that was one terrifying experience."

"What, the dog?"

"No, the woman. She's a real whacko!"

They were probably right and I realized things weren't going to get any better when one afternoon I answered the phone. It was Mr. Wainscott.

"Remember me?" he asked. "I'm Jessamyn's father."

"Of course," I said, "from the vet's waiting room. Jessamyn is the one who had the same symptoms as I had. I've been dying to ask what the doctor prescribed."

"Lots of bed rest, time to herself, no major decisions, analysis, and a light social calendar."

"I guess one out of five isn't bad," I said. "So, how are things?"

"Fine. I was calling to ask if Arlo could attend Jessamyn's birthday party. Are you there?"

"Yes," I said. "A birthday party. Where?"

"This Saturday at two. We live two blocks north of the highway next to the golf course. You can't miss it. Oh, and it's informal."

When we arrived a dozen or so dogs romped around the room.

"So glad you could come," said Mr. Wainscott.

"I must apologize for the present," I said, "Arlo ate it on the way over."

"That's perfectly all right. Gang!" he shouted, "this is Arlo. Arlo is one of Jessamyn's neighbors. Don't be frightened," he said as Arlo stood at the sink and licked water out of the spigot. "He's big for nine months. Why don't you pick Arlo up in a few hours?"

I don't know what happened to Arlo at the party, but he was never the same dog after that. One day I caught him looking at his teeth in the bathroom mirror (Jessamyn had her teeth capped).

Another time, he hopped on the bathroom scale, gasped, and refused to eat table scraps any more. One afternoon, I begged Arlo for ten minutes to go outside. He was sitting in a chair watching David Susskind.

The only time he seemed happy was in his encounter group.

The Garage Sale

There are four things that are overrated in this country: hot chicken soup, sex, the FBI, and parking your car in your garage.

What's such a big deal about pulling your car into a garage if you have to exit by threading your body through an open window, hang from a lawn spreader, climb over the roof, and slide down a garden hose before reaching the door?

Our garage was a twilight zone for garbage, the dog, old papers, boxes, excess laundry, redeemable bottles, and "projects" too awkward (big, dirty, stinking) to have in the house. So was everyone else's. In fact, there was a garage clause in most of our accident policies that if we were folded, bent, spindled, or mutilated while walking through our garage we could not file a claim.

Then one day something happened to change all of that. Helen came over so excited she could barely speak. "How would you like to go to a garage sale?" she asked.

"I have one."

"You don't buy the garage, you ninny," she said. "That's where the sale is. A woman over in the Dreamland Casita plat just advertised and I want to check it out."

A good fifteen blocks away from the sale, we saw the cars bumper to bumper. I had not seen such a mob since the fire drill at the Health Spa.

We parked the car and walked, slowly absorbing the carnival before our eyes. On the lawn, a woman was trying on a skirt over her slacks. "Do you do alterations?" she yelled to the woman who had sold it to her.

"Whatya want for 25 cents?" she yelled back, "An audience with Edith Head?"

Inside, mad, crazy, frenzied ladies fought over an empty anti-freeze can for $1.50 and an ice cube tray with a hole in the bottom of it for 55 cents.

One lady was lifting the snow tires off the family car and shouting, "How much?" Another was clutching a hula hoop over her shoulder and asking, "Are you sure this is an antique?" An older couple was haggling over a pole lamp insisting it would not fit into their car, and arrangements must be made for a suitable delivery date. It was marked 35 cents.

Outside, Helen and I leaned against a tree. "Can you believe this?" I asked, "I feel like I have just attended Alice's tea party."

"What did you buy?" asked Helen excitedly.

"Don't be ridiculous," I said, "It's all a bunch of junk no one wants. I didn't see anything in there I couldn't live without."

"What's that under your sweater?"

"Oh this. It's the only decent thing worth carrying out."

I held it up. A framed picture of the "Last Supper" done in bottle caps.

"Isn't that exquisite?" I asked.

"That is without a doubt the worst looking picture I have ever seen. Look how distorted the faces are and besides, Judas is rusting. How much did you pay for it?"

"Six dollars," I said defensively.

"*Six bucks!*" said Helen doubling over, "you've got to be kidding." As she laughed, an electric iron dropped from behind her handbag.

"What's that?" I asked.

"An iron. I really needed an extra one."

"It doesn't have a handle."

"So why do you think I got it for 75 cents?"

"Look," said a lady who had been standing at our elbow for ten minutes, "are you going to buy this tree or just stake it out so no one else can get to it?"

"No," I stammered . . . moving away.

She dug her shovel into the soil and began moving dirt.

Frankly, I didn't give the garage sale another thought until another neighbor, Grace, said to me one day, "Why don't you stage a garage sale?"

"Because spreading one's personal wares out in a garage for public exhibition is not only crass, it smacks of being tacky."

"Pauline Favor made eighteen bucks," she said.

"Get the card table," I snapped.

My husband was less than enthusiastic. "Those things are like a circus," he said. "Besides, we need all of this stuff."

"Hah!" I said, "that is all you know. This stuff is junk. One of these days we'll wake up and find the junk has taken over. We won't be able to move for boxes of rain-soaked Halloween masks, and stacks of boots with one missing from each pair, and a broken down potty chair. If you want to live like a pack rat, that's your business, but I've got to make a path through this junk—and soon."

In desperation, he gave in and the garage sale was scheduled for Thursday from 9 A.M. to 5 P.M.

At 6:30 A.M. a woman with a face like a ferret pecked on my kitchen window and said, "I'll give you 30 cents for this door stop."

I informed her the door stop was my husband who is not too swift in the mornings and if she didn't put him down this instant, I would summon the police.

By 7:30 there were fifteen cars parked in the driveway, nineteen on the lawn, two blocking traffic in the center of the street, and a Volkswagen trying to parallel park between the two andirons in my living room fireplace.

At 9 A.M. I opened the garage door and was immediately trampled to death. Grace said she had never seen anything like it.

They grabbed, pawed, sifted through, examined, and tried out anything that wasn't nailed down, but *they weren't buying.*

"What's the matter with them?" I asked.

"It's your junk. It's priced too high."

"Too high!" I exclaimed. "These heirlooms? Do you honestly think that $8 is too much for a box of candle stubs? And this stack of boots for $5 each. They don't make rubber like that any more. And besides, who is going to notice if you're wearing a pair that don't match? Dare to be different. And take this potty chair . . ."

"For twelve bucks, *you* take it," said a potential pigeon. "You can buy a new one for $15."

I wanted to hit her. "With training wheels? Why, this potty chair can take a kid right into football season. When collapsed, it will fit snugly in an Army duffle bag. It's not for everybody. Only the discerning shopper."

"You are going to have to lower your prices," whispered Grace.

Grace was right. Of course, but she should have prepared me for the personality change I was about to experience when I sold my first piece of junk.

I became a woman possessed. As one by one the items disappeared from the card tables and the nails on the side of the garage, I could not stand to see the people leave.

They bought the boots with a hole in the sole, electric toothbrushes with a short in them, a phonograph that turned counterclockwise, and an underground booklet listing the grades of Harvard Medical School graduates 1927–1949.

The junk began to clear out and I knew what I must do to keep them there. Running into the house, I grabbed dishes out of the cupboards, clothes out of the closets, and books off the shelves.

I snatched my husband's new electric drill and marked it $3. I ripped the phone off the wall and sold it for $1.75. When my son came home from school, I yanked him off his bicycle and sold it for $5.

I grabbed a woman by the throat and said, "Want to buy a fur coat for $1? I was going to give it to my sister, but she looks like a tub in it."

"I am your sister," she said dryly.

To be perfectly honest, I lost control. Grace had to physically restrain me from pricing the baby, who was being admired by a customer who cooed, "I'd like to take you home with me."

It was seven o'clock before the last car left the driveway. I was exhausted mentally and physically.

"Did I do all right?" I asked Grace.

She hesitated, "In a year or two, when you are well again, we'll talk about today."

"I don't know what happened to me," I said.

"You were a little excited."

"Are you trying to tell me I went crazy?"

"I am trying to tell you it was wrong to sell your garbage for 40 cents."

"But she insisted," I said.

"By the way," said Grace, "what's that under your arm? You bought something."

"It's nothing," I hedged.

She snatched the package and opened it. "It's your laundry!" she said, "that you keep in a plastic bag in the refrigerator. How much did you pay for this?"

"Two dollars," I said, "but some of it still fits."

8 ᘜᘜ

Law and Order

THE TEN MOST UNWANTED WOMEN
IN THE SHOPPING-CENTER PARKING LOT

DOLORES FRONKBINDER throws body over parking space to save it for a friend

DEBBIE FRUMP leaves motor running giving false hope she is ever coming back

IRIS STIGMATISM pulls into "handicapped only" parking spot with infected hangnail

WILMA WHIPLASH parks between two spaces to keep door from getting dented

ALICIA EARLY parks in a spot near door when shopping center is under construction and leaves it there

FLORENCE SYKES Alias: The Pied Piper leads a trail of hopefuls around in search of her lost car

PHYLLIS HARDHAT Woman who makes a sharp left turn into your parking place and pretends she doesn't see you

RUBY WYNETTE Alias: (See Postal Clerk) Woman with packages you follow for three hours who drops off packages and returns to shop

PAT PILL Woman who drives an emergency vehicle to the store to take advantage of parking

MARIETTA BUSCH Woman with "Jesus Saves" bumper sticker with a pedestrian clutching the hood of her car

Who's Watching the
Vacant House? Everyone.

I had only met officer Beekman on two occasions.

The first time was when I inadvertently rammed into my husband's car when I backed out of the driveway and he was summoned by my husband. (The case is still pending.)

The second time was when he helped me over a rather bad spot in my driver's test by chalking a B on the brake pedal and an A on the accelerator.

"I suppose you are wondering why I have summoned you," I said as I let him in the front door.

"Yes Ma'am," he said, removing his crash helmet and his dark glasses.

"My husband and I are going on vacation and . . ."

He held up his hand for silence and looked around him anxiously, "Are we alone?"

"I think so."

"Fine. That is the first rule. Never tell anyone you are leaving."

"I understand."

"We handle hundreds of house-watching assignments each year and the key word is: *secrecy.*"

"Don't people become sorta suspicious when they see a police cruiser in front of the house every night?"

"I don't park in front of the house every night," he explained, "I just sorta cruise by and give it this." (His head jerked like he was having a neck spasm.) "Now, the second key word is *lived-in.* Make your potential burglar believe you are home by leaving on a light or a radio playing. If you'll just tell me where you are going, when you'll be back, and give me a number where you can be reached, we'll take care of everything."

"That's wonderful," I said, seeing him to the door. As he climbed into the car I shouted, "See you in two weeks!"

He touched his finger to his lips and said, "Remember, secrecy is the key word."

Helen was the first one over after he pulled away. "Why was the police cruiser in your driveway?"

"Shhh," I said, looking around. "We're all going to Yuuck Village for two weeks and Officer Beekman is going to watch our house to see that no one burglarizes it. Don't tell anyone. He said the key word was secrecy."

For a change, my husband agreed. "That is the smartest thing you have ever done," he said. "Who are you calling?"

"Officer Beekman's second suggestion was that the house look 'lived-in.' I'm calling Margo to tell her when we are leaving so she can come in every night and turn on a different light. Then I have to call the paper boys and the dry cleaner—and the postman."

"What about discontinuing the milkman?"

"Discontinue the milkman? Why don't you just stand out in front of the house in your underwear and hold up a sign reading, 'COME IN AND BROWSE.' Thieves follow milkmen like flies follow a garbage truck. Let me handle this. I'll just have him deliver four quarts every other day like he's always done."

"Won't the crooks get suspicious when he drinks all four quarts and takes the empties back to his truck?"

"He'll just rattle a few bottles and pretend he's delivering," I sighed. "Now, where was I? Oh yes, I have to tell Mike we're leaving so he can come over and cut the grass, and Mark so he can plant garbage in our cans and put them at the curb on garbage day and . . ."

"I don't believe this," said my husband.

"You'd believe Maybelle Martin, wouldn't you? She and Dave were going to Disneyland for a few days. She dressed up her sewing form in a pants suit and a wig and propped it against the mantel with a drink in its hand. Her house was robbed the next morning. They took almost everything but the form. Do you know what gave her away?"

"Someone noticed she had a pole for legs?"

"The ice cubes in her drink melted and even crooks know no one stands around with a warm drink in his hand."

"You have told seven people already that we are leaving. How many more are you going to tell?"

"Well, I have to tell Charmaine to bring her children over to play in the yard, and Frederika said to call when we leave so she can bring her dog over on a weekend to bark. Naturally, I'll have to call my hairdresser, my cleaning lady, my insurance agent, my car pool girls . . ."

"That's sixteen."

"My Avon lady, AAA, the soft-water man, the utility meter reader, the Cub pack . . ."

"That's thirty-three."

"Of course our family vet and the check-out girls at Willard's market, my foot doctor, the guys at Bufford's service station, our minister, and Miss Baker, who does that chatty column in the *Tattler* . . ."

"Roughly, how many people are you telling we are leaving town?"

"About 683."

"Why don't you just take an ad in *The New York Times?*"

"Glad you reminded me. Grace said a great way to get phone calls while you are gone is to put an ad in the paper selling a toaster or something."

"Or you might even let a dozen insurance agents think you are in need of a good liability policy. There is nothing like a ringing telephone to scare robbers away from an empty house."

"I think you are overreacting to the entire situation," said my husband. "All these elaborate measures to make the house look lived-in are insane. If you get any more people running in and out of here, we'll have to stay home and park cars."

We both dropped the subject until a few days ago when my husband came into the kitchen where I was preparing dinner. "I met an interesting fellow today in the garage where I park my car," he said. "He arrived here two days ago from Chicago. When I introduced myself he said, "Oh, you're the fellow who is going to Yuuck Village for ten days beginning the fifteenth of next month."

"How could he have known that?" I asked, my mouth falling open.

"It seems his wife's nephew had a corn removed by a foot doctor who attended a cookout the other night at the home of our meter reader."

"Gas, electric, water, or taxi?" I asked carefully.

"It's not that important," he continued. "What was rather interesting was a story he told me regarding their vacation last summer. He said they were only gone a matter of hours when their house was ransacked. Picked clean."

"Didn't I tell you!" I shouted triumphantly. "Let me guess. They forgot to leave a radio playing low so burglars would hear sound. Or they didn't hire a cat to sit in their window. I got it. They didn't plan a party in their house while they were gone or leave bicycles lying around in the driveway."

"They did all of those things," my husband said softly.

"Then what did they forget?" I shouted.

"To lock the front door."

Suburbian Gems Police Blotter

- Stolen grocery cart spotted
- Dog complaint
- Fire hydrant buried by snow
- Officer requested for women of the moose law enforcement appreciation dinner
- Summons issued for DWI, driving with 0.10 percent or more alcohol in bloodstream and illegally parking in lobby of drive-in bank

- Woman having trouble with neighbors
- Rescue unit answered call of cat in dryer
- Went to gas up police car and pump went dry
- Report of strange-acting car. It was running well
- Call from supermarket that young male trying to purchase beer for his sister to shampoo hair
- Found door open at town hall. Nothing missing
- Woman reports harassing telephone calls from ex-husband
- Owner of dog in heat demands thirty dogs be evicted from his property
- Had brakes and drums replaced on police car
- Young boy hitchhiking claims he was running away from home. Sought assistance in crossing highway
- Bread delivery tipped over on sidewalk. Notified store manager. Restacked bread
- Report of septic tank odors
- Checked out burgled car wash coin box
- Got police car washed
- Woman reported car lights in cemetery. All three cruisers responded to call
- Women reported large dog from next door deposited a mound the size of Mt. Olympus on their lawn each morning. Requests gun permit
- Man reports having trouble with house builder. Thinks wife may have been harassed. His attorney working on problem
- Bicycle stolen while chained to bike rack
- Supermarket reports bike rack stolen
- Restaurant files missing report for twelve steaks and five bottles of booze. Possible party in progress
- Flat tire on police car fixed at garage
- Illegal burning of leaves at 8486 N. Platinum Lane
- Bad check returned to woman who thought her husband had made deposit
- Fire gutted Suburbian Gems library. Loss estimated at $143.95
- Subject observed urinating in parking lot

- Man reports kid plugging flow of creek
- Principal holding suspected drug user. Subject revealed pills to be breath mints
- Private citizen complains churchgoers blocking his driveway every Sunday. Warned of legalities in letting air out of tires
- Officer requested to speak to Rotary Club on "Crime! It's a jungle out there!"
- Officer called to investigate dirty word scratched on exit ramp freeway sign. Sign out of jurisdiction. Also misspelled
- Expectant mother requested assistance in getting out of compact car

9 〰〰

Put Your Winnebagos into a Circle and Fight!

You couldn't help but envy the Merediths.

Every weekend, they left their all-electric, three-bedroom, two-bath, w/w carpeted home with the refrigeration and enclosed patio and headed for Trailer City.

Here, these thrill-seekers parked their trailer between a tent holding thirty-five people, and a public toilet. They did their laundry in a double boiler, cooked over an inverted coffee can, killed mosquitoes that had their own air force, and watched the sun set over a line of wet sleeping bags.

We never dreamt that someday we too could escape all of our conveniences and head beyond the suburbs where the air smelled like kerosene and the streams were paved with discarded beer cans.

Then one day my husband pulled into the driveway with a twenty-one-foot trailer hooked behind the car.

It was the biggest thing that had happened in the neighborhood since home milk deliveries. The entire neighborhood turned out to inspect it.

Standing in the middle of the trailer, I felt like Tom Thumb. It looked like a miniature doll house. Those dear little cupboards. The little beds. The little stove. The miniature doors and windows. The tiny closets. What fun it would be keeping house. Of course, there would have to be a place for everything and everything would have to be in its place, but I could hardly wait to hit the open road.

"You know," said my husband, "it might be even more fun if we went with another family."

"You're right," I said. "Things are much better when they are shared."

"Are you thinking about the same couple as I am thinking?"

"Get serious," I said. "Who else would I be thinking of but Eunice and Lester?"

Eunice and Lester had moved to Suburban Gems the same time as we. Their two children were between our three agewise and there had never been a cross word between us.

"Lester is a prince," said my husband. "Why I'd use Lester's wet toothbrush."

"And I've never had a sister closer to me than Eunice," I mused. "If Eunice was pregnant, I'd volunteer to carry it for her."

We called Eunice and Lester that night and together we planned a two-week vacation. Originally, we talked about the first of June but Lester had an appointment to have his teeth cleaned and he needed a few days to get back on his feet and Eunice's horoscope forbade her to travel until her sign got off the cusp, so we juggled the schedule around and came up with the first two weeks of July.

The *Mayflower* never had a bigger send-off. The four of us packed provisions for three months. There were Eunice's astrology charts and her wok ("I never go anywhere without my wok"), and Lester's pills and ointments and of course the gear brought by their children Beezie and Wendyo: a four-by-six baseball return net and an inflated walrus (which when we tried to deflate threw Wendyo into terminal paranoia), the food and the extra linens, and the motor for the boat—but it was fun.

Then we all waved good-bye and climbed into the wagon and were off. "Isn't this going to be fun?" I said, clasping Eunice around the waist.

"Watch it!" she winced. "My kidneys."

"What's wrong with your kidneys?" I asked.

"Nothing, now that your son has his guitar out of them."

"Maybe we should trade," I giggled. "I'll take my son's guitar out of your kidneys if you take your son's bubble gum out of my left eyelash."

We both laughed so hard we almost fell out of the car.

Several miles out of town a pattern began to form. Our two families and our little travel trailer were only part of a caravan of campers which snaked in a thin line all the way across the United States.

At one point, we tried to pass a motorcycle, which was attached to a U-Haul, which was pulled by a trailer, which was hooked to a boat, which was hitched to a Volkswagen, which was being towed by a station wagon laden with vacationers.

They were all winding around the highways looking for the same thing—a picnic table. Hours passed and everywhere we went it was the same story. Someone had gotten there first. I looked at the children. Their faces were white with dust, one was coughing from exhaust fumes, and the others were staring silently with hollow, vacant eyes out of the rear window.

"Maybe," I said, touching my husband's arm gently, "we should turn back. We should never have left the suburbs to come to this God-forsaken scenic route. It's not for myself, I'm begging, but— for the children. Soon they are going to need fresh air . . . fresh fruit . . . restrooms . . ."

"Just hang on a little longer," said my husband. "I heard at the last pit stop there was a picnic area about eight miles down the road."

"Do you suppose it would have a shade tree nearby?" I asked. "Don't get your hopes built up," he said. "It was just a rumor."

We bumped along another ten miles when Eunice spotted it. "Look! A picnic table!"

Tears welled in my eyes. "All right, children, get ready. The moment the car slows down, you all jump out and run over and throw your bodies across the table until we can park and get there."

They poised their bodies at the door ready to spring when panic set in.

"There's an Airstream coming in at four o'clock," said Lester.

"There's also a four-wheel drive bearing down over the ridge," said my husband, shifting gears.

We all skidded in in a cloud of dust as the children spilled out of the cars and flung themselves on the table. When the dust had settled, we discovered we had all been too late. A dog was tied to the picnic table to stake it out for another camper.

We pulled our vehicles into a circle to plan our next strategy.

Somehow, after a dusty lunch standing around a gas pump, we all felt better and continued on toward the Ho Hum Campgrounds, arriving around dusk.

"Parking the trailer is a little tricky," said my husband. "I'd appreciate a little help."

"What are fellow-campers for?" said Lester. "I'll direct you from the front."

"And I'll stand near your left rear wheel," chirped Eunice.

"I'll stand near your right rear wheel," I said, saluting smartly, "and the children can relay any messages you can't hear."

My husband pulled up and started to back in.

"Turn your wheels," yelled Lester.

"Which way?" answered my husband.

"That way!" said Lester.

"Which way is that way?" returned my husband.

"To the left," said Lester.

"Your left or my left."

"Your left."

"Hold it!" screamed Eunice.

"What's the matter?" yelled my husband, jamming on the brakes.

"Not you," yelled Eunice, *"him!"*

"Who me?" yelled Lester.

"No, Beezie. He's making those faces at Wendyo again and . . ."

"For crying out loud, Eunice," snapped Lester. "This is no time to yell at the kids."

"Okay, when Wendyo cries, I'll send her to you."

"What did I just hit?" yelled my husband.

"Just a tree limb," I shouted.

"I can't see. It's on my windshield."

"You should have been watching for him above," said Eunice.

"It wasn't my side, sweetie," I purred.

"Turn! Turn!" shouted Eunice.

"Which way?"

"The right way."

"Not right," yelled Lester. "She means left."

"Don't speak for me, Lester," said Eunice, "I can speak for myself."

"Are we level?" asked my husband.

"What's this little hole for?" I asked.

"Where is it?" asked my husband.

"Right here in front of me," I said.

"I mean *where* is it?"

"Under your tire."

"Good heavens, that's my hook-up."

"Straighten it up," said Lester.

"Pull forward," said Eunice, "you've only got this far."

"How far?" asked my husband.

"Look at my hands," said Eunice.

"I can't see your hands," said my husband.

"I can see them," said Lester, "and she's crazy. You got another three feet back there."

"Let's just leave it," said the driver, "until it stops raining."

"It's not raining," said Lester, "you just hit a water hook-up on the next trailer."

"My God," I groaned as the water hit me, "and me without a hairdresser for two weeks."

"Moooommmmmeeeee," whined Wendyo.

"Did I tell you, Lester?" (To Wendyo:) "Tell your father."

"What is she doing out of the car?" yelled Lester.

"If you get your foot run over don't come skipping to me, Missy."

"Dad! If Wendyo is out of the car, how come we can't get out?"

"I think we're in quicksand," I yelled. "The car and the trailer are sinking."

"It is not sinking," said Lester. "The tire is going flat."

My husband got out of the car. It had taken nine people and forty minutes to help him back into a spot that was a pull-in . . . accessible by two roads.

The next morning, we all felt better about our togetherness— so much so that I decided to keep a diary.

THE FIRST DAY: This is going to be such fun. All of us have a job on the duty roster. The children are in charge of firewood. Lester is the camp doctor. Bill is in charge of camp maintenance, and I am the house mother. Eunice is the social director and is picking out songs to sing around the campfire.

The men are having a wonderful time. As Bill said this morning, "That Lester is a prince. Do you know what he is doing? He is out there fixing the motor already."

"What's wrong with the motor?" I asked.

"The pin dropped out of it in 12 feet of water at the dock."

"Who dropped it?"

"Lester did, but it was an accident. He reached back to swat a mosquito and lost his balance. Lester said he had a balancing problem."

I can believe that.

THE SECOND DAY: As Eunice was out on a nature hike with the children (they are labeling trees) Bill said, "What are you doing?"

"Washing out the public garbage cans," I said. "As Eunice pointed out, you don't know where they've been. She is so meticulous. You know, we are so lucky. Can you imagine spending two weeks with a couple of slobs? Yuuuck."

THE FIFTH DAY: Didn't mean to miss so many entries in my diary, but I've been so busy. Isn't it funny, the things you worry about never happen. I was wondering how two cooks could occupy this little kitchen. Eunice hasn't been in the kitchen but once since the night we got here. It's not her fault. Poor dear has been trying to find a store in the area that stocks bean curd cakes and lotus roots for the wok.

Lester is a klutz. I don't know how poor Eunice stands it. Always running around with a nasal spray hanging from his nostril. Right after he dropped the pin from our motor in the water, he dropped our flashlight down the only outdoor convenience. It's still down there lit. Now we can't see where we're going—only where we've been.

I have to tell myself fifteen times a day that Lester was wounded at Ft. Dix when he stapled his elbow to a private's request for transfer.

THE SIXTH DAY: What kind of animals leave hair in a brush on the kitchen table? At first, I thought it was little Beezie or Wendyo but neither of them has combed his hair in a week. It has to be their parents.

Tonight, just to break the monotony, we invited the Parkers over from the next trailer to spend the evening. Eunice told that amusing story she tells about the nun not knowing what to order in the bar and having a little booze in a coffee cup. I love the way she tells it. Eunice *is* funny. Her horoscope told her she was going to have an adventure on water. I hope so. I've carried every drop of it!

THE NINTH DAY: This trailer is driving me up the wall. There's more room in an oxygen tent and it's better arranged. The other day I took the cap off the toothpaste and had to open the window.

The refrigerator holds a three-hours' supply of meat, the oven makes one piece of toast at a time, the sink converts to a bed, the bucket doubles as a bar stool, and yesterday when Lester and Eunice slept late, we had breakfast on Lester's chest.

Tonight, Eunice sleeps with the wok!

THE ELEVENTH DAY: As I said to Bill when we undressed for bed, "How long have we known Eunice and Lester?" He said, "About six years," and I said, "Isn't it strange that we never noticed that Lester snorts when he laughs. When Eunice told that ethnic slur about the nun again, he sounded like a '38 pickup truck with water in the fuel line."

"He's a prince though," said my husband. "I mean the oil slick wasn't really his fault. He was only trying to wash the dust from our car by backing it into the lake and just accidentally hit the crankcase with a rock. It would never have happened had he not had one of his blinding migraines."

THE TWELFTH DAY: Are you ready for this? King Lester said this evening, "Why didn't you tell us the mosquitoes were so bad this time of year?"

"If Eunice had gotten off her cusp in June, there wouldn't have been any mosquitoes," I said. "Besides, my kids have taken all they're going to take from Heckle and Jeckle or whatever you call your two weak chins with the overbite."

"It's not the season," said Eunice bitterly. "It's the fact that your children are on the threshold of puberty and still don't know how to close a door."

"Speaking of doors," I said, "when was the last time you opened an oven, refrigerator, or cupboard door?"

"I suppose my braised prawn sandwiches did not meet with your middle-class taste?" she snarled.

"I don't pretend to be a connoisseur of *bait!*"

"Just a second, Erma," interrupted Lester, "if it hadn't been for Eunice's wok, we'd have starved to death."

"Only because you used my only large cooking pan to store a snapping turtle for Sneezy."

"That's Beezie!"

"It's one of the seven dwarfs!"

"Someone had to play with the children," said Lester, "since Bill was too busy cleaning out his tackle box."

"Only after you spilled the suntan lotion all over the lures, Fat Fingers."

"Hold it!" I said. "We are all exhausted from having such a good time. Let's sleep on it."

THE THIRTEENTH DAY: Tomorrow we go home. No more marshmallows catching fire and burning black. No more sand in the butter. No more bathing suits that smell like fish. No more soggy crackers.

All that is left is a stack of postcards no one mailed.

You know something? Now that I've read them, I didn't realize we had such a good time.

I wonder if Eunice and Lester could get off her cusp for a couple of weeks next year. . . .

10 ෴

Super Mom!

A group of first-graders at Ruby Elementary School were asked by their teacher to draw a portrait of their mother as they saw her.

The art was displayed at an open house.

Some mothers were depicted standing on a sailboat. Others were hauling groceries, cutting grass, or talking on the telephone.

All the mothers had one thing in common. They were pregnant.

In the suburbs, pregnancy wasn't a condition, it was the current style. Everyone was wearing a stomach in various stages of development—whether you looked good in one or not.

I frankly felt I was too short for pregnancy and told my husband so. A lot of women looked great when they were expecting. I was always the one with the hem that reached down to the ankle in the back and up to the knees in front and I forever dribbled things down my stomach. Usually, I went into maternity clothes at two weeks and by the ninth or tenth or eleventh month my drawstrings wouldn't draw and my mirror talked back to me.

Sometimes, I'd sink into a chair in my fifth month and couldn't get out until the ninth month of labor/or the chair caught fire— whichever came first.

The preoccupation with motherhood was the only thing we had in common. From then on, mothers were divided into two distinct groups: the Super Moms and the Interim Mothers.

The Super Moms were faster than a speeding bullet, more powerful than a harsh laxative, and able to leap six shopping carts on double stamp day. She was a drag for all seasons.

Super Mom was the product of isolation, a husband who was rarely home, Helen Gurley Brown, and a clean-oven wish. There was a waiting list for canonization.

The Interim Mothers were just biding their time until the children were grown. They never gave their right name at PTA meetings, hid candy under the dish towel so the kids would never find it, had newspapers lining the cupboard shelves that read, "MALARIA STOPS WORK ON THE CANAL," and secretly believed that someday they would be kissed by an ugly meter reader and turned into Joey Heatherton.

There were no restrictions in Suburbian Gems. Super Moms were free to integrate at any time they wished and when one moved in across the street, I felt the only decent thing to do was welcome her to the neighborhood.

The moving van hadn't been gone a minute when we saw her in the yard waxing her garden hose. I walked over with my nine-bean "trash" salad and knocked on the door. Her name was Estelle. I could not believe the inside of her house. The furniture was shining and in place, the mirrors and pictures were hung, there was not a cardboard box in sight, the books were on the shelves, there were fresh flowers on the kitchen table, and she had an iron tablet in her hand ready to pop into her mouth.

"I know things are an absolute mess on moving day," I fumbled.

"Are people ever settled?" she asked, picking a piece of lint off the refrigerator.

Then she waltzed in the children and seeing one lock of hair in her son's eyes, grimaced and said, "Boys will be boys!"

If my kids looked that good I'd have sold them.

"Hey, if you need anything from the store, I go every three hours," I offered.

"I shop once a month," she said. "I find I save money that way by buying in quantity and by planning my meals. Besides, I'm a miser with my time. I read voraciously—right now I'm into Cather and I try to go three or four places a week with the children. They're very aware of contemporary art. Now they're starting the romantics. Could I get you something?" she asked softly. "I just baked a chiffon cake."

I felt my face break out.

"The doctor said I have to put on some weight and I try desperately . . . I really do."

I wanted to smack her right across the mouth.

Frankly, what it boiled down to was this: Could a woman who dyed all her household linens black to save time find happiness with a woman who actually had a baby picture of her last child?

The Interim Mothers tried to get along with Estelle, but it wasn't easy. There was just no getting ahead of her. If the Blessed Mother had called Estelle and said, "Guess what, Estelle, I'm expecting a savior," Estelle would have said, "Me too."

She cut the grass, baked her own bread, shoveled the driveway, grew her own herbs, made the children's clothes, altered her husband's suits, played the organ at church, planned the vacation, paid the bills, was on three telephone committees, five car pools, two boards, took her garden hose in during the winter, took her ironing board down every week, stocked the freezer with sides of beef, made her own Christmas cards, voted in every election, saw her dentist twice a year, assisted in the delivery of her dog's puppies, melted down old candles, saved the antifreeze, and had a pencil by her telephone.

"Where is Estelle?" asked Helen as she dropped by one day.

"Who knows? Probably painting her varicose veins with crayolas to make them look like textured stockings. I tell you that woman gets on my nerves."

"She is a bit much," said Helen.

"A bit much! Would you trust a woman who always knows where her car keys are?"

"I think she'd like to be your friend."

"It wouldn't work."

"You could try."

"You don't know what you are saying. She's so . . . so organized. They're the only house on the block that has fire drills. Take the other day, the school called to tell her Kevin had been hurt. Do you remember what happened when the school called me when my son flunked his eye test?"

"You became hysterical and had to be put under sedation."

"Right. Not Estelle. She calmly got her car keys off the hook, threw a coordinated sweater over her coordinated slacks, put the dinner in the oven on warm, picked up that pencil by the phone, wrote a note, went to school to pick up Kevin, and drove him to the emergency ward."

"So—you could have done that."

"I'm not finished. In the emergency ward, she deposited Kevin, remembered his birth date, his father's name, and recited their hospitalization number from *memory*."

"I remember when you took Andy to the hospital."

"I don't want to talk about it."

"What was it again the doctor said?"

"He wanted to treat my cracked heels."

"That's right. And you had to write a check for a dime to make a phone call."

"Okay. I remember."

Actually, Estelle didn't bother anyone. She wasn't much more than a blur . . . whipping in and out of the driveway each day. I was surprised when she appeared at my mailbox. "Erma," she asked, "what's wrong with me?"

"Nothing," I hedged. "Why?"

"Be honest with me. I don't fit into the neighborhood. Why?"

"I don't know how to explain it," I faltered. "It's just that . . . you're the type of woman you'd call from the drugstore and ask what you use for your irregularities."

"All I want is to be someone's friend."

"I know you do, Estelle, and I'd like to help you, but first, you have to understand what a friend is."

"Tell me."

"It's sorta hard to understand. But a friend doesn't go on a diet when you are fat. A friend never defends a husband who gets his wife an electric skillet for her birthday by saying, 'At least, he's not one to carouse around at night.'

"A friend will tell you she saw your old boyfriend—and he's a priest.

"A friend will babysit your children when they are contagious.

"A friend when asked what you think of a home permanent will lie. A friend will threaten to kill anyone who tries to come into the fitting room when you are trying on bathing suits. But most of all, a friend will not make each minute of every day count and screw it up for the rest of us."

From then on, Estelle, neighborhood Super Mom, began to change. Not all at once. But week by week, we saw her learning how to compromise with herself. At first, it was little things like buying a deodorant that wasn't on sale and scraping the list of emergency numbers off the phone with her fingernail.

One morning, one of her children knocked on my door and asked to use our bathroom. He said his mommy locked him out.

The next week, Estelle ran out of gas while making the Girl Scout run. A few days later, she forgot to tie her garbage cans together and the dogs dragged TV dinner boxes all over her lawn for the world to see.

You could almost see her image beginning to crumble. She dropped in unexpectedly one afternoon and leaned over the divider to confide, "I have come to the conclusion there is an after-life."

"An after-life?"

"Right. I think life goes on after the children are grown."

"Who told you that?"

"I read it on a vitamin label."

"What are you trying to say, Estelle?"

"I am trying to tell you that I am going to run away from home. Back to the city. There's a life for me back there."

"Don't talk crazy," I said.

"I've tried to be so perfect," she sobbed.

"I know. I know."

At that moment one of Estelle's children ran excitedly into the room. "Mommy! Mommy!" she said wildly, "I was on the side using a toothpaste with fluoride and I only have one cavity."

Estelle looked at her silently for a full minute then said, "Who cares?"

She was one of us.

11 〰️

The Volunteer Brigade

Crossword Puzzle

ACROSS

14 nine-letter word syn. with frozen dinners, pin in children's underwear, laundry in refrigerator, five-hour meetings, no pay, no health benefits, causing head to hurt a lot.

DOWN

3 six-letter word meaning same as nine across

ANSWER

```
              P
              I
              G
V O L U N T E E R
              O
              N
```

"I Am Your Playground Supervisor"

One evening, the phone rang and a voice said simply, "We have not received your response to the mimeographed request that we sent home with your son."

"What request is that?"

"We need you for playground duty at the school."

"Please," I begged, "don't ask."

"Is this the woman who protested paid potties in airport restrooms by throwing her body across the coin slot?"

"You don't understand," I said.

"The woman who made Christmas tree centerpieces out of toilet tissue spindles and macaroni?"

"Don't . . ." I sobbed.

"Is this the freedom fighter who kept them from building a dairy bar in front of the pet cemetery with a flashing sign that read, CUSTARD'S LAST STAND UNTIL THE FREEWAY?"

"I'm only human," I sobbed. "I'll report Monday to talk about it."

On Monday, I met with Mrs. Rush, the homeroom mother. "Mrs. Rush," I began, "there are several reasons why I cannot volunteer for playground duty, not the least being I have not had my shots."

"Your old ones are good for three years," she said mechanically.

"I see. Then I must tell you the truth. I am expecting a baby."

"When?"

"As soon as my husband gets home."

"Do you have any more excuses?" she asked dryly.

"Yes. I'm a registered pacifist."

She shook her head.

"How about, 'I'm a typhoid carrier'?"

"I'm afraid all those excuses have been used before," she said. "Do you realize that only four mothers returned their mimeographed bottoms?"

"That many?" I asked incredulously.

"One mother is unlisted, one had a transportation problem, and the third one was a bleeder. We couldn't take the chance. That left you. Here is a mimeographed page of instructions. You will report Monday and good luck."

Slowly, I unfolded the yellow, mimeographed sheet. It had a picture of a mother with the countenance of St. Francis of Assisi. At her feet were a group of little adoring children. A bird was perched on her shoulder. I smiled hesitantly. Maybe playground duty wasn't the hazard the women rumored it to be.

The first day I opened up my mimeographed page of instructions:

"PLAYGROUND DUTY CONSISTS OF STROLLING AMONG THE CHILDREN AND WATCHING OUT FOR FAIR PLAY."

A group of boys parted and I began to stroll. I felt like a stoolie strolling through San Quentin between Edward G. Robinson and Humphrey Bogart.

"What are we playing today?" I asked cheerfully.

"Keepaway," they chanted, as they tossed an object over my head.

"Boys! Boys!" I admonished. "Put Miss Manieson down. She's only a sub and doesn't understand how rough little boys can play. If you want to play keepaway, I suggest you use a ball. Come on now, I mean it. I'll give you two minutes to find her glasses and return her to her classroom."

"We don't have a ball," they whined.

"Perhaps these nice boys here could share," I suggested.

"You touch that ball," said a boy who looked thirty-five years old, "and you'll wish you hadn't."

"Look," I said, returning to the boys, "why don't all of you play a quiet game. Let's ask this little fella over here what he's playing. He's sitting there so quiet."

"He's quiet because an eighth-grader just tied his hands behind his back and took his lunch money!" said a small, blond kid. "Who wants to play Rip-off?"

On Tuesday, I went to the principal, unfolded my mimeographed sheet and said, "I should like to talk about rule no. 2: Here, 'A FIRST-AID CLINIC IS MAINTAINED IN THE SCHOOL FOR CUTS, BRUISES AND OTHER MINOR ACCIDENTS.' "

"What seems to be the problem?" she asked.

"I feel they really should have some provisions for the kids too."

"We'll discuss it," she said coldly.

Wednesday was one of the coldest days in the year and I figured there would be few children on the playground. I was wrong. "Boys! Boys!" I shouted, "you must not push or shove. It says right here on my mimeographed sheet, 'SHOVING AND UNDUE PUSHING IS NOT PERMITTED.' "

"We're not shoving and pushing," they said, "we are keeping warm."

"If you keep any warmer, I will have to suspend you from the playground for three days."

"Who says?"

"My mimeographed orders say, that's who. Read this: 'A PLAY-GROUND SUPERVISOR'S ORDERS ARE TO BE OBEYED THE SAME AS THE TEACHER'S.' "

He wiped his brow. "You had me worried there for a minute."

"Is it my imagination," I said, "or do I sense you have done something with Miss Manieson?"

"She's only a sub," they grinned.

"Today's sub is tomorrow's birth-control militant," I reminded.

"So, who are you to tell us what to do?"

"I am your playground supervisor," I said, squaring my shoulders.

"So?"

"So, how would you like to go to a nice school where they make license plates?"

"And how would you like to go . . ."

I grabbed my mimeographed sheet out of my pocket, and read, "A PLAYGROUND SUPERVISOR SHOULD DRESS SENSIBLY. SHE NEVER KNOWS WHICH AREA SHE WILL BE ASSIGNED NEXT."

As I read the lips of the class bully, I had the feeling I was dressed too warmly for where I had been ordered to go.

Wanda Wentworth, Schoolbus Driver

Wanda Wentworth has been retired for about ten years now, but they talk about her still.

No one commanded the entire respect of the suburban populace more than Wanda Wentworth, who held the record for driving a schoolbus longer than any other woman in the entire school district . . . six weeks.

Every morning, fearless Wanda crawled into a schoolbus and dared do what few other adults would attempt: turn her back on eighty school children.

In the beginning, it had been a job for men only. Strong men who could drive with one hand and pull a kid in off the rearview mirror with the other. Who knew that Robbie Farnsworth could disguise his voice as a siren and liked to kill a little time by pulling the bus over to the side of the road. Who could break up a fight between two kids with bad bananas.

And then, along came Wanda. She had read an ad for drivers in the *Tattler:*

WANTED

DRIVER FOR SCHOOLBUS
SEE MAGNIFICENT SUNRISES AND SUNSETS
ENJOY THE LAUGHTER OF CHILDREN AT PLAY
BE A FULFILLED VOLUNTEER
ORPHANS PREFERRED

Few of us saw much of Wanda after she took the job. I saw her only twice: one day in the dentist's office (she had fallen asleep in the chair) and another time in the supermarket when I got a bad wheel and she whipped out her tool kit and fixed it.

"How are things going on the bus?" I asked.

"Terrific!" she said. "There's nothing to it. You just have to be strict. Let them know you mean business."

I looked at Wanda closely. Her right eye rolled around in her head—independently of her left one.

"I don't allow no cooking on the bus," she said, "even when they have a note from home. Now, I know a lot of drivers who don't mind small fires, but I say if you want a hot meal, put it in a thermos."

"I think you are absolutely right," I said slowly.

"Another thing," she said, spitting on her hair and trying to get a curl to stay in the middle of her forehead, "all notes from home have to be legit. They come up with all kinds of stuff. 'Please let Debbie off at the malt shop. Eric is spending the night at Mark's house. Wait for Lillie. She has to get Marci's nail polish out of her locker.' Any time I see a note written on stationery with a pencil or a pen, I know it's a fake. Mothers only write with yellow crayons on napkins."

"You are very wise."

"They are not dealing with any dummy," she said. "Like games. I don't allow any games on the bus."

"You mean they're not allowed to play count the cow or whip out an Old Maid deck?"

"Nope. They get too excited. We tried playing Blind Man's Bluff one day and those little devils spun me around so fast I nearly hit a tree with my bus. I just laid it on them after that. Absolutely no more blindfolding me while the bus was in motion. Actually, the time goes pretty fast," she said, folding her lower lip into a crescent and biting on it with her teeth until it bled. "By the time I pick them up and they punch everyone on the bus, and open their lunches and eat them, and make their homework into gliders and sail them out of the window, and open the emergency exit in traffic, and take off their boots and leave them under the seats, and unravel the mittens their mothers put on them, and yell obscenities at the motorists passing by, we are at school."

"It sounds like it really has its rewards," I smiled nervously.

"Oh it does. Did you hear that Tim Galloway won first prize in the science fair? He rides my bus. As a matter of fact he constructed a weather station using parts he stole off my dashboard while I was having the bus 'gassed up.' "

"That's wonderful," I smiled, "but I still don't know how you hung on for six weeks. That's longer than any other person in the history of the school. How did you do it?"

"These little gems," she said, patting a bottle of pills in her coat pocket.

"Tranquilizers?" I asked.

"Birth control," she smiled, swatting at a fly that wasn't there.

Ralph Corlis, The Coach Who Played to Lose

In the annals of Little League baseball, there was only one man who made it to the Baseball Hall of Shame five seasons in a row. That was Ralph Corlis.

Ralph was an enigma in suburban sports. He brought his two sons to a housing development two years after his wife died, and together they hacked out a life for themselves. They planted a little garden, built a little racing car in the garage, and on a summer evening would go over to the ballfield and watch the kids play ball under the lights.

It was after the third or fourth game that Ralph began to take note of the thirty or forty kids on the bench who wore the uniform, but who rarely played the game.

"What do those kids do?" Ralph asked his sons.

"They watch the team play ball."

"For that they have to get dressed up in full uniform?"

"Oh no," said his son, "they go to all the practices, work out, run, field, catch, pitch, and do everything the team does . . . except play."

Ralph thought a lot about the bench warmers and one day he approached several of them and said, "How would you like to join my team?"

When Ralph was finished, he had enough for five teams and sixteen benches. The first night they met on a piece of farmland donated by a farmer.

"This is first base," said Coach Corlis, dropping his car seat cushion on the ground, "and this is second," he continued, dropping his jacket, "and I see there's already a third base."

"But . . . it's a pile of dung," said one of his players.

"So, don't slide," said Ralph.

"Do you want to see me pitch?" asked a tall, lean, athletic boy.

"No," said Ralph. Then turning to a kid two feet tall who could scarcely hold the ball in his hand, he said, "You pitch today."

At random he assigned a catcher, basemen, infield and outfield, and said, "The rest of you—relax. On this team, everyone plays."

You cannot imagine what an impact a team where "everyone plays" had on the community. Word spread like a brush fire.

One night Coach Corlis answered his door to discover a visit from three other coaches.

"Hey, what a surprise," said Ralph. "Come in."

"What's your game?" asked one of the coaches.

"Baseball," said Ralph.

"You know what we mean," said one of the other men. "What are you trying to prove? Playing every boy who goes out for the team. How many games have you won?"

"I haven't won any," said Ralph. "I didn't think that was very important."

"What are you, some kind of a loonie? Why would you play a game, if not to win?"

"To have a good time," grinned Ralph. "You should have been there the other night when Todd Milhaus slid into third."

"Unfortunately, losers don't draw crowds," smirked the third coach.

"Oh, we don't want crowds," said Ralph. "Adults just mess things up for the kids. I heard at one of your games that a mother threw a pop bottle at her own son."

"And he deserved it," said the first coach. "He should have had his eye on second base. That kid has the brain of a dead sponge."

"He's pitching for me tomorrow," said Ralph.

"Look," said the second coach, "why don't you let the boys go? What do you want with them? They're not even winning."

Ralph thought a minute then said, "It's hard to explain, but kids go all through their lives learning how to win, but no one ever teaches them how to lose."

"Let's get out of here, Bert," said the third coach.

"Wait a minute," said Ralph. "Just think about it. Most kids don't know how to handle defeat. They fall apart. It's important to know how to lose because you do a lot of it when you grow up. You have to have perspective—how to know what is important to lose and what isn't important."

"And that's why you lose?"

"Oh no. We lose because we're too busy having a good time to play good ball."

"You can't talk sense to a man who won't even sell hotdogs at a game and make 13 cents off each dog."

Ralph Corlis's team racked up an 0-38 record the very first season. The next year, it was an even better 0-43. Parents would have given their right arms to watch the team play, but they were not permitted to view a game.

All eighty of the players used to congregate at a drive-in root beer stand and giggle about their contest. When there was criticism it was from themselves. The important thing was that *everyone was sweating.*

In the annals of sandlot baseball, there had never been another team like it. They had lost every game they played and they did it without uniforms, hotdogs, parents, practice, cheerleaders, lighted scoreboards, and press coverage.

Then one afternoon something happened. Ralph had a little nervous bedwetter on the mound who had never played anything but electric football. He wore glasses two inches thick and refused to take the bicycle clamp off his pantleg.

The kid pitched out of his mind, throwing them out at first, catching an infield pop-up and pitching curves like he invented them.

Ralph's team (it had no name) won the game 9-0.

The boys were strangely quiet as they walked slowly off the field. Defeat they could handle—winning was something else. Ralph sat in his car a long time before putting his key into the ignition. He wanted time to think.

"See you next week, Coach," yelled a couple of the boys.

But Ralph Corlis never went near the cornfield or a baseball game again. As he explained to his sons, "I couldn't stand the pressure."

Confessions of an Officer in the Girl Scout Cookie Corps

No one was more surprised than I at being named Girl Scout Cookie Captain.

I had been in the restroom at the time of the promotion.

The moment following the announcement was rather exhilarating. Mothers crowding around me patting me on the back and whispering in my ear, "If you need anything, I'm in the book," and assuring me, "This is going to be the best year ever."

Then they were gone.

And there were twenty-five little girls looking at me to lead them into door-to-door combat.

"At ease," I said, "you may chew gum if you like."

One girl blew a bubble the size of a pink gall bladder. Another one looked at her watch and shifted her weight to the other foot. The others just stared.

"Now then," I said, "I think this is going to be a great experience for all of us. I'll help you and you can help me. I have only one question before you leave today. What's a Girl Scout Cookie Captain?"

"She sells cookies," said the girl with the gum.

"And where does she get the cookies?" I asked.

She shrugged, "From her own living room."

I nodded. "I see, and how do they get to her living room?"

"A big truck dumps them there," said another scout.

"Okay, girls, I'll get it all together and be in touch."

At home, I grabbed the phone book and began calling all of those wonderful people who had volunteered to help.

Frankly, I didn't realize there were so many of life's losers in one neighborhood.

"I'd love to help, but I'm allergic to children."

"We're only a one-phone family."

"Give me a break! I'm on a diet and I'm in remission."

"I'm volunteering so much now my husband reported me missing."

"Do I know you? Oh, *that* sister!"

The first meeting of the Girl Scout cookie army went well. We discussed on what day we would take orders and on what day they must report their sales to me. I, in turn, would process the order for the entire troop and then there was nothing left to do but sit around and wait for C-Day to arrive.

It was about five weeks later when my husband nudged me out of a sound sleep one morning and said, "Do you hear something?"

"Ummm. What's it sound like?"

"Like a truck in our driveway."

We staggered to the window. By the headlights I saw them: full-grown men unloading carton after carton of cookies. "Where do you want them, lady?" they shouted.

I pointed to the living room.

When I told the girls the cookies were in they did a fantastic job of holding their emotions in restraint.

One cried, "There goes the skating party."

Another one slammed down her purse and said, "I wish I were dead."

And another one declared, "If it rains, I'm not delivering."

"It's all right, girls," I smiled, "don't hold back. You can show your excitement if you want to. Frankly, I'm just as choked up as you are. As I was telling my husband this morning as we breakfasted over 250 cartons of vanilla creams, 'This will show me to go to the restroom before I leave home.' "

The delivery of the cookies was a lot slower than I had anticipated. Hardly a day went by that I wasn't on the phone trying to contact one of the girls to pick up their cookies and deliver them.

"Hello, Marcia? I have the eighty-six boxes of cookies you ordered and . . ."

"My grandmother died."

"I'm sorry about that Marcia, but there are still the cookies."

"She was down for twenty-eight boxes."

"I see. Do you happen to know where I can get in touch with Debbie?"

"She moved."

"Where?"

"I promised I wouldn't tell you."

"What about Joanne?"

"She's dropped scouting. She's selling peanut brittle for the band now."

"Marcia! You tell the girls I'm up to my Girl Scout motto in cookies and I want them out of my living room by this weekend, do you hear?"

"Have you tried freezing them?" she asked mechanically.

"Freezing them! Sara Lee should have such a freezer!"

Stripping a captain of his rank in the cookie corps is not a pretty sight. I ripped off my armband, turned in the sign from my window that read "COOKIE HEADQUARTERS" and laid my golden badge on top of my yellow scarf.

"Do you have your records book?" asked the leader.

"I do," I said smartly. "It's all there. There are 143 cartons of cookies unaccounted for and $234 or $12.08 outstanding. It's hard to tell."

"Do you have anything to say?"

"Yes," I said, my voice faltering. "I want the record to show that I tried. When twenty-five girls literally vanished from the earth, I tried to dispose of the cookies myself. I sprinkled cookie crumbs on my salads, rolled them into pie crusts, coated pork chops in them, and packed them in lunches. I made paste out of them and mended books, rubbed them on my callouses and rough elbows, and wedged them under the door to keep it open.

"I sent them out with my bills each month, wore two of them as earrings, gave them as wedding gifts, and set glasses on them and pretended they were coasters.

"I put them under my pillow for good luck, made an abstract for the living room, dumped a canful over my compost and crumbled some of them up for kitty litter. I have a cookie rash on 97 percent of my body."

"Is that all?" asked the leader somberly.

"Yes, I'm finished."

As I started to leave the room, I could hear nominations being presented for next year's cookie captain.

I turned suddenly and took a front row seat. I couldn't take the chance of leaving the room again.

12 〰〰

"By God, We're Going to Be a Close-Knit Family If I Have to Chain You to the Bed!"

The Frozen Kiosk

When historians poke through the rubble of the suburban civilization, they will undoubtedly ponder the refrigerator mystique.

For no apparent reason, other than its functional value, the refrigerator became the meeting place of the American suburban family. It also became a frozen message center whereby anyone could drop by anytime of the day or night.

The rules of communications via refrigerator were simple: Don't write with food in your hand. If phone numbers were illegible, be a sport. Messages left unclaimed over seven years would be destroyed.

This, then, is how the suburban family communicated:

139

The Language of Refrigerator Door

"Momm. Lost my speling book. Need $2 by Munday."

"Dad. Call Doris. She says you have her number."

"Dad. Call Mom. I have Doris's number too!"

"I will be home when I get there. If not home by the time I'm supposed to be, call and tell whoever answers that I need a ride." Unsigned.

"Everybody. Don't lock the front door. I've lost my key again. Signed, the Phantom."

"MAKE ICE CUBES. NOT WAR."

"The dog made a mess in the utility room. I'd clean it up but I didn't see it."

"Mom. Call 975-5520. Could be 957-5220. Or 975-2550. They might call back."

"The creep who stole my tooth fairy money will be prosecuted!"

"Troops. Be ready to cross the Potomac at midnight. Bring change. G. Washington."

"Mom and Dad: How much is it worth to you for me to lose the notice of PTA Open House?"

Starving to Death at the Spiritual Family Feast

I got the idea from a sermon.

In church one Sunday, the Reverend said, "The dinner table

each evening should have all the elements of a service . . . a spiritual family feast whereby each one can share his day and his love with one another."

"Wasn't that beautiful?" I said in the car on the way home.

"Mom! Guess who stole the sponge out of the Holy Water font?"

"I'm telling. You know when we're supposed to shake hands in a sign of peace? Guess who pressed a dirty nose tissue in my hands then wouldn't take it back?"

"If one of you kids doesn't stop kicking the back of my seat," said their father, "I'm going to clear the car."

"Will you knock it off?" I said. "Didn't anyone hear the sermon?"

"Yeah, it was something about sharing pizza."

"It was not about sharing pizza. It was sharing your spiritual love at a family feast."

"Same thing."

"Do you know when was the last time this family ate a meal together?"

No one spoke.

"It was four years ago at Grandma's birthday."

"I remember," said our son. "I did the dishes that night."

"You did not," said his sister. "I did them because I remember we had lasagna that stuck to the pan and I had to soak it."

"Yeah, for three weeks!"

"Well, I'm not like some people who put a giant bowl in the refrigerator with a peach pit in it."

"Only because you eat everything in sight . . . including the pits."

"Look," I said, "we are long overdue. Tomorrow night, this entire family is going to sit down together and eat a meal. Only a certificate of death—a recent one—will be acceptable for a no-show."

The voices in the car became hysterical.

"I was going to practice cheers with Linda after school and then go to the library."

"You know I have ball practice until 7."

"It seems to me I have a five o'clock dental appointment and traffic on the expressway is murder. Maybe Tuesday would be a better day."

"Well, if we're not finished loving one another by 6:30, I'm going to split."

I remained firm. "Dinner on Monday. Together."

On Monday at 6 P.M. the scene was set for the Great Spiritual banquet.

It held all the giddiness of the "Last Supper."

My husband had a mouthful of Novocain and couldn't get his lips to cover his teeth.

One son appeared in stereo—a transistor in one ear and the phone in the other.

Our daughter had Linda waiting for her behind her chair.

And the other son dressed his arm in a sling to dispel the possibility of having to do dishes.

"Well now," I said, "now that we are all together, each one of us should think about sharing our day with one another. That should be an enriching experience."

"Do you know what Ramsey Phillips said were the seven words you can't use on TV?"

"Not that enriched," I said, clapping my hand over his mouth. "Dear," I said to my husband, "what would you like to talk about?"

That was a mistake.

Over the years, my husband has composed and committed to memory five standard dinner-table lectures that are as familiar to all of us as the Pledge of Allegiance. They include:

1. "WHY DON'T YOU WANT YOUR FATHER TO HAVE A LAWN?" (two minutes, forty seconds). This is a real heart-tugger in which Dad recaps his failure to triumph over bikes, sleds, plastic pools,

football games, cars, wagons, dogs, and all the little perverts who cut across his lawn just to make him paranoid.

When his eyes begin to mist, he is ready to go for options. Donate the front yard to the government for nuclear testing. Put a sentry at the driveway with a loaded rifle. Or perhaps (and this is drastic) have the kids take an interest in mowing, fertilizing, and trimming the yard so they can appreciate what he is trying to do. His zinger is, "My compost is in your hands."

2. "DO I LOOK LIKE A MAN WHO OWNS THE WATER WORKS?" (one minute, forty-eight seconds). This is a table favorite that is brought on when Dad is overcome by steam and requires oxygen when he tries to enter the bathroom. In his mind, he is convinced that he cannot afford the child who is trying to break into the Guinness Book of Records for using forty gallons of hot water to wash off a ninety-six-pound body.

This is the lecture in which he uses visuals: prunes to show feet of child exposed to too many showers, and a broom illustrating how hair dries out and cracks from overshampooing. It's a two-parter, the second half taking place immediately following dinner when he takes the group to the bathroom and demonstrates how to turn off the faucet all the way.

3. "CAPTAIN QUEEG AND THE ICE CUBES" (one minute, thirty-four seconds). The children can always tell when Daddy is going for the Ice Cube number. He appears at the table with two steel balls in his hands and for five minutes does nothing but rotate them. Then he relates with a slight smile how he has trapped the culprit who put the ice cube tray in the freezer—*empty*. When he made his drink, there were nine ice cubes in the tray. By crouching unnoticed in the broom closet, he noted four of them were used by our daughter to make a malt, three were used by Mother for a glass of iced tea, and the younger son used one to suck on and he was the culprit.

When the younger son protested there was one left, his father's face lit up and he said, "Wrong! You dropped one on the floor to melt because I slipped on it and nearly broke my back." The entire table is left to meditate on the consequences.

4. "I'M PAYING YOU KIDS AN ALLOWANCE TO BREATHE." (two minutes). This is a fun presentation because it's a group participation lecture.

"Do you know how much money I made when I was a child?" asks Daddy.

"Five cents a month," they yell in unison.

"Five cents a month," he says as if he hasn't heard them. "And do you know how old I was when I got my first car?"

"Twenty-three years old," they sigh.

"Twenty-three years old and do you know who bought it for me?"

"You did."

"I did," he says, "and have you any idea how much I had to buy with five cents a month?"

"You had to buy all your own clothes, books, tuition, medical expenses, rent, and pay for your entertainment."

"I had to buy all my own clothes, books, tuition, medical expenses, rent, and pay for my entertainment," he said. "And can you imagine what I did for entertainment?"

"Changed your underwear."

"Don't ad lib," he warns. "We really knew how to squeeze a buffalo in those days."

When three-fourths of the table asks, "What's a buffalo, Daddy?" the lecture begins to deteriorate.

5. "I DON'T WANT TO TALK ABOUT IT" (thirty minutes). This is the lecture we have all come to dread. It's the I-Don't-Want-to-Talk-about-It lecture that he talks about all during dinner.

Dad appears at the table morose, depressed, and preoccupied, picking at his food—a picture of utter despair.

Finally, one of the kids will volunteer, "If it's about the duck in the utility room."

"I don't want to talk about it," he says.

"I'm going to empty all the garbage on the back porch tonight," promises another.

"Forget it," he says.

"Hey, just because your shorts came out pink doesn't mean we can't wash them again and put a little bleach . . ."

"It doesn't matter," he says tiredly.

By the end of the dinner hour, we have all confessed to every crime to date and he is still sullen.

Finally, in desperation, I say, "If it's about the dent in the car . . ."

"That's what I want to talk about," he says.

This Monday evening, however, my husband surprised us all by introducing a new lecture. It was called, "BY GOD, WE'RE GOING TO BE A CLOSE-KNIT FAMILY IF I HAVE TO CHAIN YOU TO THE BED!" He began:

"It certainly is wonderful sitting down to a table together for a change."

"Is that it?" asked our daughter, pushing back her chair. "Can I go now?"

"No!" he shouted. "We are going to sit here and get to know one another. I am your father."

"We thought you were taller," said the son with the sling on his arm.

"I'm sorry if I haven't seen as much of you as I would have liked. It isn't easy commuting to and from the city every day. Now, we are going to go around the table and each one of you can tell me something about yourself." He looked at our daughter.

"I'm the token girl in the family. I like birthday cards with money in them, bathroom doors that can't be unlocked from the outside by releasing it with a pin, and I want to be a professional cheerleader when I grow up. Can I go now or does it have to be longer?"

"Stay put," said her father. "Next," he said, turning to our son with his arm in a sling.

"I'm the middle child in the family and am bored, depressed, neurotic, unfulfilled, and subject to pressures which will eventually drive me to my own apartment."

"Why not?" I said dryly. "You have to be driven everywhere else."

"Now, Mother," said Daddy, "it's not your turn."

"It's never my turn," I sulked. "Do you know what I think? I think you stopped loving me the day my upper arms became too big for puffed sleeves. Admit it?"

"Come now, let the boy talk."

"I have to do everything in this house," he continued. "Even though I was freed legally in 1860 by Lincoln. Take out the garbage. Let the dog out. Answer the phone. Get the paper. Change the channel on TV. Get Mom a drink of water."

"Drinking water wasn't my idea," I said wistfully.

"Hey, don't I get to say anything again?" asked the youngest. "Do you realize because I'm the baby of this family I never get to open my mouth. I've been trying to tell a joke at this table for the last three years."

Dad held up his hand for silence. "The boy is right. Take those wires out of your ears and tell us your joke."

"Well," he began, "there was this guy who stuttered a lot."

"I've heard it," said his brother, pushing away from the table.

"How do you know you've heard it? There are a lot of guys who stutter."

"I happen to know that of all the guys who stutter, only one of them made a joke out of it. Mom! Don't let him tell it. It's sick."

"It is not sick," persisted the youngest, "and was your stutterer from the South?"

"How long is this joke?"asked Linda, leaning over our daughter's shoulder. "If it's going to be much longer, I have to call home."

"You are excused to call your mother," said Dad. "Now continue with the joke."

"Well," he giggled, "this guy from the North said to the guy from the South, 'What are you doing up North?' And the stutterer said, 'Lllllooooookkinnnng for a jjjob.' "

"Didn't I tell you it was sick?" said his brother.

"Then," he continued, "his friend said, 'What sort of work are you looking for?' He said, 'Rrrrrrraaaaadddiooo aaannnouuunnnci-ing.' Then his friend asked, 'Any luck?' And this guy said (he held his sides with laughter as he blurted it out), 'Nnnnooo, whhhaaat chaance does a stttttuutttteerer have?' "

We all sat there in silence.

"That is the dumbest joke I've ever heard," said his sister.

"It's sick," said his brother.

"Are you sure you got the tagline right?" I asked.

"I've heard the joke," said his dad, "and the tagline is 'Whhat chaance hhhas a Sooooutheeeerner?' "

"Why is this family down on Southerners?" asked our daughter, leaving the table.

"I don't like your ending," said our youngest son.

"It's not *my* ending," said his father, "it's the way the joke goes."

"If you heard it before, you should have stopped me," he said, rushing to his room in tears.

"It's not my turn to do dishes," announced the last child, slipping out of his chair.

My husband turned to me. "When was the last spiritual family feast we shared together?"

"Four years ago at Grandma's birthday," I said numbly.

"Time flies when you're healing," he mused.

13 〜〜

Postscript to Suburbian Gems

It was either Isaac Newton—or maybe it was Wayne Newton—who once said, "A septic tank does not last forever." He was right.

Suburbian Gems was a real community.

So were most of the characters in this book.

Certainly, the frustrations, the loneliness, the laughter, the challenges, and especially the analogy were for real. We were like pioneers, in a sense, leaving what we knew in search of our American dream.

Some settlers found Xanadu waiting in the suburbs. For others, it was an exile at San Clemente.

For me, it was one of the most exciting times of my life: a time when my children were young, my husband ambitious, and happiness for me was having a cake that didn't split in the middle and have to be rebuilt with toothpicks.

In the beginning, it was as we thought it would be: the smell of new wood (why not, it was green), doors that stuck permanently, and the weekend battle cry that shook the countryside, "Why pay someone to do it when we can do it ourselves."

The supermarket chains hadn't arrived yet with their frozen conveniences, express lines, and red lights over the pot roast.

There was only the country store where the owner was confused by the newcomers who insisted he bag the vegetables and ran him to his grain elevators for 15 cents' worth of pellets for a pet hamster.

I remember one Thanksgiving asking the kid at the gas pump in front of the store, "Do you have Mums?" He wiped his nose on his sleeve and said, "Yeah, but she's up at the house."

I never looked at the schools that I didn't imagine John Wayne saying to Beulah Bondi, "Someday this town is going to have a real school, and a school marm, and the children will learn to read and write their sums, etc. etc."

Our kids in the beginning got choked up when Spot chased a stick and Mommy put on a new apron. (Well, what did you expect from a twenty-year-old teacher who earned $1200 a year, taught five spelling classes, two history sessions, supervised the cafeteria during lunch, was class advisor for the Future Homemakers of America, and was in charge of the Senior class play and the drill team's peanut brittle candy sale.)

Later, that too changed when children would duly report to their parents, "I'm part of an innovative enrichment program that is structurally developed to stimulate my mental attitude with muscular development, combined with a language pattern design that is highly comprehensible and sensory." (One mother advised, "Keep your coat on, Durwood, and no one will notice.")

One book on the suburbs referred to it as "Creeping Suburbia." It sounded like a disease. ("This creeping suburbia has got me climbing the wall, Margaret.") Critics credit it with weakening the family structure, becoming overorganized, isolating people of like incomes, race, social levels, politics, religion, and attitudes from the rest of the world.

It probably did all of those things and some more that haven't been dissected and labeled yet.

But no one can quarrel with the unique sense of belonging that got the suburban settlers involved in their communities.

In a few short years, it became one of the most powerful forces in this country. How they voted. How they ran their schools. How they designated their land. How they incorporated around them what they wanted and needed. How they were governed.

I only know that one morning I looked longingly beyond the suburbs to the city and said to my husband, "Got a letter from Marge and Ralph yesterday."

"When did they leave Pleasure Plantation for Crown City?"

"A week ago," I said. "Marge wrote, 'We reached the Downtown complex on the 15th. There are 17,500 units in our section, contained on 83 acres of land. There is rubble everywhere (they're still laying carpets in the hallways) and some of the elevators don't stop at our floor. None of the gift shops is open yet in the mall.' "

"The sheer guts of it," said my husband.

" 'The bus service to Ralph's office building in the suburbs is horrendous—sometimes every hour—sometimes an hour and fifteen minutes between buses. It's lonely and desolate here on the fifty-fifth floor. It's like floating in an atmosphere with no trees, no birds . . . only the wind and an occasional jet.

" 'The children have to walk to school. It will take some getting used to after busing it in the suburbs, but they're becoming used to hardships. The mail deliveries, garbage pickups, fire and police protection are nonexistent, but the strike is expected to be settled as soon as the city is solvent again.

" 'There are some bright spots. No more getting in the car to go shopping. There is a store in the building that delivers and we are fortunate enough to have our own cloverleaf exit that comes directly into the building garage.

" 'Also, it is quiet. On a summer night we can walk and breathe clean air and feel no one else is around. Tomorrow, we are going to visit a tree. It is being planted in the mall in our building. Come visit us. You can't miss us. We have a lamp in the picture window.' "

I put the letter down. "Doesn't that sound exciting? Living in a city eighty stories high. That is where the next frontier is."

"What!" shouted my husband. "And give up all of this?"

I looked around. Our "wilderness" had grown to 100,000 people, fifteen traffic lights, five shopping centers, six elementary schools, two high schools, fifteen churches, four drive-ins, a daily newspaper, and street lights on every corner.

Report cards were computerized, horses were "boarded," lube jobs on the car were "by appointment only" and there were three, sometimes four cars in every driveway.

Our garage bulged at the seams with lawn spreaders, leaf sweepers, automatic mowers, snowplows, golf carts, bobsleds, skis, ice skates, boats, and camping gear.

Our all-electric kitchen crackled with the efficiency of micro-ovens, dishwashers, ice cube crushers, slow-cooking pots, electric knife sharpeners, brooms, sanders, waxers, blenders, mixers, irons, and electric ice cream freezers and yogurt makers.

The once-silent streets had been replaced by motor and trail bikes, transistors, and piped-in music in the shopping-center parking lot and the air was thick with charcoal.

As we weighed our decision, I couldn't help but speculate how future historians would assess the suburbs—the ghost cities of tomorrow.

Poking through the rubble of that unique civilization, would they be able to figure out what 1200 bleacher seats and two goalposts were doing in the middle of a cornfield?

Would they be able to break the code of the neon signs that

flapped in the wind: "GO-GO," "CARRY-OUT," "DRIVE-IN," or a sign that instructed, "SPEAK CLEARLY AND DIRECT YOUR ORDER INTO THE CLOWN'S MOUTH?"

Would they be dismayed by the impermanence of a Nova camper with a sign in the window, "SUNSET BANK. Hours: 8 A.M.–2 P.M. WEEKDAYS. CLOSED SATURDAYS AND SUNDAYS"?

Would they probe the sandboxes and come up with a Barbie and Ken form, and figure we got sick?

Or would they piece together scraps of PTA notices, home parties, church bazaars, and little Green Stamps (thirty to a page) and ponder, "How did they survive?"

At that moment the ghosts of 100 million settlers are bound to echo, "We drank!"

If Life
Is A Bowl Of
Cherries –
What Am I
Doing In The
Pits?

For my editor, Gladys Carr,
who has the courage to laugh only when it's funny.

To my agent, Aaron Priest,
who gives 100 percent, but takes only 10 percent.

For my Mom and Dad,
(Albert and Erma Harris),
who tell everyone their daughter
is a successful dental assistant.

Contents ⋙

Introduction ⇌•:

A Pair of White Socks in a Pantyhose World

I've always worried a lot and frankly I'm good at it.

I worry about introducing people and going blank when I get to my mother. I worry about a shortage of ball bearings; a snake coming up through my kitchen drain. I worry about the world ending at midnight and getting stuck with three hours on a twenty-four-hour cold capsule.

I worry about getting into the Guinness World Book of Records under "Pregnancy: Oldest Recorded Birth." I worry what the dog thinks when he sees me coming out of the shower, that one of my children will marry an Eskimo who will set me adrift on an iceberg when I can no longer feed myself. I worry about salesladies following me into the fitting room, oil slicks, and Carol Channing going bald. I worry about scientists discovering someday that lettuce has been fattening all along.

But mostly, I worry about surviving. Keeping up with the times in a world that changes daily. Knowing what to keep and what to discard. What to accept and what to protest.

Never, in the history of this country, have worriers had such a decade as the seventies. Each year has produced a bumper crop of worrierees larger than the year before and this year promises to be even better.

Children are becoming an endangered species, energy has reached crisis proportions, marriages are on the decline, and the only ones having any fun anymore are the research rats.

You cannot help but envy their decadence.

Throughout the years, these furry swingers have been plied with booze, pot, cigarettes, birth control pills, too much sun, cyclamates, caffeine, Red Dye No. 2, saccharine, disco music at ear-shock decibels, late nights, and a steady diet of snack food.

If people haven't asked themselves these questions, they should:

How come there are still more rats than people?

How come you've never seen an iron-starved, dull, listless rat drag around the house?

Did you ever see a rat with a salad in one hand and a calorie counter in the other; yet have you ever seen a fat rat?

Have you ever yelled at a rat who couldn't hear you and couldn't outrun you?

Did you ever see a rat drop dead with lipstick on his teeth?

These unanswered questions have bothered me because everytime I turn around a new research study is taking away something that has added to my pleasure in the past, but is bound to make me sick in the future.

I heard a story about a research rat recently that makes one pause and reflect. The rat's name was Lionel. He was a pro. He had everything tested on him from artificial sweeteners to bread preservatives to foot fungus viruses to brutal subway experiments and survived them all. A researcher figured he was something of a Superrat . . . an immortal who could sustain life no matter what the odds.

The researcher took him home as a pet for his children. Within three months, this indestructible rat was dead.

It seems that one day the rat was taken for a ride in the car with the teenage son who had a learner's permit. The rat died of a heart attack.

That's what this book is about. Surviving.

1 ⇁∶∙

If You Thought the Wedding Was Bad . . .

Next to hot chicken soup, a tattoo of an anchor on your chest, and penicillin, I consider a honeymoon one of the most overrated events in the world.

It's one of those awkward times when you know everyone else had a better time than you did but you're too proud to admit it.

A Honeymoon Hall of Fame is being established at a resort hotel in the Poconos.

According to publicity, a heart-shaped alcove will feature photos, mementos and memorabilia of famed loving couples of history and fiction.

To date, they have included a recording of the Duke of Windsor's history-making declaration of love in which he renounced the British throne, early cartoons of Blondie and Dagwood, and film clips of Elizabeth Taylor's weddings.

It boggles the mind to imagine how they are going to determine who will enter the Honeymoon Hall of Fame and for what reasons, but here are a few nominations.

Ruth and Walter, who enjoyed the shortest honeymoon in his-

161

tory. Ruth shot Walter in the leg at the reception for fooling around with the maid of honor.

Sue and Ted for the most unique honeymoon in history. While Sue swam, danced, played tennis and shopped, Ted ice fished, skied, played cards and drank with the boys. While separate honeymoons don't work for everyone, it worked for Sue and Ted.

Laura and Stewart, the couple who were the greatest sports on their honeymoon. Right after the wedding, Laura discovered Stewart was out on bail for armed robbery, was coming down with three-day measles, was already married, had a son who set fires, and had taken out $75,000 worth of life insurance on her at the reception, but what the heck, as Laura explained, "Honeymoons are always a time of adjustment."

There are a lot of theories as to why marriages aren't lasting these days. The original premise was so simple. All you had to do was promise to love and to cherish from this day forward for better or for worse . . . and you asked yourself how bad could it get?

Bad never reaches it to the big stuff. It's always the little things that do a marriage in.

For example, a woman can walk through the Louvre Museum in Paris and see 5,000 breathtaking paintings on the wall. A man can walk through the Louvre Museum in Paris and see 5,000 nails in the wall. That is the inherent difference.

I don't know what there is about a nail in the wall that makes strong, virile men cry. The first time I was aware of this phenomenon was a week after my husband and I were married. I passed him in the kitchen one day while carrying a small nail and hammer.

"Where are you going with that hammer and nail?" he asked, beginning to pale.

"I am going to hang up a towel rack," I said.

He could not have looked more shocked if I had said I was going to drive a wooden peg into the heart of a vampire.

"Do you have to drive that spike into the wall to do it?"

"No," I said resting on the sink, "I could prop the towel rack up in a corner on the floor. I could hang it around my waist from a rope, or I could do away with it altogether and keep a furry dog around the sink to dry my hands on."

"What is there about women that they cannot stand to see a smooth, bare wall?" he grumbled.

"And what is there about men that they cannot stand to have the necessities of life hung from a wall?"

"What necessities?" he asked. "Certainly you don't need that mirror in the hallway."

"You said that about the light switches."

His eyes narrowed and I had the feeling he was going to zap me with his big point. "Do you realize," he asked slowly, "that there is not one single wall in this house where we can show a home movie?"

"Radio City Music Hall only has one," I retorted.

And so, the nail versus the bare wall has gone on for years at our house. He wouldn't hang a calendar over my desk because in twelve months the nail would become obsolete. He wouldn't hang the children's baby pictures because in two years they'd grow teeth and no one would recognize them. He wouldn't let me put a hook in the bathroom so I wouldn't have to hold my robe while I showered. He wouldn't let me hang a kitchen clock anywhere but on a wall stud (which happened to be located BEHIND the refrigerator).

Sometimes you have to wait for revenge. Yesterday, he reported he ran over a nail with his car.

There's an object lesson here, but I wouldn't insult anyone's intelligence by explaining it.

To love and to cherish from this day snoreward . . . forward. Why doesn't anyone think to ask? Snoring could be a real threat to a marriage, especially if it's a snore that blows lampshades off the base, pictures off the wall, and makes farm animals restless as far as fifty miles away.

The loudest snore, according to the Guinness World Book of Records, was measured at sixty-nine decibels at St. Mary's hospital in London.

Until last night.

That's when my husband broke the record by sustaining his breathing at a rousing seventy-two decibels. Seventy-two decibels, for the innocent, is the equivalent of having a cannon go off in the seat next to you in the Astrodome.

"Hey Cyrano," I yelled, "wake up. You're doing it again."

"Doing what?"

"Snoring."

"You woke me up to tell me that! If I've told you once I've told you a thousand times, I do not snore. I'd know it if I did."

"That is the same logic used by the man who said, 'If I had amnesia, I would have remembered it.' "

"What did it sound like?"

"Like the Goodyear blimp with a slow leak."

"Well, what did you expect? A concert?"

"Maybe I'll try what Lucille Farnsward tried when her husband's snoring drove her crazy."

"What's that?" he asked sleepily.

"She just put a pillow over his face."

"Good Lord, woman, that would cause a man to stop breathing altogether."

"Well, she hasn't worked the bugs out yet, but she's onto something."

"Why don't you roll me over on my side?"

"I did and you hit me."

And so it went, all through the night.

Frankly, I'm sick of all the therapist remedies that never seem to work, like self-hypnosis, earplugs and rolling the snorer off his back. These are the only remedies that bear consideration.

Change Beds

Get the snorer out of his own bed and into a strange one . . . preferably in another state.

Prolonging Sleep

This one works as well as any I've tried. Just as you are both climbing into bed, get every nerve in his body on alert by off-handedly mentioning, "The IRS called you today, they'll call back tomorrow."

Some experts believe you have to get to the root of a husband's reason for snoring. It has been suggested a person snores because he is troubled, his dentures don't fit properly, he indulges in excessive smoking or drinking, has swollen tonsils or suffers from old age.

Don't you believe any of it. A man snores for one reason alone . . . to annoy his wife. And if *that* doesn't do it, he'll resort to some other ploy to drive her crazy . . . the Sorry-I'm-late syndrome.

There are no records to prove it, mind you, but I have every reason to believe my husband was an eleven-month baby.

And he's been running two months late ever since. Through marriage (and bad association) I have become a member of that great body of tardy Americans who grope their way down theater aisles in the dark, arrive at parties in time to drink their cocktails with their dessert, and celebrate Christmas on December 26.

Frankly, I don't know how a nice, punctual girl like me got stuck with a man who needs not a watch but a calendar and a keeper.

Would it shock anyone to know I have never seen a bride walk "down" the aisle? I have never seen a choir or a graduate in a processional? I have never seen the victim of a mystery BEFORE he was murdered. I have never seen a parking lot jammed with people. I have never seen the first race of a daily double, or a football team in clean uniforms.

The other night I had it out with my husband. "Look, I am in the prime time of my life and I have never heard the first thirty seconds of the 'Minute Waltz.' Doesn't that tell you something?"

"What are you trying to say?"

"I am trying to say that once before I die I would like to see a church with empty seats."

"We've been through all this before," he sighed. "Sitting around before an event begins is a complete waste of time when you could be spending it sleeping, reading and working."

"Don't forget driving around the block looking for a parking place. I don't understand you at all," I continued. "Don't you get curious as to what they put into first acts? Aren't you just a bit envious of people who don't have to jump onto moving trains? Aren't you tired of sitting down to a forty-four-minute egg each morning?"

"I set my alarm clock every night. What do you want from me?"

"I have seen you when you set your alarm clock. When you want to get up at six-thirty you set it for five-thirty. Then you reset it for six and when it goes off you hit it again and shout, 'Ha, ha, I was only kidding. I got another half-hour.' You reset it for six-thirty at which time you throw your body on it and say, 'I don't need you. I don't need anybody.' Then you go back to sleep."

"I just happen to believe there is no virtue in being early. What time is it?"

"It's eight o'clock. You're supposed to be at work at eight."

"Yes, lucky, I've got twenty minutes to spare."

Never in my life will I hear the "Star Spangled Banner" being played. I've also had to adjust to a man who does not know how to live in a world geared to leisure.

It's a common problem. A lot of women are married to work-oholics and the trick is to get them to take two weeks off a year and just relax. Sounds simple?

I took my husband to the beach for two weeks where he promptly spread out a large beach towel, opened his briefcase and began to balance the checkbook.

I took him to a fancy hotel in a big city where he spent the entire week tinkering with the TV set trying to get the snow out of the picture.

Once I even took him to a nightclub where scantily clad girls danced out of key. After one came over and propped herself ceremoniously on his knee and tickled his chin, he turned to me and said, "We really should have the fire insurance on our house updated."

A friend of mine suggested I take him camping. "There is nothing like the wilderness to make a man relax and bring him back to nature." What did she know?

After three days in the wilderness, he had rotated the tires, mended three water mattresses, built a bridge, filled eight snow-control barrels with cinders and devised a sophisticated system to desand everyone before they entered the tent.

He went to the library to check on how the river got its name, wrote a letter to the editor of the local paper, read the lantern warranty out loud to all of us, organized a ball team and waxed the tent.

He alphabetized my staple goods, painted the word GAS on the gas cans, and hung our meat from a tree to make it inaccessible to bears and humans. (Raccoons eventually ate it.)

After that experience, I told him, "Face it, Bunkie, we are incompatible."

"Why do you say that?" he asked.

"I'm a fun-loving, irrepressible, impetuous Zelda, and you are a proper, restrained, put-your-underwear-on-a-hanger Dr. Zhivago."

"I have a good time," he said soberly.

"Do you know I'm the only woman in the world to wake up on New Year's Day with nothing to regret from the night before? No gold wedgies scattered on the stairway, no party hats on the back of the commode, no taste in my mouth like a wet chenille tongue? Only the memories of Father Time dozing over a warm Gatorade. I have had more stimulating evenings picking out Tupperware."

"That not true," he said. "What did we do last New Year's Eve?"

"From seven to eight-thirty I picked bubble gum out of the dog's whiskers. At ten-thirty you fell asleep in the chair while I drank unflavored gelatin to strengthen my fingernails. At ten-forty-five I went to the refrigerator for a drink. The kids had drunk all the mix and the neighbors had cleaned us out of the ice cubes. I poured two glasses of warm Gatorade, returned to the living room and kicked you in the foot. You jerked awake and said, 'Did you know that at midnight all horses age one year?'

"At eleven-forty-five your snooze alarm went off. You clicked your fingers while Carmen Lombardo sang 'Boo Hoo,' flipped the porch light on and off and shouted, 'Happy New Year.'

"I wish we could be like Dan and Wanda."

"What's so great about Dan and Wanda?" he asked.

"Wanda tells me she and Dan have meaningful conversations."

"Big deal," he yawned.

"It is a big deal. Have we ever had one?"

"I don't think so," he said.

Finally I said, "What *is* a meaningful conversation?"

"You're kidding! You actually don't know?"

"No, what is it?"

"Well, it's a conversation with meaning."

"Like an oil embargo or Paul Harvey?"

"Exactly."

"What about them?"

"What about who?"

"The oil embargo and Paul Harvey."

"It doesn't have to be a conversation about the oil embargo and Paul Harvey," he explained patiently. "It could be a discussion on anything in your daily schedule that is pertinent."

"I shaved my legs yesterday."

"That is not pertinent to anyone but you."

"Not really. I was using your razor."

"If you read the paper more, your conversation would be more stimulating."

"Okay, here's something meaningful. I read just yesterday that in Naples . . . that's in Italy . . . police were searching for a woman who tried to cut off a man's nose with a pair of scissors while he was sleeping. What do you think of that?"

"That's not meaningful."

A few minutes later I said, "Suppose it was the American Embassy and the woman was a spy and the nose, which held secret documents about an oil embargo between Saudi Arabia and Paul Harvey, belonged to President Carter?"

"Why don't we just go back to meaningless drivel?" he said.

"Which reminds me," I said. "Did you read that article in the magazine where it said married people are unable to respond to their differences and that is why they become frustrated? It's called the old I-don't-care, it's-up-to-you or I-will-if-you-want-to blues.

You do that a lot, and I never know how you stand on things."

"I didn't read the article," he said.

"Well, as I recall, it suggested that a husband and wife spell out their feelings using a scale of one to ten. For example, if you say, 'Would you like to go to a movie?' instead of shrugging my shoulders and saying, 'Makes no difference,' I respond by saying, 'I'm five on attending a movie. Actually I'm eight on seeing the picture, but I'm three on spending the money right now.' "

"That makes sense."

"Let's try it. What would you like for dinner?"

"Farrah Fawcett Majors."

"Not 'who,' Clown, 'what'!"

"How will I know until I know what we're having?"

"That's the point. Offer some suggestions."

"Okay, liver is a big ten with me."

"I hate liver. To me liver is a minus two and you know it. How about meat loaf?"

"Meat loaf with meat is a six, without meat but with a lot of bread, a two. However, if you feel nineish about it, I'll send one of the kids to the Golden Arches, which is emerging as a big ten."

"Would it hurt you to be a nine about meat loaf just once?" I snapped.

"You should talk. In twenty-seven years, you haven't gotten off your two once when I have discussed having liver."

"Lower your voice! We don't have to air our two's and three's to the neighbors. How about an omelet?"

"That sounds like a firm eight to me."

"Good. We agree. We're out of eggs, so you'll have to go to the store."

"The car is a nine. I'm having battery trouble. That averages out omelets to a four."

"Okay, we're down to peanut butter. It's a definite three, minus one for being cold. However, it's a plus two for nutrition plus four for not being a leftover and a minus three for being fattening. That comes out to a five. Whatdaya think?"

"I don't care," said my husband.

"I was hoping you'd say that."

There's a lot of talk about why marriages are failing, but how come so many succeed?

Some women are too old for a paper route, too young for social security, too clumsy to steal and too tired for an affair. Some were just born into this world married and don't know how to act any different.

For the woman who has any doubts about her status, just answer a few simple questions.

When your husband's best friend leans closer on the dance floor and whispers in your ear, "What are you doing the rest of my life?" and you whisper back, "Waiting for my washer repairman," you're married.

When a tall, dark, handsome stranger takes your hand and asks you to dance and you answer, "I can't. My pantyhose just shifted and with the slightest movement they'll bind my knees together," you're married.

When a Robert Redford look-alike invites you to have a cup of coffee after your evening class and you order a hamburger with onions, you're married.

When you are invited by the office single dude to join him for a weekend and bring a friend and you bring your husband . . . you're married.

When a party reveler asks, "Have you ever thought of leaving your husband" and you answer, "Where?" you're married.

No one talks about fidelity anymore, it's just something you hope is still around . . . and in significant numbers. And when the Coast Guard band strikes up "Semper Fidelis" and your husband says, "They're playing our song. You wanta dance?" you know you're married.

2

The Mother Mystique

An eleven-year-old girl once wrote:

Mrs. Bombeck,

I do not understand Mothers.

How come my Mom can hit anyone anywhere in the house at any distance with a shoe?

How can she tell without turning her head in the car that I am making faces at my brother in the back seat?

How can she be watching television in the living room and know that I am sneaking cookies in the kitchen?

Some of my friends also don't understand Moms. They want to know how she can tell just by looking at them that they had a hot dog and three Cokes before they came home from school for dinner. Or where they are going to lose the sweater they hate.

We think it is spooky the way the phone rings and before we even pick it up she says, "Five minutes!"

We all agree no one in the world has super vision, super hearing, or can smell quite like a Mother. One guy said he had a piece of bubble gum once wrapped in foil in his shoe and his Mom said,

172

"Let's have the gum. You want to tear your retainer out?"

Since you write about kids all the time we thought you could explain Moms to us.

Sincerely,
Cathie

Dear Cathie and Friends:

I found your letter most amusing. You make Motherhood sound like Jeane Dixon on a good day. (Sit up dear, and don't hold this book so close to your face. You'll ruin your eyes.)

Actually, there is no mystique at all to being a Mother. We all started out as normal, average little children like yourself, who grew up and developed the usual x-ray vision, two eyes in the back of our head, bionic hearing and olfactory senses that are sharpened by wet gym shoes. (Don't ask what "olfactory" is. Look it up in the dictionary.)

Mothers have never considered any of these senses a bonus. We call them instincts for survival. Without them we would be mortal and vulnerable. (Don't make such a face. It'll freeze that way and then where will you be?)

Someday, when your Motherhood genes develop, you too will know when someone is in the refrigerator even though you are at a PTA meeting. You will know shoes are wet and muddy when you can't even find them. You will sense your child is lying to you even while clutching a Bible in one hand, a rosary in the other and is standing under a picture of Billy Graham.

Mothers are just normal people really. We don't pretend to be perfect or to have all the answers to child-rearing.

Why, throughout the years, there are a lot of aspects of children for which I profess complete ignorance. For example . . .

Who Is I. Dunno?

Ever since I can remember, our home has harbored a fourth child– I. Dunno. Everyone sees him but me. All I know is, he's rotten.

"Who left the front door open?"

"I. Dunno."

"Who let the soap melt down the drain?"

"I. Dunno."

"Who ate the banana I was saving for the cake?"

"I. Dunno."

Frankly, I. Dunno is driving me nuts. He's lost two umbrellas, four pairs of boots and a bicycle. He has thirteen books overdue from the library, hasn't brought home a paper from school in three years, and once left a thermos of milk in the car for three weeks.

The other day the phone rang. I ran from the mailbox, cut my leg, tore off a fingernail in the door and got the the phone in time to see my son hanging up. "Who was it?" I asked breathlessly.

"I. Dunno. He hung up."

When I told my neighbor about it she said, "Cheer up. I've had an invisible child for years."

"What's his name?"

"Nobody."

"Is he rotten?"

"He makes Dennis the Menace look like a statue. He cracked the top of an heirloom candy dish, tears up the paper before anyone gets to read it, and once when I was driving the car pool, he nearly knocked me senseless with a ball bat."

"Ha!" I said bitterly, "you should have seen I. Dunno. He left thirteen lights burning the other night when he went out. I don't know how much longer I can stand it."

This morning at breakfast I said to my husband, "Who wants liver for dinner this evening?"

He looked up and said, "I dontcare."

That can only mean one thing. I. Dunno has a brother.

At What Age Is a Child Capable of Dressing Himself?

Some say when a child can reach the dirty clothes hamper without falling in, he is ready to assume responsibility for what he wears.

A child develops individuality long before he develops taste. I have seen my kid straggle into the kitchen in the morning with outfits that need only one accessory: an empty gin bottle.

There is always one child in the family who thrives on insecurities and must have her emotional temperature taken every five minutes. I call it the "Parade of the Closet." Beginning at 7 A.M. she will appear at breakfast fully clothed and ready for school. Before the cereal has stopped exploding in the bowl, she has disappeared to her room and is in another complete outfit. Four words from her mother ("You look nice today") and she is off again to her bedroom in tears for still another complete change.

She plays the same musical clothes until she runs out of clothes/ the bus leaves/her mother is institutionalized . . . whichever comes first.

There is always the kid who has an aversion to clean clothes. He is allergic to creases in trousers, socks that have soft toes, underwear that is folded, and sweaters you can sniff without passing out. He's the child who always applauds the Ring Around the Collar commercials.

The opposite is the youngster who neither desires what is in his closet nor what is in the dirty clothes hamper. He wants what has to be ironed. I have always said, "If I had nothing in my ironing bag but a diaper, that kid would wear a top hat and go to school dressed as the New Year."

Last year, we allowed our children to pack their own suitcases for our vacation. One wore a baseball cap and a pair of brown corduroys for an entire week. (We told everyone he had brain surgery.)

Another brought one coat . . . an old army jacket belonging to his father. (He looked like a deserter from the other side.) The other one packed one pair of shoes . . . a red-white-and-blue pair of sneakers with stars. The only time he didn't look out of place was under a basket in a coliseum.

Last week, all three of my children looked worse than usual as they headed for the door. "Why do all of you look so rotten today?" I asked. "Are you in a school play or something?"

"No, we're having our class picture taken."

It figures.

Haven't I Always Loved Whatshisname Best?

A woman starts thinking of a name for her baby from the minute she knows she is carrying one. She will write it out, say it aloud, try it out on her friends, and embroider it on little shirts. When the baby is born she will whisper the name softly in its ear, write it on dozens of announcements and file it in the courthouse records.

A few years and a few kids later, she can't remember who you are.

I've heard mothers go through ten or twelve names before they get lucky and hit the right one. (Once I wore my P.J.s wrong side out and my mom, thinking it was a name tag, called me Dr. Denton for a week.)

Children seem to think there is something Freudian in the entire exercise. The old if-my-mother-really-loved-me-she'd-remember-my-name trauma. This is hogwash. I love Marc . . . Mary . . . Mike . . . Mil . . . Massa . . . whatshisname with the same affection as I love Bet . . . Bronc . . . Evely . . . Mar . . . Tri . . . you know who you are.

Our neighborhood psychiatrist bears me out. He said there is nothing you can generalize from mothers who can't put a name to their children right off the bat.

It used to be a good day for me when I could remember what I called them for, let alone remember who they are.

In talking with a young married the other day, it was revealed that he was one of seven children and not once when he was growing up was he ever called by his real name. "I guess it was because there were so many of us," he said, "that it confused my mother."

I hated to shoot his theory down, but for a long while I was an only child and still got Sara . . . Bet . . . Mild . . . Vir . . . Edna. Finally, in desperation, my mother would shout, "How long do I have to call you before you answer?"

I'd yell back, "Until you get it right."

"Was I close?" she'd shout.

"Edna was somewhere in the neighborhood."

"I always liked Edna," she mused. "I should have named you that."

"Then why did you name me Erma?"

"Because it was easy to remember."

"Why Can't We Have Our Own Apartment?"

We knew the kids would take it the wrong way, but we had to do it anyway.

"Children," we said, "your father and I want to get our own apartment."

One looked up from his homework and the other two even turned down the volume on the TV set. "What are you saying?"

"We are saying we'd like to move out and be on our own for a while."

"But why?" asked our daughter. "Aren't you happy here? You have your own room and the run of the house."

"I know, but a lot of parents our age are striking out on their own."

"It'll be expensive," said our son. "Have you thought about utilities and phone bills and newspapers and a hundred little things you take for granted around here?"

"We've thought it all through."

"Spit it out," said our daughter. "What's bothering you about living with us? Did we ask too much? What did we ask you to do? Only cook, make beds, do laundry, take care of the yard, keep the cars in running order and bring in the money. Was that so hard?"

"It's not that," I said gently. "It's just that we want to fix up our own apartment and come and go as we please."

"If it's your car you wanted, why didn't you say so? We could make arrangements."

"It's not just the car. We want to be able to play our stereos when we want to and come in late without someone saying, 'Where have you been?' and invite people over without other people hanging around eating our chip dip."

"What will you do for furniture?"

"We don't need all that much. We'll just take a few small appliances, some linens, our bedroom suite, the typewriter, the luggage, the card table and chairs, the old TV you never use, and some pots and pans and a few tables and chairs."

"You'll call everyday?"

We nodded.

As we headed for the car I heard one son whisper sadly, "Wait till they get their first utility bill. They'll be back."

Is There a Life After Mine?

No one knows what her life expectancy is, but I have a horror of leaving this world and not having anyone in the entire family know how to replace a toilet tissue spindle.

It's an awesome thought to have four grown people wandering around in a daze saying, "I thought she told you how," and another saying, "If I knew she was sick, I'd have paid attention."

The tissue spindle isn't the only home skill that has been mastered by no one at our house. Consequently, I have put together a single family survival manual when Mom is gone.

Replacing Toilet Tissue Spindle

Grasp old spindle and push gently to one side where there is a spring action. The spindle will release and you discard the old cardboard. Slip on new roll and insert one end of spindle in the spring-action side and listen for a click into place.

Washing Toothpaste Off Side of Washbowl

Before toothpaste is allowed to harden/become a permanent part of the enamel, swish water from faucet over affected areas and give a gentle nudge with washcloth or hands. Sink will be ready for next slobee.

Turning on the Stove

Hot meals require a hot stove. If the stove is gas, ignite by turning dial or handle while holding match over burner. If stove is electric, take forefinger and push firmly on button of desired heat. Caution: Do not put food directly on burner, but put it in a pan first.

Closing a Door

This looks harder than it is. When door is ajar, make sure it is free of foreign objects (children, feet, packages), then grasp it firmly by the handle and give it a push until you hear it click. Slamming the door will not make it close any firmer than a push.

Turning Off a Light

The same principle is used in turning off a light as in turning it on. If it is a wall switch, you flick the switch up or down until you no longer see the light. If it is a chain mechanism, you compress chain between thumb and forefinger and give it a tug. The light will extinguish.

Operating a Clothes Hamper

Don't be intimidated because there are no dials or instructions on the lid. Bending from the waist you simply pick up a sock, a pair of pants, or a towel, lift the lid of the hamper and feed soiled clothes into it. The Good Fairy will take it from there.

Keep this manual handy for easy reference. If I have to take these skills with me when I go . . . I'm not going.

"Why Can't Our Average Little Family Get Their Own TV Series?"

The other night I was watching a situation comedy series of a typical, American family. This family laughed until they got sick.

Everytime Daddy opened his mouth, he was a scream. The mother was a stitch. And the kids were absolute geniuses at spewing out hilarious retorts. I looked around at our group. My husband was deeply depressed over the paper. He's looked like that since he let his G.I. insurance lapse. One child was on the phone insisting, "I don't believe it!" every minute and a half. Another was locked in his room with the stereo on and the other was staring morosely into the refrigerator waiting for something to embrace him.

"You know the trouble with this family? We're not funny. All the other families in the world are sitting around throwing away one-liners and having a barrel of laughs. The six o'clock news gets more laughs than we do. We've got to get with it or we'll never get our own series."

The next night as I heard my husband's car in the driveway, I shouted, "Hey Gang. Heeeeeeereeeeeee's Daddy!"

"Well," said our son, "if it isn't our father whose wallet is full of big bills . . . all unpaid."

"What's the matter with you?" asked my husband. "You're on your feet. Has your car been repossessed?"

"Dyyyyyynnnnnooooomite!" said our youngest. (I almost fell out of the chair.)

"Hey, Mom," said a son, "what do you get if you take a fender from a Chevy, the chrome from a Ford and the hubcaps from a Pontiac?" I shook my head.

"Six months!"

"A rubber hose up your nose," I said amid laughter.

"So," said my husband, "I thought you were going to straighten up the house."

"Why?" I said nudging him in his ribs. "Is it tilted? Incidentally, did you hear Mel just got a poodle for his wife?"

"I wish I could make a trade like that."

"Hey, Dad," said our daughter, "the dog just ate Mom's meatloaf."

"Don't cry," he said, "I'll buy you another dog."

My mother poked her head in the door. "Got any coffee?"

We all slumped in our chairs exhausted. Thank God for commercials.

3

Who Killed Apple Pie?

It's a frightening feeling to wake up one morning and discover that while you were asleep you went out of style.

That's what happened to millions of housewives, who one day looked into their mirrors and said, "I do not feel fulfilled putting toilet seats down all day."

Women were sick of pushing buttons. Besides, the buttons were pushing back. There was a housewife in Michigan who was vacuuming her carpet one morning and leaned over to pick an object off the floor. Her hair was pulled into the machine by the underside brush roller, causing her to fall on top of the vacuum and sustain electrical shock to the left side of her head.

They no longer bought the theory, advanced by a British Medical Association, that doing housework was the secret to female longevity and that all that exercise would prolong life.

As I was on my knees one afternoon, hoisting the bunk beds on my back and trying to put the slats back into the grooves, my husband asked, "What are you doing down there?"

"Prolonging my life," I said dryly.

"Those things fall out all the time," he said. "Why don't you get some slats that are longer?"

183

"They were longer when we got them," I said.

"Are you going to start that business about inanimate things being human? You're going bananas being cooped up in this house. You should get out more. After you get all this stuff fixed up around here, why don't you do something you've always wanted to do?"

I sat back on my knees and reflected. What I always wanted to do was run away from home. You all know the feeling. You diet for two weeks and gain three pounds. You break your bottom to get to a White Sale only to discover that all they have left are double top sheets, single contour bottoms, and King pillowcases.

Your best friend (whom you have always trusted) calls and tells you she just found out how to bake bread. Some wise guy just wrote "HELP" in the dust on the draperies.

You pick up a movie magazine in the supermarket with headlines reading JACKIE ONASSIS' SPENDING HABITS SUGGEST MENTAL DISORDER and realize you've had the same disorder for years.

The cheerleader on your high school cheer squad just became a grandmother. The supermarket just discontinued your silverware pattern and you spend forty minutes ironing a linen dress and it doesn't fit you anymore.

You drive into a drive-in bank and the car just ahead of you gets a flat. You see your neighbor going to the office and yell, "I hope you find eraser droppings in your IBM Selectric." And you can't take it anymore.

Then one day in a leading magazine, I saw a story called, "Today's Woman on the Go."

At the top of the article was a picture of a well-stacked blonde at a construction site with a group of men around her while she read blueprints to them. I noted her shoes were coordinated with her Gucci yellow hard hat.

The second picture showed her in a pair of flowing pajamas standing over the stove stirring her filet-mignon helper (recipe on page 36) while her husband tossed the salad and her children lovingly set the table.

It made me want to spit up.

I wanted to be "on the go." (I was half-gone already.) Imagine! Every morning going off to carpetland . . . to fresh bread for lunch . . . to a phone that wasn't sticky with grape jelly . . . to perfume behind each knee that spelled madness to stock boys.

And I said to myself, "There, but for the grace of a babysitter go I."

Once I made up my mind, I interviewed sitters for six months. It's depressing when you realize no one wants to be paid for what you've been doing for years for nothing. I talked with one who could only work until the children came home from school. Another believed in naps until age thirty-five, and there was one who worked for one day and quit saying, "Do you actually expect me to work in a house where the water jug looks like snow falling in a paperweight?"

Other women, I was to discover, had the same problem. A friend of mine who is a registered nurse said she had a shattering experience. She found a "gem" who was willing to sit with her children if she left explicit instructions. The first day she left the following note:

"Greg gets 1 tsp. of pink medicine in refrigerator at 8 A.M. and before lunch. He has impetigo, so wash your hands good with soap and water and don't let him use anyone else's glass.

"Paula gets 1 tsp. of orange medicine in brown bottle at 8 A.M. and at lunch. There's plenty of lunch meat, peanut butter, etc., for lunch.

"Paula has to be taken to the potty every two to three hours. There's a potty seat upstairs and a small chair in Rec. Room.

"Don't let dog in the chewing gum. He craves it but has to be taken to the vet to remove. He gets pills once a day (not birth *control) for slight infection. Get Frank (who is in and out all day long) to hold him so he will not bite.*

"Take messages. Don't use toilet in utility room. It bubbles. If you have questions, call me. Tell them you are one of the nurses if they ask."

When she arrived home, the door was marked with lamb's blood and there was a large quarantine sign tacked on it. The sitter had fled.

You have only to work once in your life to know that "Today's Woman on the Go" is pure fiction. Maybe they got the captions under the pictures switched. Maybe she wore the long flowing pajamas at work and the hard hat at home. Heaven knows, home is a Hard Hat area.

Where were the pictures showing her racing around the kitchen in a pair of bedroom slippers, trying to quick-thaw a chop under each armpit and yelling like a shrew, "All right, you guys, I know you're in the house. I can hear your stomachs growling."

According to the article, all you needed was a worksheet, with everyone in the family having his or her own responsibility, leaving Mother time not only to hold down a full-time job, but to paint, sew her own coats, ride horses, and run for the U.S. Senate.

It wasn't like that at all. I called home one evening and said, "Let me speak to your father."

"He's at the dentist," said my son. "He chipped his tooth this morning on the frozen bread."

"So who was on the worksheet to defrostthe bread?"

"I was, but I forgot my key, got locked out and stayed all night with Mike. The milkman got locked out too. There are twelve half-gallons of milk in the garage."

"Where's your sister?"

"I made her bed with her in it. She's not speaking. There are wet clothes in the washer and they're covered with a brown rash.

We're defrosting the spareribs under your hair dryer. Guess who forgot to put the dog out when he came home? When are you coming home?"

"I'll be home tomorrow. Do you miss me?"

"No, but according to the worksheet, you're on for dishes."

Sharing responsibility is what the entire movement to free women is all about. If women are ever to be appreciated, a husband should drive a car pool . . . just once.

Transporting children is my husband's twenty-sixth favorite thing. It comes somewhere between eating lunch in a tea room and dropping a bowling ball on his foot.

"Remember," I warned him before his first attempt, "they are small children . . . not mail sacks. That means you have to bring the car to a complete stop and open the door for them. Don't shout and be sure to give all six of them their own window. Good luck."

An hour-and-a-half later as he staggered through the door I said,

"So, what took you so long?"

"To begin with, old paste breath didn't want to get into the car. He said his mother didn't want him to ride with strangers. Then the name tag that was pinned to whatshername's dress fell off and she didn't know who she was. Debbie cried for three blocks because she left her Bionic Woman lunchbox on the swings. Cecil . . . I guess that's his name . . . the one who sits there and rebuttons his sweater all the time trying to make it come out even . . ."

"That's Cecil."

"He told me he lived at the Dairy Queen."

"So what took you so long?"

"Michael. Michael is the one who took me so long. He said he didn't know where he lived, so to make friends, I gave him a taffy sucker. I must have driven around in circles for thirty minutes before he said, 'That's my house.'

"Michael," I said, *"we've passed this house twenty to thirty times. Why didn't you say something before?"*

"Because," he said, *"I'm not allowed to talk with food in my mouth."*

There are some who say giving children responsibility makes them grow. There are others who contend it increases your insurance rates.

Whatever, there are some ground rules that must prevail while a mother is employed outside the home. First, when to bug and when not to bug. In other words, when do you call Mom on the phone at work?

Emergencies do arise. There's no doubt about that, but some guidelines must be established at the top of the page.

Before a child calls his mother at work he must ask himself: (1) Will Mom drop dead when she hears this? (2) Can she find a plumber after five? (3) Will she carry out her threat to move to another city and change her name?

If the answers are "Yes, No, Yes," the child might try putting the incident in a proper perspective.

For example, if there is blood to report, consider these questions, Is it his? His brother's? Is there a lot? A little? On the sofa that is not Scotchgarded? Or the eighty-dollar one that they are still making payments on? Will the bleeding stop? Was it an accident? A loose baby tooth? Can he shut up about it and pass it off as an insect bite?

Another example: When every other kid in the neighborhood decides your child's house would be a neat place to play because there is no adult at home, he should ask himself, "Do I want to spend my entire puberty locked in my room with no food and no television? Do I need the friendship of a boy who throws ice cubes at the bird? Will Mom notice we made confetti in her blender?"

Other situations to be definite about:

When a group of children decide to wash the cat and put him in the dryer and want to know what setting to use . . . CALL.

When he and his brother are hitting and slapping over the last soft drink and he wants a high level decision on who gets it, DON'T CALL.

When a couple of men in a pickup truck tell him his Mom is having the TV slipcovered, the silverware stored, her jewelry cleaned and his ten-speed bicycle oiled, CALL . . . AND FAST.

When his sister chases him into the house with the garden hose and the furniture is turning a funny looking white, RUN.

When he is bored and has nothing to do and just wants to talk, CALL HIS FATHER.

During the summer months when children are too old for a sitter and too young for sense, I find that a Primer for Imaginative Children is a must just to set down what you expect of them.

Primer for Imaginative Children

This is a house.

Vehicles are not permitted in the house.

Occupancy of this house by more than two hundred people is dangerous and unlawful. Violators will be prosecuted.

There is a dog in the house. His name is Spot. Spot likes to run and play and chase sticks. He also likes to relieve himself with some regularity. Watch Spot for telltale signs of urgency, such as jumping higher than the ceiling, gnawing on the doorknob or tunneling under the door.

It is fun to eat. See the milk? See the butter? See the lunch meat? They cannot run. They cannot walk. They have no legs.

They must be picked up and returned to the refrigerator or they will turn green. Green is not a happy color.

Hear the phone ring? That means someone wants to talk to you. Ring. Ring. Ring. When the phone rings, pick it up and speak directly into it. Say "Hello." Say "Goodbye." Say anything.

A bedroom is a special place. Find your bed each day. Try. Sometimes, you cannot see your bed because it is covered with clutter. This is not healthy. A cluttered room is a messy room. Fish die in a messy room. Mothers cannot breathe in a messy room. A messy room is unfit for humans. Many people in this house are human.

A bathroom is your friend. It is there when you need it. Lids do not like to be standing all the time. They get tired. Towels do not like to be on the floor. They cannot see anything. Ugh. Soap does not like to lie in a drain and melt. Boo.

See Mommy come home. See Daddy come home. They are walking on their knees. Be kind to Mommy and Daddy. "Look, look, Mommy, Bruce is bloody. I'm telling, Debbie. I didn't do it, Daddy."

Do you want to make Mommy crazy?

Do you want to make Daddy rupture a neck vein?

Then shape up, up, up.

The controversy of whether to work outside the home or not to work outside the home goes on. Each woman in her own way assesses what her needs are, and how they can best be met.

It must be pointed out that office procedure also has its shortcomings. Nothing is perfect. For example, one office had the following SICK LEAVE POLICY.

Sickness

No excuse. We will no longer accept your doctor's statement as proof, as we believe if you are able to go to the doctor, you are able to come to work.

Death (other than your own)

This is no excuse. There is nothing you can do for them and we are sure that someone else in a lesser position can attend to arrangements. However, if the funeral can be arranged in the late afternoon, we will be glad to let you off one hour early, provided your share of work is ahead enough to keep the job going in your absence.

Death (your own)

This is acceptable as an excuse provided (a) two weeks' notice is given in order to break in a new person for your job (b) if two weeks' notice is not possible, call in before 8 A.M. so that a sub may be provided and (c) this must be verified by your doctor's signature and your own. Both signatures must be present, or the time will be deducted from your annual sick leave.

Leave of Absence (for an operation)

We are no longer allowing this practice. We wish to discourage any thought you may have about needing an operation. We believe that as long as you are employed here, you will need all of whatever you have and should not consider having anything removed. We hired you as you are, and to have anything removed would certainly make you less than we bargained for.

Leave of Absence (rest room)

Too much time is being spent in the rest rooms. Our time study man has ascertained that three minutes, fifteen seconds constitutes a generous break. In the future, we will follow the practice of going to the rest room in alphabetical order. Those with names beginning with A will go from 8 A.M. to 8:05, 15 seconds; those with F from 8:03, 15 seconds to 8:06, 30 seconds, etc. If you miss your turn, you must wait until the day when your turn comes again.

As I was on my knees one afternoon at the office, trying to lift a filing cabinet over a piece of carpet, my boss asked, "What are you doing down there?"

"Prolonging my life. I just read a survey where it said women who worked outside the home lived a richer, fuller, longer life."

"You look tired to me," he said. "Why don't you get out of the office for a while. Go home, bake a little bread, wax the floors, visit with your children."

Between keeping house and working, I'm probably going to live to be a hundred. Or maybe it will just seem that long.

4 〜••

The Varicose Open

Well, if I had known the battle of the sexes was going to be fought on a tennis court, I wouldn't have let my knees grow together.

Looking back, it all started when Bobby Riggs became Queen of the Courts (grass, clay, and Margaret). Businessmen, housewives, students, blue-collar workers, politicians, preschoolers, everyone was "into tennis."

Heaven help you if you were new to the game. It was an uphill battle to break through the barriers of snobbery and elitism to play a game that for years had been dominated by rich kids with weak chins and straight, white teeth.

That sounds biased, but did you ever see a picture of Rockefeller coming out of a bowling alley with his gym bag, or a Kennedy tinkering with his engine just before his stock car race? On the coldest day in the midwest you could always pick up a newspaper and see one of them with a white sweater knotted around his neck, shading his eyes from the blazing sun.

As a nuevo tennis player, I felt like Belle Watling (the madam in Gone with the Wind who tried to buy respectability by giving money to a hospital). The question was could a woman plagued by varicose veins find happiness with a tennis player who was attached to his mother by an umbilical sweatband?

My first day out was a disaster. I encountered a member of the First Family of tennis who appraised me coolly.

"White is tacky," she sniffed. "Everyone but everyone who plays tennis these days dresses in colors. Tell me, who is your pro?"

"I've been getting a little help with my strokes from Leroy Ace."

She frowned, "I don't believe I've heard of him. What club?"

"The boy's club. But he moonlights from his garage."

"How well do you play?" she asked before going to the other side of the net.

"I had tennis elbow twice last week."

"That only means something is wrong with your stroke. You need help. Do you prefer string or gut?"

"I'll play with anybody," I shrugged.

"Would you like to warm up?"

"Sure," I popped a ball over the fence. "Would you believe I've only been playing for two days?"

"That long?" she said tiredly.

"What about you?" I asked.

"I played in the good old days," she said slowly, "before they opened up the courts to Democrats."

I didn't care what she said. I knew that, somehow, in this lumpy little body that tripped over lint in the carpet was a Chrissie Evert just fighting to get out.

It was just a matter of time before I developed a form, learned how to get my racket out of the press, and didn't require oxygen after each serve.

But first, I knew I would never be taken seriously as a tennis player until I learned how to pick up the ball. I summoned my son.

Now, there are few things in this world more satisfying than having your son teach you how to play tennis. One is having a semitruck run over your foot.

It's almost as if he is paying you back for letting him fall off the dryer when he was a baby . . . for putting him to bed on his fifth birthday when he threw ice cream into the fan . . . for bailing out of the car when you were teaching him how to drive. All the hostilities come out the moment you walk onto the court together.

"Okay, we're going to continue today with our instruction on how to pick up the ball."

"I know how to pick up the ball," I said.

"I've told you before, we do not pick up the ball like a gorilla going for a banana. There is a professional way and there are several approaches. You can learn with the western forehand grip. Lean over gently and tap the ball with your racket until it bounces."

Several minutes later as I was on my knees pounding the racket into the yellow optic, he leaned over and said, "It's not a snake you are beating to death. It is a tennis ball. Let's try the ball-against-the-foot method."

I stood up exhausted. "How does that work again?"

"You grip your racket against the ball and firmly force it to the inside of your left foot. Bending your knee, you lift the ball to about six inches off the ground and drop it. When it bounces, you continue bouncing it with your racket until you can pluck it off the ground and into your hand."

Gripping the racket, I forced the ball to the inside of my foot where it rolled over the foot and toward the net. I cornered it and started inching the ball up my leg, but lost my balance and fell into the net.

Approaching the ball once more I accidentally kicked it with my foot and, in a crouched position, I chased it to the corner of the court, slamming my body into the fence.

For the next fifteen minutes, the elusive little ball moved all over the court like it had a motor in it.

Finally, I leaned over, grabbed it with my hand, placed it on my leg and supported it with the racket.

"Okay," I shouted, "I picked up the ball."

"That'll be all for today," he said. "We'll spend a few more weeks on this before moving along to hitting the ball."

I put my arm over his shoulder. "Now, let me tell you how to pick the towels off the bathroom floor. You simply bend your body in the middle, grasp the towel firmly between . . ."

He was gone.

Rotten kids. They shouldn't be allowed on the courts. I got a theory about these kids who play tennis anyway . . . You know the ones. These little tiny kids who sit around swanky tennis courts in a pair of dollar-ninety-eight tennis shoes with the strings knotted, holding a tennis racket made in Tijuana and sucking on an ice cube. When they are invited to play, they squint and ask, "What do you call this thing again?"

The adults are amused. "A tennis racket."

Then the kid really starts to perform. He giggles as his pudgy little hands cannot hold two tennis balls at the same time, so he places one on the base line. He has to be told where to stand and his form is somewhere between Art Buchwald and a bullfighter with bad eyes.

After the warm-up, the personality of the kid changes. He scoops up the ball with the back of his foot, aces his opponent on every serve, runs around the court like a wood nymph, jumps the net to offer his condolences and asks for a towel.

My theory is they're beings from another planet who aren't children at all. They're forty-nine-year-old tennis players who have the body of a six-million-dollar man.

They get on my nerves almost as much as Debbie Dominant. Debbie has always been a pace setter. She was the first woman on the block with wheels on her garbage cans and chewed on her sunglasses three years before Marlo Thomas.

Two years before tennis became "in," Debbie appeared at the supermarket flushed and breathless in a tennis dress up to her tan line and white tennis shoes with a little ball fringe over the heel.

"Isn't this terrible?" she said, pushing her white hat back on her head. "I was at set point and before I knew it the dinner hour was upon me and I just buzzed in here before I could change. I had no idea I'd meet anyone I knew. I'm simply MORTIFIED!"

If she was Lady Godiva riding a power mower she couldn't have been less obvious.

Within weeks, every housewife in the neighborhood was in tennis dress not only while pushing her shopping cart around, but wearing it everywhere.

At school one afternoon, I passed a housewife in the hall who was headed for the office in full tennis attire. "Excuse me," I said, "but the girl's rest room is out of paper towels."

"Why tell me?" she asked, nervously fingering her sweatband.

"You had 'HEAD' on your T-shirt, and I figured you were a rest-room attendant."

"You're obviously not into tennis," she said stiffly.

That was the day I succumbed. I have been "into" tennis now for six months and was named Miss Congeniality in the Varicose Open.

Although my form still needs work (the body, not the game), I am proud to report I have made progess.

To begin with, I have finally mastered what to do with the second tennis ball. Having small hands, I was becoming terribly self-conscious about keeping it in a can in the car while I served the first one. I noted some women tucked the second ball just inside the elastic leg of their tennis panties. I tried, but found the space was already occupied by a leg. Now, I simply drop the second ball down my cleavage, giving me a chest that often stuns my opponent throughout an entire set.

Next, I have learned how to stall, thus throwing my opponent's entire game off. It's called the old tie-the-shoe trick. When your opponent is ready to serve, simply drop to your knees, untie your shoe, rearrange its tongue and tie it again. Baseball players use the old stall all the time. (Recently, Pat Zachry swallowed his chewing tobacco and threw up against a dugout wall. I haven't mastered at what hour I can throw up yet. Sometimes it is during a return.)

Another play is the rearrange the string number. Never take the rap for a bad return or no return. Whenever you hit a ball into the net, or miss it entirely, bring the game to a grinding halt by checking the strings of your racket, spending sometimes as much as five minutes separating them and testing their strength. This absolves you of any of the responsibility for a bad shot.

Forget all you have been told about concentration. It's overrated. Often, when there is time during one of my lobs, I yell across the net, "Your zipper is open," and have not only been ignored, but soundly punished, for my good deed.

Probably the greatest accomplishment this year has been my skill at learning how to run around my backhand. Early in my tennis career, I used to think when a ball landed to the left of me I had to use my backhand to return it. I have since learned that anything is better, including straddling a fifteen-foot cyclone fence.

No doubt about it . . . every day in every way, my game grows stronger. I saw one enthusiast the other day playing with his racket out of the press. I'll have to try that.

5 ⤜•

Profile of a Martyress

When the martyresses of our time are being immortalized, there's no doubt a shrine will be erected to the mother who holds down the homefront while her husband travels.

This courageous woman who single-handedly battles magazine salesmen, juggles car pools, stands up to TV repairmen, and whose deft fingers can find a fuse box in the darkness.

As with most heroines, there are few who are appreciated in their lifetime. One cannot possibly understand the awesome responsibility they shoulder.

That is why I should like to nominate overworked, underpatienced, unappreciated Lorraine Suggs . . . Mother Martyress.

If any of us walked for a week in her wedgies, we might have the following story to tell:

Monday she went to a parent-teacher conference alone to be told her son stole paper towels from the rest room (the girls'), wrote an obscene word in the dust on Mr. Gripper's car, and was flunking lunch. She said her husband traveled a lot and the teacher said:

"You should be glad he's working."

On Tuesday, the dog got hit by a motorcycle, the house payment

199

got lost in the mail and her daughter tried to crush a tin can with her hand like the Bionic Woman and required a tetanus shot. She told the doctor her husband traveled a lot and he said:

"You're lucky you have a car."

On Wednesday, the television set blew a tube, the car developed a wheeze and she had to cancel a night out with the girls. Her mother-in-law said:

"Be thankful you have children."

On Thursday, she was making a left-hand turn in her VW Rabbit, when a car plowed into the back of her. As she sat there crying softly, "The rabbit died . . . the rabbit died . . ." a police officer stuck his head in the window and said:

"You're lucky, lady. No one got hurt."

On Friday at the supermarket, so bored she was carrying on a conversation with a broom display, she went through the mechanics of shopping . . . lashing one kid to the basket, getting another out of the bean display where he "found" a hole in a bag of pinto beans, and on finding the third had eaten an unknown amount of fruit, offered to weigh him and anything over fifty-three pounds, pay the difference. The checkout girl in noting all the convenience foods said:

"You're lucky to have your husband gone a lot. At least you don't have to cook big meals."

On Saturday, she car pooled it to the Little Leagues, two haircuts, one dental appointment, baton-twirling lessons, the cleaners, the post office and a birthday party. As she started the power mower at dusk, a neighbor yelled over the fence:

"You're lucky. At least you get out of the house."

On Sunday, she dragged the brood to church. The baby chewed up two verses out of the hymnal, one child followed a rolling dime all the way to the altar, and the third stole a sponge from the Holy Water font.

The minister stood at the door, smiled stiffly and said:
"You should be thankful the good Lord is looking after you."

Profile of a Martyr

When the martyrs of our time are being immortalized, there's no doubt a shrine will be erected to the man who must leave the comforts of his home and travel.

This courageous soul, who sits around airports waiting for a glimpse of O.J. Simpson, and misses his plane because a security buzzer keeps picking up the foil on his gum wrapper.

This saint of a man, who spends hours in hotels trying to locate the switch that will give him light, who adjusts the shower so that it directs the spray INSIDE the tub.

As with most heroes, there are few who are appreciated in their lifetime. One cannot possibly understand the frustrations they shoulder.

That is why I should like to nominate overworked, underpaid, unappreciated Tom Suggs . . . Father and Martyr who makes his living attending conventions.

If any of us walked for a week in his shoes, we might have the following story to tell:

Monday: He checked into the hotel, which has no washcloths, a refrigerator in the bathroom growing penicillin . . . a balcony that faces a brick wall, a TV set that gets extension courses in math from the university and an air-conditioner–heater with a broken thermometer. There are no light switches. When he summoned the maid she said:

"You should be glad you're not next to the hospitality suite."

Tuesday: The hotel is a floating ark with two of everything, including elevators. There are five hundred and twenty-five rooms and fifteen hundred conventioneers. The meetings are scheduled in the Promenade room, which is on the mezzanine between the third and fourth floors and is serviced by elevator no. 1 between the hours of 3 and 4 A.M. No one knows this. He complained to another conventioneer, who said:

"You're lucky. I made it to yesterday's meeting."

Wednesday: After two days of conversing with chests that say, "Hello there, my name is illegible," he tries to call home only to find the hotel operator is unlisted. He walks to the desk, places the call and waits for fifteen minutes while his pre-schooler goes to "get mommy," five more minutes while she coaxes the baby to say, "Hi Daddy," and another twenty minutes listening to a report on how his house died due to his negligence.

The operator observes:

"You're lucky she puts up with you."

Thursday: His luggage still hasn't arrived, but there is a tracer who suspects it has never left the airport at home. As he sits in his room, trying to heat up a "rare" hamburger on a TV set that is flashing math equations, the phone rings and it is a sloshed buddy from the hospitality suite shouting:

"Hey, buddy, this beats cutting grass, doesn't it?"

Friday: He sits through five keynote speeches, comparable only to waking up in a recovery room and being asked to applaud. He still cannot find the light switch. The maid says:

"You're lucky. A man's wife down the hall arrived unexpectedly and found his light switch at 2 this morning. She nearly killed him."

Saturday he took two taxis full of clients to dinner at which a record was set for carrying on a conversation without saying one thing that was worth repeating. He called his wife again, who said:

"Thank God you have adults to talk to."

Sunday: As he calls the desk to tell them he is checking out, they inform him his lost luggage is on the way in from the airport.

As he throws up his hands, he inadvertently finds the light switch in the navel of the cherub lamp at his bedside. As he stands in the rain waiting for a cab, a driver splashes mud all over his suit. The doorman says:

"You almost got hit. You're lucky the good Lord is looking after you."

6

"Have a Good Day"

The expression "Have a good day" was born the week our oil supply was depleted, water became scarce, telephone rates went up, gasoline was in short supply, and meat, coffee and sugar prices soared. It was as if the warranty on the country had just expired.

"Have a good day" was something to say.

Ecology became a household word. My husband became a nut on recycling. Until a few years ago he thought recycling was an extra setting on the washer that tore the buttons off his shirts and shredded his underwear. Now, he sits around making towel racks out of oversexed coat hangers.

My daughter poked her head in my kitchen one day and told me my ozone was in trouble.

"Give me a hint," I said. "Has the anti-freeze leaked out of my car? Are my sinus cavities ready to crest? Or did someone flick their Bic near all the papers stored in the basement?"

"I'm talking about aerosol cans," she groaned. "I'm not going to use them anymore and you shouldn't either. Are you aware that Congress is drafting a bill that will include a ban of spray cans using fluorocarbons?"

"I wouldn't have gone so far as to take it to Congress," I said.

"Mother! Surely, you've seen first-hand how the fluorocarbons in pressurized cans can harm the atmospheric layer that screens the sun's radiation."

"You bet," I nodded. "Not to mention what happens when you mistakenly spray tub and tile cleaner on your teeth. I mean, who wants teeth that foam and deodorize?"

"I can't believe it, Mother." She smiled. "Do you realize this is the first meaningful conversation we've been able to carry on in years?"

I passed the bathroom and gave my underarms a spritz with air freshener. These may just be the only two ozones I'll ever get, and I plan to take care of them.

Have a good day. . . .

The more technology the phone company developed, the more complicated using the phone became. I never knew what complicated was until the phone company launched a campaign to save me money.

Everytime I picked up the receiver, I kept seeing the face of an operator on television with half a phone growing out of her ear admonishing, "Dial direct. Save 60 percent on nights and weekends. Lower rates on shorter distances. Talk one minute to Nashville for twenty-two minutes."

One Sunday I found myself setting an alarm for 3 A.M. and direct-dialing Nashville to a person I never liked much and talked for four minutes because I saved $1.25. It was a bargain I couldn't afford to pass up. In fact, in four weeks, I saved enough to call my sister in Ohio at a civilized hour during the week with an operator to announce me.

I put up with all of it because I knew communications were moving forward. However, I was totally unprepared one day when an operator from the phone company called to ask if I had made a long distance call to North Carolina, and if so could I supply her with the number I had called as it had not been recorded.

"How did you get my number?" I asked. "It's unlisted."

"From directory assistance," she said.

"Shame on you," I said. "That's an extra. Do you know if you had dialed me on the weekend instead of prime time during the business hours you could have saved thirty-two cents on the first minute?"

"But I . . ."

"Besides, if you call me for assistance three more times this month, you will be charged twenty cents a call. That all adds up. I assume you are calling from a business phone, which is charged full rates, which means each additional minute we talk is costing you forty cents. Frankly, dear, I'm going to do you a big favor and hang up. I don't think you can afford me."

Have a good day. . . .

The Meat Mutiny came without warning. One day, we were eating more and paying less and the next there were two hundred and seventy-eight products on the market to help our hamburger.

Housewives did not take the news sitting down. They stood outside of grocery stores eating dog food in protest. Signs went up suggesting, FIGHT MEAT PRICES. SUCK YOUR THUMB. And clever cookbooks came out to combat the crisis. (*Cook Cheap* cost $12.95.)

Overnight, butchers became the darlings of the cocktail party, replacing doctors. I hated myself for it, but I found myself playing the game like the rest of the homemakers.

"How's your rump today, Fred," I asked my butcher one day after he called my number.

He looked around cautiously. "You've been a good customer of mine for two years, Erma. Nursed our baby back to health after the flu epidemic and loaned me the money to get my store started. A man doesn't forget things like that. [I smiled.] I can arrange financing on a sirloin tip at 6 percent on the unpaid balance for thirty-six months."

"See you at our house Saturday night?" I smiled.

"You bet," he waved.

I had no shame whatsoever. "Well, if it isn't Fred Sawsil. I hate to bring this up at a social gathering, Fred, but I was wondering if you would prescribe something for a tough round steak. The meat thermometer registers normal and I've already given it two tablespoons of meat tenderizer."

He looked up tiredly. "Take two aspirins and call me in the morning," he said. "Now if you'll excuse me, I have to get back to Mrs. Beeman. She has a sty in the eye of her round."

I stood there in a daze. Somehow, it did me a world of good just to touch the hand of the man who had touched a standing rib. . . .

Standing at the meat counter day after day was depressing. I found myself looking over cuts of meat that I used to think belonged in bottles at Harvard.

"What is that?" I asked Fred one day. "In the corner of the meat case?"

"Tongue."

"Whose?"

"It was an anonymous donor," he said dryly. "This is tripe," he said, holding up a carton.

"I'll say," I said weakly.

"Have you never tried pig's feet?"

"No, you never know where they've been."

"Chicken?"

"I'll pretend I didn't hear that."

I motioned to Fred to come closer. "Listen, Fred, do you remember that rump roast you financed last week? Well, when you trimmed a little of the fat off it went into deep shock and . . ."

"I don't make house calls," he said stiffly.

"So, why don't you drop over to the house tomorrow," I said, "and I'll have a few people in and. . . ."

"On Wednesdays I play golf," he said.

Have a good day. . . .

I wanted to boycott coffee when it went to four dollars a pound. I really did, but basically I'm weak and cannot endure pain.

I knew I was paying more for three pounds of coffee than I paid for a winter coat when I was first married, but I couldn't help myself.

You cannot imagine the pressure I got from the women in the neighborhood. One morning, I practically ran to the coffee klatsch at Lois's house.

Just inside the door, Lois said, "Want a cup?"

She put an empty cup in my hand.

"Where's the coffee?" I asked.

"I never promised you coffee."

"That's not funny, Lois. Do you have any idea what I would give for a cup of coffee? I'd sell my children."

"Wouldn't we all."

"I'd sell my body."

"Braggart."

"Lois, I'd sell my bowling trophy."

"Will you get hold of yourself? We've got to stand firm together or there's no telling how high the price of coffee will go."

"Look," I said regaining my composure, "I never thought I'd admit this to anyone, but I am older than the rest of you and I lived through the Great Caffeine Drought of 1942 during the war."

"I never heard of it," said Lois.

"And I hope you never do," I said. "I saw my mother in the morning without a cup of coffee once and it's the closest to death I ever want to come. She toasted and buttered her hand and put it on my sister's plate. She bumped into a footstool with her head. She felt a draft and it was her eyelashes blinking. When she thought no one was looking, she put her head in the coffee canister and inhaled. My father caught her trying to shave her tongue. It was awful."

"It must have been a terrible thing for a child to see," comforted Carol, "but courage; it'll all be over soon."

"I know," I whimpered, "but a day without Joe DiMaggio is like a day without sunshine."

You can only be "lousy with courage" for so long. On the way back from the school after lunch, I swung the car into a drive-in and yelled, "One cup of coffee please . . . and will you take a personal check?"

Have a good day. . . .

7 ⇌•:

"Warning: Families May Be Dangerous to Your Health"

There's a lot of theories on why the American family is losing ground as an institution.

Some say it's economics . . . others say ecology . . . others blame lack of fulfillment . . . a few opt for priorities, or as one neighbor observed, "Would you want to bring a child into a world that wouldn't elect Ronald Reagan?"

I personally like the American family. It has a lot of potential. Besides, the world is not geared for two people. Twinkies come twelve to a box, kitchen chairs, four to a set, gum, five sticks to the package.

To my way of thinking, the American family started to decline when parents began to communicate with their children. When we began to "rap," "feed into one another," "let things hang out" that mother didn't know about and would rather not.

Foremost of the villains that ripped the American family to shreds was Education. It was a case of Hide-and-Seek meeting

Show and Tell . . . the McGuffey reader crowd locking horns with the Henry Miller group.

The ignorance gap that the new math created between parent and child has not even begun to mend.

Before the new math, I had a mysterious aura about me. I never said anything, but my children were convinced I had invented fire.

When we began to have "input" with one another, my daughter said to me one day, "Mama, what's a variable?"

"It's a weirdo who hangs around the playground. Where did you read that word? On a restroom wall?"

"It's in my new math book," she said. "I was hoping you could help me. They want me to locate the mantissa in the body of the table and determine the associated antilog ten, and write the characteristics as an exponent on the base of ten."

I thought a minute. "How long has the mantissa been missing?"

She went to her room, locked her door and I never saw her again until after she graduated.

The metric system was no better. Once a child knows that a square millimeter is .00155 square inches, will he ever have respect for a mother who once measured the bathroom for carpeting and found out she had enough left over to slipcover New Jersey?

And what modern-day mother has never been intimidated when she has to communicate with a child's teacher?

I don't think there's anything that makes my morning like a kid looking up from his cereal and saying casually, "I gotta have a note saying I was sick or my teacher won't let me back into school."

"I suppose it has to be written on paper," I ask, slumping miserably over the bologna.

"The one you wrote on wax paper she couldn't read. But if you can't find paper, I could stay home for another day," he said.

I tore a piece of wallpaper off the wall and said, "Get me a pencil."

The pencil took a bit of doing. After a fifteen-minute search we finally found a stub in the lint trap of the dryer.

"You sure are whipped up about this note," I sighed.

"You don't understand," he said. "If we don't have one we don't go back to school."

I started to write. "Is your teacher a Miss, a Ms. or a Mrs.?"

"I don't know," he pondered. "She owns her own car and carries her own books."

"Dear Ms. Weems," I wrote.

"On the other hand, she stayed up to watch the Miss America Pageant."

"Dear Miss Weems," I wrote.

"It doesn't matter," he shrugged. "When she has her baby we'll have a new teacher."

"Dear MRS. Weems," I wrote. "Please excuse Brucie from school yesterday. When he awoke in the morning he complained of stomach cramps and . . ."

"Cross out stomach cramps," he ordered, "tell her I was too sick to watch TV.

"Dear Mrs. Weems, Brucie had the urgencies and . . ."

"What does urgencies mean?"

"Stomach cramps."

"Don't tell her that! The last time you wrote that she put me next to the door and didn't take her eyes off me all day long."

"It was your imagination," I said. "Do you need a note or not?"

"I told you I can't go to school without it."

"Okay then, get me the dictionary and turn to the D's."

He looked over my shoulder. "What does D-I-A-R-R-H-E-A mean?"

"It means you sit by the door again," I said, licking the envelope.

Composing the note took twenty-five minutes, which was eight minutes longer than the signing of the Declaration of Independence. I wouldn't bring it up, but only yesterday I was cleaning out a jacket pocket and there was the note: unread and unnecessary.

To me, modern education is a contradiction. It's like a three-year-old kid with a computer in his hand who can multiply 10.6 percent interest of $11,653, but doesn't know if a dime is larger or smaller than a nickel.

It is like your daughter going to college and taking all your small appliances, linens, beddings, furniture, luggage, TV set and car and then saying, "I've got to get away from your shallow materialism."

My kids always talk a great game of ecology. Yet, they harbor the No. 1 cause of pollution in this country: gym clothes.

A pair of shorts, a shirt and a pair of gym shoes walked into the utility room under their own steam last Wednesday and leaned helplessly against the wall. I stood there while I watched a pot of ivy shrivel and die before my eyes.

Blinking back the tears, I yelled to my son, "How long has it been since these clothes have been washed?"

"Since the beginning of the school year," he shouted back.

"What school year?"

"1972–1973."

"I thought so. You know, I don't know how your P.E. teacher stands it."

"He said we weren't too bad until yesterday."

"What happened yesterday?"

"It rained and we came inside."

"Don't you have rules about laundering these things?"

"Yeah. We have to have them washed every four months whether they need it or not."

Carefully, I unfolded the muddy shorts, the brittle T-shirt and the socks that were already in the final stages of rigor mortis.

As I tried to scrape off a French fry entangled in a gym shoe-string, I couldn't help but reflect that this was a child who had been reared in an antiseptic world. When he was a baby, I used to boil his toys and sterilize his navel bands. I made the dog wear a mask when he was in the same room. I washed my hands BE-FORE I changed his diapers.

Where had I failed?

Under his bed were dirty clothes that were harboring wildlife. In his drawers were pairs of soiled underwear so old that some had plastic liners in them. His closet had overalls and jeans that hung suspended without the need of hangers.

Opening the lid of the washer, I felt around trying to find the gym clothes that I had just washed. I retrieved a shoestring, two labels and a clean French fry.

"What happened to my gym clothes?" asked my son.

"After the sweat and dirt went, this was all that was left."

Probably the most blatant contradiction between what a child is at home and what he is at school manifests itself at the annual Athletic Banquet.

Next time you attend an athletic awards banquet, catch the look on the faces of mothers as the accomplishments of their sons and daughters are revealed. It is as if they are talking about a different person with the same name as your youngster.

By intense concentration, you can sometimes read the parents' thoughts, as the coaches pay them homage.

"Mark is probably one of the best sprinters I've had in my entire career here at So. High. Hang onto your hats, people. Mark ran the hundred-yard dash in nine point nine!"

(Had to be nine days and nine hours. I once asked him to run out the garbage and it sat by the sink until it turned into a book-end.)

"I don't know what the baseball team would do without Charlie. We've had chatterers on the team before who get the guys whipped up, but Charlie is the all-time chatterer. There isn't a moment when he isn't saying something to spark the team."

(Charlie speaks six words to me in a week. "When you going to the store?")

"For those of you who don't really understand field events, I want to explain about the shotput. It's a ball weighing eight pounds that was thrown a hundred feet by an outstanding athlete here at So. . . . Wesley Whip."

(That's funny. Wesley looks like the same boy who delivers my paper and can't heave a six-ounce Saturday edition all the way from his bike to my porch.)

"Wolf Man Gus will go down in football annals as one of the all-time greats here at So. High. In the game with Central, Gus scored the winning touchdown despite a chipped bone in his ankle, a dislocated shoulder and a fever of a hundred and two."

(So how come Wolf Man Gus stays home from school every time he has his teeth cleaned?)

"I don't suppose anyone has better reflexes in this entire state than our outstanding basketball rebounder, Tim Rim. When the Good Lord passed out coordination, Tim was first in line."

(Tim is seventeen years old and I can still only pour him a half-glass of milk because that's all I want to clean up.)

"Tennis is a gentleman's game. This year's recipient of the Court Courtesy award is none other than So. High's Goodwill Ambassador, Stevie Cool."

(He's certainly come a long way since he tried to break his brother's face last week when he took a record album without asking.)

"The swimming team would never have made it this year without our plucky little manager, Paul Franswarth. Paul picks up those wet towels off the floor, hangs up the suits to dry, and is responsible for putting all the gear back where it belongs."

(Let's go home, Ed. I feel sick.)

It seems the more I talk with my children, the less I understand them. Take the subject of Coed Dorms.

Of all the changes parents have had to adjust to, coed dorms has probably been one of the most difficult to understand. Some dormitories have even conducted parent–student seminars where the student explains patiently, "We need a freer atmosphere where boys and girls come to know one another as friends, rather than sex objects," and the father of a freshman daughter laments, "That can't be done in a coffee shop?"

I was against coed dorms from the beginning. Not because it was a sensuous supermarket, but because I felt if anyone ever saw my son's bedroom in its natural state, I'd never get the kid married off and now my worst fears have been realized.

At Stanford, male and female students (although not given permission by the school) are using the same bathrooms. Take my word, when you see a man dribbling toothpaste and hair into a washbowl each morning and gargling like someone just pulled the plug on Lake Erie, love goes right out the window.

I know the trend is for young people to go the frankness and honesty route, but premarital clutter could stamp out marriages forever.

Men! Could you establish a meaningful relationship with a girl who put an angora sweater to dry on your last bath towel? Can you shave in a room full of steam with your face framed in a dripping pair of pantyhose? Do you really want to know how often she has to shave her legs? Could you ever be important enough to a girl to have her take the rollers out of her hair? (I swear I saw a teenage bride at her own wedding with her hair in rollers. When I asked her why she said, "We might go somewhere afterward.")

Women! Could you have a meaningful relationship with a boy who entered school in September with thirty-eight pairs of sweat sox and is just getting around to asking where the Laundromat is? Could you afford a man who uses a can of deodorant a day under each arm? Who belches before breakfast and hangs his trousers under the mattress?

As my house mother once told me when I was in college, "There is nothing that attracts the opposite sex like a busy signal . . . a locked door . . . and the word 'No.' If you want a friend . . . buy a dog."

According to the experts, if we didn't talk to our children and appreciate them every minute of the day, when they were gone we would sit in a recliner with a phone in our lap and hum all day long.

There isn't a mother alive who has not lived in dreaded terror of "The Empty Nest."

It was a long time in coming. First, you had to get the child out of bed and into a line of work.

For kids who are the most educated, well-read, best-informed people in the world, their attitude toward work is not to be believed. Next to an oarsman on a slave ship whose captain wanted to water ski, the most maligned person on the face of this earth is the teenager who has just landed his first full-time job.

No one suffers more and is appreciated less.

My son considers himself a "human sacrifice on the altar of the Church of the Establishment." He was fifteen before we could use the word "employment" in front of him. The word broke his face out and he preferred we spell it. The way he explained it to us on the eve of his marriage to a paycheck, "This is an exercise in group persecution, isn't it? All of you have run the course and now before I come of age, I have to prove that I can hack the nine-to-five number, is that it? Okay, you win. If I have to prove that I'm mature, I'll get the dumb full-time J-O-B . . . jjjj . . . jjjooo . . . jjjjoooooob!"

Maybe a lot of you know my son . . . or at least have heard of him.

He's the only employed person who has to work all day and then come home and feed himself.

He's the only dedicated teenager in North America to work when the "gang" went tubing down the river one Wednesday afternoon.

He's the first person to ever have half of his paycheck withheld for some service that he has never requested (federal income tax, hospitalization, social security, etc.). As he stated, "Someone is going to hear about this."

He stands alone as the only worker who is dominated by a senile boss (age thirty-five) who engages in office brutality by insisting he arrive on time in the mornings and after lunch.

He's the only full-time worker in the country who has not gained the respect of family and friends for his contribution to labor.

Last Saturday, I tapped him on the shoulder. "Hey, George Meany, out of the sack. It's the crack of noon."

My son rolled over. "I do not believe this is happening to a working person," he said. "All week long, I work five days a week, eight hours a day and what do I get for it?"

"You get all your meals served like a sultan, your bedroom cleaned, your clothes washed and ironed and a full-time old family retainer . . . me!"

Something tells me I'll have the first kid to retire three years before he has anything to retire from.

Once employment is attained, however, you are for the first time in your life . . . alone at last. The family structure as you know it will never be the same again.

You have weathered loose teeth, stolen bikes, team teaching, bunk beds, baton twirling, G.I. Joe, Driver's Ed., lost billfolds, Sunday night term papers, the draft, and the Doobie Brothers.

Cue the recliner and the phone . . . the Empty Nest sequence is about to begin.

As I walked into my son's empty room, I felt I was in the presence of a shrine.

Everything was intact, just as he left it. I fondled the sherbet glass with the petrified pudding under his bed . . . ran my fingers lovingly over his drum that leaked oil on the carpet . . . and cried softly as I tiptoed around the mounds of dirty underwear that didn't fit him anymore.

I made plans to preserve the room as a living memorial where I could go in the heat of the day and be by myself and reflect on the past.

Then one day as I meditated, I noticed he had an entire wall with nothing on it, so I moved the pump organ from the hallway into his bedroom. Noting the light was pretty good in his room, I also discovered by moving out his drums and storing them I could put my sewing machine in the corner with a table for cutting.

As we were making the change, my husband observed there was an entire closet free, so why shouldn't he move his clothes into the closet? By discarding five years of *Sports Illustrated* my son had saved, we found room for the Christmas decorations and the carton of canceled checks.

More and more of the family began to visit the "Temple." It became a haven for camping gear, pictures that needed framing, storage for summer lawn furniture and newspapers awaiting recycling.

The shelf of tennis trophies gave way to a supply of bleach bottles to be used by the women of the church for a project, the chest of drawers for my bicycle exerciser, and the bed was moved out of the room to create space—stored to make way for a rocker and a TV set.

Naturally, the walls were too masculine for the room, so we painted them yellow and slipcovered the rocker in a bright pink and orange.

Just before Christmas, there was a knock on the door. It was our son home for a visit.

"Hey, long time no see," said my husband. "Son of a gun. How long can you stay? Terrific. We've still got the old sofa bed in the den and you're welcome to it as long as you like."

This morning, my husband said, "How long is your relative going to stay?"

"My relative!" I shrugged. "I thought he was YOURS."

8

There Ought to Be
a Law . . .

When in the course of human events, one's sanity is in jeopardy, it becomes necessary for a lone voice in the wilderness to cry out.

It is in the name of justice for all . . . but especially me . . . that I offer the following declarations that would provide peace of mind for so many.

A Baby's Bill of Rights

Article the first: People who chew garlic shall not be allowed within three miles of a baby under penalty of drowning by spitting.

Article the second: Excessive bail shall be set for turkeys who tickle a baby's feet until he faints, or throw him up in the air after a full meal.

Article the third: Where a crime of the kidneys has been committed, the accused should enjoy the right to a speedy diaper change. Public announcements, details and guided tours of the aforementioned are not necessary.

Article the fourth: The decision to eat strained lamb or not to eat strained lamb should be with the "feedee" and not the "feeder." Blowing the strained lamb into the feeder's face should be accepted as an opinion, not as a declaration of war.

Article the fifth: Babies should enjoy the freedom to vocalize, whether it be in church, a public meeting place, during a movie, or after hours when the lights are out. They have not yet learned that joy and laughter have to last a lifetime and must be conserved.

Amendment one: No baby shall at any time be quartered in a house where there are no soft laps, no laughter, or no love.

The Hernia Amendment to the National Anthem

Few will argue that the inspirational words of Francis Scott Key are stirring enough to make Jane Fonda enlist in the Coast Guard. But something has got to be done about the melody of our national anthem before someone hurts himself.

I watched a man at the ball game the other Sunday standing tall and proud as he sang, "Oh say can you see." But by the time he got to the high-pitched, "And the rockets' red glare," the veins were standing out in his neck, his face became flushed and his voice cracked like Andy Hardy asking the Judge for the keys to the Packard.

Sensing I was looking at him, he gasped and said, "I love this country."

"Me too," I said sadly, stuffing a program in his mouth.

You take your average citizen. He sings on maybe ten or twelve occasions a year and does not have what is normally called your "trained voice." He can make "Happy Birthday to Marvin" (if they start low) and "Should Auld Acquaintance Be Forgot" and maybe a chorus of the "Beer Barrel Polka" with a few beers, but beyond that he is limited.

Me? It is my experience that everytime I go from the "twilight's last gleaming" to "the ramparts we watched" there is pain on the inside of my right leg, so I do everyone a favor by just mouthing the words. Invariably, everywhere I go, I am seated next to Beverly Sills, who comes down on "land of the free" with two notes. (The latter reached only the ears of a springer spaniel in New England.)

As I was setting down these thoughts I wondered who wrote the music to "The Star-Spangled Banner" and went to my reference book. Ironically, the music was an old English drinking song called "To Anacreon in Heaven." (Obviously, the drunks could sing the melody, but they had trouble with Anacreon.)

I personally believe there are a lot of patriotic Americans around who would like to sing "The Star-Spangled Banner" in its entirety, but who are discriminated against because they are bluebirds (singers with a range of one octave).

Would it be unreal to have one national anthem with two melodies? One for the traditionalists who can also sing Bacharach's "Alfie" without fainting, and a simple tune for those of us who sing in the cracks in the piano?

To the 3,085 ball players who chew tobacco, this could mean a lot.

Kissing by Mutual Ratification

This country has to make a hard-and-fast rule about greeting people with a kiss.

Either we all are, or we all aren't. Frankly, I gave up kissing people hello at the age of seven when my mother hired a piano teacher who chewed garlic. It was enough to make you do the *Minute Waltz* in ten seconds.

It wasn't until I began appearing on talk shows that I saw the return of the kissy-kissy. It was weird. The same persons who kissed you when you walked into the studio, also kissed you when you returned from the makeup room, the green room, and the ladies room. Not only that, but when you saw them again on the set, they acted like they hadn't seen you since World War I when they left you for dead in Paris with the fever.

Actually, kissing people hello takes some skill. First, you have to establish who is going to be the kisser and who is going to be the kissee. There should be no indecision once the kisser has decided to plant one on. He or she should grab the kissee by either the hands or the shoulders and kiss from the left (only vampires approach from the right).

If you are kissing another woman, beware of earrings that will strike you blind, jewelry that can puncture the inflated parts of your body and instant asphyxiation in a nest of stiff hair. (I was once speared and deflated by an open pin on a name card that said, "Hello, My Name Is Inez Funkhouser.")

Of prime consideration is the length of the kiss. What is considered good taste for a kiss of greeting? I have seen producers greet guests in such an enthusiastic way that I can only assume (a) he was giving mouth-to-mouth resuscitation to a dead woman or (b) they are leaving after the show to pick out the dishes.

A hello-greeting should be a quick, impersonal peck with all the passion of a sex-starved orangutan. Some kissers are so casual that while they are pecking you, their eyes are picking out the next kissee.

The person who is far-sighted encounters other problems in the kissing custom. I once embraced a water cooler for five minutes while insisting, "What do you mean I don't remember you, Florence?"

It is generally acknowledged that one woman kissing another, especially when she sees her all the time, is "senseless."

As I said the other day when I kissed a man with a toothpick in his mouth, "Ouch."

Search and Seizure Rights in the Laundry Room

I tacked a note up in the utility room yesterday that read, **"All clothes left here over ninety days will be towed away at the owner's expense and sold at public auction."**

"What does that mean?" asked my youngest.

"It means you have diapers at the bottom of your stack of clothes and you are thirteen years old. It means I am sick of watching you dress each morning over the toaster. It means your clothes have a home and I want to see them in that home."

"I've been meaning to talk with you about that," he said. "Why did you throw my blue jeans in the wash?"

"Because they were in the middle of the floor."

"Were they scrunched down to two little holes?"

I nodded. "What's that got to do with it?"

"When they're scrunched down like that, they aren't dirty."

"So, how am I supposed to know when they are dirty?"

"The dirty ones are kicked under the bed."

"Why don't you put them on top of the bed?"

"Because I don't want to get them mixed up with the clean clothes."

"Instead of sleeping with your clean clothes, why don't you take them out of the laundry room and put them in a drawer?"

"Because that's where I keep the dirty underwear I am going to wear again."

I took a deep breath. "Why would you wear underwear two days in a row?"

"Because it is my lucky underwear."

"For whom?" I asked dryly.

"I suppose you want me to put my clothes in the clothes hamper?" he asked.

"It crossed my mind."

"With all the wet towels in there my clothes would get ruined."

"You are supposed to put your wet towels on the towel rack."

"What'll I do with all your pantyhose and sweaters?"

"PUT THEM IN THE UTILITY ROOM," I shouted.

"Does this mean I lose my place dressing over the toaster?" he asked.

I planted a firm hand on his bottom. "No, it means your underwear just got unlucky."

Regulation of Interstate Shopping Cart Traffic

It is my feeling that the driving age of shoppers operating supermarket carts be raised to thirty-five. Going to the supermarket used to be an adventure. Today, it's a combat mission.

As I was telling a friend the other day, "It's a jungle out there what with all the young, inexperienced drivers and little old ladies who only drive a shopping cart on Sundays after church."

The shopping cart is the most underrated traffic hazard on the road today. To begin with, no license is required in any state to drive these little vehicles. Anyone, regardless of age, vision, physical condition or mental health can get behind the wheels. (Occasionally, no one is behind the wheels, and these little irresponsible devils slam into cars in the parking lot without a driver in sight.)

To say that they are unsafe at any speed is an understatement. Consider, if you will, their deficiencies.

1. Grocery carts are never parked. They are welded together as a group at the door and must be separated by kicking, jiggling, wiggling, and a good stiff kick in the old breadbasket. This possibly accounts for the body construction being weakened. (Yours, not the cart.)
2. A safety check would reveal there isn't a shopping cart that does not have all four wheels working. Unfortunately, all four are locked in stable directions. Three wheels want to shop and the fourth wants to go to the parking lot.
3. There are no seat belts for the children riding in shopping cart seats. Thus, it is not unusual to have them lean into your cart and eat half-a-pound of raw hamburger before you discover they are there.
4. Shopping carts should be like airplanes and nuns . . . it takes two to handle the situation. One to drive and one to gawk and read the caloric content of frozen lasagna.
5. Passing in the supermarket is hazardous because supermarket aisles are built to accommodate the width of one-and-one-half carts. Thus, we encourage the reckless driver who fears the whipped cream topping in his cart is melting and who will purposely force your cart into produce.

And here's the shocker. There are no brakes on a shopping cart.

And what is worse . . . Ralph Nader doesn't even care.

Truth in Fair Packaging of Children

We do a lot of talking in this country about "fair packaging." People like to know what they are getting before they get stuck with it.

I do a lot of thinking about how I am going to merchandise my kids. Frankly, in clear conscience, I don't see how I can let them go into marriage without slapping a sticker on their foreheads that reads: "This Person May Be Injurious to Your Mental Health."

I have visions of some poor bride coming to me in tears and saying, "You tricked me. Why didn't you tell me your son doesn't know how to close a door after himself?"

It will only be a matter of time before she discovers he is lacking in other basic skills and I will feel guilty. For example, my son does not know how to wring out a washcloth. I have held washcloth seminars in which I have demonstrated the twist-wrist action. He still insists on dropping it sopping full of water wherever he happens to be standing.

He cannot fold a newspaper after he has read it, hear a phone ring unless it is for him, put a cap on a bottle or tube, or carry on a conversation unless his mouth is full.

He hangs his clothes on a chair, has a three-months' supply of snacks hidden in his desk drawer and makes his bed by smoothing it over with a coat hanger.

Unless he changes drastically, he will be impossible to live with. He insists on having his own window in the car, calling seconds on the meat before he sits down at the table, and once confessed to a friend he does not brush his teeth until school starts in September.

No, I would be a traitor to my own sex if I did not put a tag around this child's neck reading: Boy. Eleven years old. Made in U.S.A. Height, 4′8″, net weight (including package) seventy-six pounds. Natural coloring, blond in summer, washed out in winter.

Capacity: Eight meals a day. Contains thirty-five hundred calories at all times. Artificially sweetened.

Unaffected by sun, rain and mud. Standard ingredients: 80 percent charm, 10 percent goldbricking and 1 percent energy.

Read label carefully. Take eleven-year-old boy with tongue-in-cheek, grain of salt, and a frequent checkup.

Constitutionality of Drive-in Windows

It's just my own personal observation, but I don't think God ever meant for man to do his banking, order food, or mail a letter from the driver's seat of the car.

I have noted only two cars that have swung precariously up to the position where they can comfortably do business. One was a car from a demolition derby and the other was a rental. Neither had anything to lose.

Drive-in banks intimidate me the most, possibly because I am "on camera" and quite self-conscious about having the tellers gather and exclaim, "Watch this one, Dorothy. She's the one who fell apart when her fender was ripped off last week."

Consequently, I have become something of a conservative. I pull in a good six feet from the window and when the drawer slides out I find that by opening my car door and forcing my head through my shoulder seat belt, pushing on the brake pedal with my right foot and bending my knee against the gearshift for leverage, I can slide my deposit slip into the drawer providing (a) I discontinue breathing for a while and (b) there are no high winds to circulate my deposit slip in the parking lot.

The mailboxes are something else. I never pull up to one of

them that I don't visualize a meeting of the postal department in Washington figuring out how to position the boxes.

"No, no, Chester," says the designer. "You have placed the boxes on the driver's side of the car. We mustn't pamper them. Put them on the passenger side so the driver will have to put the car in park, straddle the stick shift in the console, cup his throat over the window and just try to sail the letter into this six-inch slot."

"Then the slot should be just above the pick-up times that have become blurred and unreadable?" asked Chester.

"Higher, Chester, much higher," smiled his boss.

Yelling an order for five into a clown's mouth is something else again. Especially when you are alone. I feel like such a fool shouting until the varicose veins in my neck surface.

As my husband observed, "You don't have to go to drive-ins, you know. You can always use your feet."

Better to grow long arms.

Are Family Vacations Legal?

So many parents have been the victims of family vacations it is just possible that many of them are not familiar with some existing laws on how to handle some of the crises that arise. These are some of the most common inquiries:

The Abandon-Child Law

It is illegal in forty-seven states to leave a child in a rest room and pretend it was a mistake. Maryland and Utah are sympathetic to parents if they can produce a doctor's certificate showing mental deterioration caused by the trip. Alaska (which is quite permissive) allows a mild sedation for the children.

The New Jersey vs Kidder Law

It is illegal on the New Jersey turnpike for a child to hang out of the car window and make a noise like a siren. A decision on this was handed down in 1953, after forty-five cars (including three police cruisers) pulled over to the side of the road and tied up traffic for fifty-two hours.

The Key Decision

All fifty states have rulings regarding children who collect rest room keys as souvenirs. One of the stiffer penalties is feeding a child a quart of Gatorade and putting him outside a locked door until the key shows up.

The No-Fault Litter Law

Vehicles bearing families are not permitted to stop in the downtown area of cities having populations of four hundred and fifty thousand or more to look for a gym shoe that someone threw out of the moving vehicle. It is suggested that mothers put name tapes and full addresses on both shoes.

Anti-Noise Laws

Nearly every city (including three ghost towns in Arizona) has the noise-pollutant law. If in fact your vacationers have two radios playing at full volume, a barking dog and a father screaming, "Would anyone believe we didn't HAVE to get married," and can be heard with all the car windows up, everyone in the car can be arrested.

Safe Driving Law

It is unlawful to inflate a twenty-foot life raft in a sedan blocking Daddy's view of the road, braid his hair while he is driving in the mountains, or tie his shoes together when he is going through a tunnel.

Privileged Conversation

Conversation heard over CB radios and messages on rest-room walls repeated by children should not be grounds for shooting a child's tongue full of Novocaine unless such child dwells on same for several miles.

Regaining Single Status on an Exit Ramp

This is tricky, but some parents have opted to dissolve a family relationship on the spot by summoning legal aid. In this event, however, it is well to remember that children get custody of the station wagon.

Illegal Possession
of Junk Food

A grade school principal in the East became so upset about the lack of nutrition in the lunches the children were eating that he declared an edict banning junk food from the cafeteria.

I have a feeling the kids jammed the edict between two potato chips and two squares of Hershey chocolate and had it for lunch.

There is certainly no quarrel with the theory. Children should eat nutritionally balanced meals. But children do not take to ultimatums. I would have tried the old Accentuate-the-negative-reverse-the-positive-and-make-the-kid-think-your-idea-is-his-and-he's-driving-you-crazy approach.

Instead of an edict, the bulletin would have read something like this:

MEMO TO: School Children
RE: Nutritional Lunches

1. Carrots are illegal on school premises. Children bringing them from home will need a note from a parent giving permission to have them, or they will be confiscated by the office and held until dismissal time.
2. Locker inspection for thermoses containing hot vegetable soup or other nutritious dishes will be held periodically without warning. At that time, students are instructed to go to their lockers and stand at attention. DO NOT UNLOCK YOUR LOCKER UNTIL A TEACHER INSTRUCTS YOU TO DO SO. Thermoses will be destroyed by the custodian.
3. Because of student demand, we are selling fresh fruit by the door in the cafeteria. This is on a trial basis. If we find this

is all students are having for lunch it will be discontinued. Remember, the fruit contains sugar and Billy Tooth is watching you. To avoid congestion at fruit counter, please have correct change.

4. Teachers have reported to the office that raisin boxes and milk cartons have been found on the school grounds. We know there are students who have been sneaking nutritious foods on the premises and for this reason students have been posted and are instructed to "take names."

5. Your principal will be patrolling the lunchroom where he wants to see potato chips, candy bars, tortilla chips, soft drinks and ice cream. Remember, junk foods build soft bones, soft teeth and make you sleep a lot.

Trust me, it will work.

The Right to Declare War

I read the other day where a body that was believed to be dead was recovered from Lake Michigan. When it warmed up considerably, thaw set in and the person was alive.

Big deal.

Thanks to well-meaning merchants who set their refrigeration at wax museum temperatures, I am in a solidified state from May to September. No one even notices.

I go to a movie carrying a coat over my arm. I go to the supermarket and spend half my time warming my hands on the rotisserie. I drive my car on the wrong side of the street just to get a patch of sun on my arm. The other night at an intimate little restaurant, I said to my husband halfway through dinner, "Would you put your arm around me?"

"You wanta make love or you wanta eat?" he asked, buttering a piece of garlic bread.

"It's nothing personal," I said. "I'm freezing to death. Can you see anyone around us?"

"Not too well," he said, squinting into the darkness. "Why?"

"If everyone else is hanging from hooks, maybe we got into the food locker by mistake."

"I'm perfectly comfortable," he said, snuggling into his wool sport coat. "Maybe you're anemic or something. You should go to a doctor if you're cold all the time."

In the doctor's office, the nurse smiled and said, "Hello."

"That's easy for you to say," I grumbled; "you're wearing a sweater."

She showed me into a room where she instructed me, "Take off your clothes and slip into this." I put on a paper gown with a back exit big enough to drive a truck through and slid onto the cold metal table. A blower from over the door blew my chart right off the table. I was shivering uncontrollably when the doctor came in, took a stethoscope out of the refrigerator, and placed it on my chest. I blew on my hands and coughed.

He stood up slowly, removed the stethoscope from around his neck and walked slowly to his desk. "If I didn't know better, I'd think you were dead."

"What gave me away?" I asked.

"The tear in your eye when my breathing steamed up your glasses."

Register Camera Nuts

You will understand me when as a woman who is married to an amateur camera freak, I respectfully suggest that some kind of legislation be passed requiring a permit to carry a loaded camera.

I don't mean to overreact, but I live in fear that someday my husband will point that thing at me, forget he has taken off the lens cap, and click click! I'll end up another statistic at Fotomat.

I have been photographed walking out of a public bathhouse in a Michigan campground wearing a nightgown, curlers, and rain slicker . . . fishing around in my mouth with my fingers trying to remove a fishbone . . . and there are thirty prints floating around somewhere of me on my side in a bathing suit, that I would give up my next unborn child to get the negatives of.

The other day my husband was flipping the camera around carelessly when I said irritably, "Is that thing loaded?"

"Look," he said, "how many accidents have I had with this camera?"

"There was the time you snapped Fred at the office Christmas party trying to Xerox Miss Frampton. He threatened to rearrange your nose. Then, there was the time exposure when you nearly broke your leg trying to get back into the picture . . . and the birthday party where . . ."

"All right, so join the camera lobby and try to get them off the market."

All I'm saying is cameras shouldn't be made available to the man on the street . . . only professionals who know how to use them. The way it stands now, any child can walk right into a camera store and buy a Sunday afternoon special right off the counter . . . no questions asked. The next thing you know some innocent person is staring into the eye of an Instamatic.

"C'mon, you're making a big deal over nothing. I don't use the camera all that much. I just feel kind of important when I have a camera riding back there in the window of my pickup truck. Besides, it's sorta fun watching people's reactions when you point it at them."

He grabbed the camera and trained it on my hips, which look like I'm carrying two U.S. mail pouches for the pony express. I heard the button click.

"Fooled you. The camera isn't loaded."

One of these days he will push me too far. And there isn't a woman jury in this country who would find me guilty.

9 ⌐∵

"Gametime"

The other morning I watched five game shows in a row on television. I wanted to turn them off, but I was too mesmerized by the contestants.

The first one was a frail woman who said, "I am a simple, average housewife," then proceeded to win a toaster by humming the fight song of Bangladesh High.

The second one said she was a mother of seven, then spewed out the fuel formula for the Russian Soyuz XI space flight last year.

The third was also a "typical, suburban homemaker," who won a year's supply of tulip bulbs by answering that the Sixth Crusade in Europe was led by Frederick II in 1228. (I thought it was Billy Graham in 1965.)

After I flipped off the TV set, I sat there stunned for a minute. Not only could I not remember what I had for breakfast three hours before, but I realized that mentally I had let myself go to pot.

I prattled on at cocktail parties about Jacqueline Onassis traveling with four silk sheets, and how David Cassidy got a hickey on prom night.

My vocabulary had dwindled to three Buckley-type words: Erudite (meaning smart), which I didn't use for years because it sounded dirty. Deciduous (to lose one's leaves), which I read off a tree at the Garden Center. And noxious, which I overheard my ten-year-old use to describe my casserole. (I think it means you can't get it without a prescription.)

At card club, I broached the subject, "How in the world do those women on game shows do it?"

"They fake it," said Gloria. "Anyone can go on an intellectual crash program and change their image in five days."

"Like how?" I asked.

"First, put copies of the *London Times Literary Supplement* in your bathroom. That's status. Then when you go to the beauty shop, take a stack of books along and run your fingers across the lines as fast as you can turn the pages. Everyone will think you're a graduate of Evelyn Wood's speed-reading course.

"When you're in a crowded room, look perplexed and say in a loud voice, 'Archie Bunker? Who publishes him?' Confide to the town gossip that you had to buy a truss in order to carry the Sunday New York *Times* around.

"And above all, put together a group of one-liners for dinner parties such as, 'Isn't it incredulous that there would be fifty-seven-million, ninety-three-thousand United States dollars in circulation last year and I cannot find thirty-five-cents for a school lunch in the mornings?' "

"I don't know, Gloria," I said, "I still can't figure out how this housewife knew about Frederick II in 1228."

"Just a lucky guess," said Gloria.

"Look," said Jackie, throwing in her hand, "let me give you a piece of advice. Don't get hooked on game shows. I once watched game shows every day for a week. I began with the 'Gong Show' right after breakfast and didn't stir from in front of the set until 'To Tell the Truth' went off at seven-thirty.

"By this time I had undergone a complete personality change. I saw Nipsy Russell everywhere . . . I wanted a five-piece dinette set for remembering my own name. I pushed imaginary buzzers and shouted out for no apparent reason, 'I'll bet twenty dollars on the red.'

"Dinner was a challenge. I couldn't remember if it was door No. 1 (the oven), door No. 2 (the freezer), or door No. 3 (the cupboard). Also I couldn't seem to be able to concentrate on what anyone was saying. I'd just smile and mumble, 'I want to come back tomorrow and try for the car.'

"One game, 'Break Up a Marriage,' intrigued me. You know, it's the game where a wife tries to answer the questions the way she thinks her husband will answer and vice versa. Actually, it's a shortcut to World War III. When my husband came home I had to know, 'What would you say would be the most embarrassing moment at our wedding?'

" 'When our kids showed up.'

" 'Isn't that just like you to be cute when there are His and Her Motorbikes riding on an answer?'

" 'Okay, if you want a straight answer, when your mother arrived at the wedding in a hearse, wearing a black veil.'

" 'Maybe we'd better get it all out in the open.'

" 'Yeah, well, maybe I should give you more room.'

" 'That's terrible,' I said.

"It's turning out all right," she said. "Next week we're both contestants on a new show, 'Trial Separation.' "

Despite what Gloria and Jackie said, I still have nothing but admiration for the men and women who compete on these shows. Every week the games seem to get more involved, the prizes more fabulous and the contestants more frenzied.

I have seen these poor housewife-contestants run the emotional yo-yo from hysterical to rabid. Frankly, I don't know how much longer they can continue under the strain. For example, I watched

a new game show last week that was called simply "CORO-
NARY." It was relatively simple to follow.

A contestant was asked to select a number that corresponded
to a balloon. When she broke it, a little card fell out telling her
what she had won. It went something like this.

"Hang on, Bernice," said the moderator. "Do you know what
you have just won?" Bernice shakes her head numbly. "You have
won one hundred and twenty-five thousand dollars."

As the band plays "Happy Days Are Here Again," Bernice
jumps fifteen feet off the floor and throws her arms around the
moderator's neck and begins to weep uncontrollably.

He holds up his hand for silence. "In Italian lira, Bernice. Do
you know how much that is in American money? About forty-eight
dollars and twelve cents. Too bad, Bernice, but wait! You are
going to pick up the lira in an Italian bank. You have won three
weeks in Rome!"

Bernice clutches her chest and sways dizzily as the band starts
up again. She grabs the moderator's sleeve.

"That's Rome, New York." He grins.

Bernice slumps again, emotionally drained.

"But wait! Look what you'll be wearing to New York." The
curtain opens to reveal a four-thousand-dollar mink coat. The moderator helps her put it on. Bernice manages a weak smile and a
wave to the audience.

"Unfortunately, it's not your size. Too bad, Bernice, had it fit
you you would have walked out of here in a four-thousand-dollar
mink coat with a Swiss bank account for one hundred thousand
dollars in the pocket."

Bernice faints dead away on the floor. The moderator bends
over her. "You didn't stay conscious, Bernice. Those are the rules,
but since you've been a sport, no one goes away empty-handed.
For your consolation prize, we have a personalized pacemaker . . . let's hear it for Bernice."

The way I see it, it's only a matter of time before game-show contestants will turn pro. Naturally, they'll have to pass a complete physical indicating they are up to the pressures of competition. And they'll probably all be graduates of the Jubilance and Excitement Training schools, which will chain all over the country. Their brochure will undoubtedly go something like this.

Joe Carter's Jubilance and Excitement Seminar

Who Is Eligible?

Persons over eighteen years of age who can pass the grueling physical requirements: (a) jumping higher than Bob Barker's head; (b) ignoring the symptoms of a coronary when you have just won a trip to Athens, Georgia, and not Greece; (c) sitting four hours under a barrage of hot lights, dressed as a battery, until called upon by Monty Hall, and still becoming hysterical.

Curriculum—Whimpering and Quivering (3 credit hours)

A "must" for contestants to employ between the time they've answered the question and the time they've found out what they've won. It includes biting your lip until it bleeds, wringing hands, listening to the audience shout obscenities and rolling eyes back in head until whites are showing.

What to Do When You've Won
the Car (5 credit hours)

An in-depth study in hysteria taught by the winner of a 1953 Chevy who won it by knowing Gentle Ben's nickname.

Hugging and Kissing TV Game
Show Hosts Need Not Be Fatal
(3 credit hours)

Pressure points around the throat, cutting off breathing with your body, and lifting host off the floor are outlined.

What to Do When the Chest
Pains Come

Know which shows have oxygen and which ones expect you to be a sport about a coronary. Remember, there is no jubilance and excitement in passing out. Learn how to stay on your feet.

Look Like a Loser to the IRS

Handy tips on how to stagger by the IRS men carrying a bag of gold and still hang on to your citizenship.

Remember, game shows can hurt you. Be a pro!

What a shame. It'll be too late for Bernice.

10

Fashions and Fads That Underwhelmed Me

You always hear about fashion's success stories.

How a starlet lost an earring one night and by the next morning, the entire country was wearing one earring. Or how sweaters made a comeback in a drugstore, or a First Lady influenced how we dressed during her reign.

But what about the losers? The fashions that came in and went out the same day? The hopes and dreams of designers that were shattered by the sound of fifty million women . . . laughing themselves to death.

Some styles, for one reason or another, just don't make it.

Remember the Scratch and Smell T-shirt? This should have been a smash. The principle was great. You scratched and voilà . . . a scent was circulated that ran the gamut from perfume to pizza. Unfortunately, there were too many impostors. People scratched for status and stirred up only perspiration. This gave the official scratch and smell shirt a bad name . . . not to mention the smell.

And what about the Gladiator boots. Remember them? They

were the polished leather boots that hit just above the knee. You could look stylish in them or sit down. You couldn't do both.

The Diaper Bikini would have been a real seller if the wearers had been able to keep their weight down to eight-and-a-half pounds.

And the Fanny Sweater was a big loser. This was one of the many knit styles designed to fit a hanger and not the human body. The name was deceiving. It suggested that everyone who had a fanny should cover it with a sweater. In many instances, that's all the sweater covered and the sides and front were left wide open.

The Satin Pillow stomach just didn't make it. A few years ago, the manufacturer actually came out with a fake satin stomach that you tied around your waist for those girls who wanted to look healthy.

I looked so healthy in it, two men on the bus hoisted me into their seats and another called the police to report I was in the final stages of delivery. (The fake stomach now resides on the living room sofa.)

If there was ever a loser, however, it was the jumpsuit. This one-piece apparel has to be the Brand X of the fashion industry.

By actual count, there are only six women in the country who looked well in a jumpsuit. Five of them were terminal and the other was sired by a Xerox machine.

Just out of curiosity, I was rummaging through a rack of jumpsuits when a saleswoman approached and asked, "Which size are you looking for? Twelve? Fourteen? Sixteen?"

"Yes," I said.

"Which?" she pursued.

"All three. My bust is twelve, my waist is a fourteen, and my hips are 16."

"Try the fourteen," she said dryly. "The fitting room is behind better dresses."

The fitting room was something I had never seen before. It was a community deal . . . a large room with sixteen mirrors on the wall, a rack in the center to hang discards and a woman by the door to make sure you didn't wear out any more than you wore in.

Now a fitting room to me has always been like a confessional . . . where my body and my contrition take up the entire room. There is no room for anyone else. I looked around. All eyes seemed to be focused on one woman. She weighed about six pounds and was trying on a jumpsuit. It slid on easily, up over her hips and onto her arms. I winced as she distributed the cloth left over around her waist.

The crowd could not take their eyes off her. I had seen that look of resentment and pain on only one other occasion. It was a Charlton Heston movie just before the door slid back between the Christians and the Lions.

Inching closer, I whispered, "Lady, you better get out of here before they tear you to shreds."

It was my turn. For fifteen minutes, I tugged and inched my way into the jumpsuit and looked into the mirror. The chest was disguised as a back, the stomach strained at the buttons, the legs were numb without circulation and the hems swirled around the floor.

"How do you . . ."

"You swear off liquids after 4 P.M.," she said.

Or what about the platform shoes that brought about dizziness and nose bleeds? Also a broken leg to a thirteen-year-old girl in England, who fell off them.

Why the first time I tried on a pair of those Klutzies, I said to myself, "These shoes should have a label in them that reads, **'Warning: according to the Surgeon General's Office, these could be injurious to your health.' "**

I always thought platform shoes were something Alan Ladd

wore to make kissing easier. Then I saw them on a woman who frequents my beauty shop. At first, I tried to ignore her deformity (Mother always said, "Don't stare. They know where their problem is located"). Finally, she said, "What do you think of my wedgies?"

"I know you can walk on water in them," I said. "But what else can you do?"

"Surely you jest," she said. "For a short person such as yourself, it could change your world. They can raise you off the ground, stretch out your body and make you look twenty pounds thinner. How tall are you? And how much do you weigh?"

I had no intention of giving her my vital statistics. "Let me put it this way," I said. "According to my girth, I should be a ninety-foot redwood."

"So, you need platforms," she said.

The first pair I tried on felt great. I wiggled my toes and they sprang back like a released arrow. My ankles felt firm and I felt tall.

Then I stood up.

Easing my way across the floor, I looked into a mirror. The reflection looked like Milton Berle with a migraine.

"How come you look so funny?" asked one of my children.

"Don't talk to me," I snapped. "I am busy keeping my shoes on."

In five minutes, I felt pain. In the back of my legs, running up my hips and finally down to my toes. Within an hour, my heels were purple and my toes felt like they were being pushed through a ballpoint pen.

The physical pain is nothing when you consider that the shoes cost eighteen dollars and that I don't throw a pair away until the soles are worn thin . . . and the soles are four inches thick and by the time I get out of those orthopedic nightmares, I'll be a petrified redwood!

There is one fashion that never really comes in style and never seems to go out. Each year, some designer comes out with the organized handbag. Now, I am not into organized handbags. Let me put it another way. If Monty Hall had offered a million dollars to anyone having a 1958 baby tooth, a set of keys to a three-year-old car, a fuzzy breath mint, and a half pair of footlets in their purse, I'd be a millionaire today.

As with most vices, the only people this bothers are the reformers. The people who want to make organized handbags into law. They're the do-gooders who won't rest until you put your car keys on a clip with a flashlight at the top of the bag in a spot marked "KEYS."

Actually, one of the more zealous members of the Organized Handbag Movement is my mother. She cannot comprehend why I carry around a pack of gum with no gum in it, or what possible use I will have for two "C" batteries. For my birthday, she couldn't wait to give me one of those handbags that has a place for everything. It looked like a Post Office.

"The first thing we're going to do is to sit down and get it all organized," she said, "and you'll never have to rummage through your purse again. Give me your checkbook."

"I don't have it," I said. "I just carry a few blank checks."

"What do you record them on when you have written them?"

"My grocery tape."

"Where do you keep the grocery tape?"

"In the brown bags where I get my groceries."

"And they are . . . ?"

"Under the sink waiting for the garbage."

"I see. Well now, where's your passport?"

"My what?"

"Your passport. You know, permission to enter a foreign country."

"I only use it when I enter your grandson's bedroom."

"And here's a bag for your makeup. Where is that?"

"I'm wearing it."

"Look," she said, "why don't you fill up all these little pockets and openings yourself and surprise me."

A few days later she saw the handbag and began to check it out. I had put all my raffle tickets under TRAVELER'S CHECKS, my hair clips and single earrings under CLUB AFFILIATIONS, the trading stamps jammed in the PASSPORT pocket, a pair of fake eyelashes under MAJOR CREDIT CARDS and two worn-out washers that I have to replace were in the MAKEUP bag.

As I told her, "I hope you're happy now. I won't be able to find a thing."

Another trend I cannot bear that is destined to race to oblivion is the name-dropping signatures that adorn everything you wear these days. I know a lot of women (two) who walk around looking like billboards. Their bags carry the Gucci signature, their scarves spell out Yves Saint-Laurent, and their blouses have the name of Wayne Rogers incorporated in the design.

I never know who makes my clothes. Whoever they are, they're too ashamed to sign 'em. The closest I ever came to finding out was when I shook a pair of slacks one day and a little piece of paper fell out: "INSPECTED BY 56." I have no idea who 56 is, or where she came from, but by wearing the slacks, I got a mental picture of inspector 56. She was a former designer for an awning company until her vision started to go. When she could no longer see to attach a zipper to a tent flap, she was put in slacks. She regards slacks like a tent . . . one size fits all.

I tried to track her down, but I heard she changed her name to Inspector 94. Like I say, it doesn't bother me a bit that kids walk around in Hang Ten sweat sox with the two little feet emblem, or flaunt Levi labels coming out of their seams, but my friend is a real status seeker.

At lunch one day she gasped, "Did you see that! Violet is wearing a LANVIN blouse."

"How can you tell?"

"If you just read her chest, you can tell," she said.

"That's shabby. If people can't look at my clothes and by their style and cut know who designed them, I'm certainly not going to advertise."

"Don't give me that," she snapped. "If your dresses had a permapress label in them, you'd wear them wrong-side out."

That was a pretty rotten accusation from a woman I personally knew sat up nights drawing penguins on her husband's golf shirts. Like I told her, "You're such a snob it would serve you right if you got stuck with one of those fifty-dollar handbags that came out about a year ago. It seems a couple of designers subtly included an eight letter noun with an obscene word woven into the pattern. English-speaking women didn't have any idea that the word was smutty."

As my friend counted the letters out on her fingers, she exclaimed, "You don't have to tell me the word . . . just nod your head if I'm right. It's J.C. Penney, isn't it?"

"It is not J.C. Penney."

"You know the trouble with you," said my friend, "is that you're not open to new fashion trends. It takes a lot of courage to be different and you don't have the guts. Why, I bet you've never worn a bathrobe to a party, have you?"

"Not since the night I had my appendix taken out on the coffee table."

"Barbara Walters did," she said. "She was invited to a state dinner in the Philippines. The dinner was to begin in ten minutes and Barbara had not brought along a long dress. She was about to decline when she remembered she had a red bathrobe that would work, and saved the day. How does that make you feel?"

"Sick to my stomach."

I don't have a bathrobe in my drawer that would get me through an eighth-grade prom . . . or a house call from my doctor for that matter. Somehow, I cannot imagine myself showing up for a state dinner at the Philippines in a pair of blue scuffies, a flannel robe with a stomach button missing, spit-up on the shoulder (the baby is eighteen years old) and pockets bulging from nose tissue that smells like vapor-rub.

I even took a turn the other day through the lingerie department, and frankly I can see how they got away with it. I've never seen so many beautiful gowns and robes in my entire life.

"Here's one that's a luv," said the salesperson.

She held up a satin gown. (The last time I saw anything that narrow, there was toothpaste in it.)

"I'm afraid not. I have made it a rule of thumb that I do not wear anything to bed I have to wear a girdle under."

"What about this one?" she asked holding up a transparent bit of nylon.

"I have also promised myself that I would never wear anything in bed that you have to wear a coat over."

"What did you have in mind?" she asked.

"Something with sleeves, a turtleneck . . . and a zip-in floor."

Then she held up a robe. I have to tell you it was a knockout. "I'll take it," I said impishly.

Last weekend, I took the plunge and decided to wear it as an evening dress. Maybe my friend was right. As I entered the room . . . all eyes were upon me when my husband looked up and said, "Hurry up and get dressed. We're leaving in ten minutes."

There were other "losers" of course too numerous to mention. Who could forget the tube dress designed for the woman who wanted to be mailed somewhere, or the oriental look that lasted as long as our diplomatic relations with China lasted, or the pierced ears fad. I knew that would never last.

My daughter was crazy to have it done and I couldn't talk her out of it. I told her, "If the operation was so simple, *Good House-keeping* would have put out a kit on it."

We both went to the department store jewelry counter where they had a chair for the puncturee.

"I'll watch," I said.

When I came to, my head was in Baked Goods and my feet in Better Sportswear.

"Is it over?" I gasped.

"Yes," said my daughter, "you did fine. You passed out just after you asked the anesthesiologist what kind of anesthetic he used and he turned out to be the jewelry buyer. See my earrings?"

She flipped back eight pounds of hair to reveal a little gold ring the size of a comma in her earlobe.

It was hardly worth my scrubbing up for.

11

How to Speak Child Fluently

One evening at the kitchen table, after the dishes had been cleared away, my son sat there writing feverishly in a spiral notebook.

"What are you doing?" I asked.

"An English assignment," he said. "On things my mother taught me."

I cast my eyes downward, trying to look humble. "Mind if I read it when you're finished?" He shook his head. An hour later, I settled down to what he had written.

Things My Mother Taught Me

Logic

If you fall off your bicycle and break your neck, you can't go to the store with me.

Medicine

If you don't stop crossing your eyes, they are going to freeze that way. There is no cure, no telethon, and no research program being funded at the moment for frozen eyes.

ESP

Put your sweater on. Don't you think *I* know when *YOU'RE* cold?

Finance

I told you the tooth fairy is writing checks because computerized billing is easier for the IRS.

Challenge

Where is your sister and don't talk with food in your mouth. Will you answer me?!

Happiness

You are going to have a good time on this vacation if we have to break every bone in your body.

Humor

When that lawn mower cuts off your toes, don't come running to me.

I will never understand children. I never pretended to. I meet mothers all the time who make resolutions to themselves. "I'm going to develop patience with my children and go out of my way to show them I am interested in them and what they do. I am going to understand my children." These women wind up making rag rugs, using blunt scissors.

I firmly believe kids don't want your understanding. They want your trust, your compassion, your blinding love and your car keys, but you try to understand them and you're in big trouble. To me, they remain life's greatest mysteries.

I have never understood, for example, how come a child can climb up on the roof, scale the TV antenna and rescue the cat—yet cannot walk down the hallway without grabbing both walls with his grubby hands for balance.

Or how come a child can eat yellow snow, kiss the dog on the lips, chew gum that he found in the ashtray, put his mouth over a muddy garden hose . . . and refuse to drink from a glass his brother has just used.

Why is it he can stand with one foot on first base while reaching out and plucking a baseball off the ground with the tips of his fingers . . . yet cannot pick up a piece of soap before it melts into the drain.

I've seen kids ride bicycles, run, play ball, set up a camp, swing, fight a war, swim and race for eight hours, . . . yet have to be driven to the garbage can.

It puzzles me how a child can see a dairy bar three miles away, but cannot see a 4 x 6 rug that has scrunched up under his feet and has been dragged through two rooms. Maybe you know why a child can reject a hot dog with mustard served on a soft bun at home, yet eat six of them two hours later at fifty cents each.

Did you ever wonder how you can trip over a kid's shoes under the kitchen sink, in the bathroom, on the front porch, under the coffee table, in the sandbox, in the car, in the clothes hamper and on the washer . . . but can never find them when it is time to cut grass?

If child raising were to be summed up in one word, it's frustration. You think you're on the inside track and you find you're still in the starting gate. It's not that you expect dividends on what you're doing . . . only a few meager returns.

Okay, take the car incident. My oldest took her car to the garage for repairs last week and used my car while hers was being fixed.

For three days I sat home without wheels (which is like telling Zsa Zsa Gabor she can't have any more wedding cake).

On the day her car came back she returned my car keys and said, "Hey Mom, you owe me three dollars for the gas I put in your car."

I could not believe what she was saying. These words were being uttered by a child I poured eight hundred and eighty-seven dollars' worth of vitamins down. Paid one hundred fifty-four dollars for her old teeth under the pillow. Indulged in two thousand dollars' worth of toys (batteries extra). Footed the bill for one hundred eighty-six skin preparations to kill a single pimple. Sent to camp. Took the sink apart to find her lost class ring. Worried myself sick when she cracked an A in human sexuality.

Then I remembered a letter that a teenager had written me after she had read one of my books. Maybe that would get through to her.

"Listen to this," I said, reading from the letter.

"Parents go through life, Mrs. Bombeck, saying to their children, 'I've worked my fingers to the bone for you. I've made sacrifices and what do I get in return?'

"You want an answer, Mrs. Bombeck? You get messy rooms, filthy clothing, disheveled hair, dirty fingernails, raided refrigerators ad nauseam. You get something else too. You get someone who loves you but never takes the time to tell you in words. You

*get someone who'll defend you at every turn even though you do
wear orthopedic socks and enjoy listening to Pat Boone and changing your underwear everyday and acknowledging their presence
in public.*

*"Yes, sometimes you talked too much and sometimes you turned
away too soon. But you laughed with us and cried with us and
all the agony, noncommunication, frustrations, fears and angers
showed us that despite the need to be free and independent and
do our own thing . . . you cared.*

*"And when we leave home, there will be a little tug at our hearts
because we know we will miss you and home and everything it
meant. But most of all, we will miss the constantly assured knowledge of how very much you love us."*

My daughter looked up. Her eyes were misty. "Does that mean
I don't get the three bucks?"

In a way, I blame experts for the mess parents are in today.
They laid a ton of guilt on us so that we questioned every move
we made.

I read one psychologist's theory that said, "Never strike a child
in anger." When could I strike him? When he is kissing me on my
birthday? When he is recuperating from measles? Do I slap the
Bible out of his hand on Sunday?

Another expert said, "Be careful in the way you discipline your
children or you could permanently damage their Id."

Damage it! I didn't even know where it was. For all I knew it
either made you sterile or caused dandruff. Once I suspected where
it was, I made the kid wear four diapers just to be safe.

And scratch the wonderful "pal" theory that worked so great
with our parents. My son slouched into the kitchen one night,
threw his books on the countertop and said, "I've just had the
worst day of my entire life and it's all your fault."

"How do you figure that?" I asked.

"Just because you made me go back up to my room and turn off all the lights before I went to school, I missed the bus. Then, with all your nagging about cleaning up my room, I couldn't find my gym clothes and got fifteen points knocked off my grade."

"The gym clothes were folded in your bottom drawer."

"Yeah, well, what yo-yo would expect them to be there?"

"You've got a point."

"I hope you're happy," he grumbled. "I have failed English."

"I did that?"

"That's right. I told you I had a paper that was due before lunch and you made me turn my lights off last night and wouldn't let me do it."

"It was one-thirty in the morning."

"Just forget it. It's done. Did you have a good lunch today? I hope so because, thanks to you, I didn't get any."

"What's THAT got to do with me?"

"You're the one who wouldn't advance me next week's allowance. And more good news. You know the suede jacket you got me for my birthday last year? Well, it's gone."

"And I'm to blame for that?"

"I'm glad you admit it. All I hear around here is, 'Hang up your coat, hang up your pajamas, hang up your sweater . . .' and the one time I take your advice and hang up my jacket on a hook in the lunchroom, someone rips it off. If I had just dropped it on the floor by my feet like I always do, I'd have that suede jacket today."

"It sounds like quite a day."

"It's not over yet," he said. "Didn't you forget something?"

"Like what?" I asked.

"Like, weren't you supposed to remind me I had ball practice after school?"

"I put a note on your desk."

"Under all that junk I'm supposed to find a note! It would serve you right if I got cut. And I might just do that. I swear, I was talking to some of the guys and we decided parents can sure screw up their kids."

I smiled. "We try."

In analyzing the problem of parenting and understanding children, it would seem inevitable that this country will eventually resort to a Parental Park 'N' Swap.

I have never met a child who did not feel that he is maligned, harassed and overworked and would do better if he had Mrs. Jones for a mother who loves untidiness and eats out a lot.

On the other hand, I have never met a parent who did not feel unappreciated, persecuted, servile and would have been better off with Rodney Phipps who doesn't talk with food in his mouth and bought his mother a hair dryer for Mother's Day.

What I'm suggesting is a Sears parking lot that could be made available every Saturday afternoon, where parents and their offspring could come to look, compare and eventually swap if they felt they could do better.

When I mentioned this to my card club, they fairly quivered with excitement. "I have always wanted to 'trade up' to a child who picked towels up off the floor," said Peg.

"I have one like that," said Dorothy. "But she's a drain stuffer. If it doesn't fit down the drain she lifts out the trap and shoves it down."

"That doesn't sound so bad," said Evelyn. "I'd take a drain stuffer over a shower freak anyday. Empties a forty-gallon water tank three times a day."

"At least she's clean," said June. "I'll swap someone a long-hair who is an endangered species. Someday he's going to get lost behind that hair and never find his way out again."

"LOOK," said Peg, "I'm going to make you an offer you can't refuse. I'll offer my towel dropper for a boy who never learned how to use the telephone and I'll throw in a three weeks' supply of clean underwear."

"I'll do you one better," I said. "I'll swap or trade a quiet boy who is never late to dinner, gets up when he is called, sits up straight, has just finished two years with his orthodontist, is reasonable to operate and doesn't play his stereo too loud. No offer is too ridiculous."

The entire card table put down their cards and leaned forward. Finally June asked, "What's the catch?"

"No catch. He just knows two words . . . 'You know?' "

Everyone went home keeping what they had and feeling better about it.

When does parenting end?

It all depends on how you regard your children. Do you see them as an appliance that is under warranty to perform and when they start to cost money, get rid of them?

Are they like an endowment policy you invest in for eighteen or twenty years and then return dividends through your declining years?

Or are they like a finely gilded mirror that reflects the owner in every way and one day when you see a flaw in it, a distortion or one tiny idea that is different from your own, you cast it out and declare yourself a failure?

I said to my husband one night, "I see our children as kites. You spend a lifetime trying to get them off the ground. You run with them until you're both breathless . . . they crash . . . you add a longer tail . . . they hit the rooftop . . . you pluck them out of the spouting . . . you patch and comfort, adjust and teach. You watch them lifted by the wind and assure them that someday they'll fly . . . Finally, they're airborne, but they need more string and with each twist of the ball of twine, there is a sadness that goes with the joy because the kite becomes more distant and somehow you know it won't be long before this beautiful creature will snap the lifeline binding you together and soar as it was meant to soar—free and alone."

"That was beautiful," said my husband. "Are you finished?"

"I think so. Why?"

"Because one of your kites just crashed into the garage door with his car . . . another is landing here with three surfboards with friends on them and the third is hung up at college and needs more string to come home for the holidays."

12 ⫷⋇

"Travel Is So Broadening I Bought a Maternity Dress to Wear Home"

My husband and I are not your standard jet setters who whip over to Southern France every year to get away from the "little people."

But when our twenty-fifth wedding anniversary rolled around I said to him, "I want to go someplace where they haven't seen my two dresses."

"That narrows it down to Europe," he said.

Because it was a good day and all the parts of our bodies were working, we optimistically chose a package tour that would take us to fifteen countries in twenty-one days. It was obvious that I would need a wardrobe that was not only versatile, but could fit into a gym bag.

That's when I ran into an incredible phenomenon . . . the pre-planned, no-fault, can't miss, color-coordinated, basic wardrobe.

"This," said the salesperson, "is the Weekender. It has four basic pieces that will take you from a super casual afternoon to a formal evening. And here is the Fortnighter. It's an eleven-piece coordinated collection designed to meet all the fashion requirements of a three-week holiday. This, of course, is the Around-the-World in Eighty Days and forty-four pounds. It's twenty-two pieces that combine to make one hundred fifty-five outfits."

"This little stack of clothes weighs forty-four pounds?" I asked.

"Of course not. The clothes only weigh eight pounds. There's a thirty-six pound can of deodorant that comes with it."

"How does it work?" I asked.

"You just press the nozzle and . . ."

"Not the deodorant! The wardrobe!"

"Simple. Here is your basic pantsuit. Take off the blouse, add a vest and you're ready for polo. Take off the slacks, put on the shorts and you're dressed for bicycling. Zip the lining into the shorts, add the halter and it's a bathing suit. Take the straps off the halter and it's a bra. Add a short skirt and you're ready for tennis.

"Now, turn the blouse inside out and it's a bathrobe. Turn down the cuffs on the slacks, take the belt off the overblouse and you're in your jammies."

"It certainly is versatile," I stammered.

"Versatile! Look at the accessories. This elasticized halter can get you a sun tan, but when pulled down over the hips is a girdle. Now slip into the evening skirt, slip on this veil and you're ready to be married. Or slap a monogram on the jacket and you can pass for a member of the U.S. Olympic Chess team. The long skirt is plastic-lined. If you have to, you could convert it into a tent and live out of it for a week. Or snap out the sleeves in the overblouse and it's a caftan.

"Take off the scarf, roll down the sleeves of the blouse, put it on backward, take off your underwear and it's a hospital gown. Trust me, there are enough combinations to mix and match for eighty days."

I was ready for our adventure.

When people talk about these package tours, they are always impressed by the fact that they are a bargain. You do so much and see so much, yet they are able to offer it at prices far below domestic travels at home. In analyzing this phenomenon one morning, we both concluded one of the reasons has to be the Continental Breakfast.

The Continental Breakfast consists of a paper napkin, a knife, fork and spoon for which you have no use, a cup and saucer, a pot of coffee or tea and a container of marmalade dated, "PLEASE USE BEFORE JULY, 1936." Finally, two four-letter words that have come to strike terror in the hearts of travelers everywhere . . . the HARD ROLL.

The Continental Breakfast (literal translation: Keep out of the reach of children) has a gradual but unmistakable effect on people who eat it for a period of ten days or more.

For the first several days, partakers of the hard roll will pretend it is just the thing they need or the Famine Is Fun number. Women will pinch their waists and say, "I've been eating too much on this trip. A light breakfast is just what I need."

The truth is, the hard roll is not designed to take off weight. Even though eaten in small pieces, once in the body, it will form again in its original hard ball and build a solid wall across the hips and the stomach. After the eleventh day, hard rolls make you mean.

We had our first hard roll in Italy on July first. By July fifteenth, the group was irritable and noncommunicative. On the seventeenth, while in Belgium, my husband, in a fit of violence, grabbed a hard roll, carved his initials in it, "WLB, 1977," and sent it back to the kitchen.

By the nineteenth day, the prospect of a hard roll for breakfast forced some travelers to remain in their beds with their faces turned to the wall. Others used the hard roll to pry open their luggage, prop open their doors, or to rub stubborn stains from their shirt collars.

I seemed to be surviving the Hard Roll trauma, but I was fighting Montezuma II's revenge. (Few people realize this, but there were two Montezumas. Montezuma I is credited with lending his name to an urgency Americans refer to as the Green Apple Two-step. Montezuma II is generally known as the patron saint of gift shops. Both are unkind to foreigners.)

With Montezuma II's revenge, I would be in the country no longer than five minutes before I got severe stomach cramps, my right hand would stiffen into the shape of a credit card holder, my step would quicken and I'd rush out into the streets shouting, "How much? How much?"

Sometimes, early in the morning, I'd leave my room and wander through the hotel lobby mumbling, "I smell gift shops. I couldn't sleep."

Somehow, I was like a woman obsessed. I bought a head scarf that when worn in the rain gave me a navy blue face. I bought a toilet tissue holder carved out of wood and held by a man with one tooth. I bought keyrings, flags, bongo drums, patches, and a left-handed letter opener made out of reindeer antlers.

After a while, I couldn't sit on a sightseeing bus for longer than an hour or so before leaning over to the bus driver and saying, "Aren't we going to make a gift-shop stop soon?"

"Is it absolutely necessary?" he'd plead.

"Are you willing to take a chance it isn't?"

I bought boxes of matches, T-shirts, paperweights, pennants, and ships in bottles, small glass ducks, corkscrews, and rocks with the Lord's Prayer on them.

I bought a moose for my charm bracelet, a cocktail apron, three cheese slicers with fur handles, a Spanish doll for my bed, a small chicken coming out of a soapstone egg, ashtrays, a set of coasters, a linen calendar with months I couldn't translate, and a wild boar cookbook.

By the twenty-first day, we could barely board the plane.

Besides, I was carrying a papier-mâché donkey with a wire holder that was severing my ring finger.

I jammed a shopping bag of souvenirs under the seat in front of me.

"You're supposed to fold your snack tray up before we take off," said my husband.

"This is not a snack tray, It's my stomach."

The stewardess came by later with lunch. My husband picked up the hard roll and ran his fingers over it. There was WLB-1977 carved on the side.

We both agreed it was probably a coincidence.

13 ⚐

The Trick Is Knowing
When to Laugh . . .

A lot of people think I write humor.

But then I know a woman who thinks Marie Osmond and her relatives are depressed. As an observer of the human condition all I do is question it. I rarely find it funny.

For example, how come pens never have any ink in them except when they get in the washer by mistake and the entire laundry turns blue?

Why do they waste silicone on an ironing board cover?

How can an owner of a vicious dog look at his dog baring his teeth and know he is "smiling"?

Why is there a rectal thermometer in my sewing basket?

Why do I assume those two doves nuzzling in the trees are married? Maybe they're just fooling around.

How come the first thing I notice in a doctor's office is whether or not his plants are dead?

Okay, so maybe my threshold of laughter is low, but if you can find anything funny in the following items, I'll make a book out of 'em.

Microphones

If there is anything in this world as fiercely independent as a microphone, I don't know what it is.

I mean, imagine the year is 1775. At the Provincial Convention in Virginia, statesman Patrick Henry rises to his feet to make an impassioned plea for liberty or death. He approaches the microphone and as the entire assembly awaits his first words he asks, "Can everyone in the back hear me?"

Those seven words have preceded more speeches than the proverbial cocktail hour.

In ten years of lecturing, I have seen microphones go from an occasional passive screech to real screaming militancy. To begin with, microphones do not like to be touched by a union or otherwise. Because I am short, I tried to adjust one the other week. I gave it just a simple tweak, mind you, and it went as limp as a two-dollar permanent in a sauna. I gave the entire speech from a squatting sprinter's position.

Some microphones work great as long as you blow into them. So you stand there like an idiot blowing and saying, "Are we on? Can you hear me?" Everyone admits they can hear you blowing. It's only when you speak the microphone goes dead.

Others have a weird sense of humor. They're punchline poopers. You'll be sailing along with a three-minute story, building to a big pitch and just as you say, "So why isn't the dog drinking his daiquiri?" the microphone goes silent and you're left muttering, "Gee, I guess you had to have been there."

Some speakers spend half their lives looking for the on/off switch of microphones. There aren't any. I've looked for them under the light, on the shelf, on the side, the gooseneck, offstage. I suspect most of them are triggered by a remote control in a 1936 pickup truck in a garage across from the auditorium.

I have been warned that microphones are supersensitive and you have to talk right into them to be heard. These are usually the ones that cross you up by picking up your entire luncheon conversation including, "My God, do you mean the management is charging you ten dollars for this lunch! Has he never heard of the Geneva Convention?"

Some speakers, more secure than I, have dared to make fun of microphones. Recently, book columnist and reviewer Bob Cromie spoke in our town and opened with the traditional, "Can everyone in the back hear me?"

When someone yelled, "no" he said, "Then how did you know what I asked?"

All night long that microphone floated toward the door. Didn't surprise me a bit.

No One Wins

Did you ever notice how in reporting sports no one ever "wins" a game?

They crush, stomp, triumph, trounce, bomb, outscore, outclass, overthrow, run over, edge out, hammer and victimize, but they never use the word "win."

The other night after a sportscast where there were three assaults, four upsets, one humiliation, a squeaker, and a rout, I said to my husband, "These guys must be fed intravenously by a thesaurus each night to come up with all those words that mean 'win.' "

"They have to," he said. "You'd get bored hearing who 'won' all the time."

"But that's not the way people talk," I complained. "Can't you just see some two-hundred-thirty-pound guard being interviewed at halftime saying, 'We came to best Pittsburgh. At this moment, we're not overwhelming by as much as we had hoped, but sooner or later we hope to vanquish. After all, as Vince Lombardi said, 'subduing is everything.' "

"You should talk," he said. "How come a woman on the society pages never gets married?' "

"What are you talking about?"

"I've read those stories before. They 'exchange vows,' 'say nuptials' or 'pledge I do's,' but they never 'get married!' "

"That's different."

"Why different? We're talking about saying what we mean. When we got engaged I suppose you called up your best friend and said, 'Hey, Dottie, guess what. I'm going to plight my troth in August.' "

"I think plighting a troth is rather poetic. It's certainly not like the Raiders 'smothering' their opponents or the Jets 'clobbering' theirs."

"Hey," he grinned, "it might be fun if society pages showed as much imagination as they do on the sports pages. Can't you just imagine reading where 'Betty Schmidlapp cruised by four ugly bridesmaids Saturday to overpower her opponents and cap a victory in the Bridegroom Open in the upset of the year'?"

"This is a stupid argument," I said. "And I don't want to continue it. Just say I won and we'll forget it."

He sat there thinking.

"See," I continued. "You haven't heard the word win in so long you can't even remember how it goes."

"Let's see," he said, "let's just say in the sports vernacular you 'persuaded your opponent it was in his best interest to lose.' "

The Unmailed Letter

I found a letter to my sister the other day that I had forgotten to mail.

It just needed a little updating to send. After "The baby is . . ." I crossed out "toilet trained" and wrote in "graduating from high school this month."

And in the P.S. where I had written "I found my first gray hair today," I ran a line through gray and substituted "black."

The rest of the letter was still current. "I am on a diet as my skin does not fit me anymore. The children are rotten and I am slipping away from reality. I am going to paint the bathroom and write to the rest of the family next week."

The trouble with me is I don't like to write letters unless I have something exciting to report. I am intimidated by letter-writers whose correspondence electrifies you.

I have one group of friends who only write me once a year—from a cruise ship. They know it's going to make me spit up with jealousy and they write cute little messages that begin, "Luv: Thinking of you as we island-hop," and end with: "Must dash. A Robert Redford look-alike has been chasing me all over the ship."

Other pen-pals I can live without are the people whose children are overachievers. Their letters are filled with news of "Robbie" who just won a "Being" scholarship to Harvard. (He's so exceptional, all he has to do is sit there and breathe for four years.) There's also nine-year-old Rachel, who is competing in the Baton Olympics, makes all her own clothes, just sold her first story to *Reader's Digest*, and is going to spend her entire summer reading the Bible. And don't forget little Kenneth, who gets up during the night to change his own Pampers. (Does you-know-who still have a plastic liner in his football uniform?)

The letter-writers who bug me, though, are the ones with the stationery whose paper matches the envelopes. Sure it's easy to write a letter when you have all the equipment, but for me, it's a real hassle finding clean paper, a pencil and a stamp.

I found a letter from my sister in the mailbox today. She had crossed out "I'm glad the war is over," and substituted "Christmas." She said they loved their new Edsel, which she ran a line through and added Datsun, and added she was going to clean her oven as we were approaching a month with R in it.

My sister and I are related through recessive Writer's Cramps.

Killing Your Mother

My son never fails to amaze me. At age twenty-one, he has come up with a new way to break his neck. It's called a skateboard.

Frankly, I'm tired. I've dedicated my entire life to keeping that kid whole and at a time of my life when I should be eating chocolate sandwiches and getting up at the crack of noon . . . I'm a bundle of nerves.

It started with the two-wheel bicycle. As I ran along beside him, clutching his sweater with one hand and the bicycle seat with the other, I yelled, "You could kill yourself on this thing." Sure enough, my housecoat caught in the spokes and I almost made a wheel out of myself.

The Pogo stick was worse. As he sprang about the house, his head inches from the ceiling, I tried to shield him from falling into a lamp and he lost his balance . . . pinning me between the floor and his body, causing me severe pain.

When he wanted a horse, I tried to warn him that I just wasn't up to it, but did he listen? He did not. As I led the beast around by the reins, I was repaid for my vigilance by being stomped on by a fifteen-hundred-pound horse.

"We are not going out for football," I told him the summer of his fifteenth year. "What do you mean what has that got to do with me? I'm your mother. If you want to kill your *mother*, I can't stop you, but every Mother's Day . . . mark my words . . . you're going to feel just terrible." (I carry with me today a trick knee suffered when I ran onto the playing field with an extra mouthpiece to protect fifteen-hundred dollars' worth of braces.)

It never ended. He jumped off the high board at the pool just to give me stomach cramps and as soon as I thought I had myself under control, he came home with his learner's permit to drive. (The only boy I know who was given a ticket for speeding . . . in reverse.)

I thought all of it was behind me until the other night when he was leaving the house with this little board with the wheels under his arm.

"Where are you going?" I asked.

"Trying to find an empty swimming pool, a hill, or a paved ditch. Then I am going to balance myself on this little board up the side of it until I fall off."

I climbed on the skateboard, clutched him around the waist and closed my eyes. "Why don't you like your mother?" I whimpered.

14

I'm Laughing So Hard I
Can't Stop Crying

An interviewer once asked what the Bombeck family was "really" like. Did we seem as we are in print? A composite of the Bradys, Waltons, Osmonds and Partridges sitting around cracking one-liners.

The last time my family laughed was when my oven caught fire and we had to eat out for a week.

I did not get these varicose veins of the neck from whispering. We shout at one another. We say hateful things. We cry, slam doors, goof off, make mistakes, experience disappointments, tragedies, sickness and traumas. When I last checked, we were members in good standing of your basic screw-up family.

There is a thin line that separates laughter and pain, comedy and tragedy, humor and hurt.

And how do you know laughter if there is no pain to compare it with?

When Did I Become the Mother and the Mother Become the Child?

A nuclear physicist once figured out if a woman has a baby when she is twenty years old, she is twenty times as old as the baby.

When the baby is twenty years of age and the mother is forty, she is only twice as old as the child. When the baby is sixty and the mother is eighty, she is only 1⅓ times as old as the child. When the child is eighty and the mother is one hundred, she is only 1¼ times as old as the offspring.

When will the baby catch up with the mother?

When indeed.

Does it begin one night when you are asleep and your mother is having a restless night and you go into her room and tuck the blanket around her bare arms?

Does it appear one afternoon when, in a moment of irritation, you snap, "How can I give you a home permanent if you won't sit still? If you don't care how you look, I do!" (My God, is that an echo?)

Or did it come the rainy afternoon when you were driving home from the store and you slammed on your brakes and your arms sprang protectively between her and the windshield and your eyes met with a knowing, sad look?

The transition comes slowly, as it began between her and her mother. The changing of power. The transferring of responsibility. The passing down of duty. Suddenly you are spewing out the familiar phrases learned at the knee of your mother.

"Of course you're sick. Don't you think I know when you're not feeling well? I'll be over to pick you up and take you to the doctor around eleven. And be ready!"

"So, where's your sweater? You know how cold the stores get with the air conditioning. That's the last thing you need is a cold."

"You look very nice today. Didn't I tell you you'd like that dress? The other one made you look too old. No sense looking old before you have to."

"Do you have to go to the bathroom before we go? You know what a big deal it is at the doctor's. You have to ask for the key and walk ten miles down all those corridors. Why don't you just go anyway . . . just to get it over with."

"If you're not too tired we'll shop. Did you take your nap this morning? When you get tired, tell me and I'll take you home. You know I can't shop when you stand on one foot and then the other." (Good Lord, did you really tuck her arm in yours, nearly pulling her feet off the floor?)

Rebellion? "I'll thank you, missy, to let me make my own decisions. I know when I'm tired, and when I am I have the good sense to go to bed. Stop treating me like a child!" She is not ready to step down yet.

But slowly and insidiously and certainly the years give way and there is no one to turn to.

"Where are my glasses? I never can find them. Did I fall asleep in the movie again? What was it all about?"

"Dial that number for me. You know how I always get the wrong one."

"I'm not having a Christmas tree this year. There's no one to see it and it just dirties up the carpet for eight months or so."

"Look what I made in macrame today. I'll make you a sling in blue for your kitchen if you want." (It is reminiscent of the small hand in plaster of paris framed over the sofa.)

"Where's my flight number and the times of my planes? You always type it out for me and put it in the airline ticket pocket. I can't read those little numbers."

Rebellion: "Mother really, you're not that old. You can do things for yourself. Surely you can still see to thread your own needle.

"And you certainly aren't too tired to call up Florence and say hello. She's called you fifteen times and you never call her back. Why don't you have lunch with her sometimes. It would do you good to get out of the house."

"What do you mean you're overdrawn? Can't you remember to record your checks each time you write them?"

The daughter isn't ready yet to carry the burden. But the course is set.

The first year you celebrate Thanksgiving at your house and you roast the turkey and your mother sets the table.

The first time you subconsciously turn to her in a movie and say, "Shhhh!"

The first time you rush to grab her arm when she walks over a patch of ice.

As your own children grow strong and independent, the mother becomes more childlike.

"Mother, I did not take your *TV Guide* off the TV set."

"Did so."

"Did not."

"Did so."

"Did not."

"Did."

"Not."

"I saw your father last night and he said he would be late."

"You didn't see Dad last night. He's dead, Mother."

"Why would you say a thing like that? You're a terrible child."

("I saw Mr. Ripple and he swung me on the swings for hours."

"There is no Mr. Ripple. You made him up. He doesn't exist."

"That's not true. Why would you say that? Just because you don't see him doesn't mean he isn't there.")

"You never want to visit with me. You fiddle with those children too much. They don't even need you."

("Are you going to play bridge again? You always go out and you never have any time to read me stories!")

"For goodness sake, Mom, don't mention Fred's hairpiece. We all know he has one and having you mention it doesn't help."

("You mind your manners, little girl, and don't speak unless you're spoken to.")

The daughter contemplates, "It wasn't supposed to be this way. All the years I was bathed, dressed, fed, advised, disciplined, ordered, cared for and had every need anticipated, I wanted my turn to come when I could command. Now that it's here, why am I so sad?"

You bathe and pat dry the body that once housed you. You spoon feed the lips that kissed your cuts and bruises and made them well. You comb the hair that used to playfully cascade over you to make you laugh. You arrange the covers over the legs that once carried you high into the air to Banbury Cross.

The naps are frequent as yours used to be. You accompany her to the bathroom and wait to return her to bed. She has a sitter already for New Year's Eve. You never thought it would be like this.

While riding with your daughter one day, she slams on her brakes and her arm flies out instinctively in front of you between the windshield and your body.

My God! So soon.

Mike and the Grass

When Mike was three he wanted a sandbox and his father said, "There goes the yard. We'll have kids over here day and night and they'll throw sand into the flower beds and cats will make a mess in it and it'll kill the grass for sure."

And Mike's mother said, "It'll come back."

When Mike was five, he wanted a jungle gym set with swings that would take his breath away and bars to take him to the summit and his father said, "Good grief. I've seen those things in backyards and do you know what they look like? Mud holes in a pasture. Kids digging their gym shoes in the ground. It'll kill the grass."

And Mike's mother said, "It'll come back."

Between breaths when Daddy was blowing up the plastic swimming pool he warned, "You know what they're going to do to this place? They're going to condemn it and use it for a missile site. I hope you know what you're doing. They'll track water everywhere and you'll have a million water fights and you won't be able to take out the garbage without stepping in mud up to your neck and when we take this down we'll have the only brown lawn on the block."

"It'll come back," smiled Mike's mother.

When Mike was twelve, he volunteered his yard for a campout. As they hoisted the tents and drove in the spikes his father stood at the window and observed, "Why don't I just put the grass seed out in cereal bowls for the birds and save myself the trouble of spreading it around? You know for a fact that those tents and all those big feet are going to trample down every single blade of grass, don't you? Don't bother to answer," he said. "I know what you're going to say, 'It'll come back.' "

The basketball hoop on the side of the garage attracted more crowds than the Winter Olympics. And a small patch of lawn that started out with a barren spot the size of a garbage can lid soon grew to encompass the entire side yard. Just when it looked like the new seed might take root, the winter came and the sled runners beat it into ridges and Mike's father shook his head and said, "I never asked for much in this life . . . only a patch of grass."

And his wife smiled and said, "It'll come back."

The lawn this fall was beautiful. It was green and alive and rolled out like a sponge carpet along the drive where gym shoes had trod . . . along the garage where bicycles used to fall . . . and around the flower beds where little boys used to dig with iced teaspoons.

But Mike's father never saw it. He anxiously looked beyond the yard and asked with a catch in his voice, "He will come back, won't he?"

My Turn

For years, you've watched everyone else do it.

The children who sat on the curb eating their lunches while waiting for the bus.

The husband you put through school who drank coffee standing up and who slept with his hand on the alarm.

And you envied them and said, "Maybe next year I'll go back to school." And the years went by and this morning you looked into the mirror and said, "You blew it. You're too old to pick it up and start a new career."

This column is for you.

Margaret Mitchell won her first Pulitzer Prize for *Gone With the Wind* in 1937. She was thirty-seven years old at the time.

Sen. Margaret Chase Smith was elected to the Senate for the first time in 1948 at the age of fifty-one.

Ruth Gordon picked up her first Oscar in 1968 for *Rosemary's Baby*. She was seventy-two years old.

Billie Jean King took the battle of women's worth to a tennis court in Houston's Astrodome to outplay Bobby Riggs. She was thirty-one years of age.

Grandma Moses began a painting career at the age of seventy-six.

Anne Morrow Lindbergh followed in the shadow of her husband until she began to question the meaning of her own existence. She published her thoughts in a *A Gift from the Sea* in 1955, in her forty-ninth year.

Shirley Temple Black was named Ambassador to Ghana at the age of forty-seven.

Golda Meir in 1969 was elected Prime Minister of Israel. She had just passed her seventy-first birthday.

You can tell yourself these people started out as exceptional. You can tell yourself they had influence before they started. You can tell yourself the conditions under which they achieved were different from yours.

Or you can be like the woman I knew who sat at her kitchen window year after year and watched everyone else do it. Then one day she said, "I do not feel fulfilled cleaning chrome faucets with a toothbrush. It's my turn."

I was thirty-seven years old at the time.

Beauty

According to her height and weight on the insurance charts, she should be a guard for the Lakers.

She has iron-starved blood, one shoulder is lower than the other, and she bites her fingernails.

She is the most beautiful woman I have ever seen. She should be. She's worked on that body and face for more than sixty years. The process for that kind of beauty can't be rushed.

The wrinkles in the face have been earned . . . one at a time. The stubborn one around the lips that deepened with every "No."

The thin ones on the forehead that mysteriously appeared when the first child was born.

The eyes are protected by glass now, but you can still see the perma-crinkles around them. Young eyes are darting and fleeting. These are mature eyes that reflect a lifetime. Eyes that have glistened with pride, filled with tears of sorrow, snapped in anger, and burned from loss of sleep. They are now direct and penetrating and look at you when you speak.

The bulges are classics. They developed slowly from babies too sleepy to walk who had to be carried home from Grandma's, grocery bags lugged from the car, ashes carried out of the basement while her husband was at war. Now, they are fed by a minimum of activity, a full refrigerator and TV bends.

The extra chin is custom-grown and takes years to perfect. Sometimes you can only see it from the side but it's there. Pampered women don't have an extra chin. They cream them away or pat the muscles until they become firm. But this chin has always been there, supporting a nodding head that has slept in a chair all night . . . bent over knitting . . . praying.

The legs are still shapely, but the step is slower. They ran too often for the bus, stood a little too long when she "clerked" in the department store, got beat up while teaching her daughter how to ride a two-wheeler. They're purple at the back of the knees.

The hands? They're small and veined and have been dunked, dipped, shook, patted, wrung, caught in doors, splintered, dyed, bitten and blistered, but you can't help but be impressed when you see the ring finger that has shrunk from years of wearing the same wedding ring. It takes time—and much more—to diminish a finger.

I looked at Mother long and hard the other day and said, "Mom, I have never seen you so beautiful." "I work at it," she snapped.

"You Don't Love Me"

"You don't love me!"

How many times have your kids laid that one on you?

And how many times have you, as a parent, resisted the urge to tell them how much?

Someday, when my children are old enough to understand the logic that motivates a mother, I'll tell them.

I loved you enough to bug you about where you were going, with whom, and what time you would get home.

I loved you enough to insist you buy a bike with your own money that we could afford and you couldn't.

I loved you enough to be silent and let you discover your hand-picked friend was a creep.

I loved you enough to make you return a Milky Way with a bite out of it to a drugstore and confess, "I stole this."

I loved you enough to stand over you for two hours while you cleaned your bedroom, a job that would have taken me fifteen minutes.

I loved you enough to say, "Yes, you can go to Disney World on Mother's Day."

I loved you enough to let you see anger, disappointment, disgust and tears in my eyes.

I loved you enough not to make excuses for your lack of respect or your bad manners.

I loved you enough to admit that I was wrong and ask your forgiveness.

I loved you enough to ignore "what every other mother" did or said.

I loved you enough to let you stumble, fall, hurt and fail.

I loved you enough to let you assume the responsibility for your own actions, at six, ten, or sixteen.

I loved you enough to figure you would lie about the party being chaperoned, but forgave you for it . . . after discovering I was right.

I loved you enough to shove you off my lap, let go of your hand, be mute to your pleas . . . so that you had to stand alone.

I loved you enough to accept you for what you are, not what I wanted you to be.

But most of all, I loved you enough to say no when you hated me for it. That was the hardest part of all.

Are You Listening?

It was one of those days when I wanted my own apartment . . . unlisted.

My son was telling me in complete detail about a movie he had just seen, punctuated by three thousand "You know's?" My teeth were falling asleep.

There were three phone calls—strike that—three monologues that could have been answered by a recording. I fought the urge to say, "It's been nice listening to you."

In the cab from home to the airport, I got another assault on my ear, this time by a cab driver who was rambling on about his son whom he supported in college, and was in his last year, who put a P.S. on his letter saying, "I got married. Her name is Diane." He asked me, "What do you think of that?" and proceeded to answer the question himself.

There were thirty whole beautiful minutes before my plane took off . . . time for me to be alone with my own thoughts, to open a book and let my mind wander. A voice next to me belonging to an elderly woman said, "I'll bet it's cold in Chicago."

Stone-faced, I answered, "It's likely."

"I haven't been to Chicago in nearly three years," she persisted. "My son lives there."

"That's nice," I said, my eyes intent on the printed page of the book.

"My husband's body is on this plane. We've been married for fifty-three years. I don't drive, you know, and when he died a nun drove me from the hospital. We aren't even Catholic. The funeral director let me come to the airport with him."

I don't think I have ever detested myself more than I did at that moment. Another human being was screaming to be heard and in desperation had turned to a cold stranger who was more interested in a novel than the real-life drama at her elbow.

All she needed was a listener . . . no advice, wisdom, experience, money, assistance, expertise or even compassion . . . but just a minute or two to listen.

It seemed rather incongruous that in a society of supersophisticated communication, we often suffer from a shortage of listeners.

She talked numbly and steadily until we boarded the plane, then found her seat in another section. As I hung up my coat, I heard her plaintive voice say to her seat companion, "I'll bet it's cold in Chicago."

I prayed, "Please God, let her listen."

Why am I telling you this? To make me feel better. It won't help, though.

The Chimes

Everything is in readiness.

The tree is trimmed. The cards taped to the doorframe. The boxes stacked in glittering disarray under the tree.

Why don't I hear chimes?

Remember the small boy who made the chimes ring in a fictional story years ago? As the legend went, the chimes would not ring unless a gift of love was placed on the altar. Kings and men of great wealth placed untold jewels on the altar, but year after year the church remained silent.

Then one Christmas Eve, a small child in a tattered coat made his way down the aisle and without anyone noticing he took off his coat and placed it on the altar. The chimes rang out joyously throughout the land to mark the unselfish giving of a small boy.

I used to hear chimes.

I heard them the year one of my sons gave me a tattered piece of construction paper on which he had crayoned two hands folded in prayer and a moving message, "OH COME HOLY SPIT!"

I heard them the year I got a shoebox that contained two baseball cards and the gum was still with them.

I heard them the Christmas they all got together and cleaned the garage.

They're gone, aren't they? The years of the lace doilies fashioned into snowflakes . . . the hands traced in plaster of paris . . . the Christmas trees of pipe cleaners . . . the thread spools that held small candles. They're gone.

The chubby hands that clumsily used up two dollars' worth of paper to wrap a cork coaster are sophisticated enough to take a number and have the gift wrapped professionally.

The childish decision of when to break the ceramic piggybank with a hammer to spring the fifty-nine cents is now resolved by a credit card.

The muted thump of pajama-covered feet paddling down the stairs to tuck her homemade crumb scrapers beneath the tree has given way to pantyhose and fashion boots to the knee.

It'll be a good Christmas. We'll eat too much. Make a mess in the living room. Throw the warranties into the fire by mistake. Drive the dog crazy taping bows to his tail. Return cookies to the plate with a bite out of them. Listen to Christmas music.

But Lord . . . what I would give to bend low and receive a gift of toothpicks and library paste and hear the chimes just one more time.

Epilogue

When you're an orthodox worrier, some days are worse than others.

I pride myself on being able to handle traumas, natural disasters, deep depression, misfortune, hardship, discomfort, and readily adjust when they run out of extra crispy chicken at the carryout.

But last week, you would not believe that even a professional pessimist could have survived what I went through.

It began on Monday when the kids filed into the kitchen completely dressed.

I stood there with my iron (the one with the fifty-foot cord) and asked, "Who wants something pressed before you go to school?" No one moved!

My car with the new battery actually started. I found a parking place in front of the supermarket, got a shopping cart with four wheels that all went in the same direction at the same time, and found a sale on something edible that I needed. That night, on television, Angie Dickinson looked a little fat. I cooked a dinner that no one had had for lunch.

All of that began to make me feel a little edgy, but I figured by the next day things would surely get back to normal. They didn't. At the library, all four of the books I had written were checked out. I took a bath and the phone didn't ring. I sewed up a skirt and with two inches left to do, the bobbin didn't even run out of thread. I went to bed thinking things had to get worse tomorrow . . . they couldn't get any better.

On Wednesday, I ran for a bus and made it. The dentist said I had no cavities. The phone was ringing when I arrived home and even after I dropped my key a couple of times, I answered it and they were still on the line. The Avon lady refused me service saying I didn't need her as I already looked terrific. My husband asked me what kind of a day I had and didn't leave the room when I started to answer.

By Thursday, I was a basket case anticipating what was in store for me, but it didn't happen. My daughter told me my white socks looked good with wedgies. The checkbook balanced. No one snacked and ruined their dinners, and a film at the school, *The History of Sulphur*, was canceled.

On Friday, I was sobbing into a dishtowel when my husband tried to comfort me. "I can't help it," I said, "things were never meant to go this well. I'm worried."

"Now, now," he said patting my shoulder, "things can't go rotten all the time. How could we appreciate the bad times if we don't have a good day once in a while?"

"I know I'm going to get it," I said. "Do you know that yesterday I went into the boys' room and their beds were made? (He frowned.) And that we got a note from the IRS apologizing for being late with our refund? This isn't like us," I whined. "The bad times I can handle. It's the good times that drive me crazy. When is the other shoe going to drop?"

We heard a car turn into the garage and make the sickening scrape of a fender when it meets an immovable wall.

We looked at each other and smiled. Things are looking up.

Aunt Erma's Cope Book

How To Get From Monday To Friday... In 12 Days

For
Betsy Bombeck, Andy Bombeck, and
Matt Bombeck.
If I blow it raising them . . .
nothing else I do will matter very much.

Contents ᴨ✶ᴨ

1 ♪♪♪

How Do I Like Me
So Far?

All the way to Jill's cocktail party, I had that feeling of exhilaration . . . like when your gelatin mold comes out in one piece or you grab the door of a pay booth in the rest room just before it slams shut.

For the first time in a long time, my life was coming together. And it felt good. I no longer anguished over what I looked like. I could pass a mirror without looking at my neck and being reminded I hadn't made homemade chicken soup in a while. I had come to grips with domesticity and no longer believed that unmade beds caused shortness of breath.

My husband's infatuation with Angie Dickinson had wound down and I noted the same ecstasy he used to reserve for her pictures now appeared in his face whenever his soup was hot.

All three kids were not only speaking to us, but our twenty-four-year-old daughter openly displayed a curiosity as to how to turn on the stove.

I was becoming more assertive, refusing to "honk when I loved Jesus." I no longer inhaled around my smoker friends.

The pressures of child raising were easing off. I stopped feeling guilty for my children's colds, their overbites, or for that matter allowing our daughter to be born without pompon hands.

I stopped eating chocolates in the closet, dedicating my life to putting toilet seats down, or pretending to feel sorry for women wearing industrial-strength bras.

In my awkward way, I was reentering the human race after twenty years of Edith Bunkering it.

My husband disliked parties. He called them the Varicose Olympics where people stood around all night talking about their dogs' hysterectomies and eating bait off of little round crackers. If our social life were left up to him, the high spot of my week would have been watching the hot wax drip down on our car at the Car Wash.

My eyes fairly danced as we entered the room and I spotted my old friend Phyllis. I hadn't seen her in ages.

"Phyllis!" I shouted. "How long has it been? Do you still bowl with the League on Tuesdays?"

Phyllis set down her glass without smiling. "Bowl? That was only a transference of aggression to keep me from dealing with my realities head-on."

"C'mon," I laughed, "eighty-six wasn't *that* bad a score."

"You remember how I used to have anxiety attacks when I emptied the sweeper bag? Well, the bottom line was I was in a crisis situation I couldn't handle . . . which is what you'd expect from a Gemini, right? So, I began to read self-help books to raise my consciousness level. Right now I'm reading *Sensual Needlepoint* by Candy Summers. She also wrote *Erotic Leftovers* and *Kinky Lint*."

"*Sensual Needlepoint?*" I said, gulping my drink.

"Believe me," she whispered. "You will never make another French knot for as long as you live. By the way, you belong to the Cope-of-the-Month-Club Guild, don't you?" I shook my head.

"Every month you get a self-help book on how to improve yourself. Of course you've read *Fear of Landing* by Erika Wrong and Dr. Dryer's new book, *I Hope the Sexual Revolution Doesn't End Before I'm Drafted?*"

"Phyllis," I said, "what's happened to you? You used to be so shallow!"

She ignored my comment. "Incidentally, why are you paranoid about kissing people hello?"

"I am not paranoid."

"Yes, you are. When you approached me just now, you extended your hand. You really are inhibited."

"I'm not inhibited. I didn't kiss you because I've been eating Roquefort."

"When was the last time you told Erma how you felt about her?"

I looked over the crowd. "Erma who?"

"Erma YOU, that's who."

"You know I don't like to talk about me in front of myself. It's embarrassing."

"I knew you'd masquerade your true feelings behind cheap jokes. It's just like you to make light of something serious. But frankly, I don't know how much longer you can sit by and watch the rest of the world probe into their inner minds and understand the heights of man's nobility and the depths of his depravity."

"That's beautiful. Where did you read that?"

"In the *National Enquirer* in the express lane at the supermarket. Do you know what's wrong with you?" she asked, leaning closer. "Sex! It should be apparent to you that it's time you got in touch with your feelings. Get to know yourself. We're moving into the 1980s, sweetie, where sex dominates everything we do. You and your husband are probably just plain bored with one another. It happens in a lot of marriages. You just take one another for granted after a while."

"Phyllis, I do not believe we are having this conversation. You're the one who was too shy to tell anyone you were pregnant. You told everyone you had 'something in the oven.' You raised children who thought it took nine months to bake a pie!"

"Well, things are different now," said Phyllis. "I know that sex is something you have to work on in a marriage. You need Clarabelle Sweet."

"You mean the author of *The Sub-Total Woman?* I think I've heard of her."

"HEARD OF HER!" shouted Phyllis shrilly. "Are you serious? Women haven't been so excited about a book since *Sex Causes Fatness* came out. You know the one where the author said that making love burns up fewer calories than throwing a Frisbee? I tell you what. I'll loan you my copy if you promise to return it."

"I do not need help from *The Sub-Total Woman.*"

"When was the last time you bathed with your husband?"

"When we washed the dog."

"Do you share your husband's interest in sports? Do you create a mood for romance? Have you ever made sheets out of Astroturf?"

Phyllis was whacko. No doubt about it. I eased away and observed my husband across the room. For a man going through his metallic age (silver hair, gold teeth, and lead bottom) he did cut quite a figure. I watched him as he was joined by a girl with solar hair who was so animated I thought her face would break. As I turned, I caught Phyllis looking at me. She smiled and yelled, "Trust me! *The Sub-Total Woman* will change your life!"

2

The Sub-Total Woman

Clarabelle Sweet had been on all the talk shows touting her book, *The Sub-Total Woman*.

Clarabelle had long black hair and said things like "When a man's got cream in the refrigerator at home, he won't go out looking for two-percent butterfat."

She appeared on a sex-theme show with Merv Griffin, explained how 350 boxes of gelatin could change your life on Donahue, and made a three-bean salad on Dinah! (The garbanzo beans spelled out L–O–V–E.)

There was no doubt in my mind she had a Spanish doll nestled among the satin pillows on her bed. I figured that out after reading the Compatible Quiz.

At the beginning, it bothered me to know, without taking it, that I'd flunk. And somehow, after thirty years of marriage and three children, I didn't want to know that my husband and I had been incompatible.

But I couldn't resist it.

299

"Post Scripts to 'I DO' "

(Score yourself ten points for each correct answer)

- You and your husband are alone in a cabin for the first time since your marriage. He is nibbling on your ear. Do you (a) nibble back or (b) tell him the toilet is running?
- Your husband comes home unexpectedly in the middle of the afternoon. Do you (a) slip into something suggestive and make him an offer he can't refuse or (b) leave him there while you take the car and go to a food-processor demonstration?
- Your husband invites you to go to a convention where you will share only your evenings together. Do you (a) get a babysitter and go or (b) regard it as a great time to stay at home and paint the bedroom?
- Check your husband's driver's license. Under SEX does he list (a) male or (b) only during a full moon?
- After a long, hard day your husband drags in feeling tired and listless. Do you (a) massage his feet with witch hazel or (b) tell him all he needs is a good laxative?
- When you've had a bad day and need tenderness and understanding does your husband (a) wrap you in his arms and tell you he adores you or (b) read the paper and absentmindedly scratch you behind your ear and call you the dog's name?

I didn't have to score myself. The results were rather obvious. I had become a woman who said "I do" but didn't from the day she got her first set of car keys.

I didn't pamper my husband and I didn't serve his needs. Maybe Phyllis was right. Maybe we had fallen into a rut at a time when we needed it most.

When I thought about it, the last time he put his arms around me in a movie, I had a miniature bus caught in my throat from a Cracker-Jack box.

I'd feel like a fool padding around after him. We weren't demonstrative people. Never had been. On the other hand, what if someday he developed a craving for 2-percent butterfat? If Clarabelle Sweet's husband called her from the office every day just to pant into the phone for a minute and a half maybe it was worth it.

The next morning my husband called from the bathroom, "What's this?"

On the mirror in lipstick, I had written "65 MILLION WOMEN WANT MY HUSBAND."

"It's just a reminder, dear, how lucky I am to have you."

He studied the mirror carefully and said, "Name names."

"Don't get testy. Clarabelle Sweet says if women treated their husbands better they wouldn't wander."

"Who is Clarabelle Sweet and where am I going?"

"She's going to save our marriage. Here is your shaver, your bath towel, your soap, and your shampoo."

"Where's my rubber duck?" he asked irritably.

"And your comb, your deodorant, your clean shirt, and your trousers. Here, let me put that lid down for you."

"GET OUT OF THE BATHROOM," he yelled through clenched teeth.

Looking back on it, I never knew how being subservient could be so unappreciated. When I tried to spoon-feed him his cereal, he stopped eating. When I measured out his dental floss, he left the bathroom. When I lit a match under his chin, he blew it out and snarled "I don't smoke, remember?"

As I was standing in the driveway holding his attaché case, he said, "And lay off the vanilla."

"I'll call you at work," I said huskily. "Try to come home early."

When he was gone, I went back to *The Sub-Total Woman* for reassurance. It appeared on page 110. "In a survey of 10,000 males," it read, "almost half of them said they cheated on their wives and most said they wanted or needed some physical display of affection.

"Given a list of qualities for a partner, they arranged them in the following order:

1. "A woman with concern for my needs
2. Sincerity
3. Affection
4. Intelligence
5. Self-confidence
6. Sexuality
7. Sense of humor."

It read more like a Boy Scout handbook.

Just after lunch, I went to the phone and dialed my husband's office. The wait seemed interminable. Finally, his secretary answered and said she would put me through.

"Hello," I said, trying to make my voice sound throaty. "Could you come home early?"

"Whatsa matter?" he asked. "Do you have a dental appointment?"

"Come home early and you can have your way with me."

"Hang on a second. Another call is coming through," he said, and PUT ME ON HOLD!

I hung up the phone and went back to Clarabelle's book. "Jar your husband out of his lethargy by meeting him at the door dressed in something outrageous like a cheerleader . . . a bunny . . . or a slave girl."

A costume. Was she serious? Even at Halloween I just put brown grocery bags over the kids' heads, cut two eyes in them, and told them to tell everyone their mother was having surgery. I wasn't good at costumes.

I went through all the closets and the only thing I could come up with was a pair of the boys' football pants, jersey, and helmet. I felt about as sensuous as a bride with a lip full of Novocain, but when you're trying to save a marriage you have to go for it.

When I heard the car in the driveway, I flung open the front door and yelled, "It's a scoreless game so far."

The washer repairman didn't say anything for a couple of minutes. His eyes never met mine. He just stared at the floor and mumbled, "It says here on the work sheet that your dryer won't heat up."

I cleared my throat. "Right, come in. The dryer is next to the washer behind the louvered doors." Neither of us spoke. The only sound was of my cleats clicking on the terrazzo tile. He worked in silence and I disappeared in the other end of the house.

As I wrote him a check, he took it, shook his head, and said, "I hope your team wins, lady."

I got out of the football uniform and into a dress. Who was I kidding? I wasn't ready for the Sub-Total Super Bowl and I knew it.

I couldn't even create the atmosphere for it. We ate dinner between *Family Feud* and *Name That Tune*. The kids fanned in and out like a revolving door. The only way you could get them to turn their stereos down was to tell them you could hear the words. There were clothes to fold, purchases to discuss, decisions to be made and, of course, the electronic sleeping pill—the parade of sports.

I never realized what a holding pattern we were in until I tried to massage my husband's neck and he said, "I'll save you time. My billfold's on the dresser."

I returned to folding clothes when about eleven or so we both heard the smoke alarm go off in our bedroom.

We rushed back to see my sheer red nightgown smoking from the heat of the lightbulb on the lamp.

"Why is your nightgown draped over the lamp?" asked my husband evenly.

"I am creating a mood."

"For a disaster movie?"

"It was supposed to give the room a sexy, sensuous feeling."

"Open the window. If it gets any sexier in here, I'm going to pass out."

It was an hour or so before the smoke cleared and we could go to bed.

"Did you call me today or did I imagine it?" he asked.

"I called."

"What did you want?"

"I wanted to tell you to come home early and you could have your way with me."

"You should have left a message." He yawned and crawled into bed.

I turned on the bathroom light. The mirror still reflected "65 MILLION WOMEN WANT MY HUSBAND." I took out a deodorant stick and wrote under it WHY?

The simple fact was we couldn't be something we had never been. We were too old to change.

Besides, according to experts we were going through the best phase of our lives. The children were grown and I didn't have to cope with rainbows over the crib and knotted shoestrings. The house carried a preinflation 9-percent mortgage. And I had Mayva. Mayva was my best friend, who never went on a diet when I was fat, never told me the truth when I begged for it, and when my husband bought me a vegetable slicer for my birthday never said something stupid like "At least he doesn't drink or play around like a lot of husbands."

When Mayva saw Clarabelle Sweet's book on the hall table she nearly flipped. "You're reading *The Sub-Total Woman*? You can't be serious. Don't you know that converting your Donny Osmond night light into a strobe isn't going to turn your life around? I know what's wrong with you. You're like a lot of married couples who are floundering around in a traditional marriage that doesn't exist any more. No one paddles around waiting on one another these days. Things should be equal between you. Each of you should have a sense of self. Do you know what I'm saying?"

"No more books, Mayva."

"Listen, Pam McMeal and Richard McMeal's book *Is There a Draft in Your Open Marriage?* really spells it out. Answer me this. When was the last time you and Bill took separate vacations?"

"When we left the kids with Mother."

"You should be at a time of your life when you have an open and an honest relationship. No one dominates and no one is submissive any more. You share. You grow. You leave behind the years of sitting under your children and develop an awareness of what is going on in the world. And heaven help you if you awake one morning to discover your husband has outgrown you."

I didn't say anything for a minute, then asked, "What made you say that, Mayva?"

"It's not important," she said.

"It IS! You know something you're not telling me. What is it?"

"It's just that the other night when all of us were talking and Bill mentioned the Gross National Product you said, 'Nothing is more gross than commercials for feminine hygiene products.' "

I stiffened. "I suppose you know of a more gross commercial product?"

"Read the McMeals' book," she said. "I'll drop it off tomorrow. Believe me, it'll change your life."

A woman with twenty-six boxes of lime gelatin couldn't afford to close her mind to suggestions.

3 ♪❋♪♪

Is There a Draft in Your Open Marriage?

My son, Jaws II, had a habit that drove me crazy. He'd walk to the refrigerator-freezer and fling both doors open and stand there until the hairs in his nose iced up. After surveying two hundred dollars' worth of food in varying shapes and forms he would declare loudly "There's nothing to eat."

I used to react to that remark like a gauntlet thrown down or an attack on my honor. The remark no longer held a challenge for me. I sat at the table and continued to read my book.

"Are you reading another book on marriage?" he asked.

"What's the matter with that?"

"Nothing," he said, then added, "there's something I always wondered. How come you and Dad never lived together before tying the knot?"

I said, "Are you crazy? We got married because we didn't know one another well enough to live together."

The remark was ludicrous and we both knew it. The truth is, in a world of "limited arrangements," "meaningful relationships," and "marital concepts" his father and I were dinosaurs.

We had never negotiated the old contract, never dropped an option on one another, never comparison-shopped. We not only hadn't a clue as to where one another was coming from . . . we didn't know where we were going until one of the kids brought home the car.

We must have seemed weird in a world where young people met in a line to see *Superman*, made a commitment to one another by the intermission, and dissolved the relationship between ordering a pizza and picking it up.

I closed the McMeals' book. It was more frightening than *Future Shock*. They wrote that one out of every three marriages ended in divorce and that 75 percent of all the existing ones were in big trouble. The rest of it made marriage sound as exciting as a yogurt orgy.

After thirty years of marriage, I felt like a truss in a drugstore window—dependable, serviceable, and downright orthopedic.

Were married people an endangered species? In time would they talk of the days when men and women roamed the earth in wedlock as matched sets? Was it possible that some day cohabital living would be the sanctified relationship and marriage would be frowned on by society?

I could just see my son coming home from school one day . . . his shirt torn, blood around his mouth, sneaking to his room to avoid a confrontation.

When cornered, he'd finally admit he had a fight on the playground.

"But why?" I'd ask.

"Because Rich said . . . he accused you and Dad . . . he said you and Dad were MARRIED!"

"And what did you say?"

"I told him he was a creep. Then he said everyone in school knew it and if you weren't, then how come my last name is the same as yours? Is it true?"

When I finally nodded my head, I could see him shouting angrily, "Why can't you and Dad live together like everyone else's parents?"

I'd explain: "I'm sorry. Your father and I never wanted to embarrass you. Do you think we liked sneaking around checking into hotels *with* luggage? Wearing my wedding ring on a chain around my neck? Pinching one another in front of your friends to make them think we were not married? I'm glad the charade is over. I'm sick of going to Marriage Encounter meetings in separate cars."

When pressed as to why we did it, I'd explain we wanted to try marriage to see if it got on our nerves and if it didn't work out, we'd just quietly get a divorce and no one would get hurt that way.

I felt a chill. He was standing in front of the double doors to the refrigerator-freezer again. "What's in this yellow box?" he asked, ripping the top off with his teeth.

It was too late. The film was in his mouth.

When I thought about it, our marriage wasn't exactly made in heaven by a long shot. We had our disagreements. A little ventilation couldn't hurt. The McMeals advised couples to give one another room in their marriage to breathe and to develop as persons. They said couples should try to be more independent of one another.

As a woman who was up to her Astroturf in football, I'd buy that. How many years had I put in trudging out to the stadium every week to endure a two-and-one-half-hour sleeping pill?

Sure, men are supposed to get an emotional high out of football. But did anyone care that I've gotten bigger emotional highs out of getting a piece of dental floss caught in my teeth?

I got so bored I used to play games with myself.

I played the Fashion Alphabet with Peggy Ronstadt for a whole season. We used to alternate naming a style worn by other women in the stands from Accordion pleats and Blouses to Yokes and Zippers. The first one who couldn't come up with a style for a letter was penalized by watching the game until a first down was made.

The Hot-Dog–Cola Caper was always good for an hour or so. Disguising my voice, I'd yell down and order a hot dog and a cola from the vendor at the end of the row. Without an eye leaving the game, people passed it down an entire row of 138 people. When it got to the end they'd pass it back to the next row. I'd watch to see how many rows the hot dog and cola covered before someone finally ate it.

Another one Peggy and I always played was Stump the Fans. We'd establish a pool of a couple of bucks and the first one to figure out what the band was trying to spell out on the playing field won. (I once won eight dollars when I correctly identified a tuba player as an anchovy on a field of pizza.)

I wondered what my husband would say if I announced next Saturday afternoon that I wasn't going to the football game with him. I might just find out how secure our marriage really is.

When I talked with my neighbor Lynda, she looked shocked. "You can't be serious. You have a chance to go to a football game with your husband and you're trying to get out of it."

"What's wrong with that?"

"I'd give anything if my Jim watched football. Why, there's no healthier sport for a man in this world than a football game. Sitting out there in the bleachers with a thermos of hot coffee and a blanket over your knees, sharing . . ."

"What's he matter with you?" I asked. "You're the one who really got ticked off when you had to hire a Goodyear blimp to tell Jim you delivered him a son."

"I know. Those were the good old days. Now, every Saturday

he gets up, fills his thermos, and races toward the stadium. All he talks about are the tight ends, the line and the backfield in motion. And the kickers. He raves about the kickers."

"I thought you said he didn't like football."

"He doesn't. All he watches are the pompon girls. Fifty of them with spaghetti legs, concave stomachs, and their inflatable made-in-Japan chests. Last Saturday when the team came on the field he said, 'Let's get something to drink while the game is being played, so we'll make it back in time for halftime.' I tell you, they're ruining the sport."

"Oh, c'mon, Lynda," I said, "no one can stamp out football. It's like head colds and Doris Day . . . it will be with us always, whether we go or not. And don't tell me you wouldn't like to rewrite your marriage contract if you were given a chance."

I wrote down just a few things yesterday that really bug me about our marriage. I'm going to pin it to his pillow. Listen to this.

Takes his leisure suit . . . literally.

Puts toilet paper on the spindle with the paper coming from UNDER the roll just to annoy me.

Lied to me about ultrasuede coming from an endangered species that would ultimately cause an imbalance of nature.

Never shares with me things from the office told to him in confidence that he has sworn never to divulge.

Agrees to shop with me, then leans against the wall like he is awaiting gum surgery.

Said publicly my upper arms looked like cloverleaf rolls.

"Good Lord, that was ten years ago," said Lynda.

"There is no statute of limitations on fat-arms jokes. And in addition to all of that, he puts down my soap operas."

The latter had been a bone of contention for years. And I didn't know why. I only watched one, *The Wild and the Spoiled.*

Of course it was pure fiction. I mean, where else could you see a man who told his wife he loved her . . . with the lights on? But it held my attention.

Soaps had really changed in the years I'd been watching them. They had gone from innocent bits of fluff where the heroine served a lot of coffee and romped through a full-term pregnancy in three weeks, to abortion, alcoholism, incest, cohabital living, drugs, homosexuality, and talking back to mothers.

The heroine of *The Wild and the Spoiled* was named Erogenique. If you couldn't make it in this world with a name like Erogenique you just weren't trying.

It boggled my mind to imagine what Erogenique did on her days off *The Wild and the Spoiled*. I used to fantasize that the two of us were roommates in a New York apartment and were as different as night and day. She would rush in breathless every evening, prattling on about a new conquest who would pick her up within the hour and would I be a love and let him in.

Every time she did this, she lost her newfound desire to me. It was always the same. He would stand in the doorway, struck numb by my wholesomeness. He could have had my roommate (who didn't have a dead spot on her entire body), but he wanted me who was content to sit at home and needlepoint a flag.

When he could stand it no longer, he would reach out to pull me close—at which point I would back off and shout "If you want someone with touch control, get yourself a microwave oven."

I wondered how Erogenique would have handled thirty years with the NFL, then answered my own question.

A couple of weeks after I had decided to open my marriage to drafts, while I was watching *The Wild and the Spoiled* Lynda appeared at the door and said, "I'm dying to ask. What happened when you told your husband you weren't going to go to the football games with him?"

"He said, 'Okay.' "

"That's it?"

"That's it. Shhh, Erogenique is trying to compromise the funeral director at her stepfather's funeral."

Her sister Emma spoke: "You know the trouble with you, Erogenique, is you don't have a good feeling about yourself. You could never have a relationship with anyone because your independence has made you destructive. You don't like anyone else and you don't like yourself because there is nothing to love. You fill me with loathing and disgust!"

"Did you hear that?" I asked. "I think she's got a point. Erogenique doesn't like Erogenique. She doesn't have a good feeling toward herself."

"That's the trouble," yawned Lynda. "Everybody is trying to make you feel good about yourself. You can't be mediocre in this world any more. You have to be perfection itself. Look at that! Even the commercials are pitching it."

We watched in silence as a housewife called Mildred was being interviewed in the supermarket. The interviewer asked Mildred whether her husband preferred potatoes or stuffing with his chicken.

Mildred, who had given birth to his children, drunk out of the same bathroom glass and caught his colds, said without blinking an eye, "Potatoes. My husband would definitely choose potatoes."

When they interviewed the husband in the next scene he said, "Stuffing. I would definitely choose stuffing."

In the third scene his wife is visibly shaken as she stammers, "I didn't know . . . but from here on in I will definitely serve stuffing."

I turned to Lynda. "Gosh, I don't know," I said, my eyes glistening with excitement, "I think Bill would have chosen stuffing. What about Jim?"

Lynda looked at me tiredly. "Who cares?" she said. "I could serve him Top of the Stove Moose and he would have had it for lunch. If Mildred had any sense, she'd give that dim bulb stuffing all right . . . right up his nose!"

"What are you so upset about?" I asked.

"I'm upset because I'm sick and tired of sitting around being told how to exhaust myself and pop iron tablets. We're all being manipulated, you know. I read all about how traps are laid for consumers in a new book called *Fear of Buying*. Supermarkets are like mazes, children drive you crazy to buy things they see on TV, and advertisers have us believing the only time we experience ecstasy is when we drink coffee, take showers, chew gum, or smell laundry. I've got the book if you'd like to read it."

I shook my head.

"It's a real eye-opener."

Later that day I was emptying the waste basket in the bedroom when I saw my list of complaints for the new open marriage contract. Someone had wrapped gum in it.

Maybe I was being manipulated . . . but it beat being ignored.

4 𝔍✻𝔍✻𝔍

Fear of Buying

To tell you the truth, I had never thought a lot about what motivated me to buy.

As Bob Newhart once remarked about his friendship with Don Rickles, "Someone has to do it."

I did as I was told. I was fussy about my peanut butter, fought cavities, became depressed over yellow wax buildup, and buried my head in my laundry like I had just witnessed God.

I personally knew women who carried a quart bottle of laxative, three pounds of Mountain-Grown coffee, and a complete line of feminine products in their handbags. I never did that.

But we all believed. We believed if we converted to all the products that marched before our eyes, we could be the best, the sexiest, the freshest, the cleanest, the thinnest, the smartest, and the first in our block to be regular.

Purchasing for the entire family was the most important thing I had to do.

In 1969, a man walked on the moon. Big deal! That same year I found a pair of gym shoes that would make my son jump higher than a basketball hoop.

A birth-control pill was perfected that would make an impact on the population of the entire world. Hosanna! I discovered a little man for my toilet bowl that cleaned as it flushed.

Our government was involved in a cover-up. So what? It was enough for me to know that while I was in bed reading, my oven was cleaning itself.

My children dominated my buying habits and I knew it. They could sing beer commercials before their eyes could focus.

I remember one day standing in front of a cupboard with eleven boxes of half-eaten cereal ranging from Fortified Blinkies and Captain Sugar to Toasted Wriggles, Heap of Honey, and Cavity Krispies. They didn't snap, crackle, or pop any more. They just lay there on the shelf turning stale year after year.

I told the kids I had had it and there would be no more new cereal brought into the house until we cleaned up what we already had. I even did some fast arithmetic and figured out that a box of Bloated Oats had cost me a total of $116.53. This included repairing my tooth, which I chipped on a nuclear submarine in the bottom of the box, throwing part of the cereal to the birds in the snow, necessitating antibiotics, and the cost of packing, shipping, and crating it through three moves.

Eventually we polished off every box, only to be confronted with the most important decision we had ever made as a family: the selection of a new box of cereal.

I personally favored Bran Brittles because they made you regular and offered an African violet as a premium.

One child wanted Chock Full of Soggies because they turned your teeth purple.

Another wanted Jungle Jollies because they had no nutritional value whatsoever.

We must have spent twenty minutes in the cereal aisle before we decided on Mangled Wheat Bits because "when eaten as an after-school snack, will give you X-Ray vision."

Since the children were grown, we were still under the spell of the hard sell. I had gotten used to buying them Christmas presents that (a) I couldn't spell, (b) had no idea what they were used for, and (c) leaked grease.

Since they were older, their letters at Christmas were a far cry from Christmas past when they wrote "Dear Santa: Please leave me a new doll and a bike."

Mesmerized by some commercial, I would get a list from them that spelled out their desire right down to the catalogue number.

"An RF–60 FM stereo wireless radio chamber. Ask for Frank; five percent off list price if you pay cash."

Or "273 auto thyristor bounce flash 9–90 with head tilt for the big gift and for the stocking stuffer a couple of rolls of EX 135–30 Ektachrome ASA 64–19."

I didn't think too much about *Fear of Buying* until one night after I had lugged in twelve bags of groceries (while everyone else hid out in the john) and my husband poked through the bags and said, "What are we having for dinner? A pot of mums, a room deodorizer, a bag of charcoal, or an encyclopedia?"

That tore it. I slammed down the bag and said, "Is that the thanks I get for taking care of this family's needs? It's a jungle out there and I go into it every week . . . inexperienced people driving shopping carts, kids throwing things into your basket, coupons to clip, lists to juggle, labels to read, fruits to pinch, toilet paper to squeeze, sales to find—and as for the encyclopedias, YOU try to find the S's! Oh sure, the A to Al was a piece of cake . . . fifty-nine cents each, five thousand of them shouting 'Take me! Take me!' But just try to buy them when they're three ninety-eight and they get a limited number of S's because everyone has dropped out. All the good words are in the S's."

"You should hear yourself," he said. "Is it really that important?"

"Important? Do you want your kids to go through life not knowing the meaning of SEX, the Sabbath, Satire, Scruples, Sin and Status . . . not to mention Sales?"

"The trouble with you," he said, "is you're a pushover for every advertising gimmick that comes down the pike. They could sell you anything."

It was easy for him to say. Men didn't get the pressure from advertising that women did. I'd seen them on the tube. All men ever did was sit around grabbing all the gusto they could get, eating cereal that made them champions, and having a swell time talking to a tub of butter.

When they talked to their broker . . . everyone listened. Even the labels in their shorts danced and had a good time.

Oh, occasionally they'd run a car up the side of a mountain or slap on some after-shave and hit the ports, but mostly it was women who carried the responsibility for the entire family.

And no one cared.

If commercials were supposed to make me feel good about myself, they were failing miserably. My paper towels turned to lace in my hands. My cough medicine ran out at 2 A.M., and my garbage bags broke on impact with the garbage.

It's funny I hadn't thought about it before. I was responsible for my husband's underarms being protected for twelve hours. I was responsible for making sure my children had a well-balanced breakfast. I alone was carrying the burden for my dog's shiny coat and spritzing just the right amount of lemon throughout the house so they wouldn't pucker to death. When my daughter's love life fell through it was up to me to remind her that whiter teeth would bring him back.

I was reflecting on my responsibilities when the commercial came on of the husband who came home after a twelve-hour day, beat, depressed and exhausted. He opened the door and seventy-five people jumped up and yelled, "Happy Birthday! Surprise!"

The man grabbed his wife, kissed her, and said, "Honey, what a surprise."

She backed off from him like he was a three-day-old dead chicken and said, "What a breath! We'd better do something about it . . . and FAST!"

You would have thought that would have taken the hats and horns out of the occasion if anything would. Instead, we see them in the bathroom, where he is gargling his bad breath into remission. The last scene is one of pure joy. He has finally been allowed to attend his own party and she is beaming, knowing that she has once again saved her husband from himself.

Couldn't the big jerk tell if he had the breath of a camel? Did his wife have to do everything? I was interrupted by my husband, who came out of the bedroom holding a sport shirt. "Honey," he grinned good-naturedly, "I hate to tell you this, but there's a ring around my collar."

I looked up and snapped, "What a coincidence! It matches the one around your neck!"

I don't know what made me say it . . . only the resentment of being in charge of everyone's welfare, I guess.

I had been naive. I should have realized it the night I showered, put perfume behind each knee, and heard my husband snore in the darkness . . . thus capping the first PG-rated Aviance Night in the history of cosmetics.

I dug out the *Fear of Buying* to find out in what other ways I was being exploited. It was revealing, to say the least. It said grocery shopping is one of the last of the little-known sciences in the world. All the experts know is that it is demanding; it requires great concentration and split-second timing.

For years, researchers have been trying to pin down why women buy as they do, and they have discovered that when a woman enters the store and her hands curl around a cart handle something happens.

Their "eyeblink rate" drops to fourteen a minute, putting them in a hypnoidal trance, which is the first stage of hypnosis. Some of them are even unable to distinguish friends who speak to them.

They cover an aisle in less than twenty seconds, spending on the average of ninety-three cents a minute. Everything in the store has been researched, designed, and color coded to make you buy it. A shopper doesn't stand a chance.

The real stress situation comes at the checkout. Assuming you are able to stave off impulse buying and stick to your list, the real test comes when you unload your groceries on the conveyor belt to be tallied. Here you have candy, gum, magazines, half-price items, special purchases, balloons, breath mints, cigarettes, and fountain pens. Steady now . . . if you can hang on until the bell of the cash register sounds, your blink rate will be up to forty-five a minute and the trance will be broken. You will be able to function once more on a normal level.

Just knowing what was happening to me proved to be of enormous help.

The next time I went to the supermarket I whipped through it like O. J. Simpson making his plane. At the checkout, however, I became uneasy as I saw a line. One woman was shuffling through her handbag trying to find identification for cashing her check.

I tossed a package of razor blades into my basket.

The next woman found a hole in her bag of brown sugar and we waited while the carry-out boy went back to get her a fresh package. I added a kite to my cart.

Two more to go.

The man had a cart full of bottles that he had been saving since glass was invented. It was his fault I bought the licorice whips.

The lady in front of me only had three items, but the register tape ran out and had to be replaced. Let the patio lights and the birdseed be on her conscience.

Finally, it was my turn. The clerk began to tally up my order when she asked, "Do you want that book or are you going to read it here?"

"I'll take it!" I said.

The register bell rang up the total and I came out of my trance. But it was too late. I had a paperback of *Looking for Mr. Goodbody* under my arm.

5 ♪✳♪♩

Looking for
Mr. Goodbody

The heroines of these books were always the same. A woman, disenchanted, going through life with a nose tissue in one hand and an absorbent towel in the other, decided to go it alone.

She was always tall with "long legs that stretched luxuriously under the sheets."

Her stomach was flat, "belying her three beautiful children."

She had never known ecstasy before.

She had also forgotten about the medical school degree she held until one day when she was lining the knife-and-fork drawer with Contact she ran across it.

She felt guilty about leaving her husband with the three children, $565 a month mortgage payments, a pregnant cat, and a toilet that ran, but "she has to start liking herself" and she can only do that by taking charge of her own life.

At my age, I didn't have the stamina for a rerun. I had begun to note that my body could only do one thing at a time—digest lunch or sit upright.

I wasn't ready to assume the responsibility for the oil changes in my car. I had no curiosity as to where furnace filters went. And besides, I was too domestically geared. (Once when I saw Tom Jones performing in Las Vegas and everyone was throwing their hotel room keys at him, I gave in to an impulse and threw mine. I didn't realize until two days later I had thrown him the key to our freezer.)

Displayed along with the books on married women with a "single" wish were the marriage manuals. They were a trip. I hadn't felt so frustrated since we tried to assemble a bicycle in the closet on Christmas Eve with two washers missing and the instructions written in Japanese.

It made us wonder what we did with our time before Dr. David Reuben invented sex. (One book, *How to Build a Relationship for Pennies in Your Own Home*, even came with an applause sign for over the bed.)

But it was the testimonials to freedom that intrigued me. In a way, I was filled with envy at the heroines . . . especially their zest for living. How my life paled by comparison. All my friends seemed to be moving on to new adventures. A lot of 'em had returned to work . . . some for the money, but most because they needed the rest. Some of my friends were returning to school and the rest of them were redecorating their empty nests with white shag and mirrors.

Me? I was in a holding pattern. None of mine had abandoned the nest and there was no hope in sight.

My daughter thought the red light on the stove was a hidden camera; my son led the life of a hamster; and my other son considered employment a fad like the hula hoop and mood rings.

They were all at the awkward age.

Too old for Dr. Dentons . . . too young for Dr. Scholl's.

Too old for curfews . . . too young for me to go to sleep until they were home.

Too old to advise . . . too young not to need it.

Too old to wash dishes . . . too young to stop eating.

Too old for an income tax exemption . . . too young for Medicare.

I wish I could be like Mayva. She didn't care what her kids did as long as they had clean hands.

It seemed like I had spent a lifetime giving, loving, and sharing. And you know what giving, loving, and sharing got me? It got me a drawer full of dirty pantyhose, a broken stereo, and a wet toothbrush every morning.

It got me a camera with sand in it, a blouse that died from acute perspiration, a sleeping bag with a broken zipper, and a transistor radio that "suddenly went dead, Mom, when it hit the pavement."

Other women my age didn't have kids wandering in and out of their closets like a discount house.

They borrowed my tennis racket, my car, my luggage, and my mouthwash. And my binoculars. I had almost forgotten about my binoculars. When I asked my son what happened to them he said, "They're in my room."

"Well, why don't you put them back where you got them?"

"Why would you want to hang on to a pair of broken binoculars?"

They were driving me crazy with their irregular hours, their slovenly habits, and their lack of responsibility around the house. Besides, they had reached the point where they had learned all of my adult expressions and were using them on me.

"Are you going to clean your room today?" I asked.

"We'll see."

"It worries me when you're out until all hours of the morning."

"Big people should not worry about little people. We can take care of ourselves."

"Well, I don't like it and I'm not going to put up with it."

"Don't use that tone. You're just tired and crabby. Why don't you take a little nap and we'll talk about it when you wake up."

I had visions of my being the oldest living mother in North

America with children at home. I'd be ninety-five and my daughter would be borrowing my last clean pair of SuppHose, my sons installing an automatic Genie door on the refrigerator . . . and every Mother's Day having them chip in and buy me another tooth.

Wanda would have handled it differently. Wanda was the heroine in the book I was reading, *Wanda's Cry of May Day*. What a woman! One day she just marched out of a pillowcase bingo game and into a singles salad bar, where she ordered a spinach salad with bacon bits. Within three minutes she had struck up a relationship with a man with a tossed salad, bean sprouts, and Thousand Island dressing. She slept with him before their salads digested.

The next day she got a job as vice president of a TV network and threw herself into her work. But she couldn't forget the tossed-salad-with-bean-sprouts-and-Thousand-Island-dressing encounter.

She tried. She produced a documentary in Greece, a miniseries in Russia, and got her Ph.D. at nights. TS with BS and TI called her every day, but she knew what she wanted.

Less than ninety-six pages later she married him, settled down, and on the last page was playing pillowcase bingo and for the first time in a long time felt good about herself.

My husband and I were at the beach when I finished the last chapter. I looked down. I had buried my varicose veins beneath the sand. The flies were going crazy over my hair spray.

My husband was sitting next to me swathed in beach towels to avoid the sun, balancing the checkbook.

It wasn't exactly the surf-and-sand scene in *From Here to Eternity*.

Okay, so I was content to live vicariously through Wanda and all the others, but was it wrong to want to shift to the next plateau of my life? I approached my daughter with the problem.

"I don't know how to tell you this, but you are keeping me from shifting gears and going on to the next phase of my wonderfulness. Another year or so and it may be too late."

"What are you trying to say?"

"I guess what I'm trying to say is there are a lot of colleges away from home that provide an opportunity for a person to mingle with people from all kinds of different and exciting backgrounds. In an atmosphere of this sort, there is room to grow and to mature. Isolation from family usually forces one to take charge of one's own life, make one's own priorities, and carry them out without interference. Do you know what I am trying to say?"

She put her hand on mine. "If you wanted to go away to school, Mom, why didn't you say so? We'll manage. We'll eat out a lot."

"You don't understand," I said, biting my lip. "Life is divided into many cycles. We have an infant cycle, a childhood cycle, a teenage cycle, a married cycle, and the Grape-Nuts cycle. The end of each cycle is a little frightening because it means change and change means adjusting, but one has to move on, do you understand?"

She nodded and I felt reassured.

"It's a big decision to enter into the next cycle, but if one keeps in mind there are friends who are supportive, striking out on your own isn't bad."

"If you and Dad wanted your own apartment," she said, "why didn't you say so? We never dreamt we were getting in your way. This house has to be a lot for you. What you're saying is right. If you feel like you want to come back from time to time, we'll all still be here."

I was locked in forever with a countertop of dirty glasses, nose tissue left in jeans pockets, and corn pads that patched the water beds.

"You should be putting your own life together," I said, making one last stab at it. "You have to learn that clean pantyhose do not perpetuate themselves and the meaning of life is more than an herbal connection. If you go away to school you will be responsible for yourself. You'll find self-reliance, independence, feet! Yes, feet. There's a whole group of people out there you've never met before. They're called pedestrians."

"You are saying you want me to bug off? Split?"

"I wouldn't have phrased it that way."

"Am I getting close?"

"Your father and I love you, but it's time to move on."

"I understand," she said. "After this semester ends, I'll start shopping around for a college farther away from home."

Why was it every time I did something that was good for the kids, I felt rotten?

While in the library returning *Wendy's Pool Table Fetish and Other Fantasies* I met my friend Nancy.

We talked about my holding pattern and the exodus of my first-born, then she smiled and said, "It should be apparent what is wrong with you. You're going through your midlife crisis."

"It sounds redundant," I said.

"Believe me," said Nancy, "I know where you're coming from. You feel used up, unfulfilled, unappreciated. Your life is in the Twilight Zone. And you live in fear. Fear that your children are writing a sequel to *Mommie Dearest*. Fear of dying after you've just eaten a crummy, tasteless salad with a low-calorie dressing. Fear of going to a partner-swapping party and no one wants to swap with you."

"That's not true," I said. "I may complain but I have a fulfilling life."

"I've seen your social calendar," said Nancy. "It looks like it belongs to a shut-in. Have you never awakened in the morning, looked into a mirror, and said aloud, 'I am never going to be Ambassador to Uganda. My legs will never fit into a boot without a zipper. I will never successfully grow a Boston fern or win the *Reader's Digest* Sweepstakes. I am built like a caftan'?"

"Nancy," I said. "Whatever I am, I do not talk to myself. And I do not live in fear of anything. I am a perfectly well-adjusted person."

"Look," she said. "I've got a book that not only tells you what crisis is going to appear next in your life, it tells you how to deal with it. It's called *Packages* and each chapter deals with one little bundle after another of what is in store for you as you reach a certain age. It's like seeing your future before it gets here."

I didn't think about Nancy or the book until a few days later. As I brushed my teeth, I looked into my reflection in the mirror and for no apparent reason said out loud, "Breathes there a woman with soul so dead / Who never to herself hath said . . . My God! I'm talking to myself."

I went to the library and checked out *Packages* by Gayle Teehee.

6

Is There Life After Packages?

If there's anything my life had been, it had been predictable. You could set your clock by it. Acne at twelve, marriage at twenty-two, labor pains at twenty-six, Miss Clairol at thirty, Sara Lee at thirty-five, and turtleneck sweaters at forty.

I certainly didn't need a book to tell me the twenties had been traumatic, the thirties illusion-shattering, the forties restless and the fifties . . . my God, only two pages titled "Resignation" jammed between turtleneck sweaters and the index.

Packages didn't waste words. (I guess they figured there wasn't time to waste.) They said I was living in an age of fear. Fear of unfulfillment. Fear of what people thought of me. Fear of poor health. Fear of old age.

That wasn't true. I didn't fear old age. I was just becoming increasingly aware of the fact that the only people who said old age was beautiful were usually twenty-three years old.

In my heart I just refused to believe that Shirley Temple Black was toilet-trained. Oh, there were a few moments of sensitivity. On a trip to renew my driver's license the man behind the counter

328

asked the date of my birth in a loud voice. They tell me I slammed him against the wall, locked my forearm against his throat, and shouted, "Let us just say I'm somewhere between estrogen and death!"

Packages said I had a fear of not knowing what life held for me . . . fear of being abandoned . . . fear of being alone. Were they kidding? As a woman who once named the NFL in an alienation suit, I wrote the book on loneliness. When someone cloned Howard Cosell, I'd begin to worry.

Fear of loss of interest in sex (that was scarcely a problem to a couple who viewed an R-rated movie for the plot) and a fear of phobias.

I slammed the book shut. It was obvious. I was late for my crisis and it had started without me. Why, I didn't have a phobia in the world.

I was feeling rather pleased with myself when my daughter bounded into the house, threw her car keys on the table, and said, "Guess who's pregnant?"

"Give me a hint."

"Bunny's mother, Barfy."

"Get serious," I laughed. "Barfy is a year older than I am and two years younger than Mickey Mouse."

"Tell her. She thinks she's Bugs Bunny. I think it's neat. How come you don't have another baby? In a few years we'll all be gone. What will you do to replace us?"

"I'll get measles."

"A lot of my girlfriends' mothers are getting pregnant. They say having babies makes you feel ten years younger."

"Than what? And what girlfriends' mothers? Name names!"

"There's Wheezie's mother, Wizard. Cooky's mother, Corky, and possibly Holly's mother, Berry."

When she was gone, I slumped dejectedly into a chair. I had never been so depressed in my life. What was happening? I had an antique quilt younger than Berry. So there was one fear of midlife I hadn't counted on—Guinnessaphobia: the fear of having a baby after forty.

I couldn't do it. I didn't care what they said about caboose children being such a bonus. If it happened, I'd adjust, but under anesthesia I'd deny I ever said it.

I was too tired for a new family. I fell asleep having my teeth cleaned. I dozed at parties that dragged on until ten o'clock. I couldn't cross my legs after a big meal. One 2 A.M. feeding and I'd have bags under my eyes that would take surgery to correct.

My intellect was dulled. I didn't know any more why God wasn't married, what the inside of a volleyball looked like, or how come my biscuit dough never laughed when you punched it.

I had been there. There were no surprises. I'd spent three rainy days with three kids with chickenpox with a broken washer. I'd fainted from blowing up swimming pools. I'd traveled through three states with a bag of wet diapers under the seat and two kids in the back arguing over a piece of gum with lint on it.

I'd wrestled with strollers on escalators, fights with holy water, and hysteria on the first day of school.

A few days later I saw Barfy in the supermarket. She had that pregnant stance, like a kangaroo wearing earth shoes. She looked tired.

"Barfy!" I said solicitously, staring at her stomach. "What happened?"

"Would you believe I'm carrying it for a friend?"

"I'm sorry," I said. "It was just such a shock."

"It's okay. I get a lot of dumb questions. Like 'Good heavens, are you still walking around with that baby?' "

"I thought you were on the pill."

"We all were. Wizard, Corky, and Berry. There are no guarantees, you know. Every day someone is suing the pharmaceutical companies."

"No guarantees," I said numbly. "I'll bet your family was surprised."

"They're ecstatic," she said. "They can hardly wait until it gets here. There are all kinds of promises to change it, feed it, and play with it, but I'm afraid it'll be like Winnie's baby. You remember Winnie. Her kids promised her she wouldn't have to raise an arthritic finger after the baby was born. She was suspicious, but at age forty-three, she finally gave in. When the baby was born she called her daughter to look at it. "Well," said Winnie, "what do you think of your new responsibility?" Her daughter looked at the baby, shrugged and said, "I changed my mind. I'd rather have a new Bee Gees album."

"Gosh, Barfy, isn't it weird being in the doctor's waiting room with all the young girls?"

"Sure, but things have changed nowadays since we had our babies. They breathe them out now. Everything is natural and your husband is with you throughout the birth. Remember how it used to be?"

"Do I ever! I became hysterical and frightened and begged for sedation. And that was just the first prenatal visit."

"It's a whole new ballgame," sighed Barfy. "Super-absorbent throwaways, shoulder slings to carry them around, no bottles to fiddle with, and a new relaxed atmosphere."

"I'm sorry, Barfy, but I can't imagine a delivery without a hairdresser in attendance. That is just too primitive for me."

That night I had trouble sleeping. All kinds of pictures flashed before my eyes . . . swallowing a diaper pin at age sixty-five, having my baby push me around in a stroller at the zoo, napping during delivery, receiving a pacemaker for Mother's Day, fighting the kid for the baby food, spanking my toddler for coloring on my Social Security check, becoming the first Medicare subscriber to put in a claim for delivery.

The fact was I didn't want to look my age, but I didn't want to act the age I wanted to look either. I also wanted to grow old enough to understand that sentence.

There was definitely a youth cult in this country where people worshiped at the shrine of taut skin and shiny hair. Where only concave stomachs made the billboards and second young wives were royalty.

If you had a wrinkle, you took a snip.

If something sagged, you took a tuck.

If it jiggled, firm it up.

If it stuck out, suck it in.

If it was gray, touch it up.

New faces began to emerge among my old friends. Faces that looked like masks. In fact, I had seen more wrinkles on a baby's bottom. I remember how excited I got one day when I discovered a cosmetic stick that would erase away the lines. I erased my entire face.

According to *Packages* you were supposed to have a no-panic approach to physical aging, but it wasn't easy when all around you emphasis was put on how old you looked.

I didn't face up to my age until one afternoon when I was lying on the sofa half asleep, half absorbed in the old movie *Sunset Boulevard*, starring Gloria Swanson and Bill Holden. I had seen it a dozen times, but loved it. It was the big scene. The one where Bill Holden is leaving the aging movie star, Norma Desmond. A line in his speech nearly brought me off the sofa. He said, "There's nothing tragic about being fifty, Norma, unless you're trying to look like twenty-five."

FIFTY! NORMA DESMOND HAD BEEN FIFTY ALL THOSE YEARS? I had remembered her as ninety-seven if she was a day.

I watched in horror as she descended the staircase, the camera grinding away, the lights on her face. She was only a baby.

I turned on the bathroom light and scrutinized myself carefully.

One was always led to believe that aging was a gradual process. It just wasn't true. I went to bed one night and in the morning was struck with all the diseases of the decade I had to live through for the next ten years.

Overnight, I developed a case of LOSS OF MENU. At first I blamed candle failure. Then small print. When I had to drop the menu on the floor to see it or ask the waiter to back into a far wall until I focused, it became apparent I needed glasses.

The next to strike was REUNION ANXIETY. I had dreaded it for years, but no one could have prepared me for the moment I arrived at my reunion and one after another said "You look fantastic!"

Everyone knows when you are twenty, the greeting is "How are you?," and when you're thirty it's "What are you up to these days?" But when you're over the hill, the standard greeting is "You look fantastic!" Sometimes it's accompanied by the word "Really!," which is supposed to offer you reassurance.

PREMATURE NOSTALGIA was predictable. Day by day I watched my high school years being satirized in TV sitcoms. My clothing came back into style and the music of my youth was being imitated and satirized. For a while I tried looking blank when someone mentioned Patti Page, but it fooled no one.

The HAVE I TAKEN MY PILL YET FETISH was the hardest to adjust to. One morning I looked at the window ledge over the sink and there was a line of pills to keep me operational. They never seemed to make any difference, they were just there . . . little bottles of pills with childproof caps. Despite them I still suffered from leg cramps all night when I wore heels to a party.

My case of MEMORY DEFICIENCY became a classic. I got on a salt kick. One week I ran out of salt and made a mental note to buy it. For every week after that for about two years, I bought a box of salt because I couldn't remember if I had bought it originally. Every time I tried to remember the age of my middle child,

I had to go back to the year of his birth and count up. Memory deficiency got so bad for me, I forgot to repeat a piece of gossip I swore on my Grandmother's Grave never to divulge.

But the worst disease of my midlife was a case of INSUBOR-DINATE BODY. In my youth, my brain would say to my feet, "Take that laundry to the second floor." NOT ANY MORE. The legs rebelled and I stacked so many things at the bottom of the stairs I nearly killed myself.

I must have read the chapter on Resignation a hundred times and each time became more depressed. It sounded like I was approaching the prime of my senility.

We were going into the middle of July when my daughter announced she was going away to school in the northern part of the state. She was happy about it.

I confided to my hairdresser, Mr. Steve, about her decision: "Isn't that just like children? You devote your life to them . . . spoon-feed them, sit with them all night under a vaporizer, pack them with vitamins, straighten their teeth, curl their hair, care for them, love them, and they reach twenty or so and pick up and leave you."

"I thought that's what you wanted," he said.

"It's not what I wanted. It's what comes with my midlife cycle. Don't you understand? My life is all arranged for me. At a certain age we must shift gears and go on to the next phase of our life. I have no control over it."

"Of course you have control over your life," he said, swinging me around in my chair. "Tell me, what sign were you born under?"

I shrugged. "My birthday is February twenty-first."

"Umm, I thought so," he said. "Pisces. That explains everything. Forget all this mishmash about your life being predictable. I tell you you can control your own destiny if you just heed your sign. I swear by a book called *Get Off Your Cusp and Live!* by Jeanne Vixon. The moment I looked at you, I knew your moon was in her second decan, which added a secret longing to your Neptunian impregnability, and that the latter decan is augmented by tempestuous Mars, which offers energy and immeasurable support."

"What does that mean?"

"Either you start using moisturizer around your eyes, sweetie, or lay in a supply of wood filler!"

7 ♒

Get Off Your Cusp and Live!

Ever since I read that Eva Braun (Hitler's mistress), Judas Iscariot, and Anne Boleyn shared my zodiac sign, I could never get too choked up about Astrology.

Mr. Steve meant well, but he didn't know what a loser I was. My sun never rose on my sign. My planets were always conspiring behind my back. And my destiny always read like it had been out in the natal sun too long.

Maybe I was just bitter, but it always seemed like other people got the good signs. Their horoscopes always read "Popularity and untold wealth will haunt you. There is no getting away from it. You are irresistible to every sign in the zodiac. Give in and enjoy."

Not mine. It was always an ominous warning like "Watch your purse." "Your high school acne was only in remission, and will return the fifteenth of the month." "Don't become discouraged by your friends who will take advantage of you."

Somehow, I always felt if Mother had held on a little longer—a good month and a half—things would have been different for me.

336

Oh, I had faith in the predictions. It was just that my interpretation of my sign was not always the way it turned out. For example:

Prediction: "You get a chance today to provide guidance and inspiration."
Fact: I chaperoned thirty fourth-graders on a tour of a meat-packing plant.
Prediction: "One you thought had abandoned you is back in the picture."
Fact: We found a roach under the sink.
Prediction: "Married or single, this is a 'power' time for you!"
Fact: The heat went off for four hours.
Prediction: "You have a unique way of expressing yourself, and you could gain much satisfaction by writing."
Fact: I wrote a check to have the septic tank cleaned.

Mr. Steve didn't tell me that keeping up with my stars was a full-time job. The daily forecast in the paper was brief and scanty. I had to buy a magazine to find out my food forecast, one for my sex forecast, one for my fashion predictions, another for my travel, and still another for my decoration sense, color selection, and perfume.

I wanted to clean out my refrigerator one day but didn't dare because my sign said avoid the color green.

I canceled trips, put off foot surgery, didn't invite Virgos to my party, and on the advice of my horoscope did not handle money for an entire month. (If it hadn't been for my charge card, I'd have died.) There was so much to learn about myself. I was absolutely fascinating. I discovered women born under my sign were dynamic, confident, and into asparagus. I was an orange person, trusting, French provincial with boundless energy, and long-waisted.

One evening at a jewelry party, one of the brownies I was serving dropped on the carpet. I reached over, picked it off the floor, popped it in my mouth, and said, "A fuzzy brownie never hurt anyone."

A woman I knew only as Nicky looked deep into my eyes and nodded knowingly. "Only a Pisces on the cusp would say that."

I asked her how she knew. She said certain traits belong to certain signs. According to my birth date, I was born on a rising sign which made my destiny special. I was a wonderful home-maker, excellent cook, and fine seamstress. That wasn't a destiny. It was a sentence!

There had to be something wrong. What happened to dynamic, confident, and asparagus?

"You're on the rise," she said, "and the sun and the moon are in the direct line with the tides."

I felt like my tide had just gone out.

A cook?

Everyone knew I always threatened my children with "If you don't shape up, you go to bed *with* dinner."

A homemaker?

I wanted for Christmas what Phyllis Diller always wanted . . . an oven that flushed.

A seamstress?

I always considered a fallen button as God's way of telling us the shirt was wrong.

"You're born under a wonderful sign," Nicky gushed. "You are gentle and expect to have the least and the last. You end up with the bent fork, but you never complain. You buy a three-piece weekender outfit with a skirt and a pair of slacks and burn a hole in the jacket, but you don't care. You always come out of the rest room dragging a piece of toilet tissue on your shoe, but you don't mind."

"Why don't I mind?" I asked.

"Because it's your nature. Why I know of one woman born under your natal sign who had a son at camp. On parents' visitation day, she had flu and was seven months pregnant, but she drove the two hundred miles along a dusty road. She had a flat tire and lost her way twice. But she kept going. She made it to the camp and when all the boys were introducing their parents, her son—who was going through a difficult time of his life relating to parents—said, 'My Mom couldn't come.' Do you know what she did?"

"She killed him," I said hopefully.

"She just shrugged and said, 'I could have predicted it because my son is on the rise and I am on the cusp.' My dear, people under your sign inherit the earth."

I didn't want the earth. I wanted dynamic. Instead, I had fallen heir to the Klutzism Sign. Stumbling around life fifty-two weeks out of every year rubbing stains off my sweater, putting the wrong dates on checks, and never being able to trust myself to run the course in Better China with a shoulder bag.

What kind of a future did I have to look forward to? I locked all the doors in the car and left the top down. Broke my tooth on a marshmallow and got sucked up in my son's hair dryer and sprained my shoulder.

I liked me better when I didn't know who I was, what I was, or where I was going. Besides, my daughter had gone off to school taking with her all the small appliances, furniture, linens, bedding, TV set, typewriter, and staples.

My husband noticed it right away. "You let her pack off everything we've worked thirty years to accumulate?"

I shrugged. "What can I tell you? My sun is on the rise."

I found myself spending more time in the kitchen. Maybe I was creative and there was something in my personality I had overlooked. I bought a food processor and shredded myself to death.

I bought a microwave oven and stood by helplessly while my son's space maintainer turned to liquid when he left it in a sandwich I was reheating. I got out of the kitchen before I hurt myself.

I bought a sewing machine that did everything but answer the door, and decided to make a jacket. The darts faced the wrong way, the buttonholes were ahead of their time (no button had been manufactured for it yet). The lining grew each evening as I slept. It had been laundered three times and never been worn.

In stitching up new curtains one afternoon for my daughter's vacated bedroom, a book fell to the floor. It was called *Far Out and Far East* by Edith Marishna. On the cover was a picture of a woman sitting cross-legged, her turban-covered head tilted backward, staring toward the sky.

I knew my daughter was fascinated with Transcendental Meditation. In fact, she had even taken me to the Golden Temple of Zucchini one day for lunch. It was one of those pure-food restaurants near the local college campus where everything was either freshly squeezed or grown before your eyes. We ordered the organic bean sprouts jammed between two hydroponic tomatoes. "I think I'm going to go crazy and order a cranberry malt," I said.

A man with a turban appeared at our table and elevated the malt over his head as if it were a chalice. I felt positively sanctified until I discovered my lunch contained 1200 calories.

I had never meditated. Oh, once when I paid thirty dollars for a Halston scarf I slipped into a slight hypnotic state. But I had never meditated like the girl on the cover. The book jacket said everyone needed to create an organically oriented womb of tranquility in which to grow spiritually and pull your life together. It said I could have inner peace by controlling my own destiny. It was in my hands. I could be in control of myself by taking a few minutes out of each day and reciting a special word over and over again. The word was called a mantra.

At dinner that night my husband's fork poised over a bowl of green slime. "What's this?" he asked.

"It's puréed lettuce. I put the wrong setting on the food processor. It's easier if you eat it with a spoon."

"Do you have any idea how long it has been since we have eaten anything whole? I never see whole food any more. If I am not going to see whole food, the least you can do is to label it. Isn't there a federal law that you have to label what you are eating?"

"You don't have to shout."

"Someone should shout around here. Patterns all over the table every night, needles everywhere. Appliances whirring day and night. Weird things growing restless in the refrigerator. It's driving me crazy."

As I sat there listening to him rant, a thought occurred to me. He wasn't meek. He wasn't gentle. He wasn't resigned to pain. He certainly wasn't domestic and didn't have a long waist. AND OUR BIRTHDAY WAS ONLY TWO DAYS APART. WE WERE BORN UNDER THE SAME SIGN!

On my way to bed I picked up *Far Out and Far East* and turned on the bedside light.

It was time to get off my cusp and start controlling my own life. I was going to have inner peace if I had to break a few heads to do it.

8 ♪✳♪✳♪

Raising Consciousness in Your Own Home for Fun and Profit

For years, I have studied the phenomenon of the mother who sits down for a moment to get off her feet. From all I've been able to gather, a message goes out over an invisible network that flashes to the world "Mother is in a sitting position. Proceed and de-sit."

At that moment the doorbell will ring, children will appear holding vital parts of their anatomy, the dog will dig his paws insistently into a leg, a husband will call impatiently for help, a phone will register its fifteenth ring, a pot will boil over, a buzzer will sound, or faucets will go on all over the house, and a loud voice will shriek, "I'm telling."

The "Mother is sitting" phenomenon is probably one of the reasons meditation never really got a foothold on mothers when they were the ones who needed it the most.

All I know is I was possibly the only woman in the world ded-

342

icated to inner peace and tranquility who would end up with varicose veins of the neck from shouting.

"Tranquility" also presented another problem. It said I would need a mantra . . . a word that when repeated over and over again would transport me to a level of calmness and give me untold energy.

I called my daughter at school. "Did you get a mantra with *Far Out and Far East?*"

"Of course I didn't get a mantra. Even if I did, I couldn't let you use it. Each one is personal and given only to that person. They're secret. You have to buy them."

"How much do they cost?" I asked.

"It depends. Sometimes a couple hundred dollars."

I had no intention of paying more for a word than I paid for our first car. In discussing this one day at the supermarket with Natalie, a friend, she said she had a mantra that had barely been used. She told me she had only chanted it for three months prior to her divorce and would let it go for $12.50.

"What's wrong with it?" I asked suspiciously.

"Nothing. It's just that I couldn't do housework with my legs permanently folded. Trust me, it works. Whenever you come face to face with a situation that makes you tense, just sit down wherever you are, cross your legs, turn your palms to the ceiling, and recite your mantra over and over again."

The next day I went into my son's bedroom and was knocked against the wall by an odor. It took twenty minutes to track it down, but I finally found it. Under a stack of clothes on the chair was a doggy bag holding a chicken leg and a breast he brought home from his birthday dinner. His birthday was celebrated two weeks ago.

I felt like a fool, but I sat cross-legged in his bed, turned my palms toward the ceiling, and began to mumble my word. When the washer buzzer went off, instead of running out to get the softener in before the final rinse, I kept repeating my word.

Afterward, I felt rather refreshed and for the first time in a long time sat down to a full breakfast of orange juice, French toast, and coffee.

Later in the morning, I discovered one of the kids had left the phone off the hook. Instead of biting the phone cord in half, I just sat cross-legged in the middle of the floor, meditated, and had a cookie and a glass of milk.

That afternoon when I went to get into the car and discovered someone had left my car door open and the light had run my battery down, I squatted, recited my mantra, and was revitalized again. My newfound calm was rewarded with a piece of banana cake. When my husband came home I was eating a bowl of potato chips and drinking a diet cola.

"Aren't you pigging out a little more than usual?"

"Oh, c'mon," I said. "Maybe I have been a little more relaxed than usual but . . ."

"If you get any more relaxed, you won't be able to fit through a door."

"I don't care what you say. I've got my peace of mind."

"It's probably the only thing you can get into."

"That is all you know. How many women do you know who can still slip into the clothes they wore when they were newly married?" (It was true. Just that morning, I got into my maternity underwear and they slipped right over my hips.)

Even the boys began to notice that I was growing again. The combination of staying in the house, being alone so much, and being relaxed had turned me into an inflatable.

One afternoon when my son came bounding into the house he said, "Sorry, Mom, I didn't know you were meditating."

"I'm not."

"Then why are you sitting cross-legged on the couch?"

"I'm not sitting cross-legged. Those are my hips."

That night when I stepped out of the shower, I looked into the mirror. The soufflé of my youth had fallen. Edith Marishna and her energy. As I sat in my lotus position, I was struck by a brutal truth. It would take an Act of God to get me to my feet.

It was discouraging. Just as soon as I got my head together, my body went. It wasn't fair. All my life I had dieted. I was bored talking about it . . . bored thinking about it—and tired of planning my next meal.

As I sat there sucking in my stomach and seeing nothing move, the twelfth major religion of the world began to form in my mind.

A religion founded in the twentieth century based on the four ignoble truths:

BLOUSES WORN OUTSIDE THE SLACKS FOOL NO ONE.

ONE-SIZE-FITS-ALL IS AN INCOMPLETE SENTENCE.

IF THERE'S LIFE AFTER WHIPPED CREAM, IT'S IN THIGH CITY.

STARCHING A CAFTAN NEVER SOLVES ANYTHING.

I would call my new religion FATSU. The disciples would be every woman who has ever gone to bed hungry and who sought a destiny of pantyhose that bagged at the knee.

The day of worship would be Monday, what else?

And the daily chant would be MaryTylerMoore . . . Mary-TylerMoore . . . MaryTylerMoore . . .

I could almost see Jean Nieditch standing in the middle of thunder and lightning while the seven FATSU commandments were being flashed on a head of lettuce:

THOU SHALT NOT PUNISH THYSELF BY TRYING ON A BATHING SUIT WEARING KNEE HI'S.

THOU SHALT NOT CONSIDER GRAVY AND HOLLANDAISE SAUCE A BEVERAGE.

THOU SHALT NOT KILL FOR CHOCOLATE.

THOU SHALT NOT STEAL HALLOWEEN CANDY FROM THY CHIL-
DREN.

THOU SHALT HAVE NO OTHER MIRRORS BEFORE THEE BUT
MY SPECIAL ONES.

THOU SHALT NOT TAKE THE NAME OF COTTAGE CHEESE IN
VAIN.

THOU SHALT NOT COVET THY NEIGHBOR'S DESSERT.

Banded together, we would surpass the Shinto, Confucian, Hindu, and even the Moslem religions in numbers. Our disciples would roam the earth spreading the word: starvation. Maybe once a year we'd have a sacrifice by throwing a butterscotch sundae off a cliff. On that day we'd all fast, of course.

We'd separate our beliefs from the state, interfering only when they tried to take away artificial sweeteners.

My followers were immortalizing me in two panels of stained glass (with a wide load on them) when my husband interrupted my meditation and brought me back to reality.

"How much do you weigh now?"

I stiffened. "There are three things you never ask a woman: her age, her weight, and the date on the newspapers lining her kitchen cupboards."

"You really have spread out in the past few months. If you ask me you're spending entirely too much time sitting around the house chanting and eating. You should get out more . . . and get some exercise."

I knew it. I wondered when he'd get around to his pitch on jogging. If there is anything more sanctimonious than a man who has been jogging for eight years I don't know what it is. He wouldn't be happy until he got the entire family running around in the darkness being chased by vicious dogs and unmarked cars. Joggers were all alike, running by the house every morning like a Fruit of the Loom pageant. In all the months they huffed and puffed by the house, four abreast, drenched in their own sweat, their chests heaving in and out, I had never once seen one of them smile.

No, if I were going to lose weight, I'd do it my own way. Evelyn had a new diet she was talking about at card club. It was supposed to be a real breakthrough for dieters. I think she called it "Is Something Eating You? Or Vice Versa." After all, Evelyn was a professional dieter. There wasn't one she hadn't tried. During her lifetime she had lost 3,476 pounds. Most of it in her neck and her bust.

In her kitchen was an entire bookshelf of captivating titles . . . all current best sellers. There were:

The Neurosis Cookbook. You never outgrow your need for paranoia. Two hundred pages of new, low-calorie meals for encounter-group picnics and postnatal-depression snacks.

Did You Ever See a Fat Gerbil? This was a provocative title on how sex could make you thin by burning up 31,955 calories a year. By kissing three times a day (at nine calories each) and engaging in two amorous interludes a week (at 212 calories) you could (if you excuse the expression) conceivably lose 9.13 pounds a year.

The Mexican Quick Loss Program was relatively simple to follow. You traveled to Mexico, drank a glass of water, and ate a head of lettuce. Wear gym shoes.

There were scores more, from Dr. Witherall's flavored ice diet to *How to Face a Visit from Your Mother on 1200 Calories a Day.*

I picked up *Is Something Eating You? Or Vice Versa.* "Does this diet really work?" I asked Evelyn.

She wrinkled her brow. "Is that the one by Dr. Barnhiser where when you get so hungry you can't stand it, you get in the car and drive until you hit something?"

"I don't think so," I said. "It's the one where your emotions dictate what you eat."

"I remember," she said. "I lost five pounds and three friends on that one. Listen, if you're really serious about losing weight, why don't you go to the LUMP meetings?"

"LUMP?" I said slowly.

"It stands for Lose by Unappetizing Meals and Pressure."

"Is it a group therapy thing?"

"You got it," said Evelyn. "Once a week you go to a public meeting where you fall on your knees in front of the group and confess your caloric sins. The leader is either filled with disgust at the sight of you or rewards you with a liver malt. If you have gained, you must carry a bowling ball around for a week."

"That sounds reasonable," I said. "Maybe I'll go."

The El Gordo chapter of LUMP met once a week within a few blocks of me. I introduced myself to a group of members who were in the hallway popping water pills and removing their jewelry before they weighed in.

Following an X-rated movie—*The Birth of an Éclair*—our leader, Frances, launched into a discussion of the much-maligned staple of the LUMP diet . . . liver.

"In order for the diet to work," she said, "everyone has to consume at least sixteen ounces of liver a week." She didn't care how we disguised it.

Early in my life I had made a pact with myself. I would never eat anything that moved when I cooked it, excited the dog, or inflated upon impact with my teeth.

I didn't mind starving with LUMP's diet, but couldn't bring myself to eat anything that, when dropped on the floor, you found yourself apologizing to.

I was in LUMP's program for three weeks, during which time I did everything with liver but put a dress on it. It didn't work.

Besides, I had only lost a pound and a half—which I attributed to my less frequent trips to the refrigerator (which were slowed down when I dropped the bowling ball on my foot).

The solution to losing weight was obvious to me. I'd have to stop meditating. It was too bad, because I really enjoyed sitting cross-legged in the middle of a tense situation in open defiance of bells, buzzers, screams, threats, and the secret society to get mothers on their feet.

It was with deep regret that I called my friend, Donna, to see if she wanted to buy my mantra for $8.50.

As I left Donna, she was sitting cross-legged on the floor, her palms toward the ceiling, her head tilted to the sky, chanting "PAULNEWMANPAULNEWMANPAULNEWMANPAULNEW . . ."

I left quickly before I changed my mind.

9 ᔈᔈᔈ

The Complete
Book of Jogging

Jim Fixit's legs were the first thing I saw every morning and the last thing I saw every night.

They were on the cover of his best seller, *The Complete Book of Jogging*. For the past two years my husband had followed the gospel according to St. James Fixit. He ate Jim's cereal, took Jim's warming-up exercises, adopted Jim's form, ran with Jim in races whenever he could, and occasionally—when he thought no one was looking—lived out his fantasy by posing his legs in front of the mirror like the legs on the cover of the book.

When he wasn't poring over the pages of the book, it was on the nightstand by our bed next to the liniment.

My husband knew how I felt about physical fitness. I hated skiing or any other sport where there was an ambulance waiting at the bottom of the hill. As a golfer with a slice, I found the game lonely. And it became apparent to me long ago that if God had wanted me to play tennis, He would have given me less leg and more room to store the ball.

Despite this, I knew it was only a matter of time before he

350

pointed out that my inner peace had brought me outer fat and tried to convert me to jogging.

Joggers were like that. In no other sport were the participants so evangelistic. They talked of nothing else.

The children of runners would huddle in groups and whisper: "Who told you about jogging? Your mother or your father? Or did you learn about it in the gutter?"

Whenever a group of four would gather, someone would open the conversation with "Where were you and what were you doing when you heard that Bill Rogers won the Boston Marathon? I remember I was washing my hair when the bulletin came over the news."

One night I was dancing with one of my husband's friends when he whispered, "Sure, I could go jogging with you this weekend, but would you respect me in the morning?"

They bragged about their blisters, their Achilles tendonitis, their chondromalacia of the knee, their foot bursitis, shin splints, pulled leg muscles, back pains, and muscle cramps. Their stories made you sick you missed World War II.

I watched the joggers every morning from my kitchen window. They looked like an organized death march as they ran by gasping, perspiring, stumbling, their faces contorted with pain. I never had the urge to "cut in."

One night as I crawled into bed, I inadvertently set my root beer float on top of Jim Fixit's book. Horrified, my husband grabbed the book and wiped the jacket off with the sleeve of his pajama. "What kind of an animal are you?"

I thought then he might launch into his sanctimonious how-good-you'd-feel-if-you-got-up-at-five-thirty-and-ran-ten-miles speech, but he didn't.

I continued to reward my frustrations with food and he continued to run every day and brag about his jogger's elbow (which he got when he sideswiped a stop sign at an intersection). One morning when he returned from his run he asked brightly, "Guess who I saw running in the park?"

Before I could answer he said, "Louise Cremshaw. Remember her?"

Louise Cremshaw! We used to follow her around for shade. "Of course I remember Louise," I said. "She was the only girl in our class who had to have the sleeves let out in her graduation gown."

"Not any more," he said, grabbing for a box of Jim Fixit's cereal. "She's been running and she's a real knockout."

That did it. "Okay," I said, throwing down the dish towel. "You've won. You've penetrated the barrier of good sense. I am yours. I will start to jog. Just tell me which chapters to start reading in *The Complete Book of Jogging*."

"There are a lot of books you can read," he hedged. "There's *Inner Walking* by Tad Victor. He's the guy who wrote *Inner Bowling, Inner Roller Skating*, and *Inner Gooney Golf*."

"What's wrong with my reading your *Complete Book of Jogging?*"

"Wait until you're serious about it. Besides, you have to learn to walk before you can jog."

Inner Walking said there were two people within my body (I certainly had the stomach for it). The outer part of me was instinctively competitive. But the inner part of me needed work. I had to teach myself to concentrate and to remove self-doubts about myself and my abilities.

It said a lot of sports people used the inner theory that said within you there is a better you than you think there is. I read about the skiers who subscribed to this theory and didn't regard bumps as adversaries, but as friends. They would ski over each one saying, "Thank you, bump."

Or bowlers who threw a gutter ball would say, "Thank you, gutter, for being there." Or the gooney golf players who didn't always make the cup but were grateful that the ball didn't land in the middle of the expressway. What they were really saying is that I had to be psyched up for walking and not be discouraged.

When a boulder lodged in my shoe, I said, "Thank you, rock, for nearly severing my toe from my foot."

When a car with a bumper sticker that read "I found it" nearly ran me off the road, I said, "Thank you, car, for not strapping me to your hood to show everyone what you found today."

As I ran into the driveway, my husband said, "I thought you were supposed to be walking."

"I was," I panted, "until I ran out of Twinkies to hold off the dogs."

He said I was ready for Jim Fixit's book.

That night he brought it to the dining-room table and gently placed it before me like a chalice. In keeping with the moment, I genuflected and said a little prayer.

The big thing about jogging was that it was a pure sport. It was just you in a little pair of raggy gym shoes, a pair of shorts, and your own patch of lonely road. That was beautiful. Like a Rod McKuen poem.

It might have worked if someone had put out a pair of running trunks with tummy and thigh control, but there was no way I was going to show my legs from the knees up. I popped for a sixty-five-dollar pink velour warm-up suit.

The shoes were a little trickier. There were 147 styles, each of them priced from forty to eighty dollars. I chose a pair that gave me no arch support whatsoever but had pink shoelaces (can you believe my luck?) exactly the same shade as my pink velour warm-up suit. My handbag matched close enough.

The real zinger was the patch of lonely road. The street in front of my house was definitely out, as all the walkers were running from the dogs and the cars.

My husband told me to start a "training diary" of my distances and times and he would take me to the bike path by the canal.

The stitch in my side was sharp and persistent. I remembered that Mr. Fixit said, "No one ever died from a side stitch" and breathed deeply. I tossed in, "Thank you, stitch!"

"What did you say?" asked my husband.

I told him I had a stitch in my side, but if I considered it a friend it would go away.

He said it was probably my sunglasses that I had looped over my pants gouging me and that once we got out of the car the pain would go away.

We parked the car and I looked at the bike path. I had seen lonelier patches of road leading from Disneyland after the Fourth of July fireworks.

"Who are all these people?" I asked.

"They're roller-skaters, bikers, skateboarders, kite flyers, and joggers." It was easy to spot the joggers. They were all together in an ozone of liniment, bending and stretching and speaking fluent jogging to one another: "split times," "euphoria," "building up lactic acid and hitting the wall."

There was something different about them that I couldn't put my finger on at first. Then it hit me. There was no one there who weighed over nine pounds. I felt like stretch marks at a Miss America pageant.

A bicyclist whizzed by, nearly clipping a jogger. The jogger shook his fist and shouted at him "WEIRDO!" Somehow, the remark seemed incongruous coming from a man who was pasting adhesive bandages over his nipples to keep them from getting sore when they rubbed against his shirt.

A couple of hours later, I dragged into Edna's kitchen, where she was washing dishes. "What's the matter with you?" she asked.

"I'm not sure. I'm either experiencing a euphoric high or I'm catching flu. Can I have those leftover French fries?"

"I thought you had to watch your weight."

"I'm packing carbohydrates. I tell you, Edna, I'm exhausted trying to feel good about myself. All inner peace does is give me an appetite. Why am I telling you this? Everyone knows me like an open book."

"Not really," said Edna, rinsing plates and stacking them in the drainer to dry. "You are extremely conservative and guard your privacy. You take pains never to reveal anything about yourself so that other people have a hard time trying to help you."

"Who told you that?"

"No one had to tell me. I can tell by the way you always point your body toward the door and your knees and feet are rigid."

"Edna, my entire body is rigid because I am basted in Vaseline and I am suffering from Morton's Toe."

"What's Morton's Toe?"

"Jogging terminology. It means my second toe is longer than my big one and has turned purple and can fall off at any minute."

"Didn't anyone ever tell you you have bad body English?"

"BAD BODY ENGLISH? You're just trying to cheer me up."

"I'm serious. You show me a woman who sits like you do and I'll show you a woman who is sexually inhibited, defensive, withdrawn, and has a mind closed to new ideas."

"You can tell all that just by looking at me?"

"Sure. Why, I can tell you that Ralph there," she said, nodding toward her dog, "is unfulfilled, restless, and manifests his anxieties and frustrations in his actions."

I shook my head in disbelief. "That's really amazing. How did you figure all that out?"

"Ralph just wet on your shoe."

When I went home, I limped into the bedroom and picked up my jogger's diary. On page one I put the date, wrote under it, "Erma hit the wall and went right up it," and slammed it shut!

Next to it on the bedside table was Jim Fixit's book. I studied the cover, then stood in front of the mirror and posed my legs like his. My forty-dollar shoes were spattered with mud and Ralph. The pink shoelaces hung limp. I had oil on my beautiful pink velour pants. I hiked up the pantlegs to see if my skin was taut, the muscles firm and the knees bony. My legs looked like an unpaved road with purple rivers running everywhere.

Easy for Mr. Fixit. He hadn't carried his babies low.

10 ♪*♪*♪

How to Tell Your Best Friend She Has Bad Body English

It was probably a coincidence that the carryout boy looked at my license plates while loading the groceries and said, "I don't get it. What's TZE 403 stand for?"

"It's my license plates," I said.

"I know, but they don't make any sense."

"Are they supposed to?"

"Sure. You're the only driver I know who doesn't have something clever on her plates. Some kind of identification."

I looked up and down the line of parked cars. There were E-Z DUZ IT, I. M. CUTE, SAY AAH, PAID 4, 2 CLOSE, CALL ME, I DRINK, and FLY ME.

"My Mom's got a neat set of plates," he said. "She's got 28–36–42. I know what you're thinking, but the good numbers were already taken." He slammed down the lid. "You don't even have a bumper sticker for anything. That's unusual."

On the way home, I checked out every car on the road. He was right. Just by looking at a car you knew who was for school levies, who they voted for, their religion, their alma mater, their club affiliation, their causes, and their issues. (I could hardly wait to pass the bumper and see who belonged to the sticker that read WOMEN NEED ATHLETIC SUPPORTERS TOO.)

Maybe Edna was right. Maybe I was overly zealous about my privacy. When I thought about it, I didn't have a CB in my car to carry on a conversation with other drivers. I had never named a house or a cabin something clever like "Dew Drop Inn" and had never worn my name in gold on a chain around my neck.

I didn't personalize my blouses, towels, or stationery with my initials or send out warm, intimate newsletters about our family at Christmas.

I wore a mood ring for two weeks once, but discarded it when I looked at my American Express bill one January and went into ring failure.

I was so opposed to nametags that once when a woman slapped a gummed label over my left bosom that said, "Hello! My name is Erma!" I leaned over and said, "Now, what shall we name the other one?"

I didn't even have a telephone that answered with a clever recording that said, "Hi there. I'm really glad you called. At the sound of the beep, tell me where you're coming from and I'll call you back and tell you where it's at."

At the sound of the beep, I would go into cardiac arrest in an effort to say my name and read my own phone number off my own phone. (I once called my mother and found myself spelling my last name.) Another time I had a note to return a call and dialed the number. There was a slick voice that said huskily, "Hi, Honey. I told you you'd call. I'm out getting your favorite white wine. The key is in the usual place. At the sound of the tone, tell me what time you'll be here."

No one was a person of mystery any more.

The T-shirt craze had clearly gotten out of hand. In one day alone I encountered three propositions, four declarations, two obscene suggestions, and a word so bad I stopped the car and threw a blanket over the girl's chest.

Mother was with me one day when I stopped for a traffic light and a healthy blonde with jeans so tight her hipbones looked like towel hooks crossed in front of the car. Tucked inside was a T-shirt that read in large, bold letters SPACE FOR RENT.

We didn't say anything for a full minute. Then Mother observed, "You can say what you want, but she certainly is well read."

Well read, indeed. I could be clever if I wanted to. My car license was up for renewal. Maybe I'd go for something kinky on my plates.

"How many letters do we have to work with?" asked my husband.

"Six," I said.

"Great," said my son. "How about BEWARE?"

"Or GAS HOG?"

"Aw, c'mon," I said, "I want a plate that won't have people passing me at seventy-five miles an hour just to see what kind of a nut is behind the wheel. I was thinking more of a plate that would give me character . . . a self-description that would be unique and apply only to me."

"How many letters in DRUDGE?" asked my son.

We must have sat there another two hours trying to get a six-letter combination. Finally I said, "I've got it. How about VIT B-12? What do you think?"

"I think you have just solved the problem of the kids ever borrowing your car again."

Having personalized license plates was a step forward in revealing my mystique, but I wasn't sure I wanted people sitting around reading my entire body. According to the book Edna loaned me (*Body English Spoken Here*) it wasn't that hard to do.

Women who crossed their legs in cold weather were announcing they wanted attention. In hot weather, they were bragging.

Doctors who tapped pencils were reassuring themselves they hadn't lost them during an examination.

Men who removed their wedding rings while attending a convention in another city were saying they didn't care whether they lived or died.

Women who covered the telephone receiver when they *listened* were hearing something they shouldn't.

Teeth closing in on a dentist's hand is definitely interpreted as a hostile act.

But it worked both ways. If I could learn Body English I'd be able to read what other people were thinking even if they did not utter a single word. There was an entire section on the subtle signs men and women who are on the make exchange that was absolutely fascinating.

This was a subject I couldn't even draw on from memory. It had been too long. I wouldn't know a pitch if I struck at it.

Body English Spoken Here made me an authority. I felt I could interpret any subtlety the opposite sex threw at me. I didn't have a chance to test it until one afternoon when Mayva and I stopped shopping to grab a bite of lunch.

At a table a short distance from us were two men who glanced our way.

"Don't look at them," I said without moving my lips. "I can tell you that men mentally raise the hemline of a woman's skirt six inches if she wears lipstick."

Mayva rummaged in her handbag. "Do I have any left on?"

"If you look them in the eye and their pupils dilate, you're in over your head."

"What other goodies do you know?"

"I know that when you are flirting your eyes become less baggy, your jowls firm up, your shoulders become straighter, and you suck in your stomach without thinking about it. And if you put on your glasses, you'll look more intelligent than you really are."

Mayva gave a sharp cry. "What am I saying? Quick! One of them is coming over toward us."

"Did you cross your legs?" I whispered loudly. "That's a come-on. Or unbutton your jacket? Or moisten your lips? Tell me you didn't moisten your lips."

"I don't think so," said Mayva.

"Then just keep your head down and we'll try to undo any message our bodies sent."

A shadow crossed the table and kept going.

Mayva looked at me with disgust. "I just read the body of the man that passed us. It said 'Don't get too choked up. I'm going to the men's room.'"

Mayva could really get on your nerves and despite what she thought I still believed knowing Body English was a real plus. Especially the part devoted to the Body English of teachers. Boy, did I need that. With two children still left in high school I had to admit I was lost without an interpreter.

I didn't know what had happened to education, but within the past several years it was getting tougher and tougher to speak the language.

It was simple back in the days when teachers spoke in polite language. I didn't need an interpreter to know that when Miss Meeks said, "Bruce's personal habits have shown marked improvement" she really was saying, "He no longer wets himself every day now that he has discovered the bathroom walls."

Or "I personally hope that your son develops more self-confidence" meant he copied on every test. I knew when she duly reported, "His paper on irrigation among the Barbizon tribe was far above that expected from a fourth-grader" it translated to "How long did it take you to write it?"

But in recent years I couldn't make head or tail of what they were saying. In fact, last year's conference had been a nightmare.

When I was seated at the desk, Mrs. Vucci polished her glasses and said, "Well, let's see here what we have in the way of comments from Bruce's other teachers. According to this report, Coach Weems says he has potential but is incapable of any viable feedback. That tells us, of course, that we have a child who does not relate to social interreaction."

I nodded numbly.

"Mrs. Wormstad says he is not motivated by curriculum innovation and they don't want him to stagnate in a lockup system and they're trying to stimulate his awareness. Mrs. Rensler writes he is having behavior modification problems and they're putting him in a modular-flexible schedule. Let's hope it works.

"I personally feel we have to consider the conundrum. But seriously," she said, "it's hard to say where the burden for apathy lies, but before his achievement levels polarize, we'll counsel Bruce so he can realize his potential and aim for some tangible goals."

I had not understood one single word she had said.

"Do you have any questions?" she asked, noting my silence.

I shook my head. She wouldn't have understood the questions and I wouldn't have understood the answers. What a pair.

With Body English I might at least stand a chance. Another teacher conference was coming up in a couple of weeks and I wanted to be ready for it.

My appointment was for seven-thirty and I was early. As I poked my head around the corner of the room, Mrs. Lutz said without looking up from her desk, "I know. We all dread these sessions, don't we?"

"How can you tell that?" I smiled.

"Your reticence to appear fully in the doorway instead of inching your way into the room."

I sat down on the edge of the chair. She looked over her half-glasses and said, "There is no need to be uptight. Just sit back and relax."

"I am relaxed," I said quickly.

"No one is relaxed sitting on the edge of the chair. And stop worrying, it's not that bad."

"I don't think it's bad."

"Of course you do," she corrected. "I can tell by the way your feet are coiled around the chair legs."

This wasn't working at all. She wasn't supposed to be reading my body. I was supposed to be reading *hers.*

But I couldn't help it. The more she talked, the harder time I had to keep my body from talking. When she brought out his essay on "The Anatomy of a Belch" I sank into a fetal position and lowered my head.

When she told me he not only parked his car illegally in front of the school but told the security people he thought they had valet parking, I made a necklace out of her paper clips and chewed at my cuticles until they bled.

By the time she told me his career tests showed his future lay in shepherding, I had used every bit of Body English in the book.

It was useless to play games. She asked me if my son and I related to one another. I said nervously only through a young marriage. She said that wasn't what she meant. She was trying to establish what kind of a parent-child relationship we had.

That's when it all came out. I told her none of my children understood parents my age. They talked to me but they never listened to what I had to say. They were always too busy. I stopped telling them anything because when I did I was always in for a lecture. They never took my side.

They blamed me for everything. Never let me assume responsibility for things I could do myself. All they did was criticize. (I leaned forward.) I think they even spy on me. "Miss Lutz," I said flatly, "they treat me like an adult."

She folded my son's manila folder and leaned back on her chair. "You're not the only parent who has problems with their children understanding them," she said. "There's a wonderful new manual out called *Bringing Up Parents the Okay Way*. I don't know whether or not you can get your children to read it, but at least you'll get a better understanding of why they do and say the things they do."

I started to stand up.

"Don't forget your feet," cautioned Miss Lutz, nodding toward my legs still coiled around the legs of the chair. "That could be interpreted as some very strong Body English."

I smiled smugly. "I read a little Body English myself," I said proudly. "As a matter of fact, while you've been observing me, I've been observing you. I have come to the conclusion you are an excellent teacher, secure, in command of a situation, and will be around here for a long time."

"Not really," she said, easing herself out of the chair. "I'm eight months pregnant and am going on maternity leave next week."

Some bodies are very deceptive.

11 ৵✶৵
Bringing Up Parents the Okay Way

The trouble with my kids is they had read too many books on Parent Psychology. They thought they knew all the answers, but the truth is they didn't know me at all.

They corrected my grammar in front of my friends, told me my clothes were too young for me, bugged me about my short hair, and never tried to relate to my problems.

God knows, I had problems. I wasn't popular and wasn't with the "in" group. The in group in my neighborhood were women my age who had reentered the job scene. Every morning, I watched them from my window as they swung to their cars dressed in contemporary clothes and teetering in five-inch heels to their day in carpetland.

From my vantage point, I could only fantasize how they answered phones that weren't sticky, had lunch in a place with live plants, and talked to people who didn't respond with the same two words, "far out."

The high spot in my week was being invited to a luncheon style show where I pilfered five or six sample vials of perfume that lasted five or six minutes before the alcohol burned off.

The friends I liked my children weren't crazy about. They didn't like Yvonne, who was divorced and dated their former orthodontist, because they thought she was a bad influence on me.

They didn't like Gloria, who always came over at dinnertime and hung around while we ate, because she never seemed to have a home of her own.

And they didn't like Judy, who never cleaned her house and schlepped around in grubby clothes and greasy hair. (They said they had NEVER seen her cleaned up and she set a bad example for me.)

Sometimes I didn't know what the kids expected from me. When I needed them, they were never home.

When they were home they drove me crazy trying out their latest in parent-psychology techniques. I could always tell when they had a new theory they were trying out. I had their undivided attention.

They tried every new theory to come down the pike—active listening, effectiveness training, and transactional analysis.

I wasn't surprised to find the manual Mrs. Lutz mentioned, *Bringing Up Parents the Okay Way,* in a stack of magazines in the bathroom.

On the cover was a picture of a teenager with an insincere smile. He had put down his paper to give his attention to his mother, who was showing him something she had just read in a book.

I leafed quickly through a chapter called "How to Say No to Your Parents." I knew how. I just didn't know why. Then my eyes caught a heading called "The Middle-Parent Syndrome. What is your position in the Family?"

That was it. I was a middle parent. No wonder I was weird. I was neither the oldest nor the youngest. I was wedged in the twilight zone where no one ever does anything for the first time, says anything original, wears anything new, or is cute.

My position in the family car bore this out. When I was first married I snuggled up against my husband so close he looked like he was driving alone. When the first baby came, I moved all the way over to the door so the baby could sit between us. With the second child, I hung over the back seat and arrived everywhere fanny first so I could make sure they hadn't fallen on the floor.

With the third child, I lost my front seat and became a part of the back seat so that each child could have his own window.

When car pools became a part of my life, I was returned to the front seat, but as a steady driver. No one ever talked to me or for that matter acknowledged I was there.

When the kids began to drive, I was once more shuffled to the passenger side of the car.

Lately, I had been delegated once again to the back seat when I got a seat at all. I was on to something and I knew it as I feverishly thumbed my way to a chapter on "Growing Up." It said when we can stand alone without leaning on our children, we have indeed reached the age of independence.

It was confusing. I didn't know what I wanted. There were times when I wanted to be alone. Like when my friends dropped in. I remember one day Yvonne came by to tell me about Elaine's hysterectomy and before she could go into detail, my youngest parked himself between our coffee cups and observed, "Dogs get fat after their operation. I hope poor Elaine can hold her own."

There were other times when I wanted to be needed and leaned on.

I slammed the book shut. This particular day was definitely not one of those days. There were thirty-five unwashed glasses on the countertop by the sink. I didn't own thirty-five glasses.

The front door had not been shut all the way in two years. There were six cars in the driveway. One of them ran.

The baking soda I had put in the refrigerator to keep odors down was half eaten.

There were black heelmarks on the oven door.

The dog looked fat.

I wanted to say good-bye to pure, organic, honey-herbal scented shampoo that cost a dollar fifty an ounce and was at this moment on its side with the cap off running down the drain.

Good-bye to Linda Ronstadt and Billy Joel. Good-bye to porch lights that had to be replaced every six weeks. Good-bye mildewed towels and empty ice-cube trays and labels that read HAND WASH ONLY. Good-bye to lunch meat that dried out and curled up because no one rewrapped it.

All my friends had shed the dependency of their children and were on cruises. I know because there wasn't a day one of them didn't write me.

I was still sorting socks, skimming crumbs off the top of the water jug in the refrigerator, and every Mother's Day feigning ecstasy over a cheese shredder.

One day as my older son was looking for his glasses so he could find my purse and the other one was rearranging the dials on my car radio to a rock station, I knew what I had to do.

I took him aside and said, "You know, as a child who didn't plan for parents, you've done a pretty good job. I know I've goofed up a lot . . ."

"If it's about the cashmere sweater that shrunk, forget it," he said.

"No, it's just that we can't seem to communicate any more. We always end up shouting."

"Mom," he said. "These are the best years of your life."

I started to cry. "Kids are always saying that. The point of this conversation is why can't you accept me and not my behavior? Why do I have to be perfect? I never seem to be doing what every other mother is doing at the same time she is doing it. The time has come for me to break away and be the person I was meant to be. I think you should move out and get your own apartment."

I left him mumbling "Where have I failed?"

The next night when Gloria padded in at dinnertime and took her chair, I told her of my ultimatum.

"You're a credit to parents everywhere," she said. "I hope you're covered by Teenage Apartment Insurance."

"What's that?"

"It's a new policy for parents of young people who leave to get their own apartments. The premiums are expensive, but they cover loss of furniture up to five thousand dollars, damages to cars hauling away contents of house and restocking of the refrigerator."

"You're kidding."

"And you've got a short memory," she said. "Remember how it was when your daughter went to school? You both rattled around in here without so much as a stick of furniture. The only thing she left was an echo."

My son must have known my fears, for a couple of weeks later when he said, "I've found an apartment," he added quickly, "Don't worry. It's furnished."

My relief lasted only until we looked at it. I've seen recovery rooms with more furniture.

"Do you need a skillet?"

"What for?" he chirped. "I'm only going to be eating one meal a day at home."

Somehow he instinctively knew the roast beef nights at home and came in like he was on radar. Occasionally on these nights he'd yell from another room, "Do you want this?"

"What is it?"

"The TV set."

"Of course we want it."

"You can have the green lamp back for it."

"This isn't a park-'n-swap."

Eventually he had it all . . . the afghans my mother had made, the dishes he borrowed for a party and never returned, the typewriter, the window fan, the big pot for spaghetti, the beach towels, the four-wheel drive, and the bicycle that "is just sitting there and someone will steal it and you'll never see it again."

What really hurt was we hadn't a dime's worth of Teenage Apartment Insurance to ease the loss.

Things eased up a little after he left, with only one child in high school, but it wasn't like having our own apartment.

Gloria was with me the afternoon he became disgusted with me for not having gas in my car which he was borrowing.

"Why do you take all of that?" asked Gloria.

"It's easier than arguing. Besides, he wouldn't yell at me if he didn't love me."

"Haven't you ever heard of assertiveness?"

"Of course I've heard of assertiveness. Are you saying I'm not?"

"I'm saying if you are, you could sure use a lot more of it. Your trouble is you don't know how to say no and do you know why?"

I shook my head no and hated me for doing it.

"It's because you're very insecure about yourself. You want to be loved and you don't want to take a chance on alienating people."

"You're wrong," I laughed.

"Okay, I want you to do something for me. I want you to go into the family room and announce 'This is my house. I am my own person. I am going to be more assertive.' "

I thought about it a second, then decided to call Gloria's bluff. I went to the living room where my husband and son were watching television.

"This is my house. I am my own person and I'm going to be more assertive."

My husband looked up. "I can't read lips. What are you mumbling about? Speak up!"

I cleared my throat and started again. "This is my house. I am my own person and I'm going to be more assertive."

"Son," said my husband irritably, "turn that sound down. Your mother is trying to say something. And hurry up. State is about to score."

"This is my house. I am my own person and I'm going to be more assertive . . . if it's okay with you."

12 ♪❋♪♪

Go Suck an Egg

I called it the E. F. Hutton Syndrome.

There wasn't a morning my husband did not sit at the table and read the entire newspaper out loud to me. When he read, everyone within a ninety-mile radius was supposed to stop what they were doing and listen.

He read me the editorials, the weather in Sharon, Pa., what Dear Abby said to the woman whose husband dressed in the closet, the sports scores, why South bid seven hearts, and what Lucy said to Charlie Brown. (For no apparent reason, he made Lucy sound like Butterfly McQueen.)

The assumption was obvious. I could not read a newspaper by myself.

One day he started to read me a story of a dog who had found its way home after being lost for five years.

"Listen to this," he said. "A springer spaniel in Butte, Montana . . ."

"I read it already," I said.

". . . found its way home after five years when the family vacationed in . . ."

"The Everglades and was lost," I interrupted. It was like talking to a ballpoint pen.

372

"During his absence," he continued, "he served two years in the Army with distinction, saved a child from drowning and . . ."

"Made a drug bust in Nogales."

He looked up. "Did you know the dog?"

"I told you. I read it already."

"Well, why didn't you say so?"

My fantasy was one day to reach over with a pair of scissors and clip out the story he was reading, peek through the hole in the paper, and announce "I got my library card today."

Assertiveness had never been easy for me. In fact, I still wasn't convinced it wasn't congenital. You were either born with it . . . or you weren't.

Whenever a salesperson tried to follow me into the fitting room, I always wanted to turn to her and say, "The last person who saw me in a pleated skirt went blind."

But I never did.

I always wanted to turn to my hairdresser and say, "If I wanted hair the consistency and style of a steel helmet, I would have been a Viking."

But I never did.

But most of all, I wanted to turn to Mildred Harkshorn one day and say, "Mildred, I've had it with you and your super kids who do everything first and better than anyone else. Do you know that I just read where there is a strong correlation between over-achievers and the presence of venereal disease in the mother at birth?"

But I never did.

Mildred was a neighbor who had lived through the hedge from me for the past fifteen years with her husband, Leland, and their two children, Dwight David and Miracle. Miracle was a girl. Both could have been poster children for celibacy.

I liked Mildred. I really did. Our children had grown up to-gether, but her kids had arrived late in her life and she somehow felt that since she took so long she couldn't settle for anything less than perfection.

They were born with capped teeth, snooze alarms, and a dry wish.

That set the pace for their entire lives.

They were toilet-trained at nine months.

Every time I misted my plants, mine lost control.

They were weaned off the bottle at one year.

Mine went through a dozen nipples a week—shredded by teeth marks.

Dwight David and Miracle received awards for music festival, cheerleading, football, scholarships, and science fair.

Mine got a free ticket for a hamburger and a malt for bringing in fifty pounds of paper for the drive.

I couldn't get out of the school parking lot without Mildred tapping on the window and gushing, "I suppose your son told you about those awful SAT tests?"

My son had never spoken a complete sentence to me.

"I told Dwight David if he blew it he couldn't be captain of the baseball team. I don't care if he was elected unanimously by his teammates. His studies come first . . . by the way, did your son go out for baseball?"

My son wouldn't go out for the garbage unless we wrote him a check.

You have to be intimidated by a mother whose children never lied, never talked with food in their mouths, and wrote thank-you notes for a drink out of the garden hose when they played at your house.

If I were ever to become assertive, in my heart, I knew it had to begin with Mildred. She was at her mailbox one day when she yelled, "Hi there. How's your daughter doing in college?"

I smiled and walked over toward her. "Fine."

"What's that amusing name they call her again?"

"Suds."

"Here's another letter from Miracle," she said. "We're so close, you know. She writes me every day. Of course, I suppose your daughter does too."

"She probably dropped her Bible on her foot and can't get to the post office as often as she would like," I said.

"Maybe so," she smiled. "Some young people just simply don't feel a need for family. They view going away to school as an opportunity to break off all family ties and build an entirely new life for themselves."

I had fallen into her trap again and couldn't bring myself to talk back. What was wrong with me? Why couldn't I say what I felt?

As I walked back toward the house, I saw Helen coming home from work. "Hello there," she yelled. "Hear from your college child today?"

I would not get caught again. "Oh yes," I lied. "She writes every day."

"Is she still so dependent?" asked Helen, shaking her head. "Don't worry. She'll mature after a while and become adjusted. It just takes time for her to be her own person and not a mama's girl."

I couldn't win.

No matter what my children did, it was wrong. How come my kids were forgetful and everyone else's were "preoccupied"? Mine were fat, but other people's children were "healthy"? If mine were weirdos, theirs were "nonconformists." If mine were lazy, others were "deep thinkers." Mine flunked out, but other children were "victims of a poor teacher."

One night I was watching the Carson show when my husband told me I was sleepy and should go to bed or I'd be crabby in the morning. He turned out the light.

As I sat there wide-eyed in the semi-darkness watching the tube, Johnny introduced Dr. Eduardo Emitz, who had just authored a book called *Go Suck an Egg*.

There was no doubt in my mind that he was talking directly to me. He said being assertive isn't a luxury, it's our inalienable right. We don't have to feel guilty about it. We don't have to justify it. We don't even have to give a reason for it. Just do it.

He said there was no need to get emotional or hostile about stating your own mind. A simple way to get started was to make a list of things that bothered you and decide how you were going to handle them. He promised you'd be your own person in no time.

I turned on the light and began to make a list of things that had to change:

I will no longer sit at the breakfast table and have the paper read out loud to me.

Smokers who blow smoke in my face will learn firsthand (within minutes actually) how injurious smoking can be to their health.

I will openly yawn in front of the next person who makes me a sexual confidante.

I will no longer hang on the phone waiting for Lynda to go back and applaud her son's BM's.

I will not collect from door to door for any disease I cannot pronounce.

I will not be upset by my mother-in-law when she calls me by my maiden name.

When I return something to the department store after Christmas, I will no longer wear black and tell them the recipient died.

When summoned to school I am going to assume my child is innocent until proven guilty.

Like Dr. Emitz said, you had to build up to assertiveness. It wasn't something you did in a day; you had to take one day at a time.

I started that night when we went to a restaurant to eat. As usual, I ordered my steak well done. When they brought it to the table, I thought I detected a heartbeat.

At first I toyed with the idea of pretending it was ham, but gently I put my fork down and said, "Please take this back and cook it a little longer."

"It won't be fit to eat," grumbled the waiter.

"In that case, I won't eat it," I said firmly.

Assertiveness felt good and the more I did it, the better I felt.

I demanded my butcher take the meat out from under the pink light and show me his prime rump in the daylight.

When Mayva pinned me down as to how I liked her new blow-'n-go hair style, I told her they didn't blow it far enough.

It was several weeks later when Mildred called to tell me how Dwight David found a flaw in his teacher's theory of relativity and publicly humiliated him in front of fifty students. I started to speak, but couldn't.

"You would think a twenty-year-old boy couldn't be smarter than a big-shot college professor with all those degrees, now wouldn't you? I swear I don't know where that boy gets it from."

"Mildred," I said, clearing my throat.

"Do you remember how excited you were when your son passed his eye examination?"

"MILDRED!" I shouted. "Do you know I've just read in a magazine where there is a strong correlation between overachievers and the presence of venereal disease in the mother at birth?"

I rarely saw Mildred after that. When I did she was always preoccupied and didn't notice me or remembered something she had to do and turned the other way. As a matter of fact, the more assertive I became, the less I saw of anyone, including my mother—whom I threatened with a tongue transplant from Rona Barrett if she didn't stop relating to the children all my past sins.

What the heck. At least I liked myself for my honesty. I had finally learned how to be a good friend to myself. When I thought about it, I was my ONLY friend.

I took me everywhere. To the movies. The zoo. Long rides in the country. I dined with me over intimate dinners and turned my head with flowers and candy. I knew I was getting too involved with me, but I couldn't seem to stop myself. We got along wonderfully. I knew when to talk to me and when to shut up. I knew when I was in a bad mood and when I wanted to be alone with just me.

I praised me when I did a good job and spoiled me outrageously. There wasn't anything I could deny myself because I was such a wonderful person. If anyone had a snout-full of self-esteem, it was me. People were beginning to talk and spread rumors about my extramarital affair with myself, but I didn't care. What I felt for me was genuine. (I think I even told me I wanted to have my baby.)

I had been my best friend for about four months when I began to notice little things about me that I had never noticed before. When I laughed, I snorted like a motor that had just turned over in a 1936 Chevy. At night in bed, I drove myself crazy flipping over the pillow looking for a "cool" side. When I argued, I smiled. Do you know how disgusting it is to argue with someone who smiles?

Not only that, some of my old habits of weakness were reappearing. Just a few days before I had let someone get in front of me in the express lane with a dozen items and said nothing. I hadn't really taken charge of my own life, I had only enjoyed a temporary attack of independence. I told me if I really loved me I could do anything I wanted. Every evening before going to bed, I did as Doctor Emitz had suggested. I stood in front of the mirror and said "I love you," to which my husband would always yell, "You say that now, but will you respect you in the morning?"

One morning when I asked me for a cup of coffee and answered, "Go get it yourself!" Mayva appeared and said, "Are you talking to yourself again?"

"What do you mean again?"

"You've been doing it for months now. You don't go out any more or have anyone in. You have no friends and no one calls. You just go around here mumbling 'I'm okay. I'm not too sure about the rest of you,' and there's no one here."

"Mayva," I sighed, "in these past months I have found out so many things about myself. Through self-analysis and psychological groping, I have discovered that I am basically a boring person." She tried to interrupt. "I mean it. The other night I was telling me an amusing story that I have laughed at a hundred times and right in the middle of it, I interrupted me and said, 'What's on TV?' "

Mayva put her hand over mine. "Anyone gets bored with herself if she thinks about herself all the time. It's called the 'Me-too-me-first Syndrome.' Don't you understand? Looking out for yourself is yesterday's leftovers. It used to be in, but now it's out. No one does that any more. Today the key word is commitment. Look around you. Everyone is into causes. Sometimes when you're out, just listen to people. They have goals . . . purpose . . . principles . . . something they believe in and are fighting for. The word today is involvement."

"You're kidding," I said. "You'd have thought I would have told me if things were changing."

"You've been so isolated," said Mayva, "you probably didn't know it. You've got to get out of this house again and start living . . . see people, go places, do things. Look, if your best friend won't tell you, I will. You're self-centered and shallow."

I looked in the mirror at my best friend for the past few months and waited for her to say something.

The truth hit me. I didn't love me that much!

13 ✿✿✿

A House Divided Against Itself Cannot Stand One Another

I missed me. When I had been my own best friend, I didn't have to dress up, go out, or sit around all night listening to someone else talk.

All I had to do was get up every day and take my emotional temperature. Did I love me more today than I did yesterday? Was I really in command of my own life? Could I con myself out of doing the hand laundry for another month?

I had heard about the Me-too-me-first phase. It happened to people who read too many how-to books and became terminally strange. Was it possible I had become too obsessed with myself?

If it was, maybe—by mingling in the world of what's happening—I could find a cause that appealed to me. What better way than to give a party? I'd simply invite a couple dozen friends and during the course of the evening, some cause or project would strike my interest and I could direct my energies away from myself.

As I made out the guest list, I reminisced about the days when you simply called up your friends, put a ton of food on the table, set out the booze, and let it happen. All that had changed.

If we invited John, we had to invite three other smokers who could stand with him defiant and unified against the rest of the room.

Stella drank only vodka, twelve guests were "into white wine," and the rest of them sanctimoniously hoisted French water with a twist of lime.

Eight were vegetarians, three would eat nothing from the sea because it was tainted, and fifteen were on diets.

Lois drank eight glasses of water with her diet and had to have a straight shot at all times between her and the bathroom. Mary Ellen still had to weigh her portions on a postal scale. Elaine ran to test her urine every time she ate a carbohydrate, and Jerry brought her own concoction consisting of seaweed, olive oil, goat's milk, and cantaloupe which she stored in a Tupperware container in the refrigerator.

I couldn't seat a runner next to a lump, a nuclear proponent next to an environmentalist, a gun-control advocate next to a hunter, or a childless-by-choice next to a breast-feeder.

There should have been an easier way to get a handle on what was happening in the world and find a niche for myself.

When I saw Marj come in wearing a fur coat, I tried to propel her away from Liz, but not before Liz said in a loud voice, "My dream is to see an animal walk into a party some night dressed in a cape made out of Marj!"

I guided her into a conversation with George, who was arguing with Stan about the busing issue. I introduced Stan to Lois, who was in a shouting match with Doug about cohabital living. I thrust Lois into a group who were pro-abortion only to discover she was a Catholic, and then propelled her into a conversation with Stella. Stella, a feminist, was shouting at Sonya, who said she was happy staying home and why couldn't Stella accept that!

Liz appeared at my elbow and —nodding toward George—said, "What kind of a jerk would be against neutering animals?"

At the same time, Sonya complained she had a respiratory disorder and couldn't talk to a smoker, so I introduced her to Mary Ellen.

Doug said there wasn't one person at the party who read *The New York Times* and one woman thought a vasectomy was an operation for varicose veins. Was there no one who had an opinion on the Marvin decision!

When they were seated for dinner, my eyes glanced nervously around the table. Let's see, I had the natural-childbirth advocate next to the minister, the legalize marijuana next to open enrollment, jogger next to environmentalist, antiviolence next to the woman who didn't own a television set, the chauvinist next to the anti-feminist, and the anti-pay-toilet demonstrator next to . . . who else? Lois, who was on her seventh glass of water but couldn't tear herself away from her dinner companion's views.

The only thing I had forgotten was to put my husband, the left-hander, at the end of the table. Luckily, left-handers were pacifists.

Their conversation sounded like the Tower of Babel. Every once in a while words and phrases would surface loudly: "a new concept," "the bottom line is productivity," "at this point in time," "a positive interaction," "sexual freedom."

Mayva was right. I needed the stimulation of a cause that would put me on the other end of one of those conversations.

Later, as I was talking with Emily about volunteering a few hours a week at the Save the Whale Sperm Bank, Stella steered me to the sofa and said, "Let's talk."

She eased herself back into the cushions. "When are you going to take yourself away from all this?"

"I'm the hostess," I said simply.

"I don't mean the party. I mean all this domesticity."

I liked Stella. I also knew she never got too choked up over a "nice windy day that was perfect for drying blankets."

In fact, her wedding linens dissolved in the washer and her marriage dissolved in the courts the same week. She took that as an omen.

Like Helen, my neighbor, Stella had made the transition from the utility room to the board room as easily as napping during a piano recital.

"You're such a success," I smiled. "I'm so proud of you."

"And you could be a success too," she said. "It's a game. Men have been playing it for years. Have you read *Looking Out for You-Know-Who* by Robby Winner?"

"Stella," I said, "I just went through that number. It didn't work."

"How do you know it isn't for you? You couldn't have been serious about breaking out of the mold. Look at you!"

"Now, what's the matter with me?" I asked.

"My God, no one wears a slip any more."

"That's not true. I know a lot of women who wear slips."

"Under a see-through sweater? Get serious. Look, babe, why don't you come down next week to my office and we'll have lunch. We can talk some more. Besides, I want you to see where I work."

I had no intention of following up on Stella's suggestion until one afternoon at the Save the Whale Sperm Bank when I had hung up on my 187th obscene phone call, I called and told her I'd be by around one.

Stella was on the twenty-seventh floor of one of those office buildings that looks like it's awaiting a countdown. Her secretary led me into her office.

I had lived in smaller apartments. A huge desk held a phone with five buttons. There was a wall of bookcases and two African spears that crossed a shield on the wall behind her desk.

"I didn't know you went to Africa," I said.

"I didn't, sweetie; it's part of the trappings." She slid her glasses (the size of goggles) back over her head, giving her a Marlo-Thomas-in-the-convertible look.

"How long have you been wearing glasses?"

"I don't. Look, will you stop acting like Penny meeting Sky King for the first time? It's what I've been telling you. It's all in Robby Winner's book. You have to look like success and play the game. The tan came from a sun lamp so my clients will think I have the security to vacation in Florida during the winter. I never sweat because I wear lightweight clothes all year round and keep the thermostat at sixty-two. Coffee?" she asked.

I nodded. Her secretary brought in one cup and set it down in front of me.

"Aren't you having any?"

She shook her head. "An urgent bladder is a sign of weakness. I never indulge. You use all the tricks, honey. That chair you're sitting in . . . it's three times smaller than mine and has a soft cushion that makes you sit lower than me. Gives me an advantage. The books are all paneling. This desk set wasn't presented to me in appreciation by anyone. I just had a plaque engraved last week and it looks like I'm a recipient of something."

"Are you saying all of this is contrived, right down to your attaché case?"

"The insides smell like egg salad," she shrugged. "I cannot believe you are so naive," she chided. "We're competing in a man's world and it's serious business . . . well, maybe not all of it."

"You know something," I said, leaning closer.

"No, I was just thinking about an office party we had the other night that was rather interesting. Kay had to take Mark home."

"Who's Mark?"

"You saw him when you came in. He's the little red-haired secretary to Ms. Hamstein in Research and Development."

"You mean he had too much to drink?"

"Kay told me he was running around with a Cadillac hood ornament in his hand, shouting 'Anyone here lose a Krugerrand?' "

"Is he married?"

"Of course he's married. He probably should be at home with the kids anyway. He doesn't have to work. His wife has a good job, but it's an ego thing."

"I think office parties should be legally outlawed. What purpose do they serve?"

"Kay says it's a nice thing to do, but I don't know. Women turn into beasts when they've had a drink or two. Can you imagine those women executives plying all those struggling male clerks with drinks they're not used to? Why, even Cecil Frampton was discoing all over the place. Oh, he's got a nice figure all right. Hides it under those leisure suits. But by the end of the evening he was calling Ms. Hathcock . . . get this . . . GLORIA! And Debbie was cruising around. Marriage certainly hasn't settled her down."

"What's wrong with that?"

"I'll tell you what's wrong. She left with the new office boy and she is old enough to be his mother. There is really something pathetic about a woman who refuses to act her age. Oh sure, it may be a way out of the mail room, but he has to live with himself."

There was a silence as she shuffled through her handbag looking for her lipstick.

"I had a big week," I said. "I color-coded my leftovers."

You had to give it to Stella. She certainly had made the transition from plastic plates to power city. But she was the exception. Most of my friends didn't have such a flashy set-up. One worked in the school cafeteria, another passed out sausage samples in a supermarket, another sold real estate, and Kathy was a Girl Friday for an insulation contractor.

I rarely saw Kathy any more. She lived by a timetable. Even her headaches were scheduled. The sun never set on an empty

Crock Pot. She left the house at seven, returned at four-thirty, and her domestic schedule never missed a beat.

Kathy had certainly changed. When I knew her, she was possibly the most unorganized homemaker to ever come down the pike. She was always running out of staples like meat, milk, and toilet paper. Her gas gauge was always on E and her children were never born when she thought they were going to be. She had possibly the only twelve-month pregnancies in the history of obstetrics. Her return to the labor market was a surprise to us all. It happened one afternoon when she returned from the orthodontist. She and her husband talked it over and they decided that no way could he support two overbites on his salary.

We occasionally talked on the phone (where she answered mechanically, "Brunwilder's Insulation, Kathy speaking"), but I hadn't been to visit her since she returned to work. I didn't know the place.

Just inside the door was a large mirror. Over it was a lettered sign that read STRAIGHT TEETH MEAN SACRIFICE.

The house was decorated in Early Memo. You couldn't see the refrigerator door for the instructions on it.

- NOW HEAR THIS . . . When the floor becomes adhesive, MOP IT.
- There is no known navy-blue food. If there is navy-blue food in the refrigerator, it signifies death.
- Setting the table is not considered child abuse.
- Anyone eating an entire can of albacore white tuna packed in water for a snack must be prepared to work out financial arrangements.
- An open refrigerator door and the furnace going at the same time are incompatible.
- Look upon one glass carried from your bedroom to the kitchen as "one small step for man, one giant leap for mankind."
- Today is a new day. Throw away something off the countertop.

- The dog's business is EVERYONE's business. Even when you don't see it, clean it up.

In the utility room was another memo:

- You are standing in a utility room.
- Clothes are washed, dried, and ironed here.
- Hand washables left over ten years will be sold.
- Spaghetti inside the washer can be traced.
- Small brown dots on clothes that smell like a wet possum should be dealt with immediately.
- Match every sock with something. Color, texture, and size is not important.
- Do not shake out gym clothes as they trigger the smoke alarm. Process them immediately.
- Do not take the chill off the room by turning the iron to the COTTON setting.
- One pair of jeans is considered a "mini" load.
- Clothes do not have feet. They cannot skip, run, or walk. They must be carried to your respective bedrooms.

The bathroom memo read:

- Towels in the bathroom are yellow. REPEAT. Yellow. If they appear in any other color, drop them into the nearest clothes hamper.
- A word about gravity. A shampoo bottle when lying on its side with the cap off will eventually empty into the drain. Just because there's 35 pounds of hair in the drain, there is no need to shampoo it.
- Flushing is an equal-opportunity job. Simply press finger firmly on the lever and push. If water "runs" longer than 15 hours, jiggle lever gently.
- Hair dryers left on and shut up in a drawer serve no purpose. Turn them off.
- The management requests you conserve towels. No more than

one for hair, one for the right arm, one for the left, and one for the body. Somewhere, there is a war on.

• The mystery of disappearing soap has been solved. A discovery made in 1903 revealed soap, when submerged in water, will dissolve.

• FIFTY-MINUTE SHOWERS CAUSE ACNE.

After visiting with Stella and Kathy the thought of going home was depressing. My surroundings didn't exactly have the stamp of success written all over them. My meat always overthawed and ran down the stove. There was a mountain of "hand washables" in the utility room with baby sweaters near the bottom. Someone had written in the dust on the coffee table, "For a good time call Leah 555–3049." I cannot remember when there was a pencil by the phone.

Why didn't I take pride in my work? Homemaking, if you did it right, was just as creative, just as vital, and just as professional as what women were doing outside the home. Besides, it was one of the few jobs left where you could have an urgent bladder and not lose respect.

As for the extra money they made, I could run my home like a business if I tried. Why, I could save thousands of dollars just passing up convenience foods, clipping coupons, saving stamps, pumping my own gas, and grooming the dog.

Could there be a book on how to run a home more efficiently and save money? Does the Pope work Sundays?

The phone rang at the Save the Whale Sperm Bank. I listened for a minute or two, then said, "If you knew ANYTHING about whales, sir, you'd know that is physically impossible!" and hung up.

14 ∫❋∫❋∫
Living Cheap

The bookstore was bulging with books on how to save money. It seemed strange to me that they were on a table marked Current Fiction.

Leading the list was the current best seller, *How to Dress a Chicken* (From Separates to Basic Weekenders), followed by *How to Perform Home Surgery Using Sewing Basket Notions*, and my favorite, *How to Build a Summer Cabin Using Scraps Ripped Off from the Neighborhood Lumber Yard*.

I didn't want to get too specific. I just wanted a general book on how to save money by doing things around the house myself. The clerk recommended one that had been selling briskly called *Living Cheap*.

The book cost $23.95, but she said if I followed the advice in the first chapter alone, I'd recoup my original investment in a week.

The first chapter told me if I saved coupons I could cut down on my food bills as much as twenty dollars a visit. They were wrong. The first week, I saved thirty dollars using coupons that I had clipped from every paper and magazine that came into the house.

By having coupons I got an extra carton of cat food . . . an extra bucket of swimming-pool chemicals . . . an extra carton of infant strained lamb . . . and a huge savings on calf's liver.

The only problem was we didn't have a cat, a swimming pool, or a baby, and we all hated liver.

Double-stamp hours made a lot of sense. If I went to the store between 7:30 and 8:45 on a Wednesday morning following a holiday and was among the first ten shoppers to buy the manager's special and come within two minutes of guessing when the cash register tape would run out on the express-lane register, I'd receive double stamps, which when the book was filled would give me ten cents off a jar of ice tea that made my kidneys hurt.

I licked and pasted until the family said my mouthwash just wasn't cutting my glue breath.

I tried creative things with my leftovers, disguising everything with a blanket of cheese and a sprinkling of parsley to kill the taste.

Some of the suggestions were just not practical, like "Don't shop when you're hungry," which eliminated all the hours when the store was open.

I soon tired of trying to disguise cheap cuts of meat to look like something wonderful. (The chicken necks lashed together like a Polynesian raft set adrift on a sea of blue-tinted rice just didn't do it for me.)

Moving quickly to Chapter 2, I discovered I could create an exclusive health spa in my own home for pennies. If there was anything I needed help on it was my body. I neglected it shamefully. The only equipment I had was a phone that rang every time I got into a hot tub.

At the shopping center I decided to blow a few bucks on one of those pulley exercisers that you attach to your doorknob.

Fifteen minutes a day, said the directions, was all it took to lose inches. It was midafternoon when I started to mix together all the concoctions to restore my youth.

First, to give my hair shine, I separated three eggs, beat the yolks with the juice and grated rind of a lemon, and massaged it into my hair. I topped it off with egg white which had been beaten stiff.

Next, two bunches of mint leaves were blended with body lotion and applied to my face and entire body. Slipping a towel over me, I opened the refrigerator door and removed a bowl of ripe avocados to which olive oil had been added and plunged my fingers into them to make my nails hard. The last thing I did as I stretched out on my back on the floor was place a sliced cucumber over each eye to tighten the skin.

Attaching the pulley to the door, I slipped my wrists into the loops of the exerciser. Slowly at first, I stretched my arms down to my side and felt my mint-covered leg being pulled up over my waist.

I must have lifted and lowered my legs for five or ten minutes when I experienced pain—pain that can only be caused by a door slamming on my skull.

"Anyone home?" asked my husband. He always looked at me when he said that.

I tried to sit up, but a cucumber slid down into my towel.

"I was going to ask if you were all right," he said, "but I have just answered my own question."

"You don't understand," I said. "I have just saved fifty or sixty dollars in beauty treatments at some expensive spa. I am using the secrets of the stars."

"Don't look at me," he said. "I won't tell a soul what I have just seen. Is there dinner? Or are you it?"

I got to my feet, clumsily clutched my towel, and started toward the shower. "That's the thanks I get for trying to save you money.

I've been working my fingers to the bone scrimping and saving and doing things around here myself just to cut down a little on expenses and that's the thanks I get."

"I know," he said. "And I loved the chicken-neck rafts. It's just that if you really wanted to help and save money, you could start with the car."

"What do you want me to do for it?"

"For starters, you could learn how to use the self-service islands. That would save a couple of pennies per gallon. And when gas is scarce, you could take time out of your day and have the car gassed up. That would really help."

He didn't know what he was asking. He was talking to a woman who, every time she tried to pull on the car lights, inadvertently released the hood. A woman who had driven for years with the rear-view mirror turned in at lip level. He was talking to a driver who started to pull out of a gas station one day when a man knocked loudly on the car trunk.

When I jammed on the brakes he said, "Ma'am, here's your gas cap. They forgot to put it on."

"Thank you," I said, dropping it into my handbag.

"Aren't you going to put it on your gas tank?"

"If I were," I asked cautiously, "where would I put it?"

I couldn't remember the last time I got gas. He had been getting it to and from work, so I mentally blocked out fifteen minutes on my schedule to pop in and pop out.

Thinking I was in a right-turn lane of cars, I eased around the thirty or forty cars ahead of me and pulled in just in front of a Volkswagen convertible. The man in the car jumped out and tapped on my window.

"Whatya think we're in line for? Demolition Derby?" I had seen that look on a face only once before and vowed I'd never forget it. It was a movie with Rod Steiger, who was playing the part of Pontius Pilate just before he sentenced Jesus of Nazareth.

"Don't worry," I smiled. "I'm not in the full-service line. I'm pumping my own gas."

I think it was then that he threatened to braid my lips. I took my place at the end of the line and played the radiator game with the rest of 'em. (Each one chipped in a quarter and the one whose radiator boiled over first got the pot.)

Several hours later when I pulled up to the pump, a guy with a clipboard said, "What time is your appointment or are you a standing?"

"A standing what?" I asked.

"A standing appointment for your gas."

"You're kidding."

"No. We take a certain number of appointments per day. There's a shortage of gas, you know."

"I'll tell you what. If you'll fill my tank I'll give you a four-piece place setting, consisting of a dinner plate, bread-and-butter plate, and a cup and saucer of the popular Toughware in the wheat pattern."

He relaxed his clipboard and picked his teeth with a matchbook cover.

"Wait a minute. If you put in ten gallons, I'll give you a Styrofoam cooler and a set of glasses with baseball heroes of the forties complete with signatures."

When he started to walk away shaking his head I yelled, "How about a rainbonnet in a handy travel case and balloons for your kids?"

With a lot of luck, I had just enough gas to make it home. I had blown three hours for nothing. I couldn't believe it. There weren't any impulses left in the world any more. Every Thursday, the beauty shop; every six months, the dentist; every year, the gynecologist; every April, H & R Block; every three months, my son's guidance counselor; every five weeks, the Avon lady; every Thursday, garbage day; every three hours, the grocery.

Now I was saddled with a 3:30 P.M. odd-numbered day every other week except when the month had five weeks in it, standing at the gas station for a fill-up, tune-up, lube job, and tire check.

No wonder my husband wanted me to take on the car. It was a full-time job.

A lot of my friends talked about the energy crunch and how it was affecting their lives. Most of all, the crisis was reflected in how far they could go for their vacations.

According to *Living Cheap*, there was an answer to the problem. You simply planned a wonderful "at home" vacation.

Imagine, no turning off 138 necessities of life, leaving instructions for your neighbors, jamming the family into a car, and setting off for Mosquito Larvae Lake or Kneespread, Texas, to God knows what awaits you.

No husband hostile because he could only make ten miles a day. No children hostile because their knees touched. No mother hostile because all she had to look forward to was a handbag full of quarters in a flying-lint laundromat.

My husband was suspicious about an "at home" vacation, but my son was downright surly. I told him: "How would you like to vacation in a place with great weather, two ovens, good food, a bedroom for everyone, TV privileges, and indoor plumbing? Close to swimming facilities, shopping areas, and all your friends?"

"It sounds like home to me," he grumbled.

"Let us think of it as Disneyland," I smiled. "The kitchen is Adventureland, the utility room is Frontierland, the garage is Tomorrowland, the bathroom, Main Street, U.S.A., and the bedroom, Fantasyland."

"We can take a lot of minitours and see our own state," I added, "and for the first time relax and get to know one another when we aren't racing around in a tense crisis situation. And look at all the money we'll save."

The first day of the vacation, I had a few chores for my husband, just to "pull the house together," that he had been putting off.

This included fertilizing, rolling, seeding, and mowing the lawn, adjusting the TV antenna on the roof, painting the exterior of the house, installing a humidifier in the crawl space in the hall closet, wallpapering two bedrooms, fixing a leak behind the washer, and—if there was time—stripping the kitchen cabinets and staining them a lighter color so the kitchen wouldn't seem so dark.

On the morning of the second day, I received a phone call from Mona and Dick Spooner from Billings, Montana, and their two little boys, Ricky and Richie.

They were passing through town when Mona remembered her old friend whom she had not seen since nursery school. When I asked her who the old friend was she said it was me. Naturally, I invited them to stay a few days.

They unloaded five years of laundry, fifteen suitcases, and a cooler that leaked water on my wax buildup.

During the next three days we became authorities on the Spooners.

The boys were just learning English and had not gotten to the three most beautiful words in the English language, "Close The Door!"

We discovered Richie could bounce a ball steadily against the house for 146 hours without stopping.

Dick was a finalist in the gargling Olympics.

Mona's only mental stimulation was sitting in front of the TV set in her baby-doll pajamas trying to answer the questions put to guests on *The Newlywed Game* and turning to Dick saying, "Am I right, baby?"

Ricky would not drink water out of a glass until it had been wrapped in transparent wrap like the motels.

Richie liked to throw rocks in the toilet because it bubbled when he did that.

Mona was allergic to domesticity and let me do the laundry because she wasn't "into electricity."

Sticky . . . I mean Ricky swiped a pillowcase full of our knick-knacks (seashells, ashtrays, and coasters) and stuffed them under the spare tire of their station wagon so we didn't know how to reclaim them without a scene.

The Spooners stayed for four days, which just about took us to the end of our vacation. The visit—counting short trips, entertainment, extra food and drink, and an eighty-dollar plumbing bill to turn off the bubble machine, set us back $450.

Somehow *Living Cheap* lost its credibility for me after the Spooner Experience. I didn't feel like buying clothes secondhand, shopping garage sales, or haunting park-'n-swaps.

I was bored with being clever. Who cared if I saved all the little containers of hot sauce from Mexican carryout or painted my varicose veins in Crayolas to make everyone think I was wearing textured stockings? No one.

Mother was visiting one afternoon when she saw the book on the back of the commode in the bathroom.

"Whose *Living Cheap*?" she asked as she came down the hallway and entered the kitchen.

"No one's any more," I said. "I'm out of my Brand X period and am between self-improvements at the moment."

"If you ask me, there's never been anything wrong with you that a little organization couldn't cure. You're always running around at the last minute like a chicken with her head cut off . . . going in nine directions. You can't seem to get it together."

"I do all right."

"Do you want to go through your entire life being 'all right'? Have you ever been on time for anything? Never!" she said, answering herself.

"If you heard the 'Star-Spangled Banner' you wouldn't recognize it. You've never seen a first inning, a first race, the first act, or the opening of anything in your life.

"Look at this house . . . coffee cups in every room . . . stacks of magazines . . . shoes under everything . . . dog dishes in the living room . . ."

"It's a candy dish."

"The dog's eating something out of it. Did you get that little brochure about a course at the high school at nights called 'Tidying Up Your Life' or something like that? You ought to look into it. Lord knows you could use some help. When was the last time you tossed out the notes on your refrigerator door?"

"Mother! I'll thank you not to come in here and criticize the way I keep my house. If you must know, every time I come in I check the refrigerator for messages. I read them and throw them away."

She moved in closer to the refrigerator and removed a card that was yellow and faded. "Did you overlook this reminder to take your Edsel in for service? It says here they'll give you a full tank of gas and a set of dishes if you act before June 30, 1959."

15 ❧

Tidying Up Your Life

I was late for the Tidying Up Your Life class.

But it wasn't my fault. The roast was frozen when I put it in the oven at five, there wasn't a clock in the house with a time that matched, and two traffic lights were against me.

Luckily, the class was being held at the high school near me. I eased into a seat by the door and looked around. There were a dozen or so adults who had gathered to put some system back in their lives.

The woman across the aisle smiled and whispered "I'm Ruth." Her socks didn't match.

A man behind me asked if I had a pencil he could borrow. Another man asked to be excused as he had left his car lights on.

It was obvious I did not belong here. They were all a bunch of losers who couldn't function with any semblance of order or priorities in their lives.

I shuffled through my handbag and finally resigned myself to reading without my glasses what the teacher, Ms. Sontagg, had written on the blackboard. It was a quiz on how organized we really were. One set of questions was for the men, the other for the women. We were to score one to twelve points for each answer.

1. Are candles in your house a touch of romanticism or the major source of light because you forgot to pay your utility bill?
2. Are you still living out of moving cartons when you have been in your home [check one] (　)five years (　)ten years (　)fifteen years or more?
3. Can you put your hands on the Christmas cards you bought for half price in January?
4. Is your mail stored in one spot or do you use it as a dustpan when you sweep the kitchen floor?
5. Do you put groceries away after each visit to the store or use them directly from the car?
6. Do you often misplace things you use regularly—like door keys, handbags, glasses, or children?
7. Do you forget important occasions like birthdays, dental appointments, rabies shots for the dog, or Christmas?
8. Can you open your closet door without hurting yourself?
9. Would you feel comfortable letting guests wander through your house unattended?
10. Do you accomplish what you want to in a given day or are you always asking "What day is this?"

I leaned over to borrow Ruth's glasses (they were held together with a paper clip) and answered the questions the best I could. My score was deplorable. But that didn't prove anything.

I got by. After all, I had been a writer from my own home for over fifteen years and never missed a deadline. That kind of discipline was bound to take its toll on my personal life. It certainly accounted for the sign on my front door, HOUSE OUT OF ORDER.

Ms. Sontagg said that during the next week we should try to pull together one facet of our daily routine and make some order out of it. In other words: Think Organization.

I walked out with Ruth, who offered to drive me to where my

car was parked. (She had also arrived late and had parked her car in a towaway zone.) We discussed our frailties.

"The trouble with me," said Ruth, "is I'm a perfectionist. Do you have a coathanger?"

"What for?"

"I locked my keys in the car. I'm one of those people who can't settle for mediocrity," she explained, taking off her necklace and making a loop in it to pull the button up. "Easy now . . . I got it!" she smiled. "Do you know I even used to iron diapers? The only reason I'm taking this class is so I can learn how to compromise. If I don't, I'm going to drive myself crazy. What's your problem?"

"It's my mother," I said. "She thinks I need organization. She plans her next headache."

Ruth nodded. "I know the type."

"Her spices are alphabetized. She cleans splatters from her stove every time she uses it. Every year she changes her closet over from winter to summer."

"You're kidding!"

"No. I have never seen my mother carry a suede handbag in the summer. She's what I call a box-saver."

"What's that mean?"

"It's the difference between youth and old age, I think. When you're young you believe that somewhere around the next bend is always a box when you need it. Old age never wants to take that chance."

"You know, I think you're right," nodded Ruth.

"She's got boxes inside boxes. I've received scarves in a stationery box, a blouse in a shoebox, and once on my birthday I got a small pendant in a box marked 'Rectal Thermometer.' Every Christmas, I get something from Mother in a Neiman-Marcus box. It's the same box. My mother has never been in Neiman-Marcus in her entire life.

"Neat little boxes . . . stacked neatly in her neat little closet,"

I rambled, "boxes for transporting cakes, hamsters, laundry, and picnic supplies. Boxes for mailing. Boxes for storing. Boxes for starting fires. Boxes for sleeping dogs, snapshots, and memorabilia. Boxes for rainy-day projects. Boxes for boots by the door. Boxes to keep the baked beans from spilling over the car trunk. Boxes for a child's birthday present . . . boxes in boxes . . ."

"Well," said Ruth, "it's been nice talking to you. See you next week in class."

"I guess so," I hesitated.

"The first rule of being organized," smiled Ruth, "is to keep an appointment book with you at all times." She took out a little green leather book titled CALENDAR and leafed through to the date. "Let's see," she said, "next Tuesday would be the sixteenth and the class starts at seven. I told you I'm a perfectionist," she said, slamming the book shut.

Under CALENDAR . . . embossed in gold . . . was the year 1976.

At the second session of Tidying Up Your Life, I looked for Ruth, but she never appeared. It was too bad, because we dealt with something that had long been a mystery to me: how to make the paperwork easier around the house.

I had a desk, but it was always cluttered and I mixed my business and personal papers together.

My checkbook hadn't been balanced in years.

Ms. Sontagg's suggestions were exciting. She said that for every check I wrote I should be recording it in a little booklet that fit right inside my checkbook. There was space on it for the date, the check number, who it was written to, and the amount.

Now, wouldn't you have thought that someone would have come up with that idea years ago? It certainly simplified knowing what your balance was at all times.

Ms. Sontagg gave us a home assignment. She said during the next week she wanted us to clean out one closet. "Be ruthless," she warned. "Throw out and keep nothing you are not using. We all have a tendency to accumulate things we don't need, but are reluctant to throw away. Do it!"

As she talked, I knew what I had to do. Clean out my husband's closet. It was a storehouse for all seasons.

Every time I opened the door it was like being in a time capsule. His first pair of long trousers. His knickers that he received his First Communion in. His double-breasted suit that he graduated in. His Nehru jacket. They were all there, along with his double-runnered ice skates, bowling ball, kite, composition books from college, old report cards, roadmaps (listing the original thirteen colonies), and fifteen years of back issues of teachers' magazines.

He had a thing about his possessions. Once I tried to pack for him for a vacation and he became quite testy and told me he could do it himself. His luggage weighed a ton. It should have. He was prepared for any occasion. If he won the Nobel peace prize, he had the clothes for it. If he was taken prisoner, he had the clothes for it. He could commandeer a torpedo boat through a squall, barter clothes for mules and guides into a remote jungle, and he had the wardrobe for it. He carried clothes for snorkeling, discoing, safaris, high teas, low ceilings, clothes for lounging, and clothes to leave behind as tips.

In tossing out his clothes I followed the three basic rules to a tee. (1) Have I used or worn it recently? (2) Will I ever use or wear it again? (3) Does it have any sentimental value to me?

Since it was his closet, the decisions were relatively simple.

It was with a feeling of exhilaration that I called a local organization that employed reformed gamblers and had an outlet store for used merchandise. They backed up the truck and I waved good-bye to clutter.

I knew the exact moment my husband discovered what I had done. You could have heard him in the next county. "What have you done with my clothes?"

"I have sent them to that big Trick or Treat in the sky."

He shook his head slowly. "Not my pants with the pockets in them? Not my lucky sweater that I was wearing when the war ended? Not my penny loafers?"

He needn't have carried on so. Within a week, the truck was back with all the items from his closet with a note saying "We're needy . . . not desperate."

I missed a couple of sessions of Tidying Up Your Life, but when I went back for the last meeting I saw Ruth.

"Where have you been?" I asked.

"I told you I'm a perfectionist," she said. "I went home from the first class and started to dress all of my daughter's naked dolls. It took longer than I thought. Are you getting your life together?"

I assured her I was. My turkey roaster was stored on a shelf so high you got nosebleed from it. I had hooks on every door in the house, shelves in every bit of closet space, and was so efficient I was putting sanitized strips across the johns every time I cleaned them. I even ventured into my son's bedroom.

"How long has it been since you were in there?"

"Nineteen seventy-six. He had flu."

"How old is he?" asked Ruth.

"He's a senior in high school."

"Then he'll be going away to school next year?"

"I guess so. We haven't talked about it. I'm afraid I don't relate to my son very well. He's the last one at home and we seem to come from different worlds. Somewhere I've failed him."

"Good grief! You put hooks on his doors and a basketball hoop over his clothes hamper. What does he want from you? Socks that match?"

"He doesn't want anything. That's the problem. It's probably my fault he doesn't spend more time at home. When he's there all I do is yell at him. I complain because I have to pick up after him all the time."

"What's wrong with that?"

"I yell at him for coming in late. I yell at him for wrecking the car. I yell at him for not getting a job. I yell at him for bad grades."

"So what's the problem? You want more choices?"

"You don't understand, Ruth."

"Oh, I understand all right," she said. "You're suffering from terminal guilt. How do you want to be remembered when you go? With a tombstone that stands upright and is chiseled with A MOTHER WHO CARED ENOUGH TO NAG or one that lies flat on the ground like a doormat with a WELCOME so everyone can step on it?

"You're on a guilt trip, my friend, and it's time you started living your own life. You should be like me. Two years ago I saw the light. I had just finished reading a book called *I'll Give Up Guilt When I Stop Making You Feel Rotten.* My son was cooking breakfast one morning when he broke the yolk in his egg. He yelled, 'Mom! Here's another egg for you to eat' and proceeded to break a fresh egg into the skillet for himself. At that moment I came to terms with myself. I announced, 'From this day forward, I am never going to eat another egg with the yolk broken.' "

"That's a beautiful story," I said.

"And it could be *your* story. Things are changing. We don't have to feel guilty any more about things that are supposed to be. Get the book and read it. Listen, it's been fun. I don't know about you, but I've gotten a lot out of this class. From here on in, my life is going to be orderly. I'm going to think before I talk; plan before I act; act before I procrastinate. I think I've got it all together now. So long, Edna."

"That's Erma," I said.

16 ৵৵

I'll Give Up Guilt When
I Stop Making You
Feel Rotten

I'd been giving a lot of thought to my tombstone lately and was
torn between

IF YOU DON'T HAVE A HAIRCUT
I CAN'T HEAR YOU
or
OVERDOSED ON IRON
AND RUSTED TO DEATH 19–

Ruth had mentioned the word I never wanted to hear or for
that matter deal with, *guilt*. She didn't know it but I was an
authority on guilt. Had there been a Guilt Olympics, I could have
won the Decathlon hands down. All ten events:

1. The ten-ring dash for the telephone call from Mother. Why
   did I instinctively know it was from her and let it ring while

I got a cup of coffee and a calendar before I picked up the receiver?

2. The kitchen-table broad jump. Whenever anyone looked around and noticed salt/steak sauce/mustard/catsup/sugar bowl or anything missing, I jumped up like a gazelle and ran for it like I had springs in my underwear.

3. The thirty-minute nap. When I heard a key in the door, I'd jump up, throw cold water on my face, smooth my clothes, pull the bedspread taut, stagger into the kitchen, and throw an onion in the oven. When my husband mentioned the chenille marks on my face, I'd lie and say, "It's bad skin."

4. The finish-off-the-leftovers event. Sometimes, I'd do a by-pass right at the table where, instead of scraping the leftovers off into the disposer, I'd stuff them down Erma. Other times, I'd put them in a holding pattern in the refrigerator and try to inhale all of them by the next "grocery day."

5. The Sunday-night "paper due on Monday" dash. Faced with a child with a paper that had been assigned on the first day of school but had been put off, I felt obliged to borrow reference books on "The History of String" from a person who lived across town on a street that changed names three times after you left the expressway.

6. The draperies-can-be-cleaned-again-and-they'll-look-like-new hurdles. For six years I sacrificed new draperies for baton lessons, a root canal, ten-speed bicycle, low-calorie camp, classical guitar, and two snow tires.

7. The new-puppy throw-up. Despite repeated opposition to a new puppy, I gave in and ended up with a new lifestyle: contemporary dog hair with wall-to-wall urine and a barking doorbell.

8. The javelin throw through the heart. The first one home in the evening would look me straight in the eye and say,

"Anyone home?" When I'd say, "I'm home," they'd say emphatically, "I mean ANYBODY!"

9. The non-Mother billfold. I'd want to die every time someone whipped out a billfold that unrolled like a giant tongue with 187 snapshots of their children. As I rummaged through a half stick of gum, a claim check for the parking lot, a piece of material I was matching, and a Kennedy half dollar, I'd explain lamely, "I sent my children's pictures out to be cleaned."

10. Fifteen-hundred-meter run. From wherever I was, I threw in my hand/ran up the aisle/stopped the game/stopped eating/quit talking/and hit for home so I could be there when I heard those wonderful words of praise from my children: "You'd better be home. I forgot my key."

I figured out long ago that guilt was like mothers. Everyone in the world had at least one. And it was passed down like a torch to the next generation. When you thought about it, a mother traditionally cried at weddings, but when there was a birth, there was always that crooked little smile on her face that said, "You're about to get yours."

I didn't have a friend who hadn't heard of her mother's thirty-six hours of hard labor, her stretch marks that would never tan, and how their appearance in this world at the same time as the Depression was "probably a coincidence, but we'll never be sure, will we?"

By the time I was twenty-five I had a list of things I was going to regret for the rest of my life that covered a wall.

"If you let that baby cry while you polish your nails, you're going to regret it for the rest of your life."

"If you don't get out of that bed and take an antibiotic and go to school to see Andy dressed as a grain of wheat in the Thanksgiving pageant, you are going to regret it for the rest of your life."

"If you don't curse gravy and become a born-again cottage-cheese disciple, you are going to regret it for the rest of your life."

"If you don't go with your husband on that fishing trip to Raw Waste Lake, where the cabin has a wood stove and the land temperature is 92 degrees and the lake temperature is 50 and has leeches, and pretend you are having a good time, you will regret it for the rest of your life."

If I had a dental appointment, I felt guilty. If I was sleepy and had to go to bed early, I felt guilty. If we ran out of toothpaste, I felt guilty. If someone asked me for the time and my watch had stopped, I felt guilty.

I apologized to the washer repairman who removed a pair of training pants out of the hose for forty-two dollars for not having the child toilet-trained.

I apologized to a baby sitter for not having better television reception and fresh lemon for her cola.

I even apologized for bothering a recording that told me to call back the next day when the office was open.

Of all the sins I committed in the name of sanity, possibly none was regarded with so much loathing and disgust as the mother who did not get up in the morning to get breakfast for her family.

It was unthinkable . . . un-American . . . and downright unconscionable.

I had always thought if training films were shown to brides contemplating marriage, the one that would have saved a lot of them from embracing matrimony would have been the one on the mother getting her family out of the house in the mornings.

It was a study in guilt.

I got blamed when the milk was warm and the bread was frozen and the kitchen floor was cold on their bare feet.

It was my fault that their homework was not finished because I made them turn off their lights at 1 A.M. and go to bed.

I assumed the blame for the gym clothes not being dry because I left them in the washer all night instead of setting the alarm and putting them in the dryer.

If a fork was bent, I got it.

If they yelled at me that they needed a note to get back into school after being ill and I didn't get it to them by the time they closed the front door, let it be on my conscience if they were sent home.

If I made them make their beds and they didn't have time to go to the bathroom, then all day their headache would be my fault.

If they dawdled and missed the school bus, it was my punishment to drive them to school and pick them up afterward.

After they had left I viewed all the food left on their plates. If I ate it, I went off my diet and was considered a bimbo. If I threw it away, I was wasteful and was considered a bad wife.

I was a cheap shot. Everyone knew it. I couldn't get out of a conversation without someone saying, "You paid full price for it?" "You carried the baby the full nine months?" "Get serious. You couldn't have gone through four years of college without learning how to play bridge." "You didn't breast-feed? How tragic."

By the time I was thirty, I knew enough about guilt to start spreading a little of it myself. After all, how would my children know anything about it if I didn't set an example?

Since I had always been lousy at long speeches and shouting, I opted to use the nonverbal guilt medium. These forms have always been grossly underrated but are really quite effective.

I started out with the time-honored, no-fail, classic one: sighing.

Whenever one of the kids would fill up a glass to overflowing, I would sit there in absolute silence looking like I had just been told the rabbit died. Then slowly (don't hurry it) I would take a deep breath, deep enough to make my chest rise and get a catch in my throat, and then let it out slowly.

When this is done unhurriedly and with feeling, you can just feel the rottenness of the accusee.

Another favorite was the pantomime with limited dialogue. It's a little dramatic, but it works. When one of my children informed me he was going on a picnic on Mother's Day with his friend's family, I would square my shoulders (this is important; it denotes courage) and give a very weak smile. Then without commenting one way or another, I'd go to the sewing basket and get a piece of black fabric and begin to drape his empty chair at the dinner table. (By this time he should be feeling so miserable he has the phone in his hand.) Now you're ready for the zinger. Smile painfully and say, "Have a good time, son."

My ace in the hole was the "I'll do it myself" number.

When I asked my husband or one of the children to take the garbage cans to the curb and they didn't respond right away, I'd paddle out in the darkness in a pair of bedroom slippers (preferably in the snow), a coat that didn't fit, no hat and no gloves, and begin to drag the cans noisily to the driveway inch by inch . . . HOLDING MY SIDE.

It was important in this operation to say little . . . just wince, strain, and occasionally yell to a neighbor, "How lucky you are to have people who love you."

One afternoon I announced to my husband and son that the television antenna had blown off course. No one moved. I rattled around in the garage for the ladder, dragged it to the side of the house, and slowly ascended to the roof. I must have sat up there three-quarters of an hour waiting for someone to follow me. I had just confirmed my suspicion. Ruth was probably right. It was time to read *I'll Give Up Guilt When I Stop Making You Feel Rotten.*

The book was two years old, but it was still twenty years ahead of where I was. The author, Jim Preach, said it was time adults let go of traditions. Relationships were changing. The days when a family existed as a matched set were gone. Never had there been a time when individuals flourished and there was no need to feel guilty about its passing.

Already I felt better. Just knowing that I was no longer responsible for clean underwear if my son had an accident was a weight off my mind.

Jim also said that a lot of guilt stemmed from setting goals too high not only for yourself but for others. You cannot always agree, he said, but at least you can try to understand.

"If you're at odds with your children, don't make them feel guilty for their actions and yourself feel guilty because you don't agree, just keep lines of communication open and establish some kind of rapport."

It wasn't easy advice. Children and parents were living in different worlds. The new morality was like future shock and I couldn't get used to it. Could a girl who suffered from terminal contrite when she drove a boy to lust by wearing patent-leather pumps find happiness in a home where her kids watched *The Flying Nun* and figured they'd made their Easter duty?

I wasn't the only parent who felt it. We talked about it a lot. What we thought was a normal communication gap had become a cultural cavern that widened every day.

While parents prattled on about writing notes of thanks for graduation gifts, the kids weren't even planning on showing up for the ceremony.

While parents were rousting their kids out of bed and laying the responsibility for cutting the grass on them the kids were smoking it.

One afternoon I answered the phone. It was a girl asking for my son. In my time a girl never called a boy unless she was asked to pass on a homework assignment or was inviting him to the cotillion.

To show my displeasure at the custom, I sucked in my breath slowly in preparation for my "sighing" number. My son looked at me sharply and I smiled even when my face turned blue.

17 ♪✳♪♪

Contemporary Etiquette That's AWRIIIITE

There's a special place in heaven for the chaperones where the sun always shines, varicose veins dissipate, and the bar never closes.

I had enjoyed a self-exile from school activities for several years, mainly because I figured I had served my time. I had gone to camp and eaten raw chicken cooked over a tin can punched with holes, chaperoned a group of sixth-graders through a meat-packing plant, and sat through summers of Little League softball games that were real squeakers: Giants, 87–Dust Devils, 34.

When Mrs. Bitterly, the advisor of the senior class, called me to help chaperone the prom, I instinctively started to decline. Then I changed my mind.

I got out my trusty book of etiquette to brush up on what a chaperone did. It said: "The presence of an adult guards our young people from possible foolishness or from involving themselves in situations from which they are not mature enough to extract themselves."

That didn't sound so bad. And after all, what better way to

413

understand today's young people than to spend an evening with them.

It's logic like that that fills nursing homes.

To begin with, my son said he wasn't going to the prom. It cost too much to rent a suit, the evening was a bore, and, besides, no girl had asked him yet.

Mrs. Bitterly called a meeting of the chaperones for the following Wednesday to fill us in on what to expect.

"If any of you has a hearing problem," she said, "let me know now."

A woman said, "I can hear perfectly."

"Then you may be excused," she said. "We are looking for people whose hearing is already impaired. By the end of the evening the music could conceivably make you lose your appetite, make you nauseated, or render you sterile. Those of you proficient in lip-reading skills will do well.

"Now, we are doing away with the hand stamp this year. We used to stamp the hand of every guest at the prom. When they went out and came back the stamp showed up under a fluorescent lamp. However, last year, Mrs. Miller had trouble with a few older rowdies who crashed the party and had the stamp tattooed on their tongues. She didn't feel she should quarrel with this.

"I cannot stress enough: be sure of your authority. When you walk into the parking lot and discover three hoods who do not attend the school ripping off a car and have a tire iron in their hands, make sure you have a better threat than, 'You know this makes you ineligible for the Robert Frost poetry awards in the spring.'

"If you are going for a 'bust' of any kind, make sure you are familiar with the facts. Two years ago, a guidance counselor summoned an emergency unit, two police cruisers, and a priest for a boy who had just thrown two Tic Tacs into his mouth to improve his breath.

"You may dance if you like but know that the current craze is disco and if you do not have a flight plan filed, you could hurt yourself.

"Lastly, how do you know when the prom is over? First, there will be a ringing sensation in the ears and the band will be gone. Your eyes will no longer smart from Clearasil and your car will be the only one left in the parking lot . . . if you are lucky."

Personally, I thought Mrs. Bitterly overreacted. Other than the fact that for a few days following the prom I answered the phone and it wasn't ringing, I did fine. The kids seemed to have a good time. Maybe it was my success with the prom that prompted me to approach my son and ask him about his future.

"I've been checking into it," he said. On his desk were catalogues from every school you can imagine; none of them sounded familiar. I leafed through a few of them: Diablo Karate School . . . Electronics Institute and Tape Deck Installation . . . and College of Transcendental Bowling.

"Are you serious about these?"

"I've eliminated a lot of them," he said. "Especially the ones behind the Iron Curtain. Their football teams are lousy."

"Well, why don't we check out a few?" I said. "Your father and I could go along and we could make a vacation out of it."

I have spent better vacations in intensive care.

The first school was out because it was twenty miles from the ski slopes.

The second school was out because their football team lost six games the previous year.

The third school was out because they had a grading system.

The fourth school we looked at, he loved. I expected John Belushi to fly through a window any minute dressed in ham and cheese. The rooms looked like cells with terminal mildew. A girl in a bathrobe was walking her dog in the corridor. Someone was cooking illegal brownies.

"How many ironing boards do you have?" I asked.

A hush fell over the entire dorm.

"What are the posted hours that you have to be in at nights?"

A hush fell over the entire campus.

"Where is your house mother?"

A hush fell over the entire state.

They weren't guilt-stricken. They were all laughing themselves to death.

I couldn't pretend to be anything but confused over the change in relationships. "Roommate" had an entirely different connotation, as did "companion," "associate," and—as one of my daughter's friends listed the unwed father on the birth certificate— "significant other person."

I remember going to a wedding of the daughter of a friend. The bride wore something old/something new/something borrowed/ something blue and it was the same thing. A pair of jeans. She had met her husband when he was living with her girl friend. I remember the organ played a hymnlike melody that was hauntingly familiar. I couldn't identify it. Then it came to me while they were exchanging their vows. It was "Days of Wine and Roses."

The next time I went to the library, I asked if there was a book on modern manners and morals and the librarian recommended *Contemporary Etiquette That's Awriiite.*

In checking over the index, I discovered things had changed since Amy Vanderbilt recommended shaking hands with your gloves on until your engagement had been formally announced.

There was a chapter on dating: how long does a boy keep a girl waiting until he finishes dressing.

Weddings: what to do when the groom is still married.

Entertaining: when to wear shoes and when to carry them.

Grooming: the six occasions in your life when you shave your legs.

Houseguests: explaining "meaningful relationships" to your sixty-five-year-old mother who insists on putting your roommate in a Big Boy recliner for the night.

Getting a job and other obscenities.

Introductions: explaining to a fourth-grade teacher why you have two sets of sons the same age who are related through divorce.

Why wouldn't children be different? Most had been conceived during a commercial break on the late-night movie, weaned on every new concept in education ever devised, nurtured on social change that affected the entire world, and sustained on a diet of sex, violence, realism, and independence.

Who would have thought that I would be sitting in a movie with my high school son and when the sex in the movie reached gasping proportions, he would lean over to me and say, "Why don't you go out for some more popcorn, Mom?"

That was my line when he asked which one of the dwarfs was Snow White's husband.

Who would have guessed after twenty-five years of vitamins, shots, and regular checkups that your children would accuse you of poisoning them with bleached flour, sugar, additives, and butterfat and would sit around telling you in explicit detail how hot dogs are made?

For a while after I leafed through the book I took on a new air. Whenever my son mentioned something that was supposed to shock me I responded with "Really!" or "Awriiite" or "Far out."

There was nothing that could shake me up. If he related a particularly grim movie to me I shouted, "Go for it." If he played a record at 97 decibels I yelled, "Could you turn that up? I love the words."

If he told me he skipped a day at school, I took a deep breath and said, "You're not the only one."

Finally one day he said he was not going to get a job this summer because he wanted time to get in touch with his feelings and find out where he was coming from.

I changed into a parent right before his eyes.

"I don't know where you're coming from," I shouted. "But I know where you're headed. The same place you were last summer . . . getting up at the crack of noon. Every time I shook out the bedclothes, there you were. Every time I walked in front of the TV set, there you were. Every time I followed the beam of light from the refrigerator door, you were at the end of it.

"For your information, Peter Pan, you are getting a job this summer. Say it slowly at first . . . let it roll over your tongue and you'll get used to it . . . j o b . . . J O B . . . JOB. It's an old establishment expression meaning to have some pride in yourself, some productivity, pulling your own weight, having a reason for getting up in the morning and being tired enough to go to sleep at night.

"For someone who abhors materialism, you sure demand a lot of it . . . for someone who is turned off by pollution, you sure contribute to it. For someone who is a pacifist, you sure know how to start an internal family war. So, get off your duff tomorrow and get a job!"

My son didn't say anything for a full minute. He just smiled and shook his head. Then he said, "You talk pretty good."

"What do you mean by a crack like that?"

"I mean all this time all you ever did was look at me and frown and sigh a lot. I never knew what you were thinking. I just felt rotten."

"You mean you don't feel rotten now?"

"Yeah, but now I know *why* I feel rotten. I never knew before."

"I guess old Jim Preach was right."

"Are you still plowing through all those self-help books?"

"Don't knock 'em. Someday I'll get it all together."

"You know what your trouble is," said my son. "You try too hard. You're going through the old 'Be a winner' routine. When I was younger, I used to think winning was everything. It isn't. Don't sweat it. Just lay back and let it happen. Take life as it comes. The important thing to remember is Be Yourself."

A few hours later he brushed by me in the kitchen. He was wearing his father's tennis shorts, a T-shirt he filched from the school's lost and found, and carried his brother's tennis racket. He grabbed my car keys off the countertop and winked. "Remember what I said. Be yourself!"

18 ♪❋♪♪

I Don't Care What I
Say . . . I Still Like Me

It had been all of three months since I picked up a how-to book.

A lot of people I know eased off reading them gradually, but I knew if I was to kick the habit I'd have to stop reading them cold turkey and live just one day at a time.

It wasn't easy. I was surrounded by social self-help readers who couldn't wait to pick up a volume and offer me one. Tonight would be my first big test.

We were going to a cocktail party at Jill's house. My husband hated cocktail parties. He said people drank too much and it was like talking to a traffic light . . . a blinking red eye, and in five seconds they sped off to another corner.

I felt pretty wonderful. My daughter was giving up television for Lent this year instead of me. My older son had shaved and no longer looked like a Lincoln penny, and that very day we had just gotten a letter from our younger son at school (*Mom* was spelled with two o's, but what the heck, he was only a freshman).

The entire family was pleased that I had stopped improving

420

myself and was back to my old ways. I loved everyone else better than me, was insecure about my job, had no idea what I was feeling or why and almost never listened to my body.

There had been withdrawal symptoms after I had stopped reading self-help books. I knew there would be. I was checking out in a supermarket one day when I glanced down at a headline near the checkout stand. The article was topped by IT'S 11 O'CLOCK! DO YOU KNOW WHERE YOUR ANXIETIES ARE?

My palms became sweaty, my throat dry, and instinctively I dug into my handbag for my glasses. My husband came by just in time, steered me toward the door and said, "You need a drink."

It was strange standing in the middle of Jill's living room. I couldn't help but reflect this was where it all began . . . exactly one year ago.

A voice at my elbow interrupted my thoughts. "Hi! Have a drink?"

It was Phyllis.

"Of course," I smiled.

"How about a cheese fluff?"

"Thanks."

"How about a book on *Can You Handle Your Biofeedback During a Full Moon?*"

"Good-bye Phyllis."

"Wait a minute!" she shouted. "Even the Pope approves biorhythms."

"I don't care if they're at the top of the charts, I am not going to get involved in another self-help book."

"As you stand there talking," said Phyllis, "your frustrations, your tensions, and your conflict translate into specific events taking place inside your body."

"I am leaving you, Phyllis. You're going to look like a fool standing here talking to yourself."

"God forbid your biorhythms could be out of sync, but it happens. You could be in one of your critical days. There's always the possibility you could meet with a freak accident."

"I am just saying good-bye to one."

"Why are you so sore?" she persisted.

"Because ever since you turned me on to *The Sub-Total Woman,* my life has not been the same."

"Then it's true. You are having trouble with your marriage."

Rita overheard our conversation and said, "Listen, sweetie, Dan and I swear on the Camp of the Close Encounter and Massage Village about fifty miles north of here. It's a wonderful shared experience of personal learning. And you don't have to worry about a wardrobe—if you get my drift."

"No, really, Rita, our marriage is just fine. The kids have all left home and . . ."

"Did I hear you say you're going through the Empty Nest trauma?" asked Natalie. "Some people make the transition smoothly, but you're going to have to be careful. You're a child-geared person. We've always known that. You were always fulfilled by kids . . . baking the funny cakes for their birthdays, buying a bolt of material and dressing them all alike like wallpaper, and you always had a sign in front of your house for as long as I can remember: FREE KITTENS. Have you read *Nest of Tears: Handling a Child's Rejection?*"

"Natalie, listen to me. I am not rejected. At my age it's predictable . . ."

"Listen to her," said Marcia. "At her age. Why, I've got a cookie sheet older than you. Don't be so insecure. You're not all that unattractive. Nothing that reading *Look Like a Million Dollars for Only Half That Amount* couldn't cure."

I reached out and grabbed *Can You Handle Your Biofeedback During a Full Moon?* and ran my hand over the cover. I could feel beads of perspiration on my forehead and my hand shook. Could I stand to have it start all over again?

The raising of my consciousness level seemed so innocent at first I promised myself I could stop raising it anytime I wanted to.

The lies about how many self-help books I was reading a day.

The excuses I made when I sat at the breakfast table and read just a few more pages from *How to Get Rich During a Democratic Administration* before I could start my housework.

The day my husband found *Suppressing My Primal Scream* hidden in my hosiery drawer.

The night I had too much to read and embarrassed my family by standing on a coffee table reciting from *How to Engage in Perversion as a Hobby.*

Did I want to go back to that?

I handed the book back to Phyllis. "Thanks, but no thanks. I am going to be myself."

"You're kidding," said Marcia. "Without any help from anyone?"

"That's right."

"You're going against the tide," said Natalie. "No one is themselves these days. It just isn't good enough. Everyone is into some kind of a transitional flow."

"You're copping out," snapped Phyllis. "Sure, it's easy to sit around and just let things happen, but the bottom line is groping! How can you be happy if you're not miserable?"

Natalie was right about one thing. I was out of the mainstream. There were "color parties" in which everyone in the neighborhood was invited to be analyzed and effective colors were suggested for them to wear and to decorate their homes with. But no one asked me.

A speaker at Town Hall discussed how to survive an audit from the IRS using tranquilizers that you could buy over the counter, but I wasn't invited.

Phyllis even gave a party for all dogs who were born under the Gemini sign. My dog was the only Gemini in the block who wasn't there.

I didn't see any of them until one day in the book department I looked up and there was Phyllis.

She was holding a book called *I Don't Care What I Say . . . I Still Like Me*. She seemed surprised to see me.

"So how's Polly Perfect? Still handling your own anxiety attacks, struggling with your birth traumas, and treating your neuroses out of your medicine cabinet?"

"I'm doing okay," I smiled.

"I suppose it's a waste of time to point out that this new book is a brilliant insight into the Id? It tells how through conscientious self-analysis a person can achieve happiness without a lot of inner conflict and mythological mishmash. It facilitates and utilizes an entirely new concept in living experience."

"That translates to 'be yourself.' Right?"

Phyllis looked surprised. "Right. Did you read it?"

"Phyllis," I smiled, "I wrote it."

Author's Note ∫❋∫❋∫
The Pursuit of Happiness

Our forefathers didn't know what they were laying on us when they penned the Declaration of Independence.

Life and Liberty were pieces of cake compared to the Pursuit of Happiness.

I have lived this book for over a year and never knew how miserable I was until I tried to find out why I was happy. Oh, I knew I was bored, depressed, neurotic, inhibited and unfulfilled, but I figured no one is perfect.

During the last year I have come to grips with midlife, found inner peace, fought outer flab, interpreted my fantasies, examined my motives for buying, dissected my marriage, charted my astrological stars, and become my best AND ONLY friend. I have brought order to my life, meditated, given up guilt, adjusted to the new morality, and spent every living hour understanding me, interpreting me, and loving me—and you know what? I'm bored to death with me. If I never hear another word about me it will be too soon.

I have no more curiosity about myself. No more drive to make

425

me a better person. No more patience to find out what I am feeling.

If I never see the words "input," "concept," "feedback," or "bottom line," it will be all right with me.

If I ever say the words "share with you" or "at this point of time in my life," I hope my saliva runs dry.

After a year of reading sixty-two self-help books and articles, I have discovered something interesting. You don't find happiness. It finds you.

If you are married, you're supposed to be happier than those who are not. If you control your life and have the wherewithal to do it, you're supposed to be happier. If you love and are loved back you're supposed to be happier. Financial security will make you happier (I've suspected that for a long time).

I have discovered something else. We are not permitted to be depressed any more, nor are we allowed to age.

Already people are beginning to wonder where have all the old people gone? They've gone underground because we live in a time when we must go through life like a miracle fabric: drip-dry and wrinkle-free. If your hands look as young as your married daughter's, you can get on a commercial. If you are seventy and can do a time step, you get a shot on the Carson show. If you saw the Civil War and can wave a flag, you get a standing ovation.

The "Is Everybody Happy?" syndrome is just as bad. I used to wallow—no, nearly drown—in wonderful funky days of despair when nothing went right, and I loved it. Those down-in-the-dirty-pits days when I was unappreciated, overworked, underpaid, and had split heels from not wearing socks in the winter.

I couldn't win. My hair wouldn't curl. The hot water heater rusted out. My best friend's husband got a promotion. My child dropped a typewriter that belonged to the school. Someone asked me if my youngest was my grandchild. The car door froze shut on my morning to drive.

Maybe those days were why I appreciated the ones where my

gynecologist said I just had flu, and the dryer only needed a fifteen-cent fuse.

This book is not a put-down of all self-help books. It focuses on the absurdity of paying $12.95 for a cookbook that tells you how to save money. It points out how ludicrous it is to read a book on guilt that threatens, "If you don't read this, you'll regret it for the rest of your life." It takes on the books that take 362 pages to tell you, "Stop listening to advice and take control of your own life."

After reading sixty-two books and articles on how to deal with oneself, I realized something was missing . . . a sense of humor. I cannot believe that people look into the mirror that reflects their actions and behavior and keep a straight face.

There is a paragraph from Gail Sheehy's *Passages* that seems to sum up a flaw most of us have when we pursue happiness: "Would that there were an award for people who come to understand the concept of enough. Good enough. Successful enough. Thin enough. Rich enough. Socially responsible enough. When you have self-respect you have enough, and when you have enough, you have self-respect."

Aunt Erma's Cope Book fulfills a fantasy for me. I always wanted to be an authority on how to do something . . . ANYTHING! For years, I watched the Dr. Joyces, the Dear Abbys, the Mrs. Clarabelles, and the Miss Americas come to grips with the problems of life head-on.

After a year of research, it became apparent to me—the only "how-to" book I had enough expertise to write was "How to Get from Monday to Friday in 12 Days."

In her infinite wisdom, my mother offered yet another observation on my months of self-examination, devotion to improvement, and quest for happiness. She said, "I'll be glad when you hit menopause. It'll take your mind off your problems."

Motherhood
The Second Oldest Profession

There are a lot of proper names in this book.
None of them is real with the exception of
my mother's, whose name is Erma.
If there is a name the same as yours,
it is pure coincidence.

ERMA BOMBECK

Contents ❧❧❧

Introduction ❧❧

I was one of the luckier women who came to motherhood with some experience.

I owned a Yorkshire Terrier for three years.

At ten months, my children could stay and heel. At a year, they could catch a Frisbee in their teeth in mid-air. At fifteen months, after weeks of rubbing their noses in it and putting them outside, they were paper trained.

Some women were not so fortunate or realistic. They viewed motherhood from a safe distance.

At a baby shower I was attending one evening, the new mother-to-be gasped, "Did you see the story in the paper about the woman who forgot one of her children in a laundromat restroom? And she dares call herself a mother! How disgusting! What kind of a mother would . . ."

"What kind of a mother would . . ." It was a familiar phrase. Ten years and three children earlier, I had used it myself with just the right blend of shock and disapproval.

Now, I personally knew seven mothers who had tried the same thing.

"Mother" has always been a generic term synonymous with love, devotion, and sacrifice. There's always been something mystical and reverent about them. They're the Walter Cronkites of the human race . . . infallible, virtuous, without flaws and conceived without original sin, with no room for ambivalence.

Immediately following birth, every new mother drags from her bed and awkwardly pulls herself up on the pedestal provided for her.

Some adjust easily to the saintly image. They come to love the adulation and bask in the flocks that come to pay homage at their feet on Mother's Day.

Some can't stand the heights and jump off, never to be seen again.

But most mothers just try to figure out what they're supposed to do . . . and how they can do it in public.

Motherhood is the second oldest profession in the world. It never questions age, height, religious preference, health, political affiliation, citizenship, morality, ethnic background, marital status, economic level, convenience, or previous experience.

It's the biggest on-the-job training program in existence today.

Motherhood is not a one-size-fits-all, a mold that is all-encompassing and means the same thing to all people.

Some mothers give standing ovations to bowel movements. Other mothers reserve their excitement for an affair.

Some mothers have so much guilt, they cannot eat a breath mint without sharing it. Other mothers feel nothing when they tell a kid his entire pillowcase of Halloween candy got ants in it . . . and eats it herself.

Some mothers cry when their thirty-year-old daughters leave home and move to their apartments. Other mothers sell their twelve-year-old son's bed when he goes to a long scout meeting.

I've always felt uncomfortable about the articles that eulogized me as a nurse, chauffeur, cook, housekeeper, financier, counselor, philosopher, mistress, teacher, and hostess. It seemed that I always read an article like this on the day when my kid was in a school play and I ironed only the leg of the trouser that faced the audience, knitted all morning, napped all afternoon, bought a pizza for dinner, and had a headache by 10:30.

For a long time, I was afraid to laugh at the contrast, for fear no one else would.

Anticipating the question of which mother am I in this book, I will tell you. There's a little bit of all of them in me. Rose's humor, Janet's frustration, Mary's emptiness, and oh, yes . . . Cora's awe.

All of them are real in every sense. They are not the nameless, faceless stereotypes who appear once a year on a greeting card with their virtues set to prose, but women who have been dealt a hand for life and play each card one at a time the best way they know how. No mother is all good or all bad, all laughing or all serious, all loving or all angry. Ambivalence runs through their veins.

This book was written too late for Judy, a mother in her early twenties I met a few years ago through brief correspondence. Judy was incarcerated in a Southern prison for the unspeakable crime of killing her child. Withdrawn, unable to communicate, and living in her own particular hell, she passed time in solitary confinement reading some of my earlier books. After she had read and reread them, she wrote to me, "Had I known mothers could laugh at those things, I probably wouldn't be where I am today."

What is certain is that there is probably not one of you who has not at some time of your life demanded an answer to the question "What kind of a mother would . . ." It's an old phrase, conceived in innocence, carried with pomposity, and born of condemnation. It is not until you become a mother that your judgment slowly turns to compassion and understanding.

Let none of you who read about the mothers in this book judge them until you have walked in their shoes of clay.

Erma Bombeck

1 ❧❧

So You Want to Be a Mother!

One of the biggest complaints about motherhood is the lack of training.

We all come to it armed only with a phone number for a diaper service, a Polaroid camera, a hotline to the pediatrician, and an innocence with a life span of fifteen minutes.

I have always felt that too much time was given before the birth, which is spent learning things like how to breathe in and out with your husband (I had my baby when they gave you a shot in the hip and you didn't wake up until the kid was ready to start school), and not enough time given to how to mother after the baby is born.

Motherhood is an art. And it is naïve to send a mother into an arena for twenty years with a child and expect her to come out on top. Everything is in the child's favor. He's little. He's cute and he can turn tears on and off like a faucet.

There have always been schools for children. They spend any-where from twelve to sixteen years of their lives in them, around other children who share the experience of being a child and how to combat it. They're in an academic atmosphere where they learn how to manipulate parents and get what they want from them. They bind together to form a children's network, where they pool ideas on how to get the car, how to get a bigger allowance, and how to stay home when their parents go on a vacation. Their influence is felt throughout the world. Without contributing a dime, they have more ice cream parlors, recreation centers, playgrounds, and amusement parks than any group could ever pull off.

They never pay full price for anything.

How do they do it?

They're clever and they're educated.

Some people think mothers should organize and form a union. I think education is the answer. If we only knew what to do and how to do it, we could survive.

It's only a dream now. But one of these days there will be a School for New Mothers that will elevate the profession to an academic level. What I wouldn't have given for a catalogue offering the following skills.

Creative Nagging 101: Learn from expert resource people how to make eye contact through a bathroom door, how to make a senior cry, and how to make a child write you a check for bringing him into the world. More than 1,000 subjects guaranteed to make a child miserable for a lifetime. "Sit up straight or your spine will grow that way" and "Your aquarium just caught fire" are ordinary and boring. Creative Nagging gets you noticed! Child is furnished.

Seminar for Savers: No one dares call herself "Mother" until she has learned to save and hoard. Squirreling away is not a congenital talent, as formerly believed. It can be learned. Find out where to store thirty pounds of twist ties from bread and cookie packages, old grade-school cards, and boots with holes in the toe. Learn how to have a Christmas box for every occasion by snatching them from a person before they have taken the present out of it. Learn why hangers mate in dark closets and observe them as they reproduce. Mature language.

Investments and Returns from Your Children: Frank discussions on how to get your children to believe they owe you something. Each day mothers let opportunities for guilt slip through their fingers without even knowing it. The child who was ordered to "call when you get there" and doesn't can be made to suffer for years. Find out how. Special attention is paid to Mother's Day and the child who once gave a $40 cashmere sweater to a girl he had known only two weeks, while you, who have stomach muscles around your knees, received a set of bathroom soap in the shape of seahorses. Class size is limited.

Perfection: How to Get It and How to Convince Your Children You've Got It: The art of never making a mistake is crucial to motherhood. To be effective and to gain the respect she needs to function, a mother must have her children believe she has never engaged in sex, never made a bad decision, never caused her own mother a moment's anxiety, and was never a child. Enrollment limited to those who have taken "The Madonna Face Mystique."

Legal Rights for Mothers: Know the law. Are you required to transport laundry that has been in the utility room longer than sixty days? Do you have the right to open a bedroom door with a skewer, or would this be considered illegal entry? Can you abandon a child along a public highway for kicking Daddy's seat for 600 miles? Are you liable for desertion if you move and don't tell your grown son where you are going? A panel of legal experts will discuss how binding is the loan of $600 from a two-month-old baby to his parents when there were no witnesses.

The History of Suspicion and Its Effects on Menopause: Due to popular demand, we are again offering this course for older mothers. How to tell when your child is telling the truth even after her nose has stopped growing. The following case histories of suspicion will be discussed: Did Marlene really drop a Bible on her foot, keeping her from getting to the post office and mailing the letter to her parents? Did twenty dollars really fall out of your purse and your son found it and kept it and didn't know how it got there? Was your son really in bed watching Masterpiece Theatre when he heard a racket and got up to discover 200 strangers having a party in the house and drinking all of Dad's beer?

Physical examination required.

Threats and Promises: Four fun-filled sessions on how to use chilling threats and empty promises to intimidate your children for the rest of their lives. Graduates have nothing but praise for this course. One mother who told her daughter she would wet the bed if she played with matches said the kid was thirty-five before she would turn on a stove. Hurry. Enrollment limited.

Note:
Guilt: The Gift That Keeps Giving has been canceled until an instructor can be found. Dr. Volland said his mother felt he had no business teaching others when he ignored his own mother.

2 ❧

Donna (Donna Reed Show), **Harriet** (Ozzie and Harriet), **Barbara** (Leave It to Beaver), **Shirley** (Partridge Family), **Marjorie** (Make Room for Daddy), **Jane** (Father Knows Best), **Florence** (The Brady Bunch)

What Kind of a Mother Would . . . Tip the Tooth Fairy?

Among them they had twenty-two children, six husbands, and three maids. For two decades, during the Fifties and Sixties, they were role models for every mother in the country.

They looked better cleaning their houses than most of us looked at our wedding.

They never lost their temper, gained weight, spent more money than their husbands made, or gave viewers any reason not to believe they were living out their lives in celibacy.

They never scrubbed a toilet, were never invaded by roaches, never shouted, and no one ever knew what they did between the time their families left in the morning and came home in the evening.

Every week you viewed a miracle—seven out of seven women who got their figures back after having children.

Their collective virtue was patience. There was no situation too traumatic for them to cure with milk and cookies, no problem that could not be resolved in twenty-four minutes, plus four minutes for commercials and two minutes for theme and credits.

I often wondered what would happen if one of their children had slammed a fellow student against the paper towel machine in the school restroom and extorted his milk money.

There's no doubt in my mind:

Donna would have called a family conference.

Barbara would have met Ward at the door and said, "Dinner's ready."

Shirley would have taken away his drums for a week.

Marjorie would have changed her nail polish.

Harriet would have sent Ozzie out for ice cream.

Jane would have invited the rip-offee to dinner.

And Florence would have her live-in bake extra brownies.

It was the age of God, Motherhood, Flag, and Apple Pie. All you had to do to be a mother was to put on an apron.

No one did it better than the prime-time mothers.

I was one of the not-quite-ready-for-prime-time mothers.

I never wore hose around the house all day, nor did I know anyone personally who did.

My kids were the ones the prime-time mothers forbade their kids to play with or else they would get into trouble.

I never ironed my husband's pajamas.

If I raised my hand to wipe the hair out of my children's eyes, they'd flinch and call their attorney.

We all knew prime-time mothers were too good to be true. (I once bragged that I saved a diabetic's life by throwing my body in front of a Donna Reed rerun.) But God, how we wanted them to be.

I had a fantasy once about Jane.

She had one of those pantyhose-on-backwards days. You know, the kind when you don't know if you're going or coming. Betty had borrowed and sweated in her new Christmas sweater, she discovered a nude calendar stashed between Bud's mattress and his dust ruffle, and Kathy hadn't spoken to her for three days.

Her mother volunteered the advice, "You should be more strict with those children," and the ground was real mushy around their septic tank.

The bank called and said she had written a check to cover an "overdraft," the cleaner called to say the patches fell off Jim's favorite jacket, and someone sprayed an obscene set of directions on her picket fence.

The fantasy always ended with Jane standing in the middle of the mess and delivering a four-letter word before she fell apart. I felt rewarded somehow.

Whatever the television mothers were, they got the message across that they were doing something important. They were the hub of the family that held it all together. And it only took thirty minutes a week to do it.

It was the not-ready-for-prime-time mothers who questioned it in the late Sixties.

They questioned the long days. The lack of fringe benefits. The run-and-fetch syndrome. The question, "What kind of a day did you have?" and the answer that fell on deaf ears.

It started out as a ripple of discontent, gathering momentum through the Seventies. By the Eighties the dissidents were a force to be dealt with, as fifty-two percent of all mothers had jobs outside the home.

Whatever happened to the Insulin Seven: Donna, Barbara, Shirley, Harriet, Marjorie, Jane, and Florence? They disappeared beneath a tidal wave of reality.

Oh, occasionally one of them returns to the tube in mid-afternoon on reruns. There are few mothers home to watch them at that time, only latch-key children, eating pizza in front of the set, who must wonder what indeed they are . . . these dinosaurs in aprons who roam the Earth smiling wisely and pouring milk.

Ironically, I miss them in spite of their maddening perfection. And I envy them a little because they seemed so fulfilled.

I ask myself why. Maybe it was because they got paid so well for being a mother and the season lasted only twenty-six weeks. Maybe it was because they only had the kids for thirty minutes a week and then they could send them back to wherever they came from.

Maybe it was even a little applause when they did a difficult scene.

Or maybe . . . maybe it was because they never had to face life between the hours the family left in the morning and returned in the evening.

Prime-time mothers.

Fade out.

End of show.

End of an era.

3 ❧❧❧

Frank

What Kind of a Mother Would . . .
Go an Entire Day without Shaving?

On October 15, 1979, Frank Rutledge became the mother of Adam, fourteen; Caroline, twelve; and Teddy, age six, thus becoming the first suburban mother in Rochester with a mustache who wasn't on estrogen.

The new role came out of a conversation six months earlier, when Frank confessed he was "burnt out" from working at the ad agency. He was sick of cereal boxes that tap danced and termites wearing tutus. All he wanted to do was to stay home and work on his novel.

His wife, Ann, was ecstatic with his decision. She had missed the sexual revolution, arrived late for the women's movement, let the kids borrow her self-esteem, and refused to begin her midlife crisis until she lost ten pounds. The idea of going anyplace where she didn't have to cut up everyone's meat titillated her.

They agreed to try it for a year. Ann would go to work and sell office supplies and Frank would stay home and write. It seemed like a simple decision. After all, the President of the United States had been working from his home for years.

There were, however, a few appreciable differences.

1. The President of the United States was never summoned from a high-level phone conversation that could alter the course of history to hear a voice yell, "We're out of toilet paper!"
2. Pest-control men did not shuffle through the White House spraying his feet with insecticide.
3. The First Lady never called from her downtown office with instructions for him to "go to the garage. Turn the power mower on its back and just under the right rotary blade see a serial number. Copy it down and call it in to the repair shop so we won't get caught again when the grass needs cutting."

By November 22, after a month of chasing escaped gerbils and listening all day to "I'm telling," Frank ripped the blank piece of paper out of his typewriter and made a second decision.

He decided to put off writing his novel. Instead he would keep a diary on his experiences as a house-husband.

It would sell. He knew it would. He couldn't go into a bookstore without seeing an entire section of books on domestic drolleries, the covers showing frazzled-looking women in aprons and dogs nipping at their heels. After all, how many men had experienced what he was going through? It would be a book of humor. He would call it, "A Frank Look at Mothering." (God, he loved the title.)

It should also be noted that on November 22, 1979, Rochester, New York, began its coldest winter on record, with eighty-nine inches of snow falling in a six-month period.

At first Frank loved the snow. Sitting at his typewriter, he would call to one of the children as they scurried past his door and patiently explain there were no two snowflakes alike. He even insisted they trace the patterns of ice that they made on the glass.

On December 3, school was closed due to "an act of God."

For the next ten days, Frank was charged with the responsibility of keeping three children from killing one another. He found himself saying nothing while watching Teddy force a button up his nostril.

He watched Caroline color his marriage license and all he could mumble was, "Stay in the lines."

He was numb as he observed the chandelier over the dining room table shake as Adam used his bed for a trampoline.

The house had wet clothes drying all over it and smelled like a wet possum in heat.

By December 30, 1979, Frank had scribbled only three entries in his diary:

1. There is no God.
2. Cute Teddy story. He can't say "spaghetti." Pronounces it "gasphetti." Needs work.
3. Ann got me trash compactor for Christmas. (This was crossed out and a note made, "No humor here.")

There were a few entries after that. "January 15, 1980: Loneliness in suburbs is a myth. Teddy is on half days and changes clothes eight times between 8 AM and bedtime. He has a costume for everything, from watching Captain Kangaroo to spitting on sister's dessert. I have not been alone in the bathroom since October.

"Jan. 17: Have much to learn. Beverly from next door was here having coffee when I started to clear the table and scrape leftovers into garbage can.

"She said no one throws away anything straight from the table. It is written somewhere no one buries garbage 'before its time.' Garbage, if it's made right, takes a full week.

"Jan. 26: Tried new liver casserole from *Better Homes and Gardens* (serves six, takes sixteen minutes to make). Blew budget on mushrooms, scallions, Brie, and Cabernet Sauvignon.

"Ann had it for lunch.

"Caroline's teacher called. I'm a homeroom mother.

"Feb. 1: *Better Homes and Gardens* lied. The liver serves sixteen over a six-day period. Beverly made it too, only she left out the scallions, Brie, mushrooms, and liver.

"Feb. 27: I am losing my mind. Everyday I put a dozen or so pairs of socks into the washer. When the washer is shut off, there is only one sock left out of each pair. Adam, Caroline, and Teddy are ticked off about socks and want to know where they go. I told them they went to live with Jesus. I hate my job."

During all of March and April, Frank did not record anything in his diary. In March, the house died. It wasn't a pretty death. The dryer went out the night Teddy had a virus and threw up on three sets of sheets, the washer gave out two days later, followed by the water heater, the vacuum sweeper, and the steam iron. The car battery went dead on the very day Frank was carpooling eight seventh graders on a field trip through a meat-packing plant. And he missed "General Hospital."

Besides, no one noticed what he did. Or even cared. Ann popped in one night with three extra guests for dinner. She didn't even notice that he took the bent fork.

Spring was supposed to come to Rochester in April but it couldn't land because of the snow. There was nothing for Frank to live for. No white sales. No sun for a tan. He was getting fat. And the kids were making him squirrelly.

One night, after Ann had missed dinner with them all week and they were getting ready for bed, she said, "Did I tell you I've been promoted and I think I'm suffering from Success Anxiety?"

"Feed an anxiety, starve a fever," mumbled Frank.

"What's wrong?" she asked.

"Nothing," said Frank. "Everything's perfect. I can't get any-one to help me void eggs for Teddy's class to decorate for Easter. I get as far as 'Could you help me suck six eggs?' and they hang up. Adam is the only fourteen-year-old in North America who does not have an alligator on his shirt and you fall asleep in a chair every night. We never talk anymore."

"What is it?" asked Ann, tired. "Do you want to redo the house?"

"That's right," said Frank. "Toss me a couple of new sofa pillows and I'll go away."

"Look, why don't you get a new hair style?"

He chewed on his fingernail. "I'm trying to let it grow. I told you that!"

"I know," said Ann. "Let's take a vacation. Just the two of us."

"May 17: Trip was a bummer. Instead of being off by ourselves, we met another couple from Ann's office. She and Phyllis talked shop all night. Jack was childless. All he talked about was sports, his job, and his boat. We had nothing in common. Besides, I missed the kids and cut it short to get back in time for Caroline's baton-twirling recital. She only touched pits once!

"May 26: God, I'm bored. Finally stored the Christmas orna-ments. Beverly has decided to have the implants. I wish I could do something drastic to change my appearance. I have no appetite, I'm tired all the time, I don't feel well in the mornings, and if I didn't know better I'd think I was . . . my God, what am I saying?

"May 29: School is out for the summer. Beverly told me about a wonderful camp. It's out of the city and has fresh air and tons of activities that develop skills. It lasts for two weeks but it helps everyone to be around contemporaries and do something else be-sides watch game shows and eat popcorn all afternoon.

"I'd love to go, but who would keep the kids?

"Aug. 24: Can't wait for Ann to get home so I can tell her about Reflexology. A woman in the beauty shop where I have my hair cut said I can clear up my sinuses by rubbing the back of my toe.

She said every organ in my body is projected onto a corresponding spot on the sole of my foot.

"Aug. 25: Ann said it's unnatural for someone to sit around playing with their feet. We don't relate to each other anymore. What I do is never important."

Late one evening in November, Frank flipped off the kitchen light and slowly made his way to the dining room table where Ann was paying bills.

"You're a fool," she said sharply. "Why don't you make the kids do the dishes?"

"Because I found a piece of gasphetti on my plate the other night."

"So, someone was a little careless."

"Ann, we use those dishes every night and we haven't had gasphetti in three weeks."

"You're going to have to learn to be firm."

"Ann," said Frank after a long pause, "write me a check."

"For what?"

"For me."

"Frank, what do you want a check for? If you need something, just take it out of household."

"I want to know that I am worth something."

"You're serious, aren't you?" said Ann, putting down her calculator.

"Do you know that one day last week I didn't hear one human voice all day? Everyone I talked to was a recording—the bank, the elevator, your office, the school, a wrong number. You used to be able to call a wrong number and get a person."

"You're tired, Frank. You should take naps."

"I cook food and someone eats it. I make beds and someone wrinkles them up again. I scrub floors and someone tracks mud on them. It never ends."

"That's what the job is all about," said Ann.

"It's not the job," said Frank. "I remember when I used to come home from work and the kids would say, 'Hi, Dad.' Do you know what they say now? They come in and look me right in the eye and say, 'Anyone home?' *I'M* HOME, DAMMIT! I'M A PERSON! And they don't see a person anymore."

Ann shook her head. "Look around you, Frank. You've got a nice home, a yard, three children, freedom to do whatever you want all day. You've got your own car, enough appliances to open up your own store, a wife who takes care of you, and a pound and a half of credit cards. I give up! I don't know what you men want!"

4 ❦❦

Connie

What Kind of a Mother Would . . .
Go to Her Grave Thinking ERA
Stood for Earned Run Average?

Connie paused over her job application blank and rubbed her eyes. She was tired. She should never have stayed up to watch the end of the Miss America pageant, but she was glad she did. How often do you get a chance to see history being made? Imagine. A Miss America who was only 5'2". There really was a God.

As she resumed filling in the blanks, she saw the black that had rubbed off on both fingers. "Terrific," she said out loud. She had just smeared her eye shadow and probably looked like a raccoon. She always forgot she had the stuff on.

All of it was new to Connie. The pantyhose every day, the bag that matched something, the wrinkle eradicator that she put under her eyes in an attempt to erase the damages caused by two teen-agers, and of course her new diet: one divorce and 700 calories a day.

PLACE OF LAST EMPLOYMENT. Connie could barely remember.

AGE. Somewhere between estrogen and death.

454

MARITAL STATUS. She spit on her finger trying to get the black to come off.

Connie had been born married. She and Martin exchanged vows right out of high school. They did everything by the book. Bought the house, had the two planned children, went to Florida on the summer rates, and saved two years for a home freezer.

She wasn't happy and she wasn't sad.

Then one day she was at the airport seeing a friend off when she overheard a woman talking about her husband who had just passed away. She said, "The house is so quiet. There is no one to talk to . . . no one to fix things . . . no one whose presence you feel as you sleep . . . no one at the table to share your food or your day and no one who makes you feel 'alive.' "

Connie froze.

The woman had just described her life with Martin!

After the divorce, she tried a variety of jobs from her home: babysitting for friends, housesitting for neighbors, and selling cosmetics on commission. (What a joke! She couldn't even eat a ham sandwich wearing lip gloss.)

She needed a full-time job. And after three months of trudging from one office to another she made a major discovery. She wasn't qualified for anything, and she had no goals.

Goals. How she wished she had one besides being able to cross her legs in hot weather. Miss Arkansas had a great goal last night. She wanted to work for World Peace and stamp out hunger throughout the world. She started to write it in, then stopped. Maybe it sounded pretentious.

Connie took a deep breath and checked her résumé. It would have put an insomniac to sleep.

"Miss Sawyer will see you now," said the receptionist.

Miss Sawyer looked like all the other personnel managers Connie had been meeting for the past several months. Her makeup was impeccable, her hair looked like an unmade bed, and she wasn't a day over twelve.

"You have no college," said Miss Sawyer.

Connie cleared her throat. "I was going to take some classes at the junior college, but I couldn't find a parking place."

"You didn't check the box marked sex," Miss Sawyer said, as if she were grading a term paper.

Connie wanted to say, "only during a full moon," but decided against it. "Female," she said. Miss Sawyer checked it off.

"Your experience is limited," she observed. "Have you no computer experience?"

"I got married right out of high school," Connie answered.

Miss Sawyer shook her head. "I'm afraid you're just not qualified for anything we have, but we'll keep your application on file and if anything comes up, we'll call you." She reached for her phone (a personnel trick), signaling that the interview was over.

Connie sat in the parking lot, her head bowed over the steering wheel. She was too angry to cry. Not qualified for anything! Who said so? A child, not unlike her own, who should have known better, said so. She had wanted to say to the infant behind the desk, "I know you! And you know me! Didn't I hold you in my arms, nurse you, powder your behind? Didn't I feed you and hang crêpe paper for your birthday parties? I went to your class plays and took your pictures and clapped the loudest. I went to your science fairs and walked for hours while you explained how bread mold can cure cancer.

"I listened to your piano recitals, balanced your meals and made out the budget. I learned how to sew and to cut hair. I helped hamburger before anyone knew it could be helped. I made a thousand decisions in one day, counseled you, kept you well, and gave you stability. I listened to you when you talked, I laughed with you when you laughed. And I cried with you when you cried. Now my whole life hangs in balance and you ask me what I'm qualified for."

Angrily, Connie got out of the car and returned to the office where she stood before Miss Unmade Bed.

"Did you forget something?" Miss Sawyer asked coldly.

"Yes. I forgot to tell you that early this morning an interviewer told me I was too quiet. Two hours later, another said my eyebrows showed negativism and wanted to know if I could drive under pressure. I have been told if I could get a number 2 license I could drive an airport shuttle or if I were a size nine, I could rent cars. An hour ago, a girl in front of me with a mouth like Emmett Kelly and an IQ the same size as her bust got the job.

"Let me tell you who I am, Miss Sawyer, and what I'm qualified for. I'm a thirty-five-year-old woman who was a professional wife and a mother for seventeen yers and I was very good at it. If you will kindly get me two extra sheets of paper, I will be glad to list my background and my skills!"

5

Everybody Else's Mother

She has no name. Her phone number is unlisted. But she exists in the mind of every child who has ever tried to get his own way and used her as a last resort.

Everybody Else's Mother is right out of the pages of Greek mythology—mysterious, obscure, and surrounded by hearsay.

She is the answer to every child's prayer.

Traditional Mother: "Have the car home by eleven or you're grounded for a month."

Everybody Else's Mother: "Come home when you feel like it."

Traditional Mother: "The only way I'd let you wear that bikini is under a coat."

Everybody Else's Mother: "Wear it. You're only young once."

Traditional Mother: "You're going to summer school and that's that."

Everybody Else's Mother: "I'm letting Harold build a raft and go down the Ohio River for a learning experience."

A few mothers have tried to pin down where Everybody Else's Mother lives and what background she has for her expertise on raising children. They have struck out.

458

The best they can come up with is a composite that they put together by pooling their information.

As close as can be figured out, Everybody Else's Mother is a cross between Belle Watling and Peter Pan. She likes live-in snakes, ice cream before dinner, and unmade beds. She never wears gloves on a cold day and voted for Eugene McCarthy. She is never home.

She's never been to a dentist, hates housework, and never puts her groceries away. She sleeps late, smokes, and grinds the ashes into the carpet with the toe of her shoe.

She eats jelly beans for breakfast, drinks milk out of a carton, and wears gym shoes to church because they're comfortable. She never washes her car and doesn't own an umbrella.

Everybody Else's Mother moves a lot and seems to be every-where at the same time. Just when you think she's moved out of the neighborhood, she reappears. She is quick to judge and has handed down more decisions in her time than the Supreme Court has in the last 200 years. She has only one child and a friend who "was a dear" carried it for her.

She has never used the word "No."

If Everybody Else's Mother showed up at a PTA meeting and identified herself, she would be lynched.

From time to time, the existence of Everybody Else's Mother is questioned. It is probably wishful thinking. Does she exist?

Oh yes, Virginia, she really does. She lives in the hearts of children everywhere who have to believe that somewhere there is an adult on their side. Someone who remembers the frustration of needing to belong to a peer group at some time of your life to do the forbidden . . . just because it's there.

Just because one has never seen her, does that prove she's not there? Would one question the existence of monsters that appear in bad dreams or tigers that crawl on the bed in the darkness and disappear when the lights go on?

Everybody Else's Mother is very real and for a few years she's a formidable opponent to mothers everywhere. Then one day she disappears. In her place is ninety pounds (give or take) of rebellion and independence, engaging in verbal combat, saying for themselves what Everybody Else's Mother used to say for them.

It's called Puberty. There's nothing like it to make you yearn for Everybody Else's Mother. She really wasn't such a bad person after all.

6 ❦

The First Day of School for "The Baby"

What Dina Said:

"Mike, I don't know what you're scared of. Mother's going to be right here when you come home. My goodness, you've got a nice little yellow bus to ride and your own lunch box and your name pinned on your sweater. Now what could go wrong?

"You're a big boy now, and you have to act like one. You're going to make all kinds of new friends. Now you march right out there and sit on the curb and stop acting like a baby. You don't have a thing to be frightened of."

What Mike Didn't Say:

I don't know anything.

I have new underwear, a new sweater, a loose tooth, and I didn't sleep last night. I'm worried.

What if the bus jerks after I get on and I lose my balance and my pants rip and everyone laughs?

What if I have to go to the bathroom before we get to school? What if a bell rings and everyone goes inside and a man yells, "Where do you belong?" and I don't know?

What if my shoelace comes untied and someone says, "Your shoelace is untied. We'll all watch while you tie it"?

What if the trays in the cafeteria are too high for me to reach and the thermos lid on my soup is on too tight and when I try to open it, it breaks?

What if my loose tooth wants to come out when we're supposed to have our heads down and be quiet? What if the teacher tells the class to go to the bathroom and I can't go?

What if I get hot and take my sweater off and someone steals it? What if I splash water on my name tag and my name disappears and no one will know who I am? What if they send us out to play and all the swings are taken? What do I do?

What if the wind blows all the important papers that I'm supposed to take home out of my hands? What if they mispronounce my last name and everyone laughs?

Suppose my teacher doesn't make her D's like Mom taught me?

What if the teacher gives a seat to everyone and I'm left over? What if the windows in the bus steam up and I won't be able to tell when I get to my stop?

What if I spend the whole day without a friend?

I'm afraid.

What Mike Said:

"See ya."

What Dina Didn't Say:

What am I doing, sending this baby out into the world before the umbilical cord is healed? Where's all the relief and exhilaration I'm supposed to feel? If only I hadn't been so rotten to him all summer. "Go play! Get out of the house! Take a nap! Why don't you grow up?"

I think I blew it. I talked too much and said too little. There are no second chances for me. It's all up to someone else.

Now it's my turn. My excuse for everything just got on that bus. My excuse for not dieting, not getting a full-time job, not cleaning house, not re-upholstering the furniture, not going back to school, not having order in my life, not cleaning the oven.

It's the end of an era. Now what do I do for the next twenty years of my life?

These walls have been so safe for the last few years. I didn't have to prove anything to anyone. Now I feel vulnerable.

What if I apply for a job and no one wants me?

What if changing toilet paper spindles is my maximum skill?

What if I'm kidding myself about writing the book that I told everyone is inside me?

What if I can't let go of my past? It's only 8:15 in the morning.

I'm afraid.

7 ⟡⟡⟡

Pacifier Pioneers

A group of mothers was discussing the ten most significant contributions to the quality of their lives one night. Most of the suggestions were quite predictable: penicillin, fire, electricity, the automobile, not to mention The Pill, polyester, and ten-foot phone cords.

I don't care what women say, the number one choice for me is the pacifier. How many women would be with us today were it not for that little rubber-plastic nipple that you jammed in a baby's face to keep him from crying?

Today, it's as much a part of a baby's face as his nose or ears, but thirty years ago the pacifier was considered a maternal crutch, a visual that screamed to the world "I can't cope."

I was a closet pacifier advocate. So were most of my friends. Unknown to our mothers, we owned thirty or forty of those little suckers that were placed strategically around the house so a cry could be silenced in less than thirty seconds. Even though bottles were boiled, rooms disinfected, and germs fought one on one, no one seemed to care where the pacifier had been.

We found them under beds, buried in sofa cushions, thrown in ashtrays and lost in the garbage. No child ever got sick from "fooler around the mouth."

I kept the pacifier a secret from my mother for as long as I could. But one day she dropped by unexpectedly and demanded, "What is this?"

"It's a pacifier."

"Do you know that if you keep using this pacifier, by the time this baby is four years old, her teeth will come in crooked and her mouth will have a permanent pout?"

"Do you know, Mother, if I do not use that pacifier, I may never permit her to become four?"

We American pioneers of the pacifier have given it the respectability it deserves. After all, what other force in the world has the power to heal, stop tears, end suffering, sustain life, restore world peace, and is the elixir that grants mothers everywhere the opportunity to sleep . . . perchance to dream?

8 ⊸⊸⊸⊸

Who Are Harder to
Raise . . . Boys or Girls?

If you want to stir up a hornet's nest, just ask mothers, "Who are harder to raise—boys or girls?"

The answer will depend on whether they're raising boys or girls.

I've had both, so I'll settle the argument once and for all. It's girls.

With boys you always know where you stand. Right in the path of a hurricane. It's all there. The fruit flies hovering over their waste can, the hamster trying to escape to cleaner air, the bedrooms decorated in Early Bus Station Restroom.

With girls, everything looks great on the surface. But beware of drawers that won't open. They contain a three-month supply of dirty underwear, unwashed hose, and rubber bands with blobs of hair in them.

You have to wonder about a girl's bedroom when you go in to make her bed and her dolls have a look of fear and disbelief in their eyes.

A mother once wrote me to agree. She said that "after giving birth to three boys, I finally got a girl on my fourth try. At first, she did all the sweet little things I longed to see. She played coy, put her hands to her face when she laughed and batted her eyes like Miss Congeniality.

"Then she turned fourteen months and she struck like a hurricane. When she discovered she could no longer sail down the bannister and make my hair stand on end, she turned to streaking. I'd dress her ever so sweetly and go to the breakfast dishes. Before one glass was washed, she'd strip, unlock the door and start cruising the neighborhood. One day, the dry cleaner made a delivery and said, 'My goodness, I hardly recognized Stacy with her clothes on.'

"As she got older, she opened her brother's head with a bottle opener for taking her dolls and called the school principal a 'thug' to his face.

"I am pregnant again. I sleep with a football under my pillow each night."

I knew of another mother who said, "Boys are honest. Whenever you yell upstairs, 'What's all that thumping about?' you get an up front reply, 'Joey threw the cat down the clothes chute. It was cool.'

"When my daughter is upstairs playing with her dolls I yell, 'What are you girls doing?' She answers sweetly, 'Nothing.'

"I have to find out for myself that they're making cookies out of my new bath powder and a $12.50 jar of moisturizer.

"Her pediatrician advised me to 'not notice' when she insisted on wearing her favorite outfit for four months. How do you ignore a long dress with a ripped ruffle, holes in the elbow and a Burger King crown? How would you handle it if you were in a supermarket and the loudspeaker announced, '*Attention Shoppers.* We have a small child in produce wearing a long pink dress with a gauze apron, glittery shoes and a Burger King crown'? Our third child was born recently. Another girl. I told the orderly to pass maternity and go straight to geriatrics. I rest my case. God knows it's the only rest I've had in six years."

Whether mothers want to believe it or not, they compete with their daughters. They recognize in them every feminine wile in the book because they've used it themselves. It worked on "Daddy" when you used it, and it'll work again with your daughter. ("Daddy, you do believe that a tree can swerve right out in front of a car, don't you?")

Girls mature faster than boys, cost more to raise, and statistics show that the old saw about girls not knowing about money and figures is a myth. Girls start to outspend boys before puberty— and they manage to maintain this lead until death or an ugly credit manager, whichever comes first. Males are born with a closed fist. Girls are born with the left hand cramped in a position the size of an American Express card.

Whenever a girl sees a sign reading, "Sale, Going Out of Business, Liquidation," saliva begins to form in her mouth, the palms of her hands perspire and the pituitary gland says, "Go, Mama."

In the male, it is quite a different story. He has a gland that follows a muscle from the right arm down to the base of his billfold pocket. It's called "cheap."

Girls can slam a door louder, beg longer, turn tears on and off like a faucet, and invented the term, "You don't trust me."

So much for "sugar and spice and everything nice" and "snips and snails and puppydog tails."

9 ✿✿✿

Donna

What Kind of a Mother . . .
Runs a Wedding—in Three Hours,
Forty- three Minutes and Sixteen Seconds?

It was the moment every mother of the Seventies prayed for.

The phone rang and the voice said, "Mom, guess what? Barry and I are getting married!" (Hallelujah!)

Married. Her friend, Sophie, had a son who had short hair, but he wasn't . . . married. Another friend, Eileen, could boast a daughter who still shaved her legs and waited for someone to open the car door for her, but even she wasn't . . . married.

Married. It was like a dream come true for Donna. Just think, soon her little girl would have unpaid bills, unplanned babies, calls from the bank, and substandard housing. All the things a mother dreams of for her child.

Not only that, Donna would become the first mother-in-law in her bridge club. She couldn't believe that after two years of co-habitation, it was finally happening.

Then Donna hesitated. What if this were another "commitment"? Her mind raced to a meadow. A van painted with serpents.

Grace Slick coming from a tape deck. Organic juice out of Dixie cups. Guests smoking the lawn.

As if she were reading her mother's mind, Lynn said, "Don't worry, Mom. It's going to be a traditional wedding."

Tears welled in Donna's eyes. A real wedding. Stuffed mushrooms, cutaways. A string quartet. Silver pattern. Tapered candles. Barry Manilow. Navel-length corsages.

The bride-to-be's father was less exuberant. "Who's Barry?" he asked.

"I forgot to ask."

"What do we know about him?"

"What's to know? He's the man who's going to marry (hallelujah!) our daughter."

"He has some nerve, after they've been living together all these years."

The invitation arrived within the week. It was shaped like a runner's shoe.

Lynn and Barry
Invite You to Their
Marathon of Nuptials
Saturday, June 18, at 2 PM
at Jackie's Body Shop.

Guests will assemble in Central Park and
run 10 K's with the bride and groom
to Jackie's place.
Dress optional: Running or aerobics attire.

Donna and Mel looked at the invitation in silence. They were stunned. Mel spoke first. "This isn't an invitation to a wedding. It's the opening of a gym. We're not going."

Instinctively Donna stiffened. "Maybe you're not going, but my only daughter is being married (hallelujah!) for the first time and I'm not about to miss it. Tomorrow the bride's mother is going shopping for her outfit for the wedding, with or without the bride's father."

The next day, Donna looked at her reflection in the fitting room mirror. She had experienced dizziness in a fitting room on only one other occasion, and that was the day she tried on a bathing suit wearing knee-hi hose. Today was a close second. Plum tights that glowed from the strain of a million fat pockets of cellulite fighting to get out were covered by a pink leotard that rode high over the hips. A matching pink headband tried valiantly to keep her forehead from falling into her eyes. She looked at the leg warmers and prayed she wouldn't have a hot flash. She knew that if she so much as cleared her throat the crotch would bind her ankles together.

Poking her head outside the curtain, she said to the salesperson, "On second thought, I think the groom's mother is wearing this. I think I'll go for the blue velour warm-ups. A daughter only gets married (hallelujah!) once."

Her last stop was a sports center where a young man fitted her with running shoes. As she peeked into the X-ray machine to check the stress points on her new shoes, she asked, "By the way, young man, how far is 10 k's?"

"It's 6.2 miles," he said.

On the way home, Donna smiled to herself and mused, "He must have misunderstood. Probably thought I said Circle K."

Mel knew he was being stubborn, but he wasn't as forgiving of his daughter's independence and life-style as Donna. Around 8:30 PM on June 18, as he had done every five minutes that evening, he peeked through the Venetian blinds and spotted Donna emerging from a cab.

She limped noticeably while pressing her hand firmly on her backside.

"Where have you been?" he demanded.

"Oh Mel, you should have been there. It was wonderful. I started off at the park with everyone else and then I fought off three dogs, nursed two blisters, and finally hitched a ride with a motorcyclist who was going right by Jackie's Body Shop.

"Your daughter looked beautiful. They stood in front of a wall of mirrors and pledged to love one another forever as much as they did today, keep their bodies fit, and with God's love, both qualify for Boston with a 2:42.

"The groom's mother wore a T-shirt that read JOGGERS DO IT BETTER and the minister had Band-Aids on his nipples to keep his shirt from irritating them as he ran.

"I ate a lot of health food, and met a lot of people—one woman who said her daughter was married in a free parachute fall over Omaha and had to pack her own parachute. We've having lunch next Tuesday. Just before Lynn left she took me aside and said if she continues to run thirty to forty miles a week she won't ovulate and so I shouldn't expect any grandchildren right away. She said that's the first meaningful conversation we ever had in our entire lives.

"Barry is built like the U.N. building and sells air conditioners at Sears. Oh, I was the only one there carrying a handbag, and I think I pulled a hamstring, but Mel . . . our daughter is . . . married!" (Hallelujah!)

10 ✿✿ Hair

Every hundred years or so, the Earth shifts and goes into another cycle. I missed the Stone Age, the Ice Age, and the Glacial Period, but I was here for most of the Age of Hair.

It was the best of times and it was the worst of times.

Like most mothers, I devoted my life to the length of my son's hair. He would come down for breakfast and say, "Good morning," and I would reply "Get a haircut. One egg or two?"

We would be standing in church, and as the priest encouraged us to "extend to one another the sign of peace," I would turn to him, smile reverently, and say, "Get a haircut, weirdo."

It was all we ever talked about. We argued about barbers and the length of time between haircuts. We argued about the price of shampoo, the limitation of hot water, how he was screwing up our septic tank, and how we'd never unload him at the altar if he insisted on looking like Walter Matthau in drag.

He would come home and try to tell me the barber gave him a Timothy Leary trim.

"It looks more like a King Kong clip to me."

"What's a King Kong clip?"

"A light trim on your hands and ankles."

473

"There's no pleasing you," he shouted.

"Try!" I shouted back.

I always thought I was fair. I told him, "Hair can be as long, as shabby, and as dirty as it wants to be. It can be braided around the head five times or hang down to the tailbone in a pony-tail . . . as long as it's on someone else's son."

The more I talked, the longer the hair became and the more fragile our relationship became.

In twelve years, not once did I give his hair a rest or miss an opportunity to harp on how he had disappointed me as a son.

Then one day he came into the kitchen and said, "When's dinner?"

I said mechanically, "You've got time to get a haircut. It's at 6:30."

He said, "Okay."

I nearly fainted.

When he returned, his hair was neatly trimmed and cleared his ears. We both smiled awkwardly. Like strangers on a blind date.

"So, what's been going on?" I asked.

"Not much," he stammered. "What about you?"

I had no idea what a large part of our relationship had been based on such intimacies as, "How long does it take you to wash that mop?" "How are you financing your shampoo these days?" "Did you know Attila the Hun once wore that style?"

There was absolutely no rapport between us. His hair had been the only thing that had kept us together . . . the only common ground of communication we had.

I began to remember the good times . . . the time we ragged him about his hair on a vacation from Gary, Indiana, to Salt Lake City, Utah. The time really flew.

I recalled the time I told him I had enrolled him in a Miss Radial Tire competition and he had won.

Oh, I tried new lines of communication like, "You live like a hog," "There is no boy so tall as the one who stoops to pick up a towel," and "Don't ruin your dinner with that junk!" But somehow it wasn't the same.

We had lost that wonderful hostility that parents need to relate to their children.

Then one day he came home from school and my face lit up. "What's that disgusting bit of hair around your mouth and chin?"

"I'm growing a beard," he said.

"And sit at my table, you're not. I cannot believe that's the chin I used to spend hours wiping the saliva and oatmeal from. Why are you doing this to your mother?"

"I'll keep it trimmed."

"Hah. You show me a man with a beard and I'll show you what he had for lunch. It smells like pizza right now."

"All the influential men of the world have had beards, like Moses, Christ, and Burt Reynolds."

"You forgot King Henry VIII, Lenin, and Satan. I'll be honest with you. You look like one of the Seven Dwarfs."

"I knew you wouldn't understand," he said, slamming the door.

At least the beard would take us through Christmas vacation.

11 ❧❧❧

Sharon

What Kind of a Mother Would . . .
Wash a Measuring Cup with Soap
After It Only Held Water?

Everyone said Sharon was a terrific mother.

Her neighbors said it.

She painted the inside of her garbage cans with enamel, grew her own vegetables, cut her own grass every week, made winter coats for the entire family from remnants, donated blood and baked Barbara Mandrell a doll cake for her birthday.

Her mother said it.

Sharon drove her to the doctor's when she had an appointment, color-coordinated the children's clothes and put them in labeled drawers, laundered aluminum foil and used it again, planned family reunions, wrote her Congressman, cut everyone's hair and knew her health insurance policy number by heart.

Her children's teacher said it.

She helped her children every night with their homework, delivered her son's paper route when it rained, packed nutritious lunches with little raised faces on the sandwiches, was homeroom mother, belonged to five car pools and once blew up 234 balloons by herself for the seventh grade cotillion.

Her husband said it.

Sharon washed the car when it rained, saved antifreeze from year to year, paid all the bills, arranged their social schedule, sprayed the garden for bugs, moved the hose during the summer, put the children on their backs at night to make sure they didn't sleep on their faces, and once found a twelve-dollar error in their favor on a tax return filed by H & R Block.

Her best friend said it.

Sharon built a bed out of scraps left over from the patio, crocheted a Santa Claus to cover the extra roll of toilet paper at Christmastime, washed fruit before her children ate it, learned to play the harpsichord, kept a Boston fern alive for a whole year, and when the group ate lunch out always figured out who owed what.

Her minister said it.

Sharon found time to read all the dirty books and campaign against them. She played the guitar at evening services. She corresponded with a poor family in Guatemala . . . in Spanish. She put together a cookbook to raise funds for a new coffee maker for the church. She collected door to door for all the health organizations.

Sharon was one of those women blessed with a knack for being organized. She planned a "theme party" for the dog's birthday, made her children elaborate Halloween costumes out of old grocery bags, and her knots came out just right on the shoelaces when they broke.

She put a basketball "hoop" over the clothes hamper as an incentive for good habits, started seedlings in a toilet paper spindle, and insulated their house with empty egg cartons, which everyone else threw away.

Sharon kept a schedule that would have brought any other woman to her knees. Need twenty-five women to chaperone a party? Give the list to Sharon. Need a mother to convert the school library to the Dewey Decimal System? Call Sharon. Need someone to organize a block party, garage sale, or school festival? Get Sharon.

Sharon was a Super Mom!

Her gynecologist said it.

Her butcher said it.

Her tennis partner said it.

Her children . . .

Her children never said it.

They spent a lot of time with Rick's mother, who was always home and who ate cookies out of a box and played poker with them.

12

Louise and Estelle

What Kind of a Mother Would . . .
Lose Her Amateur Status by
Turning Pro?

Next to hot chicken soup and vitamin C, Louise considered breakfast with her children as the most overrated ritual in American culture.

What was so great about sitting around a table with two surly kids fighting over fifteen boxes of unopened cereal?

She relented once a year. She called it her Annual Christmas Breakfast with Mommy, complete with candy canes and favors. The rest of the time Louise worked at staying out of their way.

She had discovered early that she was not like other mothers. It disgusted her to take knots out of shoelaces with her teeth that a child had wet on all day. She was bored out of her skull sitting around buying hotels for Park Place with funny money. She was not fulfilled walking around with a handbag full of used nose tissue handed her by her children to dispose of.

Housework didn't do a lot for her, either. Neither did the women who talked about it. She refused to break out in hives just because someone had found a way to get spaghetti stains out of plastic place mats. One day when the group was talking about Heloise's eighty-seven uses for nylon net, Louise snapped, "Why don't we just make butterfly nets out of it, throw it over ourselves, and check in at a home?"

Her goal in life was to hire a woman who would come in and sit with her children while she worked.

Her husband would not hear of it. "Give me a reason," he kept insisting.

"I'm bored," said Louise.

"That's not a reason," he said. "That's a symptom. You should keep busy."

Maybe he wanted her to lie like Elsie Waggoner, who said she got a part-time job to buy her daughter's Barbie and Ken dolls a wardrobe to go to Ohio State for the weekend.

In desperation, Louise did the next best thing. She volunteered.

It didn't take long for word to get out that Louise was "easy." She'd chair anything. She'd save animals she hadn't even heard of, raise funds for diseases she couldn't pronounce, and sit through three-hour meetings where the only decision made was where to have the next meeting.

In 1973 she set a record for volunteering more hours in a year than any other woman in the community.

She also set another record . . . unofficially. Louise hired and fired more babysitters in a year than any other woman in the history of women's liberation.

Louise demanded a woman who would read to her children and play games with them when they were bored.

She wanted a woman who would be there to share their day.

She wanted a woman who would bake them cookies, mend their broken toys, and kiss their scraped knees.

She wanted Julie Andrews flying around with an umbrella for a buck an hour.

The list of women who worked for Louise Concell would fill a book. There was Mrs. Crandel, who was a soap opera addict and between noon and 2 PM the world stopped.

There was Mrs. Sanchez, who made gin ice cubes and was discovered only when one of the children had a lemonade stand and every kid in the neighborhood slept through three meals.

Carol from the university lasted only a week, when the children began quoting from a Cheech and Chong album, causing Louise's teeth to go numb.

In the fall of 1979, Louise and her husband succumbed to temptation—a paying job that would take all her energies and time. She was chosen to serve as director of the Tinkerbell Child Care Center. Louise was ecstatic. She would have more responsibilities than she had ever had before, and for the first time there would be a price tag on her worth. She began a serious talent search for a surrogate Mother of the Year.

That's when she found Estelle. Estelle was too good to be true. She was young, had two children of her own, knew how to entertain them, feed them, and discipline them with firmness and love. She also drove.

Estelle had been a single parent for two years and had been through an entire alphabet of government services and organizations. At the moment, she was enrolled in the Social Awareness Program for Black Women that met in the church social hall every Wednesday.

She dropped her children, Glenn and Missy, off at the nursery in the room next door and took her place at a long table holding the Craft of the Day.

Today's project was simple enough. All she had to do was paint a cigar box and let it dry. Then take pieces of macaroni, dip them in paste, and place them on top of the cigar box. When it was completely covered, she sprinkled the entire box with sequins and, *voilà*, a jewelry box.

The only problem was she had no jewelry.

Estelle fingered the macaroni slowly and wondered about her life. What did she have to show for her two years at SAPFBW? A macramé pot. A crocheted Mexican hat that fit over a bottle of Tabasco sauce, a picture of an English cottage in bottle caps, and a piggy bank made out of a bleach bottle.

And now the pasta experience.

Angry with herself, she grabbed the bag of macaroni, took it home, cooked it and vowed to find a job.

Estelle loved her children and didn't want them to suffer for her restlessness. She had heard good things about the Tinkerbell Child Care Center.

"Do you have any questions about us?" asked Louise Concell. "After all, that's what I'm here for."

"Do you keep the children busy?" asked Estelle. "I mean, I don't want a place where they nap all day long."

"I think you'll find we have a superb activities program," said Louise.

"What about the teachers? My kids have never been away from me for any length of time."

"They love them as they do their own. Trust me," smiled Louise.

"I want someone around my children who doesn't consider it just a job but who really wants to be with them."

"I understand perfectly," said Louise, smiling. "We close at 6:15. Is that a problem?"

"Actually, I don't have a job yet," said Estelle. "I wanted to try the children out here while I start looking."

Louise pushed her glasses to the top of her head. "Have you thought of child care?"

Estelle shook her head.

"You see, I have two young children at home and I was looking for someone to sit with them. Do you mind if I ask you a few questions?"

"That's what I'm here for," said Estelle.

"I would want planned activities for the children so they're not watching the tube all day. They have such a low threshold of interest. You know, busy work."

"I've had plenty of experience with that in the last couple of years." Estelle smiled.

"My children would have to like you. You see, I've always been a mother who has stayed at home, and they're not used to being around anyone else."

"I've always been good with children. Trust me."

"This is difficult for me to explain," said Louise, "but my children have always been rather special to me and I don't want someone who is just being with them for money, but someone who really loves them and wants to be with them."

"I know where you're coming from," said Estelle.

So it was in September, 1980, both Louise and Estelle became "career mothers" . . . for minimum-wage scale.

They both wiped noses, changed diapers, rocked babies, hummed lullabies, and made bloody fingers well again with the touch of their lips.

Neither could explain why being paid for it made such a difference.

13

How I Spent My Summer by Laura Parsons, Age 11

I spent my summer the same way I spent my winter. I'm a mini-mom. When my mom is away at work, I take care of my younger brother and three sisters.

A mini-mom's job is boring.

I take my brother and sisters to the bathroom when they don't want to go.

I wash their faces when they jerk their heads away.

I wipe their runny noses when they don't want them to be wiped.

I put them to bed when they're not sleepy.

And when they follow their "real mother," I grab them around the neck and hold on tight until they turn purple.

There is a lot of hitting and spitting with the job.

I wish I had never been born first.
I thought it would be neat, but that's before
I found out that I would be the first to reach
the top shelf and have to get glasses down . . . the
first to know how to button, tie and zip . . .
the first one to be old.
I wish I could be a "sitter" instead of a mini-mom.

Sitters get neat snacks and tips if the
house isn't wrecked. They get treated like a sister.

Mini-moms get blamed if someone turns
the garden hose on in the living room and punished
if someone eats the bananas mom was saving. We're
treated like mothers.

Being a mother really grosses me out. I hate
wiping someone after they go to the toilet. I
hate it when I call a thousand times and
they pretend they don't hear me. I hate not
having any time to be by myself.

They like their real mom better than they like
me. I don't care.

I wanted to run away from home, but my
mother would kill me if I went out on the
highway before they put a traffic light in.

I don't want to be a mother. Ever.

14

The Five Greatest American Fiction Writers of All Time (Who Just Happen to Be Mothers)

Eileen Whorf
(Author of the Poetry Club Letters)

September 16, 1978

Mrs. Loretta Flake
Bramblebush Acres
Norman, Oklahoma

My Dear Mrs. Flake:

I cannot tell you how surprised and shocked I was to learn that I had been nominated to succeed you as president of the Walt Whitman Poetry Club.

Especially since I attended only one of your meetings as a guest. Although I am honored to be considered, it is with great regret

486

that I must decline to serve as your president next year.

I know you will understand when I tell you I am terrified to get up before anyone to speak. It's a congenital shyness that I have learned to live with, but it certainly would not serve the best interests of the Walt Whitman Poetry Club.

Gratefully,
Eileen Whorf

September 21, 1978

Dear Loretta:

Thank you for your letter of insistence. I do agree that the more one speaks, the more comfortable one becomes. However, there is still another reason why I cannot serve as your president. I haven't told anyone (even my husband) about a small cyst on my right toe. It is probably benign, but we never know and I would not have your membership suffer because of my infirmity. I know you will keep my little secret.

Trustingly,
Eileen Whorf

September 26, 1978

Dear Loretta:

If perseverance were little drops of rain, you would have drowned weeks ago. I know I could count on the understanding and support of your membership, and thank you for reminding me of the Cyst Leave of Absence in the by-laws. However, there is a possibility that Mr. Whorf is being transferred to another country, in which case it would be impossible for me to commute to the monthly meetings of the Walt Whitman Poetry Club. Surely there is some-

one in your membership worthy of the honor you have tried to bestow on me with such force.

Regards,
Eileen Whorf

October 1, 1978

Dear Loretta:

You and your membership astound me with your generosity, and although I know you are willing to allow me to serve as your president until we move out of the country, there is still another reason.

I don't drive.

Anticipating your reply, I don't like to ride with anyone either.

Regards,
Eileen Whorf

October 4, 1978

Look, Loretta, I don't even know who Walt Whitman is!

Eileen Whorf

October 7, 1978

Loretta:

I accept.

Eileen Whorf
Reluctant President of the
Walt Whitman Poetry Club

Barfy Whitcomb
(Author of the annual
Christmas Newsletter)

Christmas, 1982

Dear Friends and Relatives:

Heigh Ho, everyone.

Another year has gone by, and it's time to bring you up to date on the Whitcombs.

Our Lewiston took his college entrance exams and was accepted at Harvard. (Sob. Sob. Sixteen seems so young to go to school so far from home.) Bob and I will drive him to Boston, as he is talking about taking his Russian icon collection with him. (You can't tell children anything!)

As you can see by the enclosed picture, Melody has certainly filled out. She is following in her mother's footsteps at Seward High by being named head of the Pom and Flag drill team. The head of Pom and Flag is automatically named Prettiest Girl in the Class and Homecoming Princess at the Farewell Waltz. The theme this year is "Some Enchanted Evening." You're going to die, but that was exactly the same theme as the year I was Princess! Couldn't you scream?

Bob has had another promotion since last year's letter, putting us in another tax bracket (ugh). I am busy with my volunteer work. Last year I gave seventy-four phone hours to soliciting baked goods for the Bake-A-Rama. I was named Top Call Girl by the League.

In June, the Whitcombs "roughed it" on a camping venture. Imagine traveling six hundred miles with no Cuisinart! Our camper was forty-five feet long and Bob went crazy trying to back it into a spot in the campgrounds. Melody said it was what he got for not going where there was valet parking. Melody is a stitch. (Three of her quotes have been used by Reader's Digest.)

I must say it was a trip to remember. We saw a bird eating bread off a picnic table and one day visited a discount house. You have to admit, Barfy Whitcomb married adventure!

Tragedy struck the household in August. Chelsey, our prize-winning poodle, was raped by a German shepherd who forced his way in through the mail drop. No one fought harder for her honor than Bob.

Bob and I went to State for our twentieth reunion. You can imagine my shock when the usher directed us to the "student section." Everyone wanted to know what we did to stay so eternally young. We don't do anything special. We just eat properly, exercise regularly, and are rich.

I want to thank all of you who commented on last year's letter. (You know, the one where I paraphrased all the Whitcombs' achievements to "The Night Before Christmas.") It's gratifying to know that someone appreciates what it takes to get something to rhyme with "opulence."

> *Joyeux Noël*
> *Feliz Navidad*
> *Merry Christmas*
>
> > *Barfy and Bob*
> > *Melody and Lewiston*
> > *Chelsey and Bruno*

Billie

(Author of letter to former classmate regarding impending visit)

April 12, 1982

Dear Sal:

What a surprise to hear from you. I can't believe it was three years ago since you and your family last visited. But then I counted back to when I got the sofa recovered and new mattresses (is Tommy toilet-trained yet?) and the car repainted, and you're right. Three uneventful years.

Since you are such a good friend, I know you will understand when I tell you we are sorry we are not going to be home when you pass through this time, even though you did not pin your visit down to a definite date. There are so many reasons, I hardly know where to begin.

First, Mother has become a problem. Whenever she has a "spell," we must run. I know this sounds vague and mysterious, but I'll explain later, when I have more time. It's sort of like your little Warren. Does he still love to watch fire?

Bill and I may go around the world all summer. Nothing definite. It's still in the planning stages and will depend on whether business picks up at the gas station and if he can get time off and we can scrape the money together and you know how it is.

If we stay home, we may paint the entire house inside and out, and you know what a mess that can be when you're visiting. (Especially if your Mona locks herself in the bathroom and mixes her "secret potion" in the toilet bowl.)

The children are also thinking of going to camp and it certainly wouldn't be any fun for your little cherubs to sit around with nothing to do. (Our Michelle still talks about your Myron using her for a dart board.)

I cannot believe there are so many circumstances converging to keep us apart. It was so hard to say good-bye to you the last time.

Please call us just before you come so I can bring you up to date on our plans.

Love,
Billie

P.S. We may be moving.

Grace Reingolt
(Author of letter to the president of Roy's Sonic TV and Appliance Center regarding broken handle on refrigerator door)

June 4, 1982

Dear Roy:

On March 21 of this year, for no reason, the handle of our refrigerator door fell off. Neither my husband Stoney nor I was in the room at the time.

We called you the morning of March 21, at which time your serviceman Duane came to check it out. He said there was no way the handle could have come off by itself, as the three-inch pin in it was bent double. Now I ask you, who do you think did it? Certainly not my husband or I, who were watching "Dukes of Hazzard," and certainly not our four-year-old son Budro, who was swinging from the spare tire in his bedroom at the time of this unfortunate event.

You have always been fair in the past. You may recall when a tube of toothpaste for no reason manifested itself in the lint trap of our dryer and a live dog wearing pantyhose wrapped around the pulsator in the washer, obviously there before it left the factory.

I suppose you are used to these apparitions, but to us they smack of poltergeist. Wishing to save you the trouble of replacing the handle, we have contacted our insurance company who said it would have to be an act of God in order to make a claim. (He obviously has never had an evening when he was separated from his gusto by a door without a handle!)

I am sad to report the warranty ran out on the refrigerator eighteen years ago next month. However, knowing how you want

to protect your reputation for fairness, we look for an early set-
tlement at no cost to us, the victims.

Regards,
Grace Reingolt

Melissa Johnsey
(Author of advance instructions to her mother who will be babysitting Bo, her six-week-old daughter)

Mom—

Please have more light bulbs for changing crib and bumper pads before Bo arrives. Last time the supply was inadequate.

Have on hand four boxes of daytime diapers for a 15-pound infant.

One gallon skim milk. Make sure the date is recent for fresh-ness.

Plenty of moisturized towels and plastic bags for dirty diapers.

Bottles can be washed in the dishwasher. However, nipples and caps must be done by hand. Push water through hole in nipple to make sure it works. Gas bubbles can be painful to an infant.

Phisoderm soap.

Vanilla ice cream.

Two plastic pails and a large basket for laundry. Commercial washer and dryer may be used.

No pets in room being occupied by the baby.

Phone must be off the hook while baby is sleeping.

Rectal thermometer should be shaken down after each use and stored in alcohol.

Do not place crib under duct.

Keep toys in plastic bag when not in use.

Sprinkle baby powder on hands and not directly on area to be powdered.

Be sure to put hand behind her head to support her.

Don't tickle, play hide-and-seek, or patty-cake in excess. Levity makes her spit up.

Check occasionally for fever. (Emergency numbers on separate sheet.)

It's your grandchild. Relax and enjoy her. The three hours will pass in no time.

Love,
Melissa

15

Julie

What Kind of a Mother Would . . . Die and Not Take You with Her?

Had Julie not been the deceased, it was a funeral she would have loved.

The minister, in his desperate struggle for an analogy of comfort, said to her three sons sitting rigid in the front row, "Think of your mother as the spirit leaving the body. The shell is here, but the nut is gone."

The organist forgot the music and the only song she knew by heart was "Days of Wine and Roses."

And her middle son, Steve, flew in from school with only the shoes on his feet . . . a pair of red, white, and blue Adidas with stars that glowed in the dark, which he wore with a three-piece brown suit.

It was hard to believe Julie was dead at forty-eight, the victim of a "kind" cancer that acts quickly and with accuracy.

Chuck, the eldest, had been in his apartment when his grandmother called with the news. All he had been told until then was that his mother had been "a little tired lately."

She had been so proud of her son, "the television mogul." Actually, he was a prop man for a sitcom, but his degree had been in cinema and he spoke the language.

Every time they were together, he couldn't resist showing off. "What movies have you seen lately, Mom?"

JULIE: " 'The Seduction of Miss Marple' and I loved it . . ."
CHUCK: "It missed making a statement."
JULIE: "Up to a point. Of course, the one I really liked was 'Trilogy: Blood, Sex, and Violence.' It was breathtakingly . . ."
CHUCK: "Stargins had a concept. It just didn't work."
JULIE: "Dull. You're absolutely right. I thought 'Slime' was really gross . . ."
CHUCK: "Beautiful, sensitive film."
JULIE: ". . . grossed a million and was worth every penny."

How could he have been such a superior jerk? Now it was too late to say he was sorry. He had had no right to put her down. He fingered the letter in his pocket addressed to him in his mother's hand and opened it slowly. It was her last message to him. He unfolded the pages carefully as if to savor them.

Dearest Chuck:

Since this letter is for no one's eyes but yours, I can tell you that I always loved you best.

Maybe it was because you were the first miracle to stir inside me. The first hint of my immortality.

You were a part of the lean years for your father and me . . . the part that brought laughter to poverty, warmth to cold, success to failures.

You were the original model. There would be others who would come after you who might blow bigger air bubbles, burp louder, talk earlier, walk faster, or "go potty" sooner, but you did it first.

You may have suffered a bit from our inexperience with open pins, clumsy baths, and overprotection, but you got something better. You got our patience, our stamina, and our youth.

You got the part of us that was the best we had to give. Our struggle and our triumph over it. You were Hamburger Helper. You were redeeming bottles for movies. You were fresh grandparents who woke you up when you were asleep to rock you to sleep. You were six volumes of baby pictures and a set of encyclopedias. You were house calls for gas pains. You were strained lamb. You were the beginning. You were wanted and you were loved.

Mama

Chuck folded the letter quickly as Steve slid in beside him.

"Did you get a pen knife with those?" he snapped, nodding toward the red, white, and blue jogging shoes.

"No, a Frisbee."

Steve took a deep breath and tried to focus anywhere but on his brothers. He hadn't been able to look at Chuck since he had read the letter his mother sent him. He had never known she had felt that way about him or even why.

Steve had worked on being a maverick. Every time he screwed up, his mom always took him aside and said they understood, but they didn't. Not really. A couple of years ago, they took his other brother Tim to visit Chuck at school for a weekend and left him in charge of the house.

Why couldn't she have blown up like any other mother would have? Instead, the night they returned, she said, "Want to tell me what happened?"

"What makes you think anything happened?" he asked.

"The thirty neighbors standing around in their nightclothes

watching three police cruisers parked on our front lawn and the dog that is wearing my underwear. A lucky guess."

"I had a party."

"According to the police report you had a 746."

"What's a 746?"

"I'll read it to you. 'Blocking off street for a parade without permission. Illegal parking of two Porta-Johns on a carport, holding an assistant principal against his will, and unlawful assembly of 150 people in a house built as a single family dwelling.' "

Why had he been so stupid? All he had to say was "I'm sorry" and she'd have forgiven him, but he couldn't say it. Now he'd never get the chance. He felt the letter. It was still there. How could she have known him so well?

Dearest Steve:

You must have suspected, but I will say it anyway. I have always loved you best.

You drew such a stupid spot in the family and instead of caving in, you became all the stronger for it. How I did admire your fire, your independence, and your impatience. You may have worn faded, played with chipped toys, and never in your life did anything first, but you rose above it.

You are the child we relaxed with and enjoyed. The one who made us realize that a dog could kiss you on the mouth and you wouldn't die from it. If you missed a nap, you wouldn't get sick. If you sucked on a pacifier until age two, your teeth wouldn't grow in a circle.

You were a part of our busy, ambitious years. The time when priorities and values can get so mixed up. But you reminded us of what we were all about and put us back on course when we strayed.

You were the sibling that unseated the only child. You were spaghetti and meatballs at eight months. You were checking accounts written down to twenty-seven cents. You were shared birthdays. You were arguments over bills. You were the new house we couldn't afford. You were staying home on Saturday nights. You took us away from tedium, rescued us from boredom, and stimulated us with your zest for life.

You were the constancy and were loved.

Mama

Tim stared at his brothers sitting with him in the pew. His suit was tight. At fourteen, it didn't take him long to outgrow anything.

He felt sorry for his brothers. They had missed a part of their mother that only he knew. When they lived at home, she gave and they took. For the last year Tim gave and she was helpless to do anything but accept. Thank goodness he had had that year to make up for all the grief he had given her.

He had hated being the "baby." He had hated the comparisons, the loneliness, the protectiveness, the references to "our second family." He lived in a house where all his parents did was diet and watch animal documentaries.

The only time he saw sugar was when his brothers came home for a visit. Then there was a lot of talk about "being a family again." What did they think he was? A computer?

His brothers had had it all. A father who played touch football after dinner. A grandma who bought them digital watches for their 10th birthdays before she got "practical." A mother who had been too busy to alphabetize their baseball cards and put them in files.

Over the past year, they had talked out all the resentment inside him. The letter his mother had left said it all.

Dearest Tim:

A mother is not supposed to have favorites, but I have always loved you best.

Just when your father and I thought youth had left our lives, you came along to remind us we had something left to give. You darkened our hair, quickened our steps, squared our shoulders, restored our vision, revived our humor.

You were our second chance to enjoy a miracle from God.

You grew so fast in such a short time—or maybe it was that we didn't want to think about time. You fell heir to broken baseball bats, trains that wouldn't run, a refrigerator full of yogurt, midlife crises, and a baby book with nothing in it but a recipe for Apple Brown Betty.

You also fell heir to the one thing we never counted on: our mortality.

With you, we discarded the rules and experienced what a baby is all about. It was like seeing one for the very first time. It's a love one cannot describe.

I have loved you for your thirty-five-year-old patience, your ninety-year-old compassion, and your fifty-year-old practicality, but mostly, I love the fourteen-year-old boy who wore them awkwardly, but proudly.

You were the culmination and were loved.

Mama

As the last strains of "Days of Wine and Roses" faded, two women left from the back of the church.

"Didn't it just tear your heart out to see those young boys of hers without a mother?"

The other woman leaned closer and whispered, "I heard the medical bills took all they had. She didn't leave those boys a thing."

16 ❧❧❧

The Special Mother

Most women become mothers by accident, some by choice, a few by social pressures, and a couple by habit.

This year, nearly 100,000 women will become mothers of handicapped children. Did you ever wonder how mothers of handicapped children are chosen?

Somehow, I visualize God hovering over Earth selecting His instruments for propagation with great care and deliberation. As He observes, He instructs His angels to make notes in a giant ledger.

"Armstrong, Beth, son. Patron saint, Matthew.

"Forest, Marjorie, daughter. Patron saint, Cecilia.

"Rutledge, Carrie, twins. Patron saint . . . give her Gerard. He's used to profanity."

Finally, He passes a name to an angel and smiles, "Give her a handicapped child."

The angel is curious. "Why this one, God? She's so happy."

"Exactly," smiles God. "Could I give a handicapped child a mother who does not know laughter? That would be cruel."

"But does she have patience?" asks the angel.

"I don't want her to have too much patience, or she will drown in a sea of self-pity and despair. Once the shock and resentment wear off, she'll handle it.

"I watched her today. She has that sense of self and independence that are so rare and so necessary in a mother. You see, the child I'm going to give her has his own world. She has to make it live in her world and that's not going to be easy."

"But Lord, I don't think she even believes in you."

God smiles. "No matter, I can fix that. This one is perfect. She has just enough selfishness."

The angel gasps. "Selfishness? Is that a virtue?"

God nods. "If she can't separate herself from the child occasionally, she'll never survive. Yes, here is a woman whom I will bless with a child less than perfect. She doesn't realize it yet, but she is to be envied.

"She will never take for granted a spoken word. She will never consider a step ordinary. When her child says 'Momma' for the first time, she will be witness to a miracle and know it. When she describes a tree or a sunset to her blind child, she will see it as few people ever see my creations.

"I will permit her to see clearly the things I see—ignorance, cruelty, prejudice—and allow her to rise above them. She will never be alone. I will be at her side every minute of every day of her life because she is doing my work as surely as she is here by my side."

"And what about her patron saint?" asks the angel, his pen poised in mid-air.

God smiles. "A mirror will suffice."

17 ❧❧❧
Ginny

What Kind of a Mother Would . . .
Get a Sitter and Go Bowling on
Mother's Day?

The moment the dog started barking Ginny knew her sister was coming.

In seven years, he had tried without success to sink his teeth into her thighs, but Peggy's thighs were just too ambitious, even for a full-grown Doberman.

"That dog should be owned by an attorney," snapped Peggy. "You'd think in all these years he'd know I'm related. Where's B.J.?"

"Watching 'Days Of Our Lives.' "

"What could a fourteen-month-old baby get out of that?" she said sharply.

"A cheap thrill," sighed Ginny. "Nothing more."

Peggy shot her sister a look of disapproval and knelt down before the small child, who was propped up in a seat. "Hello, B.J.," she shouted. "It's Aunt Peggy. Remember Aunt Peggy? Of course you do."

"You don't have to shout," said Ginny. "He's retarded. Not deaf!"

Peggy slipped out of her coat. "You're not in another one of your moods, are you? You look tired around the eyes."

"You want Brooke Shields? Come after lunch. Coffee?"

"Sure. Hold the sugar. I'm cutting back. Hey, did Sue call?"

"What's she selling?" snapped Ginny.

"What made you think she was selling anything? She just wants to invite us over for an evening of shallow conversation and a fattening dessert."

"Sue never serves cashews without a reason. She's always hustling something—plants, plastics, jewelry. Call me cautious, but I'm always suspicious when someone invites me over for dessert and then says, 'Oh by the way, wear clean underwear and bring your checkbook.' "

Peggy took her handbag off the table and hesitated. She didn't know if this was a good time or a bad time to give Ginny the column she had clipped from the newspaper on mothers of handicapped children.

She unfolded the column slowly. "Got something for you. As soon as I read it, I thought of you."

"Don't tell me. I've been named Miss Congeniality in the Pillsbury Bake-Off."

"I was going to save it for Mother's Day, but I think you need it today. Read it."

Ginny took a deep breath and began to read in a sing-song voice. "Most women become mothers by accident, some by choice, a few by social pressures, and a couple by habit." Her head jerked up. "She forgot a bottle of Tequila in the back seat of a Toyota." She continued reading. "This year nearly 100,000 women will become mothers of handicapped children. Did you ever wonder how mothers of handicapped children are chosen?"

Ginny put the column down. "I'm throwing up already."

"Keep reading," Peggy ordered.

Ginny's eyes moved quickly across the lines without emotion. When she had finished reading the article, she threw it on the table, and said, "It's crap."

"I thought you'd like it," sighed Peggy.

"Does she have a retarded child? Then who gives her the right to tell me how to feel? I'm sick of being patronized. It's tough enough having to deal with all this without someone trying to put a halo on me."

"I just thought . . ."

"This is reality," she interrupted. "Look at it. This is the only house on the block that will never have a swing set or a path across the yard. I'm a mother whose kid will never play in the toilet. Never tug at my leg when I'm on the phone. Never tear up my favorite magazine. Never run away from home stark naked. He'll never play patty-cake. Never pull my hair. He'll never even know my name."

"It sounds like you could use a night out. I'll sit if you want me to."

"I'm not looking for cute messages to stamp on tea towels. I'm madder than hell, don't you understand?"

"Don't you go to those meetings anymore?"

"What? Those group misery sessions where everyone sits around and tells you God never gives you more than you can handle? Well, I've got a flash. He overshot the field. I'm drowning, Peggy."

"You have to get out more."

"Don't you think I know that?" She sipped at her coffee. "I'm sorry, Peggy. It's just that I'm so scared. I can handle it now. I really can. Rob has been great. And Mom and Dad have been wonderful. Sometimes I forget how disappointed they must have been. But I'm worried about the long haul. I know what B.J. will be like ten years from now, but what will I be like? I don't like what bitterness does to people. I just want to be special to someone. Look, I didn't mean to take off, but every time I read something like this—"

"I understand," said Peggy, getting up. "Listen, I only stopped by for a minute. Need anything?"

Ginny shook her head and saw her sister to the door. "I'm sorry. Come back when I'm a human being." They put their arms around one another.

After Peggy left, Ginny looked at B.J. He sat quietly as "Days Of Our Lives" told a sensual story of greed, avarice, and carnal pleasures. Ginny stooped and wiped off his face with a piece of tissue, then stuffed it up her sleeve. "Well, what'll we do today, Tiger, play indoor volleyball?"

As she stood up, she caught her reflection in the mirror and paused for a closer look. She was stunned by what she saw. A thirty-year-old woman with hundred-year-old eyes. Eyes that were dull and listless. Eyes that held no joy. Eyes that looked but never seemed to see anything that interested them. Eyes that reflected no life—only pain.

Quickly, she turned away from the mirror and gathered up the coffee cups. Her eyes caught the phrase on the clipping, "When her child says 'Momma' for the first time, she will be witness to a miracle and know it."

She knelt beside B.J. "Look, B.J., there's something I've got to tell you. I'm no saint. It's important to me for you to know that. I have cursed you for my guilt, my exhaustion, and my life. I have questioned why both of us were born. I haven't figured out yet why He brought us together. I only know there is something special between us, something I can't even explain to Rob. I couldn't bear it if you were not here, or if you had never been.

"In the mirror just now I saw myself as you must see me—beaten and angry. I'm not like that. Honest. Sometimes, I think I'm the one who's handicapped." Ginny eased B.J. out of his sling chair and held him close as they both looked into the mirror.

"B.J., I've never made any demands on you. I've never asked you for anything, but right now, I want you to say 'Mama.' I know it's not going to be perfect, but try. Just make a sound. Grunt. Burp. Anything!"

The saliva came out of the corner of B.J.'s mouth. No sound came forth. Then Ginny noticed his eyes. They stared back into hers in a way she had never seen before. They didn't focus right away, then they looked at her for the first time. There was awareness in them, interest, recognition. He knew who she was!

Rob wouldn't believe her. No one would, but B.J. had just spoken his first word with his eyes. He had called her "Mama."

There were tears in her eyes. She took the article and shoved it into the stove drawer. It was still crap, but there *was* something to that miracle part.

18 ❧❧❧

¿Se Habla English?

When my son entered the first grade, his teacher asked to see me. She began our meeting by telling me, "He verbalizes during class, periodically engages in excursions up and down the aisle, has no viable goals and seemingly no definitive conception of his role expectation. Peer pressure seems advised at this time."

"Are you trying to tell me my son is goofing off?"

"I would not have expressed it in the vernacular, but you are correct."

When he was in the third grade, a teacher at open house opened his folder and announced, "To categorize the problem as simply as I know how, your son has challenged group management techniques, our academic expectations, and our sense of efficacy with his declining attention span, which at this time does not occupy a position of priority."

I took a shot and figured he was goofing off.

In the fourth grade he was still goofing off, but he was described as "lacking the basic skills of competency and languishing in his academic environment, even though he has not attained his cognitive limits."

In the sixth grade, I had a long talk with his teacher, who said, "Your son has potential, but is incapable of any viable feedback. You tell me—what are we to do with a child who does not engage in social interaction, does not respond positively to established concepts, and persists in interruptive behavior? I'm sorry to come down so hard, but certainly you can understand the ills and lacunae of contemporary education."

I didn't even understand good-bye.

In the eighth grade, my husband answered the phone one night and did a lot of nodding. When he hung up, he turned to me and said, "Guess what? Our son is not motivated by curriculum innovation. They're apprehensive about his stagnating in a lock-step system, and they're trying to stimulate his awareness. What do you think it means?"

"I think it means he's goofing off."

He was in his sophomore year when he was diagnosed as "having problems that indicate behavior modification, perhaps in a modular-flexible schedule on which an aggressive monopolizer would diminish his role and force him to accept a lesser role in a nonpunitive, restraining, yet pleasant way."

At the beginning of his senior year, my son's adviser summoned me to her office and said, "Well, it's that time when we have to consider the conundrum, isn't it?" She laughed so I laughed too.

"It's hard to say where the burden for the lack of motivation and apathy lies, but before your son's achievement levels polarize, I thought we should have a little talk.

"Hopefully we can open options so he can realize his potential and aim for some tangible goals. Although accreditation is near at hand, I wanted to emphasize his need for upward mobility if he is to succeed on a postgraduate level."

On the way out, I leaned over to the secretary and said, "English! Do you speak English?"

She nodded.

"What was she talking about?"

"Your son is goofing off," she said flatly.

I don't know if education has helped my son or not, but it has certainly improved my vocabulary.

19 Dottie

What Kind of a Mother Would . . .
Hang Up on E.T.?

Dottie Fedstrom was a no-nonsense mother who raised her children by the rules.

Dottie Fedstrom made the Marine Corps look like an exercise in Show and Tell.

She was born to mother. She had hands like thermometers, two sets of eyes that could look through doors and tell at a glance when a child was constipated or lying. She had a nose that could smell chocolate on the breath of a child in another state with his head buried in a pillow.

Dottie had six daughters. She called them The Gang. She bought them white socks (one size fits all) and brown oxfords which were passed down from one sister to the next. Once she bought two bolts of navy corduroy and made each of them a jumper and had enough left over to make drapes and spreads for their bedrooms. (As one of her daughers observed, if you didn't smile, she wouldn't know if you were in your room or not.)

If one daughter wanted oatmeal for breakfast, they all got oatmeal. If one got the measles, Dottie made sure they all got them. If the first to get a watch lost hers, then none of the others would be trusted with one.

Whether they were twenty or two, they all had the same curfew and the same allowance, and got the same doll, the same sweater, album, and hair dryer for Christmas. Dottie didn't play favorites.

It surprised no one when the girls married young. They were as predictable as their mother. Eventually, Dottie was down to one daughter, Nicky.

For three years Nicky heard:

"I don't know why you don't let your hair grow like your sister Leslie's. You'd look good in that style instead of looking like a twelve-year-old boy."

"When Pammie had your room, she had that real pretty pink spread. I think it's still around here somewhere. I'm going to dig it out for you."

"Does your teacher know you're Wendy's sister? She should have recognized the dress. It was Wendy's favorite."

"You're exactly like your sister Leah. She never could manage her money either. Every week she wanted an advance on her allowance."

"You and Alice were never good judges of character."

"You'd better snap it up. All five of your sisters were married before their twenty-first birthday."

Nicky was destined never to do anything original in her entire life. She had been sired by a Xerox machine set for six copies.

Her wedding was predictable—a carbon copy of her sisters'. The dress was the same design; the flowers came from the same florist, the food was from the same caterers, the cake from the same bakery. She received from her parents the same gift her sisters had received: a toaster oven and two goose-down pillows.

As she waited in the small room at the back of the church before going down the aisle, her mother appeared with the same tearful face she had displayed at the weddings of her sisters. She cupped Nicky's face in her hands and whispered her last piece of advice (which had also been given to Nicky's predecessors): "Be yourself or you'll never find happiness."

20 ᘓᘓᘓ

Two Be or Not Two Be

GRAND RAPIDS, MICH.—Robin Hawkins could be the little girl they had in mind when they named it the "terrible twos": the toddler has, by actual count, racked up nearly $3,000 in damages in two months.

First, it was the plumbing, then the dishwasher, the refrigerator, and the family car. None has escaped the $2,862 rampage of Rowlf and Bernie Hawkins' two-year-old daughter.

Robin's trail of terror began at the toilet, a familiar trouble spot for toddlers. A stuffed animal, named Alice the cat, got dunked, drowned, and flushed.

Hawkins, who dutifully has kept track of Robin's exploits, neatly tallied the expenses in a yellow tablet: $62.75 for the plumber, $2.50 for Alice.

That was only the beginning.

Robin's decision to give Teddy Bear a bath—atop the heating element in the dishwasher—cost her father $375 for repairs, $25 for smoke damage and, of course, $8 for the teddy bear.

Then there was the refrigerator. It seems Robin stuck some magnetic letters in the vents just before the family left home for the weekend, burning out the motor. The cost: $310 for the refrigerator, $120 in spoiled food and $3.75 for the magnetic letters.

"That evening, we sat down to watch TV," said Hawkins, an East Grand Rapids police officer. "Robin had twisted the fine tune so far that it broke inside."

The repair bill: $115.

The next day, Mrs. Hawkins went to pick up her husband from his second job as a part-time officer in Sparta. She left Robin sleeping in her safety seat, with the keys in her purse inside the car.

"We heard the car start up, and we ran outside just in time to watch the car start down the street." Hawkins said.

The car ran into a tree. Cost: $1,029.52 in repairs.

A few days later, Robin tried to play some tapes in the family stereo. Cost: $36 for tapes and $35 for tape-deck repairs.

Shortly after that, the Hawkins (sic) parked their car halfway in the garage after a shopping trip and, because they were planning to unload groceries, decided to leave Robin strapped in her safety seat.

"My wife had the keys, so figured everything was OK," Hawkins said.

Everything was OK, until they heard a loud noise and went outside to find the automatic garage door bouncing off the hood of the car with—guess who?—locked inside the car, pushing the remote control. The bill: $120.

Robin also lifted $620 out of the cash register at a supermarket, drilled fifty holes in the walls of a rental property owned by her parents, painted walls with nail polish and slipped the garden tractor out of gear so it rolled down the driveway narrowly missing a neighbor out on a walk.

"Some day, when she comes and asks me why she isn't getting any allowance, I'll show her this," Hawkins said, waving the yellow pad containing an itemized list of his daughter's damages.

21 ❧❧❧

Brooke

What Kind of a Mother Would . . .
Buy Vanilla a Fifth at a Time?

Every time Brooke visited her sister, she never sat down without first running her hand over the chair.

The whole house was like a giant playpen inhabited by five active children with sticky hands, pacifier lips, and something running from every opening in their faces.

The house was a dump! A lone goldfish swam around in an Old Fashioned glass, the three silver iced tea spoons she'd gotten her in her pattern for her anniversary were stuck in the flower bed, and she could have sworn she saw a rainbow over the baby's diaper.

Both of them had been raised in an atmosphere of fine china, good books, oriental carpets, and cloth napkins. Somewhere, her sister had lost her way.

In six years of marriage, Brooke and her husband Clay had done a lot of thinking about how their child would be raised. Like every stick of furniture in their white and chrome townhouse, their two-seater sportscar, their his-and-her careers, and their club membership, their baby was planned.

Brooke would conceive in February, after the holiday parties were over, still be slim enough in May to work on her tan, and deliver in time to have the family portrait taken for the Christmas card.

Brooke and Clay made only one mistake.

They made promises to each other that new parents should never make:

Their baby would *not* dominate their lives.

They would never stoop to plastic.

They would never put their coffee-table books or art glass out of the reach of their child.

They would be able to take their child anywhere and not be embarrassed.

They said all of this in public where people could hear them.

Somewhere it is written that parents who are critical of other people's children and publicly admit they can do better are asking for it.

Other self-righteous people who have defied this law included: Mia Farrow, who was delivered of "Rosemary's Baby," Lee Remick, who birthed Damien in "The Omen," and the parents of Lizzie Borden.

It came as no surprise to anyone except Brooke when she went into labor a month early at the Halloween party at the club and was rushed to the hospital where she gave birth to Wesley.

Her timing was lousy. She had gone to the party dressed as a nun.

Brooke stubbornly insisted Wesley wasn't a bad little boy, he was just "accident prone." He started each day like one of those battery-driven cars that you put on a track and it doesn't stop until it hits something and self-destructs. Brooke was fond of capping each trauma with, "Wesley is just 'all boy.' "

By the time Wesley was six, his medical charts read like the first eighteen chapters of a first-aid manual. He drank paint tint and urinated Melody Blue for a week. He pulled a bubble gum dispenser on himself, fell out of his crib, swallowed a penny, cut his lip on a waste can, got his foot caught in a shopping cart and had to be torched out of it, ate a plastic banana, and bit a rectal thermometer in half.

He gouged himself in the eye with his own finger, broke his arm while watching TV, was bitten by a hostile turtle, fell on the ice and caused a boil on his tailbone, forced a golf tee in his ear, and made a bet he could swan-dive into two and a half feet of water, and lost.

Brooke made so many trips to her local emergency ward, they sent her cards when Wesley was well.

Through it all, never once did Brooke publicly admit defeat. Other children could watch TV and "waste time." Wesley could do it and be "curious and searching." Other kids could shove people out of the way and be "aggressive." Wesley could do it and be "ambitious." When other children took money from their mother's purse without her permission it could be construed as "stealing," but when Wesley did it, it was "reinforcement of the mutual trust between them."

Early in June, Brooke smiled stoically when her obstetrician told her the scanner revealed she was carrying twins.

Normally, that kind of news would have given a mother pause for reflection, but not Brooke.

She stopped on her way home to buy fresh flowers for the table.

She called her husband to tell him the news and thanked goodness the silver pattern of the baby spoon was open stock.

She called her sister to tell her their season opera tickets were still intact, even if the babies came early.

She told Wesley the news and sent him to the neighbors to play.

She retired to her room with a bottle of vodka and was not seen until 4 PM the next day.

22 ❀✿❀

Born to Crisis

Some mothers are born to crisis.

They're ready for it. They sit around in color-coordinated outfits, with their car keys in one hand and a first-aid manual with illustrations of pressure points and CPR in the other.

When a child comes screaming in the back door, "Mommy! Mommy! Mikey has a bloody boo boo," this mother calmly instructs her oven to cook the dinner by six, backs the car (filled with gas) out of the garage, and off they go to the hospital.

She's always at the reception desk when I arrive with my child, who is wrapped in a dirty dish towel and wearing a pair of pajamas that I was going to use for a dust rag as soon as I ripped the snaps out.

She rattles off her insurance number by memory as I wrestle with my child's name and age, finally pinning his birth down to the year we paid off the freezer.

As she quietly goes to the waiting room holding the *Saturday Review of Literature* under her arm, I am checking every phone return for a dime to call my husband, Whatshisname.

One of the most difficult jobs of child-raising is knowing when your child needs medical attention and when he doesn't. Or as

519

we say at the wine-tasting parties, "Be not the first on your block to race a case of constipation to the hospital, nor the last to call the pharmacist for a compound fracture."

There is possibly no guilt in this world to compare with leaving a sick child with a babysitter. The sitter could be Mother Teresa and you would still feel rotten. There is something about having your child throw up without you that is difficult to live with.

I once spent more time writing a note of instructions to a babysitter than I did on my first book.

Dear Miss Tibbles:

The suppositories are in the refrigerator next to the meal worms. The meal worms are for the lizard, who eats breakfast when everyone else eats breakfast. The suppositories are for Bruce's nausea. He will work against you, but persevere. Please return them to the fridge as they are better chilled. The antibiotic is to be given every 12 hours. Bruce is crabby at the 3 AM medication and he will spit it in your face, but remind him it is for his own good. Be firm! The baby aspirin are in the medicine chest on the top shelf. Start early, as the cap is childproof and difficult to remove. Simply depress the cap and twist at the same time in a counterclockwise movement until the arrow reaches the indentation and then, using your thumbnail, flip up. If you cannot get it off, give it to Bruce. He can whip that sucker off in two seconds flat.

He has not been able to tolerate solids yet, but try him on some gelatin and crackers. If he throws up, stop feeding him solids.

Mrs. Bombeck

Pediatricians are no help. Year after year, they dole out instructions that are some of the best comedy material being written today.

"Make sure he keeps it down" is a classic. And how about "Don't let him scratch." (That's like telling the Pope to buy a leisure suit.)

"Keep him quiet and in bed" is another goodie, but my all-time favorite is "Watch his stool."

Do you know of any mothers personally who have ever followed that advice? My son swallowed a nickel once. I was ready to declare it a tax write-off and forget it. My mother was outraged. "You have to take that child to a doctor and see where it is lodged. It could be serious."

The doctor examined him and through X-rays discovered the nickel had "traveled." He then turned to me and with a serious face said, "Watch his stool."

"Why would I want to do that?" I asked.

"For the nickel."

"Money is no object to us. We own our own home and have a microwave oven."

"It's not the money," he said. "Don't you want to know what happens to it?"

"Not that badly," I said.

There are some things you just don't ask a high school graduate to do.

23 ❧❧❧❧

Cora

What Kind of a Mother Would . . .
Have Her Maternity Clothes Bronzed?

Cora is an important character in this book. Mostly because adults do a lot of kidding about children.

Complaining is a mother's escape hatch. That's why you hear a lot of, "Go out and play in the traffic" or "Marrying your father was my first mistake. You were my second." And on a bad day, "If God had meant for me to take you to church, He would have put restrooms at the end of each pew."

It's important that you meet Cora in the examination room at her gynecologist's. There's always something intimidating about the place.

Maybe it's because you're sitting in a chilled room in a paper dress (you've set drinks on a bigger piece of paper) waiting to discuss intimate things with a man who is two years younger than your cookie sheet.

On this day Cora cleared her throat and wished her feet looked better. The heels were cracked and her toenails needed cutting. She wished her whole body looked better. Since she stopped smoking six months ago, her body looked like an avocado. Even when she sucked in her stomach, nothing moved. Maybe he could give her a diet.

She reasoned she was stupid to come. There probably was nothing wrong with her. She was just tired. And probably ready for the estrogen connection.

The examination lasted less than three minutes and after a couple of questions and a few notations, the doctor smiled and said, "Congratulations: you're going to become a mother."

Cora looked him in the eye for the first time since he came into the room. "I'm going to become a what?"

"Mother," he said. "As in Teresa, McCree, and Nature."

She threw her arms around his neck and for a reason that made no sense to either of them said, "Thank you!"

Cora couldn't believe it. For years she and Warren had tried everything. They had kept charts, burned candles, sought adoption, and even gone into debt (which everyone said was a sure-fire way to get pregnant). Nothing. Motherhood eluded her.

"You know I'm thirty-eight," said Cora, anxiously.

The doctor was without expression. "If you'd waited another year, the birth could have been covered by Medicare, not to mention *The New York Times*. Your uterus is tilted, so we're going to take some precautions."

Eleven weeks into her pregnancy, Cora climbed into bed and remained there until the birth of the baby six months later.

She ate her meals from a tray that Warren prepared every morning, watched soaps and game shows, read, and entertained the parade of soothsayers who wanted to relieve her of her happiness.

Her mother said, "Tell me again. What happened?"

Her sister-in-law said, "Are you aware the kid will take your social security card for Show and Tell?"

Her husband offered to lace her bran with Valium.

Her neighbor warned she'd feel different when the kid sat around connecting liver spots on Mommy's arms.

Her paper boy said, "I thought you were the oldest mother in North America, but I looked it up in the *Guinness Book of World Records* and there was a woman who gave birth when she was 57 years and 129 days."

Her former boss told her that the expression, "Children keep you young," was first said by a nineteen-year-old mother in Milwaukee who denied saying it when she turned twenty-two.

Somewhere in this chapter it should be said that most children are wanted. For every child abandoned in a bus station, there's a list of adoptive parents who have waited and prayed for years to hold a baby.

For every woman who has an abortion there are women who are fighting for both of their lives against stiff odds.

For every mother who complains how much a child costs, how much trouble they are, and how much different their lives would have been without them, there are thousands of women who would not have been whole without them.

In May, Cora delivered a healthy six-pound, five-ounce son. She had never known before, nor would ever know again, such a feeling of exhilaration.

There is a lot of Cora in most of us. More than we like to admit. At whatever age, we are awed by the miracle that stirs inside us. We are filled with joy and wonder by the process that gives us our immortality. Why are we so reluctant to admit it?

24 ✿✿✿✿

Stepmothers with Bad P.R.

Snow White's Stepmother

It was Queenie White's first marriage.

At thirty-seven, it was something she thought would never happen. Sometimes she had to pinch herself to make sure it wasn't a dream. She was married to a successful king, with a castle in the suburbs and a small beautiful child who looked like something out of a Pampers ad.

It should have been idyllic, but it wasn't. Snow resented her for marrying her father. Why couldn't it have been just the two of them? They were happy before she came along. At the wedding Snow had informed her new stepmother that she was wearing something old, something new, something borrowed, something blue. The symbolism was all wrapped up in one garment—a pair of raggy, faded jeans.

Queenie knew Snow was spoiled, but she was resigned to patience and never burdened her husband with the problem.

When Snow gave a slumber party at the castle for the jousting team, she covered for her. She took the blame for the dent in the King's carriage. She kept silent when she saw Snow and some friends smoking the croquet lawn.

One day she looked at her image in the mirror and said aloud, "Mirror, mirror on the wall, who's the stupidest of them all?" Before the mirror opened its mouth, she knew the answer.

Things couldn't continue. She dropped by Snow's room.

"Snow," she said softly, "we're not close and I don't know why."

"Because you're heartless and cruel," said Snow. "And you wish I'd split because I'm a constant reminder of how beautiful my mother was."

"I'd like for us to get along because we both love the same man and he deserves better," said Queenie.

"Stick it in your mirror," said Snow. "You think I haven't caught you carrying on a conversation with it? You're weird!"

"Do you have any idea what love really is? It's caring enough to tell you the truth even at the risk of losing your love. Why don't you get your act together? Stop dressing like trick or treat. Get some order to your life. Enroll at junior college. Volunteer. Or I'll tell your father what you've been up to."

That night, fearful that Queenie would make good her threat, Snow headed for the forest outside of San Francisco. She spotted a small cabin in the clearing, occupied by a commune. It was the first time she had ever checked in anywhere without a reservation. For the next three years, Snow played the guitar, grew her own vegetables, and made owl macramé planters for a local florist.

There is probably no guilt in this world to compare with that of a stepmother who has driven a child away from the family hearth. Queenie tried daily to find her.

Then one day a courier brought word from Snow.

Queenie duly reported it to her husband.

"We've found Snow."

"That's wonderful," said the King.

"Not so wonderful," said Queenie. "She's living in the forest in a commune."

"So, it could be worse. She could be living with a man."

"She's living with seven of them. All dwarfs."

"I want her home," said the King.

Snow returned with a husband, a baby, and asked to be reinstated in the family.

The couple and their child slept on mattresses surrounded by candles in sand, drank goat's milk, and ate sunflower seeds. They meditated and chanted all day long.

Queenie stood in front of the mirror one day and said, "Mirror, mirror on the wall, what must I do to survive it all?"

And the mirror answered, "Drink!"

Cinderella's Stepmother

Her name was Buffy Holtzinger.

But to the world of fairy tales, she was identified only as "Cinderella's mean, evil, ugly stepmother."

Buffy attracted losers like a white dress attracts spots. First there was Ray, who left her high and dry with one small daughter and another on the way. And then there was Eugene, who brought his daughter, Cinderella, to the marriage, then split to get in touch with his feelings.

Buffy was one of the first working mothers in her neighborhood. She held no illusions that she was a "real" mother (a fact which Cinderella reminded her of at least fifteen times a day). She worked. She came home. She shouted until she had varicose veins of the neck. She fell into bed. There was no doubt in her mind that if she continued raising three teenaged girls by herself she'd end up like Rapunzel sitting in a tower braiding her hair. She had to get them married off if she were to survive.

Her two natural daughters were bad enough. They were surly. They lounged around the house all day reading the *Palace Enquirer* (a gossip rag) and waiting for someone to spoon-feed them.

Goofing off Buffy could handle. But it was Cinderella's active imagination that drove her up the wall. From the beginning, Cinderella played with the truth like most kids play with their gum— stretching it, rearranging it, hiding it, and disguising it. She told her teacher in the third grade that her "stepmother" made her play outside naked in the snow. She told them her stepsisters got silk dresses for Christmas and she got a certificate to be "bled." She told everyone her stepmother hated her because she was pretty and made her wax the driveway.

One night, when Buffy was needlepointing a sampler that said, "YOU HAVE TO KISS A LOT OF TOADS BEFORE YOU FIND YOUR PRINCE," she summoned Cinderella to talk.

"Cinderella, why do you say things that aren't true?"

"I don't," said Cinderella defensively. "I do everything around here. I'm nothing but a slave. You like your kids better than you like me. Daddy and I were happy before you came along. If he were here, things would be different."

"All of us have chores," said Buffy tiredly. "And if all of you get them done you can go to the ball next Friday night. How would you like that?"

"Who are we kidding here?" snapped Cinderella, as she headed for the door. "You'll think of something to chicken out. The pots won't be sparkling enough or the floor won't shine enough. I hate you and I hate your stupid warts!"

"They're not warts! They're moles!" shouted Buffy after her.

The next Friday was predictable. Buffy's two older daughters made a stab at finishing their chores, but Cinderella was doing her Butterfly McQueen number. She flicked a speck of dust off with her finger, blew on it, and went on to the next brick.

Buffy called her bluff. "That's it! I made a rule and I'm going to hold you to it. You're grounded."

Several hours later no one was more shocked to see Cinderella at the ball than Buffy. She grabbed one of her daughters and said, "How did she get here?"

She popped another cheese puff into her fat cheeks. "She's telling everyone a fairy godmother made a coach out of a pumpkin, a coachman out of a white rat, footmen out of lizards, and horses out of frightened mice."

"Oh God," moaned Buffy. "Tell me she didn't say that to the reporter from the *Palace Enquirer*. They're going to put her away in a ha ha house. You tell her to get herself home or she won't be able to sit down for a week."

Cinderella met a shoe salesman that night at the ball and married him several months later. Happiness continued to elude Buffy when Cinderella submitted a manuscript to a publisher called *Stepmommie Dearest*. The title was changed to *Cinderella* and the book became an instant best seller.

It is credited with saving millions of women from a second marriage who are now living happily ever after.

Hansel and Gretel's Stepmother

Wilma met Hansel and Gretel's father at a woodcutters' convention and it was magic. They liked the same music, the same food, and the same jokes. No one was surprised when, three days later,

Wilma gave up her job as a secretary to marry Herb and go live with him and his two children in the forest.

From the beginning, Wilma sensed that the children resented her presence. They set the table for three. They coughed on her porridge so she couldn't eat it. And one night they put a dead wolf in her bed.

"Maybe they're getting too much sugar," she suggested to Herb. "They seem so hyper."

"Nonsense," he said. "They're just active little children. Try to have a little fun with them."

Wilma tried. She took them on picnics and they tied her to a tree. She read them little stories and they put a candle under her dress. Finally, Wilma faced the problem realistically. They were the type of children who would kill both parents and make you feel sorry for them because they were orphans.

When she told Herb that something had to be done about their behavior, he said, "So, what's your solution?"

"I think we should take them out into the forest and dump them." Seeing the horrified look on his face, she said, "I'm only kidding, Herb. Can't you take a joke?"

But just at that moment, a plan began to form in the warped little minds of Hansel and Gretel . . . a plan to get Wilma out of their lives for good. They planned an outing in the forest where they purposely got lost. When they returned, they told their father Wilma tried to ditch them. The only way they had found their way back was by dropping crumbs. "She's never liked us," said Hansel. "Things were wonderful before she came," said Gretel.

The next week, they once again planned an outing with their stepmother, and this time disappeared forever, sealing Wilma's fate.

Several days after their disappearance, the little cottage was overrun with authorities taking fingerprints, looking for clues, and questioning Wilma and Herb until they were incoherent.

"There was a Rosemary's Baby quality about those two," said Wilma. "Something I couldn't put my finger on."

"They were just active little children," Herb growled.

"You weren't here the day they strapped 138 pigeons to their arms and said they were going to fly to South America," said Wilma. "I'm telling you, Herb, those kids were weird."

"Are you saying you're glad they're gone?" asked the inspector.

"I'm saying I think they planned to run away," said Wilma.

"Then why did we find crumbs of bread a few feet from the house? Is that the act of children who want to stay lost?"

Wilma had no answer. The case against her was too strong for her defense. She was a stepmother who had never displayed any real affection for her two charges. At one point during the trial, when someone mentioned that these two little children would never be seen again, Wilma laughed uncontrollably.

She was sentenced to life in prison for the questionable demise of two small innocent, helpless children.

Wilma was considered quite mad by those around her and incapable of communication. However, one day in the prison library, Wilma's eyes caught sight of a small story on an inside page of *The New York Times*. It seemed that two small children were being sought for shoving an old woman into an oven. They had conned their way into her home by telling her they had been abandoned in the forest by a wicked stepmother. After they did the old lady in, they ripped off all her treasures and escaped on the back of a white duck.

A chill went through Wilma's body. She wanted to stay where she was forever. She felt safe there.

25 ❧❧❧

Pat

What Kind of a Mother Would . . .
Go in Search of Her Daughter's "Real Mother"?

So you're Joanie's "real mother."

I've made a million speeches to you in the bathroom mirror. They were all brilliant.

I thought you'd be taller. You always seemed taller when we talked about you. And you always looked like Barbara Stanwyck to me. Don't ask why.

We've talked about you a lot. As soon as Joanie—that's your daughter's name now—was able to focus, we told her she was adopted. We told her her real mother loved her so much that she was unselfish enough to give her up to someone who could give her all the things she couldn't. That's true, isn't it? No, never mind. I don't want to know.

Forgive me for staring. It's just that all my life, I've wanted to see what a "real" mother really looks like. Joanie always seemed to know you better than we did. You know, "My *real* mother wouldn't have done that" or "My *real* mother wouldn't have said that." That kind of thing.

I guess first off I should thank you for giving birth to our child. I don't know how we would have gotten through life without Joanie. Children make your life important.

There's probably a lot of things you want to know about Joanie. Is she beautiful? Is she smart? Is she happy? Does she play the piano? I guess I owe you that.

It's funny. I've always wondered about my debt to you. Things like how *much* do I owe you? When is the debt paid? And when do I become "real"?

It's only fair that if you hear all the good stuff, maybe you have to hear the bad stuff. There were bad times, you know. Did you know that our—your—daughter almost died from an asthma attack when she was eight? I thought about you that night as both of us gasped for every breath together under that vaporizing tent. I said to myself, "Where in the hell are you now, *real* mother?"

Why am I doing this? Why am I so angry at you? I've always known you did what you thought was best. I can tell by the look on your face that you honestly don't know what you did that I think is so terrible.

I'm not sure myself. I only know that when you went away you took a part of our child with you that we can't give her. You took away her history!

Without a past, she's been adrift on a sea of frustration, sometimes afloat and sometimes sinking, and she doesn't even know what port is home. Is she allergic to penicillin? Did her grandfather have red hair? Is she part Irish? Was she conceived in love? Was she really wanted? Is there someone out there who bears her likeness?

It's been difficult for all of us. How can any of us go forward until we know what is behind us?

Love? People talk about it like it's the universal Band-Aid for all physical and emotional ailments. Well, there's one thing it can't cure. The rejection by a woman who gave her life.

We tried. The photo albums, the birthday parties, the instant set of grandparents, but in her heart she stands like a waif on the outside of a family, never feeling like she really belongs on the inside.

I look at you and I don't know why all these years I've felt threatened by the ghost of a "real mother."

You want to know what "real" is?

Real is what gets a part-time job to pay for a baton that lights up.

Real is what hears, "I hate you" and still says, "No."

Real is what sits up until 3 AM when she has the car out and it's raining.

Real is hurting when she's in pain and laughing when she's happy.

Real is emergency rooms, PTA's, music that deafens, lies, defiance, and slammed doors.

Real is what shows up every day!

I'm shouting and I don't know why.

I do know why. All these years, you have been the object of my love and gratitude, frustration and pain, blame and compassion. But mostly you have been the object of my envy. You had that wonderful experience that I would have given anything to have. The movement inside me of a girl child who would one day look at me and see me as "real."

No one can give it to me. No one can take it away from you.

It is there.

26 ❧

Five Classic Motherhood Speeches

Written, Choreographed, and Staged for
Amateur Presentation
(*Advanced Mothers)

1. "Why you cannot have a snake for a pet."
2. "So you've decided to pierce your ears."
3. "Do you know what time it is?"
4. "You want to borrow my <u>WHAT?</u>"
*5. "Don't pretend you don't know what this is all about. <u>YOU</u> know!"

1. "Why You Cannot Have a Snake for a Pet."

SCENE: Kitchen table, where a large mound of cookies sits on a plate next to a pitcher of cold milk. Mother exudes love throughout monologue.

Mother: "Sweetheart, you know that Mommy and Daddy love you very much. We would certainly never say no to your having a snake. After all, we love animals as much as you do. We just want to talk about it first.

"Have a cookie.

"Our first concern, of course, is for the snake. You know how prejudice and ignorance haunt them wherever they go. Could you stand to walk into a crowded room with your little friend and watch it empty out in three seconds? Of course not. It would break your heart.

"And they're so small. What if someone stepped on one of them with a large rake or accidentally dropped a boulder on him? It wouldn't have a chance, now would it? Sometimes, snakes have been known to give Mommy a start. Remember the one in the back yard last year that was thirty-five feet long, had fangs that dripped human blood, was pregnant, and had the capacity to open doors with a passkey?

"You may remember it as smaller, but Mommy doesn't forget things like that. Have another cookie.

"He'd be difficult to paper-train, and the poor little thing couldn't bark when he wanted to be let out or walk on a leash at the shopping center. He couldn't even chase a ball and pant.

"Sweetheart, we want a snake just as much as you do, but what kind of people would we be to deprive him of a normal life, if you get my drift. Don't you think he'd want to date and have a family and do all those things you can't do in a hermetically sealed Mason jar?

"Have all the cookies you want, dear.

"I wish serpents had a better image. You know and I know that they are just as afraid of us as we are of them. I mean just because we never saw a snake spot a human being in the grass and hyperventilate and sink into a coma doesn't mean they don't have feelings.

"Then it's settled. You tell _____ (name of playmate) it's nice of him to think of you and to want to give you his snake, but a snake needs the stability of a family unit.

"I know. It may seem like we are a stable family unit, dear, but tell him if that snake comes into this house, your mother is running away from home and never coming back!"

2. "So You've Decided to Pierce Your Ears."

SCENE: Mother is seated at center stage, engaged in something domestic like reading the *American Journal of Tooth Decay* and making notes in the margins.

Daughter enters stage left.

Daughter: "What would you say if I told you I was going to pierce my ears?"

Mother (putting book down and marking spot): "My feeling is that your body is your own and if a girl wants to punch holes in her earlobes with an ice pick, it's strictly her own business. After all, darling, we don't live in a Victorian age anymore. This is _____ (current year). Every woman is a human being in her own right and it is her decision to make and if you are thinking of piercing your ears it will be over my dead body! I did not pump you full of vitamins and fix your feet to have some bungling butcher perform back-street surgery on my only daughter.

"I suppose _____ (name of daughter's best friend) is going to do it. I know she's your best friend and you'll hate me for saying this, but _____ (name of daughter's best friend) seems to have cast a spell over you. Don't misunderstand me. She's a nice girl, but I don't relish the idea of your going under the needle with a girl who plays with her gum and never washes her hands after she plays with the dog. The next thing she'll have you tattooing butterflies on your shoulder blades.

"I wasn't going to tell you about _____ (name of person she doesn't know) but she pierced her ears and suffered a concussion. She'll never be right. Had her ears 'done' in the main aisle of _____ (leading department store), passed out, and hit her head on a footstool in Better Shoes.

"You do what you want with my blessing. Why not? I'll be dead soon anyway."

3. "Do You Know What Time It Is?"

SCENE: Mother is alone on stage with television set flashing test pattern. A clock with large face is located on table next to her. She is facing the door when son or daughter walks in.

Mother: "I don't want to know where you've been, what you've been doing, or who you've been doing it with. It's late and we'll discuss it in the morning. (Turns off TV set and all the lights except one.)

"Do you honestly think that by not talking about it it's going to go away? (Son opens mouth to speak.)

"Don't lie to me! I would rather you go to bed and say nothing than to stand there and tell me you ran out of gas or the car broke down. I don't want to talk about it tonight or I'll say something I'll be sorry for. Go to bed. (Races him to landing of stairs/hallway, blocking entrance to stairs.)

"Do you have any idea what it is like to be a mother and sit here half-crazed for seven hours, hoping against hope that you were in an accident and had amnesia and that when the ambulance passed the house you heard your dog barking and it triggered your memory? I cannot believe you had the nerve to walk in here without a scratch on you and expect me to understand.

"Please, not another word. I'm exhausted. (Turns off light and follows him upstairs.)

"You know what really hurts? I've been sitting in that chair for seven hours making myself sick and you don't even have the courtesy to phone and say, 'I'm all right. Go to bed.' If you didn't want to talk to me, you could have paid someone to do it for you. Go ahead, say it. You didn't ask me to wait up. I wondered when you'd get around to that. I'm supposed to have a little switch that clicks on and off? On, when it's fun to be a mother. Off, when it's five o'clock in the morning? (Bathroom door slams and she stands outside it.)

"Well, I don't know about you, but I'm going to bed. The doctor says I need at least eight hours of sleep a night. Easy for him to say. He's never had an ungrateful son. Never sat there for seven hours trying to figure out what two people could possibly do at five in the morning. (Bathroom door opens and son goes to bedroom door and closes it.)

"I know you want me to hear your story—if you have one. I personally think we'll be a little more rational in the morning. If you want to apologize, I could heat up the chili."

4. "You Want to Borrow My <u>WHAT?</u>"

SCENE: Mother is busy while child hovers nearby, uncertain. Mother has a distinct advantage and is in charge of this situation.

Mother: "I know that look. You're standing there because you want to borrow something. If it's my hair dryer, you've already got it, unless it grew legs and walked back into my bathroom. I'm not a selfish person. You know that. I don't mind if you borrow something as long as you return it in the same condition as I loaned it to you.

"Take my luggage. Which you did, literally. What did you carry in it? Scrap iron? The whole frame is bent. And my camera will never be the same since you dropped it in the sand. Every picture we develop comes out looking like a puzzle.

"Remember my tennis racket you borrowed three years ago? You never did replace the string you broke. Lucky it's the one in the middle, and I never hit the ball there.

(Refrain: I'm-not-a-selfish-person speech.)

"I wouldn't mind lending you things if you took care of them. I guess I don't have to remind you of my good white blouse that you promised not to sweat in and did. The only place I can wear it now is to funerals where I don't have to raise my arms.

"The trouble with kids is they don't know the value of what they're borrowing and don't have respect for it.

"Do you remember how you returned my car the last time you borrowed it? It had trash all over the back, mud on the tires, catsup on the steering wheel, and I don't have proof, but I know the clutch had been violated.

"You want to borrow my WHAT? Sit down! Let me tell you why I'm going to say no."

*5. "Don't Pretend You Don't Know What This Is All About. <u>YOU</u> Know!"

SCENE: Anywhere. Mother's face is a mask that reveals nothing and reacts to nothing that is said. *This is important*, lest the child

*Speech for Advanced Mothers with years of experience.

know what you are talking about. Keep clues broad. Interest is sustained by slamming doors, dropping plates on the table, and kicking the dog.

Mother: "Well, I hope you're satisfied. You've done it again. Don't pretend you don't know what this is all about. *You* know. How long before you were going to tell me about it?

"Did it ever occur to you to check with me first? That's it, play dumb. You're dumb like a fox. You knew what this would do to your _____ (person, place, or thing). You've done it before.

"I'd like to say it doesn't matter, but it does. Well, no use crying over spilled milk.

"And don't play Miss (Mr.) Innocence with me. You know very well what I'm talking about. It's not the first time you've disappointed me and I'm sure it won't be the last. If you want to talk about it, I'm here to listen. If you don't, tough biscuits.

"I'd like to think you'd promise not to do it again, but I know you won't, so forget it. You want a hint as to what I'm talking about? That's a joke. Do you mean to stand there and tell me you haven't the foggiest notion of why I'm angry? That's rich. Really rich.

"Okay, I'll play your little game. Tuesday! Is that enough of a hint? You know you should be an actress (actor). I am looking at an Academy Award performance here. You can make your eyes as big as a spare tire, but you won't convince me you don't know what I'm talking about.

"I'm going to say this once and only once. If you ever do it again, you're going to have to answer to a lot more people than me.

"You have anything to say? Any apologies to make? Any promises?

"You know something? I'll never understand you."

27 ❦❦❦

Sarah

What Kind of a Mother Would . . .
Rather Be Rich and Thin Than Pregnant?

There are three things in this world that people refuse to accept: an incurable bad back, directions without a map, and a woman who does not want a child.

Sarah did not want a child. She was thirty-two, happy with her marriage, happy with her job, and happy with her life. What she was unhappy about was the people around her who seemed to feel her choice not to have children was their business.

People like her mother, her sister Gracie (mother of five), her best friend Dodie, and her gynecologist, who reminded her, "You're not getting any younger." (Who is?)

One day, in a moment of intimacy when she and her mother were alone, Sarah attempted one last time to explain to her mother why she preferred to remain childless.

"Try to understand, Mom," she said. "I'm not against children. I'm just against them for me. For Gracie, it's fine. She's a born mother. I just don't want to go through life with little gates all over the house and a bathtub full of ducks and boats. People who

542

have children change, and it's scary. They lose a part of themselves that I don't want to lose. It's like someone flipping a switch. All of a sudden you're not a person anymore. You're attached to another human being. Separate them and they both die.

"I don't want to be an extension of someone else's fever, someone else's hunger, pain, disappointment, and frustration. I had a wonderful childhood, but when I was a child I never began to appreciate all your work and sacrifice. What did you get out of it? A lot of slammed doors and a wooden pig that held recipes for your birthday.

"If I had children, Mom, I'd be having them for all the wrong reasons—because you wanted to be a grandmother or Steve wanted someone to carry on his name or I couldn't stand the pressure of people wanting to know why I don't have children.

"I don't think I'm selfish. I'm certainly not bitter or angry. I just feel I have a choice and I have every right to make it. Do you understand?"

Her mother nodded.

The next morning, in a planned moment of intimacy, Sarah's mother called her other daughter, Gracie, and said, "I think I know why your sister doesn't want a child."

Gracie glued the receiver to her ear. "Why?"

"Well," said her mother, "I don't pretend to understand all of what she said, so I'll quote verbatim. She's scared! It's that simple. The idea of having a baby scares her spitless, and besides, she doesn't want all the mess around the house, like rubber boats and gates.

"She made it pretty clear that if I want to be a grandmother again, it's in your ballpark, since you love the crud detail. Besides, she said with her luck she'd catch a fever from them and probably eat every time they ate and weigh a ton. Does that make sense to you?"

"Perfectly," said Gracie.

Within the hour, Gracie called Dodie, Sarah's best friend, and said, "Hold on to your hat. You know how none of us could figure why Sarah shouldn't have a child and be as miserable as the rest of us? Well, Mom talked with her this morning and she finally confessed."

"What's her problem?" asked Dodie.

"I couldn't believe it when Mom told me. Sarah is afraid of losing her shape! She never weighed over 115 pounds in her entire life."

"I think I've heard about that," said Dodie. "It's called sagophobia. It's a fear of the entire body falling down around your knees."

"And listen to this," interrupted Gracie, "she said that if anyone in the family should have a packful of kids, it's me. How do you like that? She said I've always got a houseful of old gates and soldiers and boats all over the place, but I'm used to it.

"She didn't say it in so many words, but Mom guessed the real reason is that Sarah is up for promotion and she can't afford to pass it up. I'm not too shocked, are you?"

"Not really," said Dodie.

When her husband came home, Dodie handed him a drink and said, "You'll never guess what Sarah's sister told me today."

"Surprise me," said Bob, opening up the paper and burying himself behind it.

"She said Sarah wants a baby, but they can't afford one. And all this time she's been putting up such a brave front and all, pretending she didn't want one. Gracie said she's up for promotion if she can keep her weight under 115. I don't know what they're going to do if she doesn't get it. Obviously, Steve's job is on shaky ground. They won't even be able to adopt. I wonder why they bought a boat? Are you listening to me?"

"I heard every word," said Bob.

Several days later, while playing handball with Sarah's father, Bob said, "Congratulations. I hear Steve and Sarah are adopting a Korean child and going boating this summer if he can turn his career around."

That night, Sarah's father said to her mother, "Have you talked to Sarah lately?"

"Not in the last day or two."

"I heard the strangest rumor at the gym today. Something about Sarah wanting to adopt, but Steve doesn't want to. Does that make sense to you?"

"Perfectly," said his wife.

Exactly one week from the time they had their "little talk," Sarah's mother paid her daughter a visit, looked her in the eyes, kissed her on the cheek, and said, "I want you to know that whatever your decision for your future, your father and I will support you a hundred percent. I know now why you said the things you did and we love you for it."

As Sarah told Steve that night, "Imagine my thinking my mother wouldn't understand a word of what I was saying. Sometimes I think we underrate mothers."

28 Motherese

It's a language unto its own, spoken and passed down from one mother to another.

There are hundreds of phrases. The following ones will get a mother through the first seventeen years of a child's life.

Oldies But Goodies

THIS IS GOING TO HURT ME WORSE THAN IT HURTS YOU.

WHEN YOU GROW UP, YOU'LL THANK ME FOR BEING SO STRICT.

WE'LL SEE.

DON'T TALK WITH FOOD IN YOUR MOUTH. ANSWER ME!

I'M DOING THIS BECAUSE I LOVE YOU.

NEVER MIND, I'LL DO IT MYSELF.

I'M NOT GOING TO SPEAK TO YOU AGAIN.

LITTLE PITCHERS HAVE BIG EARS.

CHILDREN SHOULD BE SEEN AND NOT HEARD.

NO SENSE CRYING OVER SPILT MILK.

DO YOU BELIEVE EVERYTHING YOU HEAR?

I'LL GIVE YOU SOMETHING TO CRY ABOUT.

KEEP YOUR HANDS WHERE THEY'RE SUPPOSED TO BE.

On Age

WHY DON'T YOU GROW UP?

SOMEDAY YOU'LL BE OLD.

YOU'RE NOT GETTING ANY YOUNGER.

YOU'LL GROW UP FAST ENOUGH. WHEN I WAS YOUR AGE . . .

WHEN ARE YOU GOING TO ACT YOUR AGE?

I'LL TREAT YOU LIKE AN ADULT WHEN YOU START ACTING LIKE ONE.

YOU'LL ALWAYS BE MAMA'S BABY.

Guilt Grabbers

I'M GOING TO SEND ALL THAT FOOD YOU LEFT ON YOUR PLATE TO ALL THE STARVING ARMENIANS.

DO YOU WANT MOMMY TO LEAVE THE HOUSE AND NEVER COME BACK?

IF YOU SLEEP WITH DOGS, YOU GET FLEAS.

YOU'RE GOING TO DRIVE ME TO AN EARLY GRAVE.

BE GLAD I'M SCREAMING. WHEN I STOP . . .

THIS IS THE LAST TIME I'M GOING TO BEG.

WE'RE NOT ASKING YOU NOT TO GET MARRIED. WE'RE ASKING YOU TO WAIT.

JUST KEEP PLAYING WITH MATCHES AND YOU'LL WET THE BED.

THAT'S WHAT YOU GET FOR NOT LISTENING.

I'M ONLY ONE PERSON.

Great Exit Lines

JUST WAIT TILL YOU HAVE CHILDREN OF YOUR OWN!

DO YOU THINK I WAS BORN YESTERDAY?

IF YOU DON'T LISTEN, YOU'RE GOING TO HAVE TO FEEL.

THAT DOES IT. I'M SENDING YOU TO REFORM SCHOOL.

WHERE DID I FAIL?

WHY ME, GOD?

Philosophical Bon-Bons

YOU MADE YOUR BED, NOW LIE IN IT.

I MAY NOT ALWAYS UNDERSTAND YOU, BUT I AM ALWAYS WILLING TO LISTEN.

WHAT'S A MOTHER FOR BUT TO SUFFER?

FOOL ME ONCE, SHAME ON ME—FOOL ME TWICE, I'LL KILL YOU.

IF YOUR GIRLFRIEND JUMPED OFF THE BRIDGE WOULD YOU DO IT TOO?

IF YOU FALL OFF THAT SWING AND BREAK A LEG, DON'T COME RUNNING TO ME.

29 ❧❧❧

Janet

What Kind of a Mother Would . . .
Have Joan Crawford for a Role Model?

It was a masculine house. You could tell just by looking at the outside of it that inside all the toilet seats were up.

The yard looked like a missile site. The front door was held open by flyers and throwaways. Someone had drawn a sixth finger on the HELPING HAND sign in the window and added, ALL MAJOR CREDIT CARDS ACCEPTED.

The driveway looked like a used car lot. Janet's compact brought the total number to six. As she balanced four bags of groceries, she kicked open the door with her foot. The dog nearly knocked her over trying to get out.

God, wouldn't you think they'd get a clue that the dog wanted out when he tunneled under the door? Janet's eyes took in the kitchen.

Breakfast cereal had hardened in the bowl. The butter had turned into a beverage. The kitchen phone was off the hook. The TV was blaring. Mechanically, she put the milk in the refrigerator before moving down the hall. At a bedroom door she yelled, "Mark! Turn that stereo down or put on your headphones."

When he didn't answer, her suspicions were confirmed. The music fed into his ears and blared out of his nose. The next stop was her bathroom, where she pushed in the lock button and caught a glimpse of herself in the mirror. She wasn't your basic Oil of Olay success story. At forty-six, Janet's hair was coming in Brillo gray and zinging out in every direction. Every muscle in her body had surrendered to gravity. (She dropped out of aerobics class when the only thing she could touch were her knees to her chest . . . and only because her chest met her knees halfway.)

This had been the worst day of her life! Her best friend was happy because she was going on a cruise. The elastic broke on her maternity underwear (she wasn't pregnant), and her dentist had just informed her her gums were receding. Someday she'd put her body together.

All her friends had, but then all her friends didn't have three full-grown sons at home squatting in the nest with knife and fork poised, waiting for her to come home from work each night and drop something from the microwave into their beaks.

The children of her contemporaries were long gone. They were living with someone, bumming around with guitars on their backs, having babies, or wrestling with high interest rates.

At first, she was flattered that her kids never wanted Mother's Day to end. That was before Joan Crawford became her role model. Now, she just felt used.

The porch light had been burning day and night for three years.

The refrigerator held empty milk cartons, dried out lunch meat, and empty ice cube trays.

They borrowed her hair dryer, camera, luggage, car, and money without asking.

They kept hours like hamsters.

They were still small, dependent children in big hairy bodies with deep voices.

What was she supposed to do? Turn her back on them when they needed her? Was it John's fault his marriage hadn't worked out? Cindy had seemed so perfect for him. They had everything in common. Both loved raw pizza dough, both were left-handed, and both liked the way Liza Minnelli sang "New York, New York" better than Frank Sinatra.

It should have worked.

Then there was Peter. At twenty-four (two years younger than John) he was well on his way to becoming the oldest living schoolboy in North America. He had changed his major twelve times, having passed only two things last semester: human sexuality and his eye test.

As for Mark, Janet was convinced his future was shaped when, in her eighth month, she got caught in a revolving door. It was to have a serious effect on her youngest. His first words were "hello-goodbye."

Their relationship had never been good. She honestly never knew why. When anyone asked her how many children she had, she'd say, "Four. John, Peter, Mark at home, and Mark away from home."

Mark at home was miserable. He was the most negative kid Janet had ever set eyes on. There was no pleasing him. No one ever cooked his favorite food. Everyone picked on him. He hated his room. He hated his clothes. He hated his life.

For the last three years, he'd worked on and off, but mostly he sat in his room strumming his guitar and waiting for a dish to rattle.

Janet slipped into her robe and gave a last glance in the mirror. Would there ever be a day when she and George would pick at a salad by candlelight and hoist a glass of white wine without him saying, "My God! Smell this. This glass was used for creme rinse."

As she turned to run water for a quick shower she saw it. Her bottle of Gossamer Gold shampoo that contained pure organic honey herbs and H-D phylferrous additive that was to make her a legend in her own time was on its side with the cap off. All $4.69 of it had gone down the drain. She had hidden it carefully behind the Ace bandages and a box of Midol and "they" had found it.

That shampoo was more than her ticket to *fat*, sexy hair. It was her last bastion of privacy, her only selfish indulgence that separated her from all that *gusto!*

She had had it with their insensitivity, their noisy mouths that every night at the dinner table attacked food like scissors, their mildewed towels, their tennis balls under the brake pedal.

She was sick of hearing a siren in the middle of the night and not being able to go back to sleep until all the cars were in. She was exhausted from sharing their lives and their problems. As a mother, she had stayed too long at the fair.

Outraged, she stomped out of the bathroom and beat with both fists on Mark's door. When no one answered, she barged in. He was propped up in bed, bare-chested with his headphones on, strumming his guitar.

"Did you wash your hair today?" she demanded.

He shook his head.

"You're lying. I know fat, sensuous hair when I see it."

"Okay, so I borrowed some shampoo. I'll pay you back."

"The Martins are going on a cruise. My elastic broke, my gums are shrinking and you're going to pay me back."

"What are your gums shrinking from?"

"My teeth!"

"I suppose you're gonna rehash how much my teeth cost and how ticked off you were when I dated the girl with the overbite."

"I was ticked off because the woman was thirty-three years old and it was her eleven-year-old daughter who had the overbite."

She looked around the room. Like its occupant, it was half child, half man. The wrestling trophy from his junior year in high school was on the nightstand along with a suspicious letter that said FINAL NOTICE and had a return address of Municipal Court, Division of Traffic. Clothes dotted the floor, newspapers were draped from chairs, and a sherbet glass with something brown in it was under the bed. "This room is a dump!" she said. "How can you breathe in here? It's June, for God's sake, what's your ski sweater doing out?"

Mark looked at her closely. "Why don't you get it over with? Tell us all to leave."

"What are you talking about?"

"Boot us out. Clean house."

"Don't think it hasn't crossed my mind." She looked desperately for a place to sit down. "I've tried to be a good mother, Mark. And a patient one. I really have."

"You've been a good mother," he said evenly. "So finish your job."

"What do you mean finish my job?"

"You chickened out. All our lives you told us what to do, how to do it, and when. You've done it. You don't have to prove anything anymore. It's graduation day. Say goodbye to us and get on with your life."

"You have no right to say that to me. I've been through it all with you kids—from exhaustion to anger to guilt and back again."

"You're at martyrdom and you've been there a long time. How long can you keep bucking for Mother of the Year?"

"Is that what you think? Then why don't you move out?"

They sat there for a long time.

Finally Janet said, "What will you do? Get a job? Get married?"

"You always said there was no one good enough for me."

"That was before I knew you showered in your underwear." She smiled.

They looked at one another for a long time.

"Mom," said Mark, "I'm scared."

"Me too," said Janet, closing the door.

Her hands were shaking and she felt like she was going to cry. What if fat, sexy hair and independence were overrated? She squared her shoulders. "What the heck. Joan Crawford made it in 'Mildred Pierce.' "

30

If You Can't Stand the Heat . . . Turn Off the Stove

In a Sunday school class one morning, the teacher asked, "And what did the disciples say before they ate the fish?"

A five-year-old boy in the front row waved his hand vigorously and said, "I know. They said, 'These fish got any bones in them?' "

As a mother who has dedicated her life to force-feeding her children, I have every reason to believe this story is gospel.

Kids are without a doubt the most suspicious diners in the world! They will eat mud (raw or baked), rocks, paste, crayons, ballpoint pens, moving goldfish, cigarette butts, and cat food.

Try to coax a little beef stew into their mouths and they look at you like a puppy when you stand over him with the Sunday paper rolled up.

I got so much food spit back in my face when my kids were small, I put windshield wipers on my glasses.

I read a survey once that said fifty-eight percent of the children interviewed resented the fact that parents make them eat food they don't like.

My children always had an unusual diet. They tolerated hot dogs only when they cost $1.50 in the ballpark, hamburgers that were 1/15 inch thick and suffocated in secret sauce, charred marshmallows that were speared on a bent coat hanger, and anything left under a car seat longer than fifteen days.

In general, they refused to eat anything that hadn't danced on TV.

By mid-1970's, I faced up to a cold, hard fact. Home cooking was dead! A victim of nutrition and a well-balanced diet served up by a mother.

Show biz food was in! Hamburgers with cute names, catchy songs about tacos, and free balloons with every shake. I did what any red-blooded American mother would do. I fought back.

I installed golden arches above the stove with an electric scoreboard and focused a red light on the pie to keep it warm.

I added a lighted menu and a drive-in window and served everything in a bag that leaked coleslaw and contained a two-inch plastic fork.

I served pizza wearing a straw hat and a cane. And when their attention began to lag, I propped my mouth open with a fork and let them yell their order into it, but it didn't work.

There's just something exciting to a child about eating in a car that smells like onions every day of the year.

For the next several years, we ate all of our meals in the car.

Then one day, our son said a curious thing. He said, "Didn't you tell me I could eat anywhere I wanted for my birthday?" We both nodded. "Then I want to eat at home."

"Well, I don't know," I said, looking at my husband. "Can we afford it?"

"Sure, what the heck, it's his birthday."

On the night of the birthday dinner, everyone even looked different. They were taller.

"Hey, look at this," said one of the boys. "What do you call these?"

"Silverware," I said. "That particular piece is a knife."

"Neat."

"And these are plates."

"I've never eaten in a place where you can take your dog before," said our daughter.

As the family sang "Happy Birthday," our son said, "Could we do this again next year? Maybe sooner?"

As I tossed the china noisily into a trash barrel, I said, "Let's not get carried away. We'll see."

31 ❧❧❧
"Every Puppy Should Have a Boy"

The ad in the paper said the puppy was "partially housebroken."

That is like being "partially pregnant."

Sylvia should have known better, but she was one of thousands of mothers every year who give in to family pressure and get a dog.

The first thing Sylvia did was to set up house rules. Anyone who saw the little puddles or dog bombs first was to clean it up. Then, you were to rub his nose in it and put him outside. No one was to feed him at the table. He was to sleep only in his own bed in the utility room. Everyone would take turns putting him out and bringing him in. Praise him when he did good, punish him when he did bad.

The first week, Bob's feet never touched the floor. He was the darling of the Forbes household.

The second week, they were less enthusiastic about his being there. (One of the kids even told him to "shut up!" when he yapped in the middle of the night.)

By the third week, Bob was Sylvia's dog. She fed him, bathed him, and let him in and out fifty times a day.

One night four years later, Sylvia heard her sons whispering. One was saying, "You better clean up Bob's mess." His brother answered, "It's my year not to see it. You didn't see it last year."

She gathered the family together and said, "I thought all of you should know that we are going to be in the *Guinness Book of World Records*. Our living room carpet is now one large, continuous wall-to-wall stain. The bottom line is, I am getting a new carpet and Bob goes. Please, I don't want anyone to say anything until I am finished. Try to see Bob as I see him—a twenty-eight-year-old man in a shaggy fur coat who watches television for six hours every evening and never leaves the room for a commercial, if you get my drift.

"He knows nothing of nature. He has never seen a tree, a blade of grass, a curb, a low chair leg, or a car tire.

"He has no curiosity as to why the velvet on the chair is so hard for him to reach or why they make a shag carpet so difficult to balance yourself on on three legs.

"I have tried everything, including sawing a hole in a $300 door that lets out the heat in the winter and the cool air in the summer. Bob is out!"

Even though Sylvia went on to be elected to the U.S. Senate, write three books, and give the commencement address at Harvard, she will always be remembered as the selfish mother who put carpet before compassion.

32 ❧❧❧

Treva

What Kind of a Mother Would . . .
Deny Having Grandchildren Three Times Before the Rooster Crows?

Treva hadn't spoken a word since they left the baby shower. As her daughter Gloria struggled to find a comfortable spot for her stomach under the steering wheel, Treva knotted her nose tissue into a ball, lost in her own thoughts.

They centered on Gloria's mother-in-law, Gayle. That woman had been bad news ever since her son married Gloria two years ago. Even at the wedding she was a royal pain. A bridegroom's mother is supposed to wear beige and keep her mouth shut. Everyone knows that. But not Gayle. She whipped around the reception like Mrs. Astor's pet horse, leaving Treva in the kitchen to slice ham like a field hand.

And the gift of a honeymoon to Acapulco made their bathroom heater look sick!

To make matters worse, Gloria thought the sun rose and set in the woman's backyard. Now she was trying to take over on the baby her daughter was carrying—Treva's first grandchild!

"You're quiet, Mom," said Gloria. "Did you have a good time? Can you believe how many prizes Gayle won? Imagine getting twenty-three words out of the word BASSINET. You never said how many you got."

"One," said Treva—"ASS!"

"Mother!" she said. "Shame on you." Then, following a silence, "Did you hear that Gayle is going to videotape the birth of our baby?"

"Pull the car over. I'm going to throw up," said Treva.

"Mom," said Gloria softly, "there's no reason for you to be jealous of Gayle. It's your grandchild too and both of you will get equal time with it."

"Jealous! Is that what you think I am?" Treva laughed in a high-pitched voice. "Don't be ridiculous. The baby won't be able to tell us apart, except I'll be the grandmother who bought him a stuffed teddy bear and Gayle will be the grandmother who bought him the San Diego Zoo. Let's drop it. How do you feel about ham?"

"Compared to what?" asked Gloria.

"I'm trying to figure out what to have for Christmas dinner."

"Mom! It's five months away. We haven't had Thanksgiving yet."

"Thanksgiving is settled. We're having your favorite, turkey."

Gloria slowed down and lowered her voice. "Mom, we've been through all of this before. Chuck and I just can't go on every holiday hopping from one house to another eating for four people— five this year. I'm going to weigh 500 pounds trying to keep all of the parents happy."

"Look, if you want to go to Gayle's, just say so. I've lived with disappointment before, I can do it again."

Gloria stopped the car and turned toward her mother.

"Mom, do you remember the old story about the wise king and the two women fighting over a child?"

Treva shook her head stubbornly.

"Each woman claimed the child was hers. Finally, the wise old king put the baby on a table before him, picked up a sword and said, 'Very well, since neither of you can decide, I will cut the baby in half.' At that moment, in an unselfish act of love, the real mother rushed forward and said, 'No! Give the baby to her.' At that moment, the king knew who the real mother was. Do you understand what that story is saying, Mother?"

Treva looked at her daughter with tears in her eyes. "It is saying Gayle kept her mouth shut and gets custody of the new grandchild and I get stuck with a twenty-pound turkey and a ten-pound ham!"

That night in bed Treva couldn't sleep. She kept seeing Gayle, who began to look like Rosalind Russell as Auntie Mame, waving from a cruise ship with her grandchild by her side and throwing streamers and promising to write.

She hated herself for being so competitive, but her arms ached to hold a baby once more. She had never adjusted to the empty nest. Maybe if she set up a nursery in the spare room, Gloria would leave the baby here on weekends. New parents always need time to themselves. Perhaps she and Mel could even take their grandchild to Florida with them and build sand castles on the beach.

She fell asleep fantasizing about a tall dark stranger saying, "You don't look old enough to be a mother," only to have her blush and say, "I'm not. It's my grandchild!"

Treva . . . Ten Years Later

The minute they heard Gloria's car in the driveway, Treva and her husband swung into action with all the precision and efficiency of the Lippizan cavalry.

Treva whipped the planter off the coffee table and put it in the hall closet, locked the bathroom door, shoved a bowl of candy under the lounge chair, put the dog in the utility room, and took the knob off the TV set and dropped it in her pocket.

Her husband Mel covered the sofa with plastic, put his bowling trophy on top of the refrigerator, blocked the entrance to the basement with a kitchen chair, put the toaster cover over the phone, and closed the lid on the piano to cover the keys.

Then both put toothpicks in their mouths to announce they had just eaten.

They broke their own record—one minute, thirty-six seconds.

Gloria dragged in with her four children under eight years of age and fell into a chair. The children scattered as though they ran on batteries, except Jeffrey, who sat in the middle of the floor and screamed.

"What's the matter with him?" asked Treva.

"He's teething," said Gloria tiredly.

"Have you tried a little whiskey on the gums?" asked Treva.

"I had a belt just before I came and I feel better," said Gloria.

"So what brings you to the neighborhood?"

"Nothing in particular. You got any crackers?" she asked, going to the kitchen and flinging open the doors. "Would you look at this. Wild rice! There was never any wild rice when I lived at home."

"You hate rice."

"I might have developed a taste for it if I knew it cost this much. So what time are you having Thanksgiving dinner?"

Treva and Mel exchanged glances.

"Ah, we're not going to be home this year for Thanksgiving, dear," Treva said quickly. "We're going out. Mel, check on Danny, the toilet's running."

"Do you know how long it's been since we've spent a holiday together?"

"What about Gayle?" asked Treva. "Gloria! Where is Jeffrey's diaper?"

"He just started taking it off when it has a load in it. Go get your diaper, Jeffrey. I know . . . poopoo. Gayle? They're going on a holiday cruise again. If I didn't know better, I'd feel no one wanted us for the holidays."

"Sweetheart, you don't want to chew on that cassette. Give it to Grandma. And don't cry!"

"Mother, when you take away something, you have to give her something else."

"I'm about to," said Treva, raising her hand.

"It's a shame you don't have that roomful of toys like you used to. That kept 'em busy. Do you really use that room for a chapel?"

"There isn't a day I don't go in there and meditate," said Treva. "What about Gayle? Does she still have her nursery-away-from-home?"

"No, she converted it to a tack room three years ago."

"A tack room in the house?"

"Doesn't matter. They don't have horses anyway. Well, listen, I've got to get going. You'll call on Thanksgiving?"

"Of course I will. Melanie! That's Grandma's dusting powder and it cost $12.50 a box. You must leave it here. You can visit it the next time you come. Melanie, don't take that lid off! Please!"

"You want me to clean it up?" said Gloria.

"No, I can do it when you leave," said Treva. "Take care of yourself, dear, and . . . don't turn your back on them."

As the car pulled out of the driveway, Treva and Mel mechanically and without words went about a ritual they had done many times before.

Treva put a sponge in each hand and began moving quickly through the rooms sliding her hands up and down the door frames, the refrigerator, and the cabinets. She let the dog out of the utility room, put the knobs back on the TV set, and brought the planter back into the daylight.

Mel wheeled out the sweeper and vacuumed up crumbs and

dusting powder. He retrieved his bowling trophy from the refrigerator and turned off the spigots in the bathtub. The candy went back on the table.

As Treva picked three Band-Aids off the wall in the foyer, Mel rubbed out a white spot on the piano bench where a wet glass had been.

As Treva headed for the chapel, Mel said, "Remember that first Thanksgiving when Gloria didn't come home and you draped her chair in black bunting and put her picture in the empty chair?"

Treva winced. "Give it a rest, Mel."

33 ❦❦❦

Anonymous

AUTHOR'S NOTE:
I cannot possibly improve or add anything to this
anonymous letter received in May, 1982, from
a mother in upstate New York.
She belongs in this book.

Dear Erma:

*You feel like my best friend. The only thing that surprised me
was to find out that I am taller than you.*

*Anyway, I have something I want to talk to you about. There
is no solution to this. I just want to let you know we exist, we are
human too and we hurt with the helplessness I can't begin to
describe.*

*I belong to a group of people that doesn't even know it's a group.
We have no organization, no meetings, no spokespersons, we don't
even know each other. Each of us, as individuals, are way in the
back of the closet with the rats and cockroaches. We may not even
be any different from our neighbors. We look the same, talk and*

act the same, yet when people know our secret, they shun us as lepers.

We are the parents of criminals. We too love our children. We too tried to bring them up the best way we knew how. There is small solace in reading of a movie star or politician's kid being arrested. It helps but little to realize that our pain is not confined to the poor. (Although studies have shown that a rich kid is more likely to be sent home with a reprimand from the police, where a poor kid will wind up in jail.)

We are the visitors. Mother's Day, Christmas, our kids cannot come to us, so we go to them. For some of us, the hurt is so unbearable, we cut out the cause—we give up on them. Some parents don't visit, don't write, don't acknowledge the living human being they bore.

I have not yet given up on my son, though the court has. I still cry, and plead, and encourage and pray. And I still love him.

I search my memory. Where did I fail him? My son was planned, wanted, and was exactly the all-around kid I had hoped for. I spent lots of time with him, reading stories, going for walks, playing catch, teaching him to fly a kite. We went to church together every Sunday since he was 4. He did all right in school and his teachers liked him. He had lots of friends, and they were always playing ball or going fishing, all the regular kid things. He was on Little League. I went to every game. He won a trophy for All-Stars. He was just a regular kid.

That's only one. Mine. There are thousands of them. Criminals with ordinary childhoods. We, their parents, trying to live ordinary lives. And maybe being ostracized by family members and certainly by society. ("Maybe it's contagious!")

Tomorrow is Mother's Day. My son is running from the police. I didn't do it, I don't condone it, nor try to justify what he did. But I still love him, and it hurts.

I hope you can find room in your heart to accept us, who love the children society hates.

I'm sure you understand why I just cannot put my name. Thanks for letting me get it off my chest.

"Mom"

And I know you know that this is not a made-up letter. I'm real. I wish I weren't. Happy Mother's Day.

34 ✿✿✿

"Don't You Dare Bleed on Mom's Breakfast"

A lot of things have been done in bed in the name of love . . . but nothing comes close to the traditional Mother's Day breakfast in bed.

On this day, all over the country, mothers are pushed back into their pillows, their bird of paradise (which blooms every other year for fifteen minutes) is snipped and put in a shot glass, and a strange assortment of food comes out of a kitchen destined to take the sight out of a good eye.

A mixer whirs out of control, then stops abruptly as a voice cries, "I'm telling."

A dog barks and another voice says, "Get his paws out of there. Mom has to eat that!"

Minutes pass and finally, "Dad! Where's the chili sauce?"

Then, "Don't you dare bleed on Mom's breakfast."

The rest is a blur of banging doors, running water, rapid footsteps and finally, "You started the fire; *you* put it out!"

The breakfast is fairly standard: A water tumbler of juice, five pieces of black bacon that snap in half when you breathe on them, a mound of eggs that would feed a Marine division, and four pieces of cold toast. They line up on the bed to watch you eat and from time to time ask why you're not drinking your Kool-Aid or touching the cantaloupe with black olives on top spelling out M-O-M.

Later that night, after you have decided it's easier to move to a new house than clean the kitchen, you return to your bed, where you encounter beneath the blanket either (a) a black jelly bean, (b) a plantar wart, or (c) a black olive that put the O in M-O-M.

And if you're wise, you'll reflect on this day. For the first time, your children gave instead of received. They offered up to you the sincerest form of flattery—trying to emulate what you would do for them. They gave you one of the greatest gifts people can give: themselves.

There will be other Mother's Days and a parade of gifts that will astound and amaze you, but not one of them will ever measure up to the sound of your children in the kitchen on Mother's Day whispering, "Don't you dare bleed on Mom's breakfast."

35 $\infty\infty\infty$
"Is Anyone Home?"

In 1981, Miriam Volhouse was the only full-time, stay-at-home mother in her block. She was also named in the school records of seventeen kids who listed her under IN CASE OF EMERGENCY CALL . . .

Occasionally Miriam was tempted to join her friends in an outside job, but she resisted because she considered herself a conscientious mother and "rapping" with one's children was important.

Each evening when Miriam heard a door slam, she'd yell, "Mark, is that you?"

"What do you want? Buzz is waiting. We're going to shoot baskets."

"Can't we just sit and have a conversation?"

"I gotta go," he'd say.

Miriam would pour two glasses of milk and put cookies on a plate and grope her way through the dark living room. "You in here, Ben?"

"Shhhhh."

"So, what kind of a day did you have? I'll bet there are a lot of fun things you'd like to share. I tried a new recipe today and . . ."

"Mom! Give me a break. I'm watching 'M*A*S*H!' "

When another door slammed, Miriam would race feverishly in time to see Wendy writing a note, "Don't wait dinner. Choir practice."

"Wendy, I want you to know I'm here if you want to rap about anything . . . like I want to know how you feel about life."

"I'm for it," she said, pulling on her coat, and then added, "Mom, you've got to get something to do. You can't lean on your kids all the time for companionship."

As Miriam drank both glasses of milk and ate the plateful of cookies, she felt rejected. No one was ever home when she was. Kids shouldn't have parents, if that's how they're going to treat them. What if something happened to her? Who would know? They were selfish and thought only of themselves. She couldn't remember the last time they sat down and talked with her about her problems or her day. How did other mothers get their children to talk to them?

She found out. Miriam got a job.

Every day between 3 and 6 PM Miriam felt like an 800 number for free records. Her kids were on the phone to her every three minutes, each time with a new trauma. She couldn't get them to stop talking. In desperation, Miriam posted a list of rules regarding phone calls.

1. If there is an emergency, ask yourself, "Will Mom drop dead when she hears this? Can she find a plumber after six? Will she carry out her threat to move to another city and change her name?"

2. If there is blood to report, consider these questions: Is it yours? Your brother's? Is there a lot? A little? On the sofa that is not Scotchgarded?

3. When every kid in the neighborhood decides the house would be a neat place to play because there's no adult at home, ask yourself, "Do I want to spend my entire puberty locked in

my room with no food and no television? Do I need the friendship of a boy who throws ice cubes at birds? Will Mom notice
we made confetti in her blender?"

4. Only a fool calls his mother and says, "There's nothing to
do."

One night, as she was racing through the kitchen and running
the hamburger through the dry cycle to thaw and delegating chores
to the kids, her son said, "If you're not going to stay home and
take care of us, how come you had children?"

Her other son said, "There's no one here anymore when I come
home from school. You used to bake cookies."

Her daughter said, "Sometimes I think mothers are selfish.
They don't share any of their innermost thoughts with you, like
how they feel about life . . ."

"I'm for it," said Miriam, tossing the salad.

36 ❧❧❧

Primer of Guilt
"Bless Me, Everybody, for I Have Sinned"

A   Abandoning children and responsibility, leaving them helpless and alone with a $200 babysitter, a $3,700 entertainment center, a freezer full of food, and $600 worth of toys while you and your husband have a fun time attending a funeral in Ames, Iowa.

B   Buying a store-bought cake for your son's first birthday.

C   Cursing your only daughter with your kinky red hair and your only son with your shortness.

D   Dumping cheap shampoo into a bottle of the children's Natural Herbal Experience, which costs $5 a throw.

574

E Explaining to "baby" of family why the only thing in his baby book are his footprint, a poem by Rod McKuen, and a recipe for carrot cake.

F Flushing a lizard down the toilet and telling child it got a phone call saying there was trouble at home.

G Going home from the hospital after hysterectomy and apologizing to kids for not bringing them anything.

H Hiding out in the bathroom when the kids are calling for you all over the house.

I Indulging yourself by napping and when caught with chenille marks on your face telling your children it's a rash.

J Jamming down the sewer three newspapers you promised your child with a broken arm you'd deliver for him.

K Keeping Godiva chocolates in TEA canister and telling yourself kids don't appreciate good chocolate.

L Laundering daughter's $40 wool sweater in hot water.

M Missing a day calling Mother.

N Never loaning your car to anyone you've given birth to.

O Overreacting to child who found your old report card stuck in a book by threatening to send him to a box number in Hutchinson, Kansas, if he talks.

P Pushing grocery cart out of store and forgetting baby in another cart inside until you have turned on the ignition.

Q Quarreling with son about homework only to do it for him and getting a C on it.

R Refusing to bail out daughter who lives by credit cards alone.

S Sewing a mouse on the shirt pocket of son who is far-sighted and telling him it's an alligator.

T Taking down obscene poster from son's bulletin board just before party and substituting brochure for math camp.

U Unlocking bathroom door with an ice pick when a child just told you he's not doing anything only to discover he's not doing anything.

V Visiting child's unstable teacher at school and telling her, "I don't understand. He never acts like that at home."

W Writing a postdated check to the tooth fairy for a buck and a half.

X X-raying for a swallowed nickel only after you heard it was a collector's coin worth $6.40.

Y Yawning during school play when your daughter has the lead—a dangling participle.

Z Zipping last year's boots on your son when you know they will never come off without surgery.

37 ❧❧❧

Rose

What Kind of a Mother Would . . .
Give Up Sighing for Lent . . . When She's Jewish?

Rose had been playing the game of "musical mother" for over five years now. Next to the lottery, it was the biggest game of the twentieth century. It required anywhere from two to eight players. The rules were simple.

Take one widowed mother and spin her around until she comes to rest with her daughter in Florida. Daughter in Florida has four months to con her brother in Chicago to take her. Brother in Chicago keeps her until he can spread fifty pounds of guilt on his sister in California.

The mother always loses. Rose had logged more air miles than a space shuttle astronaut.

Ever since the death of her husband Seymour, four years ago, Rose changed bedrooms every four months. She fantasized about a rest home and allowed herself the luxury of contemplating a room of her own—a place where she could talk when she felt like it and be surrounded by other people with irregularity problems.

Her children wouldn't hear of it. They had a responsibility to take care of her and she had the responsibility of enduring it.

Every night, no matter where she was, Rose indulged in the practice of calling on Seymour's presence for a nightly conversation.

Florida (July)

"So, it's Florida. It must be July. How are things with you, Seymour? Irene, Sam, and Sandy met me at the airport. Your grandson is a scarecrow. Twelve years old and he can't weigh more than fifteen pounds. How could he when there's nothing in this house to eat? All the bread is frozen and every box in the cupboard has grains of wheat growing on it and NATURAL stamped all over it. I don't want to worry you, but he'll be dead by Chanukah.

"I'm in the guest room, as usual. Remember the recovery room just before you died? Same decorator. They store everything here. I sleep next to a ping-pong table and an ironing board that hasn't been down since they moved here.

"Nothing has changed with Irene. Her ice cubes still smell like melon, and she thinks dust was put here to measure time. Where did we fail, Seymour? It's a good thing you aren't here to see it. The woman doesn't even wash her dishes in sudsy water and rinse them before putting them into the dishwasher.

"I have to go now. Irene is having theme week in the kitchen and tonight it's Korea's turn. I starve to death with chopsticks. See you later when the rates go down. That's a joke, Seymour."

Florida (October)

"You there, Seymour? So, how do you like my hair? Irene thought I ought to wear it pulled straight back and into a bun. I think it makes me look older. If you think it makes me look older, give me a sign, like lowering the humidity here to 96.

"I fainted twice today. Do you remember those copper-bottomed pots and pans we gave Irene for a wedding present? You wouldn't believe, Seymour. I saw them today and said, 'Tell me those aren't the pots and pans your father and I bought you.' She said, 'What's the matter with them?'

"I said, 'Would it kill you to sprinkle a little cleanser on them each time you use them? You weren't raised to let your bottoms go.'

"Nothing much happening. I paid my health insurance. Irene and Sam wanted me to go with them to the Levines' for dinner, but the last time we went out I was washing out cups in the sink and they were in the car blowing their horn at me and I almost passed out. It isn't worth the aggravation.

"I heard Sam on the phone talking with Russell, so it looks like I'll make my annual visit to Chicago. A lot of people winter there. Stay well."

Chicago (November)

"Hello, Seymour. Guess who? There something I've got to know. When you went to heaven, did you have a five-hour layover in Atlanta? If you did, I'm not coming.

"Your son looks good. Barbara looks as good as can be expected. The children still have no necks. I wonder why that is. Russell has a neck. My theory is that all four of them are cold all the time and trying to keep warm.

"Barbara and I play thermostat roulette each night. I don't see how she stands it. She said the other night, 'It's healthy to sleep in a cool room.' I said, 'Who sleeps? I'm afraid to nod off or I'll never wake up again.' You remember that movie where it happened to Ronald Colman, don't you?

"So, the woman tries. Four children. She has her hands full trying to get David toilet trained. She got him a little potty seat that plays music when he tinkles. It should play 'The Impossible Dream.'

"And she waits on me hand and foot. Fills up my plate, does my laundry, reminds me to take my pills and turns my bed back into a sofa every time I go to the bathroom.

"Playing any golf? Talk to you soon."

Chicago (February)

"Be honest with me, Seymour. Is it me? Or are the winters getting longer? I stood at the window today and for the life of me couldn't remember what green grass looked like. I asked Barbara and she just stood and looked at me. She probably can't remember, either. I paid my health insurance. Mostly, I watch a lot of soap operas. It's a shame you can't see them. They're enough to start your heart beating again. Went to the dentist today and he said I should have my bridgework redone. Hang onto your billfold, Seymour. It will cost $4,000.

"When I told Barbara she said, 'You're seventy-two years old. What do you want to get your teeth fixed for?'

"Russell talked with Judith today. He said she's lonely after the divorce and wants me to visit.

"All of a sudden, I feel very old and very tired. Maybe when I get to California, the smog, brush fires, floods, and earthquakes will cheer me up."

California (March)

"I know I just got here Seymour, but I had to talk with you. Our Judith has had a face lift. At forty-three, how far could it have fallen? I thought she looked different when I saw her. She has a surprised look on her face twenty-four hours a day.

"Your grandson Marty and I had a long talk coming in from the airport. I told him about my bridgework and he said the same thing you did—'Go for it.' "

California (April)

"Seymour, we've got to stop meeting like this. That's a joke. It's good to hear you laugh. I made a friend today. You know how I hate dryers, so I took a couple of Marty's shirts and stretched a line out back. I met a woman visiting her son next door and—are you ready? She hangs shirts by the tails, too, instead of the collar.

"She invited me to a funeral tomorrow. I might go . . . just to see something sagging again. You'll probably find out anyway, and I want you to hear it from me. Judith is dating a man called Patrick. I said to him, 'What's your family name?' He said, 'Murphy.' I said, 'What was it before?' He said, 'Before what?' I don't think he's Jewish. Why am I being punished?"

In May, Rose was suspicious that her life was about to change. Usually her trip to Florida was confirmed by this time.

There had been phone calls. A lot of them. Judith talked with Irene and Sam in low, serious voices at night. Russell and Barbara talked with Judith, who nodded occasionally and said, "I noticed."

In June, Judith summoned her mother to the kitchen for a talk. The entire family had noticed behavior that was "erratic." Barbara expressed concern that Rose stood near a window in Chicago and mumbled, "Admit it, God, Chicago was a big mistake!"

Irene had reported tearfully that she peeked in her room one night to find her in deep conversation with the ping-pong table. It was their consensus that Rose should be put in a home.

* * *

The room was sparse, but Rose could fix that. She'd get her rocker out of storage and some pillows and glassware she'd saved. But before she unpacked, she had to get in touch with Seymour. "You there?" she asked looking toward the ceiling.

"Listen, you're not going to believe this, but I had to go to Atlanta to get here. I'd have thought California to Colorado would have been a straight shot, wouldn't you?" Out of the corner of her eye, Rose noticed another resident of the home who had dropped by. "Wait a minute, Seymour, there's someone here."

Her visitor said, "You're talking to Seymour? My husband died two years ago and talks about a Seymour all the time. Does he play golf? What's his handicap?"

38

"Do I Have to Use My Own Money?"

When the history of guilt is written, parents who refuse their children money will be right up there in the Top Ten.

When do you give it to them? And when do you stop? I read somewhere that you should set up an allowance system to instill in your children the basics of self-esteem.

I paid my kids to close their eyes, blow their noses, breathe in and out, clean out their cages, pick up their towels, keep their feet on the floor, and, one New Year's Day, when my head was very sensitive to sound, I offered one of them a blank check if he would stop smacking his lips.

By the time the kids hit puberty, they were filthy rich. The reason they were filthy rich is that they never spent their own money on anything.

Somehow I never got over the feeling of knowing he had $2,500 in his savings account and I got a paper doily basket with three black jelly beans for Mother's Day.

It was always "sticky" as to what they were financially responsible for.

Take the area code 602 with a 1 in front of it my son once dated. I mean, a 1-602 wasn't across a whole country from 602, but it was far enough away to run our phone bill up to $35 a month in long-distance charges.

It was a marriage made by Ma Bell between two people who shared such insights as:

"What are you doing?"

"Nothing. What are you doing?"

"I don't want to interrupt you if you're doing something."

"I told you I wasn't doing anything."

"You sure?"

"I'm sure."

"So, what are you doing?"

We never had to worry about the physical part of the relationship because they were never off the phone. He would set his alarm to call her in the morning. At night I would go into his room and remove the phone from his ear as he slept. It was like hanging up an umbilical cord. As soon as they left each other after school in the afternoon, he would shout, "I'll call you when I get home." I offered to feed him intravenously.

One day I approached him with the phone bill and suggested he pay for it with his own money. He smiled and said, "You think this is just some infatuation, don't you? You don't realize this is a person I genuinely care for and want to spend the rest of my life with. She's important to me and very special. There isn't anything I wouldn't do for her."

"I'm glad to hear you say that," I said, "because according to this bill you owe us $84.10 in long-distance telephone charges."

He never talked to her or saw her again.

All parents set their own goals as to when the Open Purse policy ends with their children.

Ours ended the day we knew in our hearts that our son's savings account was the only thing between us and welfare benefits.

We made a speech: "We know you won't understand this now, but someday you will. We no longer want to deprive you of the poverty you so richly deserve. The Happy Days Are Here Again Bank of Prosperity is closed! Money is not related to love. It's only a shallow substitute. What you really need is a ton of self-respect."

He sat there for a while in silence. Finally he said, "Do I have to buy it with my own money?"

We smiled. "It's the only way you can buy it."

39 ❧❧❧

The Spirit of
Christmas . . . and
Other Expenses

Every year, one of my children wants a game for Christmas. It is always one for which the demand exceeds the supply by about 355,000.

Every kid in town has it on his list.

The game is touted on television, beginning in June, with the approach that if it is not under your tree on Christmas Day you are an unfit parent and your child will grow up to rob convenience stores wearing pantyhose over his face.

By September, your child has built up to such a pitch that if he doesn't get this game, he may give up breathing. He assures you it is the only game he wants. Now the pressure is on you to find that game. For the purpose of avoiding a lawsuit, I will call the game Humiliation, fun for the entire family, order no. 170555354, batteries not included.

By October, every store in your area is sold out of Humiliation, with no hope of getting a new order in. But the television teasers go on, showing a typical American family with Mom, Dad, and 2.5 children sitting around a table playing Humiliation until they pass out from joy.

Forget baking fruitcake, buying a Christmas tree, entertaining with wassail, caroling, sending out Christmas cards, or decorating the house. Every morning as soon as the alarm goes off, your feet touch the floor and you give the battle cry, "Find Humiliation today!"

By mid-November, you have driven 1,800 miles in search of the game, following tips from friends that a discount house in the northern part of the state has two left, or a toy dealer has one under the counter that is damaged but negotiable.

Several times you are tempted to get a game that is a rip-off of Humiliation, like Mortify or Family Conceit, but you know in your heart it wouldn't be the same.

If you're lucky (?), just before Christmas you race a little old grandmother to the counter and snatch the last Humiliation game on Earth from her fingers, buy batteries and put it under the tree.

On Christmas night, while you're picking up all the paper, ribbon, and warranties, your eyes fall on Humiliation, still in the box, the $49.95 price tag shining like a beacon.

The kids are playing with a cardboard box and snapping the air pockets of plastic packing material. Humiliation had its minute and now it's gone.

Why do we do it?

How are we manipulated into buying toys we cannot afford and are interesting for a matter of minutes? Several reasons: For one, parents are basically insecure and have to buy affection, and second, we are cursed with short memories.

We refuse to stop and reflect on toys past that have been discarded.

Like the horse. Remember him? He was brown and sucked up eighty gallons of water a day through his face. He was a lot of fun and lived with us for three years. Every time the farrier came to shoe him, it cost $45. No one wanted to pick the manure out of his feet because it was "gross." He attracted flies and disliked the sensation of anything on his back. He was ridden twelve times.

Or the ping-pong table. It was a big table that held books, coats, dirty laundry, lunch bags, stuff that had to go to the cleaner, and stacks of old newspapers. You couldn't see the TV over it, and it eventually went to the garage, where it warped.

From Christmas past came a full set of leather-bound, gilt-edged encyclopedias containing 3,000 illustrations. These were supposed to bring a new level of culture to the family, and I recollect were used twice: first to point out pictures of Eve, who was naked in Volume V, and second, to hold open the door when the new sofa was delivered.

I recall the plastic inflatable swimming pool that was to bring the whole family closer together. It was officially dedicated on the morning of July 5 and officially closed on the evening of July 5, when it was noted that a small boy in the neighborhood had drunk five glasses of grape drink and had not left the pool in twelve hours.

The ice hockey sticks were biggies and are still in the closet awaiting the arrival of the Canadian Salvation Army. They fell from favor when it was discovered they did not have training wheels on them and worked only when someone stood upright on ice skates.

I try to be a good mother, a loving mother, a considerate mother, who wants to see her children happy.

That's too bad. Shallow and unfeeling is a lot cheaper.

40 ❧❧❧

Mary

What Kind of a Mother Would . . . Tell Her Children If They Didn't Come Home for Christmas, She'd Be Dead by New Year's?

The four of them had been poring over the luncheon menu for fifteen minutes in total silence.

It was a waiting game to see who would ask the question first. Iris broke the ice. "Is anyone going to have the popovers?"

The question was ludicrous. Does Zsa Zsa Gabor refuse a proposal of marriage? No one in their right mind would come to Neiman-Marcus's tea room in Atlanta and not order popovers.

"I don't know," mused Mary. "I'm cutting back, but maybe I'll have one just to be sociable."

The waitress shifted to the other foot. "You want your usual two baskets?" Everyone nodded.

How long had they been coming here? Twice a year for the last twelve or fifteen years? They gathered every June 3 on Jefferson Davis's birthday and January 10 to commemorate the birth of Robert E. Lee.

A lot had happened in those fifteen years. Their roots had gone from black to gray and back to black again. Their children had gone from home to husbands and come home again. Their husbands from office to retirement to home, and their cars from station wagons with bad clutches to coupes with bad clutches.

"Another round of sherry from the bar?" asked the waitress.

"Why not?" said Charlotte. "After all, this is a festive occasion."

"Has anyone heard about Evelyn Rawleigh?" asked Iris.

"What happened?" asked Bebe.

"Well, she went through a series of the most awful allergy tests ever, only to discover she's allergic to ultrasuede."

They gasped as a quartet.

"I'd get a second opinion," said Bebe.

"How tragic," said Charlotte. "Is there nothing they can do for her?"

"Nothing," sighed Iris. "And the worst of it is she won't leave the house. She thinks everyone is looking at her."

The waitress returned with the sherry and Bebe made the toast, "To Robert E. Lee, who won the war. So, did everyone have a good Christmas?"

"I know Iris did," said Charlotte. "As usual, your Christmas Newsletter was inspired!"

God, how they all hated those Newsletters. Iris should have made *The New York Times* best-seller list for fiction. Who else had kids who were toilet trained at seven months, guest conductor for the Atlanta Symphony at six, and sent thank-you notes in French? Their family picture on the letter made the Osmond family look depressed. Was it their imagination, or did their teeth get straighter every year?

"Well, I had the best Christmas ever," volunteered Bebe. "Dede had us all over at her house. What a dear she is! I couldn't love her more if she were my own daughter. What about you, Mary? Any of your children come home?"

Home! Jeff had sent her a plastic salad spinner that you put your lettuce into to twirl all the water out. He called on Christmas Eve from Vail, where he'd gone with his family to unwind. How tightly wound could a thirty-four-year-old salesman of after-shave lotion get?

Jennifer had sent her an expensive executive organizer handbag with eighty-three compartments for the woman on the go. The only problem was she wasn't going anywhere.

Robin had been the biggest disappointment. She had sent salt and pepper shakers shaped like unicorns and a note that said, "These remind me of you and Dad. I love you. Robin."

The group was waiting for her answer. "You know how busy they are, but as usual they were too extravagant. Imagine designer chocolates when I told them I was counting calories."

Bebe summoned the waitress and ordered another round of sherry. Then, turning to Charlotte, she asked, "So how does Walter like retirement?"

Charlotte forced herself to smile. She had married Walter for better or worse, but not for lunch. From the day he retired he had taken over her kitchen like a carpetbagger. The first week he was home she entered her kitchen and asked, "What do you think you are doing?"

He said, "If God permits me to live long enough, I am going to clean your exhaust fan. If I had run my office like you run your kitchen, Charlotte, we'd have starved to death years ago."

So Walter had alphabetized her spices and she drank to "festive" occasions, which in recent months had included National Foot Health Week, the dedication of a sewage plant, and the day she got her fur out of storage.

"I never knew retirement could be so wonderful," she said and whispered to the waitress, "Bring the bottle."

"Is everyone as bored with TV as I am?" asked Iris. "I mean, you can't turn on a show anymore without all those disgusting people kissing with their mouths open."

"They're all doing it," said Bebe. "Even Carol Burnett."

"By the way, Iris," said Mary, "how's your daughter?"

Iris winced. At thirty-two, Constance had racked up two marriages, two meaningful relationships, one child, and a state of bankruptcy. On the Christmas Newsletter, this was translated as "Connie is in St. Louis working on a novel."

Charlotte nearly knocked over a glass of wine, catching it just in time. She put her finger to her lips, signaling secrecy. "Don't tell Walter. Did I tell you the other day he met me at the door and shouted, 'You have exactly three hours to do something with this yeast before the date on it expires'? I told him to take that yeast and . . ."

"Popovers, anyone?" asked Iris.

"You think you got problems," said Bebe. "That Yankee daughter-in-law of mine doesn't even trust me to diaper the baby. She said things have changed. The plumbing looked the same to me."

Mary spoke slowly and deliberately. "Do you ever get the feeling that none of this happened? That we put in thirty years of our lives and have nothing to show for it?"

"I love my children," said Iris defensively. "Even the ones who are shacking up."

"Mine never really knew me," Mary mumbled, as if talking to herself. "I never let them. I couldn't. I had to set the example. I had to make sure they saw only the best. I never cried in front of them. I never laughed when I wasn't supposed to. In all those years they never saw me without hair spray. What do you think of that?"

"That's wonderful," said Iris.

"That's lousy," said Mary. "Do you know what a unicorn is? It's a mys . . . mystical . . . weird animal with a horse's body and a horn on top that everyone needlepoints. Sort of aloof and unreal. There's nothing there to love. That's how Robin sees me. A unicorn. I was never real."

"What are we supposed to do with the rest of our lives?" mused Charlotte. "One minute there weren't enough hours in the day to do all I had to do. And the next thing I know I'm dressing all the naked dolls that belonged to my daughter and arranging them on the bed. Did you ever iron a bra for a two-inch bust? We're too young to pack it in and too old to compete for our own turf."

"Would we have done things differently if we had known then what we know now?" asked Charlotte.

For a full minute no one spoke.

"I'd have talked less and listened more," said Bebe.

"I'd have eaten more ice cream and less cottage cheese," said Charlotte.

"I'd never have bought anything that had to be ironed or was on sale," said Iris. "How about you, Mary?"

"I'd have been more human . . . and less unicorn."

Mary filled her wine glass and made a toast. "To the sainted mother of Robert E. Lee, who on this day gave birth to a legend. What do you want to bet that for Christmas she got a plastic salad spinner?"

41 ❧

Ethel

What Kind of a Mother Would . . .
Sentence Her Eighty-two-year-old Mother to
Chez Riche, a $2,000-a-month Nursing Home?

Ethel refused to believe her mother was approaching senility.

She rationalized a lot of eighty-two-year-old women ran away from home every week, sat in parked cars talking to themselves, and threatened to name Cary Grant in a paternity suit.

She would not listen to anyone who advised her against keeping her mother at home with her. Not her doctor, her minister, her husband, nor her Aunt Helen who insisted, "Face it, Ethel, Jenny has one oar out of the water. She's my sister and I love her too, but I'm telling you normal people don't give out cans of tomato paste for Trick or Treat."

Ethel was defensive. "It's my fault. The kitchen was dark and she grabbed the first can she saw."

The burden of her mother's future was awesome to Ethel. When did the responsibility revert to her? Was it at her father's funeral three years ago when she put her arm around her mother and promised to take care of her? No, no, it was long before that that the mother became the child and the child became the mother.

She had started hearing echoes from her childhood soon after she was married.

"Mother! Aren't you ready yet? The doctor won't wait, you know." (Ethel! Don't dawdle. School will be over by the time you get there.)

"Come over Wednesday and I'll give you a permanent." (Hold still, Ethel, and I'll pin up your hair so you'll have curls.)

"Try this dress on, Mother. It'll make you look younger." (I don't care what you say, Missy, that dress is too old for you. Try this one.)

"Mother will have the fruit plate. She thinks she wants the veal parmesan but she'll be up all night." (I know a little girl whose eyes are bigger than her tummy.)

Her mother resisted at first, then fell easily into the role. After a while, when the memory went, Ethel was dialing phone numbers for her mother, filling her coffee cup half full, and automatically holding out her arm whenever she brought the car to a stop.

The transfer of authority was complete.

The lapses of her mother's memory were erratic. One minute Jenny could recall bite for bite what she had to eat forty years ago at a dinner at the VFW. The next minute, she was referring to her grandson as "Whatshisname." Ethel couldn't count the number of times her mother had thrown out the inside of the percolator with the grounds.

In time, she turned quarrelsome, irritable, and downright hostile toward Ethel. She announced to anyone who would listen that Ethel was stealing her blind and was trying to do her in by putting something bitter in her bran. She told her sister Helen, "I'd rather die of irregularity than be poisoned."

One night before guests, she tearfully told them she had been tortured beyond belief by her daughter, who had made her watch an Ali MacGraw film festival on TV.

The accusations broke Ethel's heart. Things came to a head one day, when her husband brought Jenny home from the polls where she had just voted. "Something has got to be done about Jenny," he said.

"What's the matter?" asked Ethel.

"She just voted Democrat. She'd die if she knew that."

Eight months later, Ethel checked her mother in at the Tranquil Trail Nursing Home. As they carried in her suitcase, Ethel observed, "It's a nice room, Mother."

"It's bugged," she said, "and it's dinky. Why didn't you just put me on an iceberg and let me drift out to sea. That's what Eskimos do."

"I wouldn't do that, Mother," she said tiredly.

"I suppose you've sold all my cut glass. You'll be old some-day."

"I'm old now, Mother."

"That's true. Did you pack my fur coat?"

"It's July. You don't need it now. I'll bring it to you when it gets cold."

"You've said *that* before. Why don't you admit it. You sold it."

Ethel leaned back in the chair and rested her head. Was there anything left in her but frustration, hurt, and shame?

She was doing a terrible thing. She was abandoning her own mother, putting her in the hands of strangers. Her mother had sacrificed her entire life to raising her and now Ethel was turning away from her responsibilities. But she was so exhausted trying to relate to a person she didn't even know.

Her mother was living in a strange new world and had been for some time. It was a world that allowed the past to enter but not the present or the future. She had tried, but she couldn't reach her there. Nor did she want to. She wanted the old world. The way it used to be when her mother was softer and in control.

Would these strangers understand her mother's world?

An attendant came in and said, "Jenny, you got everything you need?"

"Did you steal my watch?" asked Jenny, her eyes narrowing.

"You bet. Was it valuable?"

Jenny stood toe to toe with her and searched her eyes carefully. "I got it from Cary Grant. I named him in a paternity suit and he tried to buy me off."

"Same thing happened to me with Clint Eastwood," said the attendant.

Together they walked out the door as Jenny whispered, "Clint Eastwood. Is he the one who squints all the time?"

Ethel watched them for a while, then wiped the tears from her eyes and put herself together. Maybe it would work. Maybe she was a constant reminder to her mother of the old world, the one that had left her suspicious and confused. Maybe that's why she lashed out at her with such anger. Oh well, she would think about it tomorrow, when she brought her mother's fur coat to her.

42 ❧❧❧

Erma

What Kind of a Mother Would . . .
Reply When Asked What It Was Like to Give Birth to
Erma Bombeck, "It's a Rotten Job, But Someone
Had to Do It"?

This book would not be complete without a chapter on my mother, who at this moment is leafing through it to see if she is mentioned.

Words that flash through my mind when the word "Mother" is mentioned include: box saver, gravy on diet bread, right words in wrong places ("Your grandfather migrained here from Ireland"), candidate for first tongue transplant, courage, abounding love.

My mother was raised in an orphanage, married at fourteen, and widowed at twenty-five, left with two children and a fourth-grade education. According to her height and weight as listed on the insurance charts, she should be a guard for the Lakers. She has iron-starved blood, one shoulder that is lower than the other, and she bites her fingernails.

She is the most beautiful woman I have ever seen.

I never can remember exactly how old she is, so I set it at thirty-three and forget it.

In the years I was growing up, there were good times and bad times, but when I presented her with three children, our relationship stabilized. There is no doubt that the grandchildren offered her the answer to her prayers: revenge.

No one is more supportive of the First Amendment guaranteeing freedom of speech than I am, but the "gag rule" seems to get more attractive all the time.

When my kids are around, Grandma sings like a canary.

I never thought she'd turn on me. When I was sinking in a sea of diapers, formulas, and congenital spitting, Mother couldn't wait to pull her grandchildren onto her lap and say, "Let me tell you how rotten your Mommy was. She never took naps and she never picked up her room and she had a mouth like a drunken sailor in Shanghai. I washed her mouth out with soap so many times I finally had to starch her tongue."

At other times, she is on my side and her presence is comforting.

Once, when I was in my twenties, I remember standing in a hospital corridor waiting for doctors to put twenty-one stitches in my son's head and I said, "Mom, when do you stop worrying?" She just smiled and said nothing.

When I was in my thirties, I sat on a little chair in a classroom and heard how one of my children talked incessantly, disrupted the entire class, and was headed for a career making license plates. I said to her, "Mom, when does it end?" She said nothing.

When I was in my forties, I spent a lifetime waiting for the phone to ring, the cars to come home, the front door to open. I called her and whined, "When does it stop?" There was no answer.

By the time I was fifty, I was sick and tired of being vulnerable and worrying about my children. I wished they were all married so I could stop worrying and lead my own life. But I was haunted by my mother's smile and I couldn't help remembering how she looked at me with concern and said, "You look pale; you all right? Call me the moment you get home. I worry about it."

She had been trying to tell me what I did not want to hear: "It never stops."

When my first book came out, she went with me to New York, where my baptism on television was to be "The Tonight Show." I was terrified. As she was zipping me into my dress, I said, "I don't think I can do this," and she turned me around and said, "If you're going out there and try to be something you're not, you're right. You'll fall flat on your face. All you can do is to be yourself."

I went out that night and took her advice. I was myself. And I bombed so bad it was ten years before I ever got on the show again.

When I confronted Mother, she said, "What do I know? I just came along to shop at Bloomingdale's."

There's a lot to admire in my mother. The wonder she sustains . . . even at the age of thirty-three. She is still impressed with people, curious about new things, and excited about Christmas. Her openness is not to be believed. One day, a reporter from a supermarket tabloid knocked at her door and wanted to know anything about her daughter that the public didn't know. Mother invited him in, gave him coffee, told him my life story—beginning with the labor pains—in great detail. By the end of three hours (she was up to toilet training), his teeth were falling asleep and as he begged to leave, Mother insisted he take a bag of homemade raisins. He never came back.

I suppose every child remembers some special virtue their mother has—some piece of wisdom that has saved them from disaster or a word that made the path infinitely easier.

I love my mother for all the times she said absolutely nothing.

The times when I fell flat on my face, made a lousy judgment, and took a stand that I had to pay dearly for.

God knows I've made every mistake in the book, from the time

I bought a car with 87,000 miles on it to the time I made a decision to tell my boss, "I don't need this job."

Thinking back on it all, it must have been the most difficult part of mothering she ever had to do: knowing the outcome, yet feeling she had no right to keep me from charting my own path.

I thank her for all her virtues, but mostly for never once having said, "I told you so."

Epilogue ✿❀✿❀

When the Good Lord was creating mothers He was into His sixth day of "overtime" when the angel appeared and said, "You're doing a lot of fiddling around on this one."

And the Lord said, "Have you read the spec on this order?"

She has to be completely washable, but not plastic.

Have 180 movable parts. . . . all replaceable.

Run on black coffee and leftovers.

Have a lap that disappears when she stands up.

Have a kiss that can cure anything from a broken leg to a disappointed love affair.

And have six pairs of hands.

The angel shook her head slowly and said, "Six pairs of hands . . . not possible."

"It's not the hands that are causing me problems," said the Lord. "It's the three pairs of eyes that mothers have to have."

"That's on the standard model?" asked the angel.

The Lord nodded. "One pair that see through closed doors when she asks, 'What are you kids doing in there?' when she already knows. Another here in the back of her head that see what she shouldn't, but what she has to know, and of course the ones here in front that can look at a child when he goofs and reflect, 'I understand and I love you' without so much as uttering a word."

"Lord," said the angel, touching His sleeve gently, "come to bed. Tomorrow . . ."

"I can't," said the Lord, "I'm so close to creating something so close to myself. Already I have one who heals herself when she is sick . . . can feed a family of six on one pound of hamburger . . . and can get a nine-year-old to stand under a shower."

The angel circled the model of The Mother very slowly. "It's too soft," she sighed.

"But tough," said the Lord excitedly. "You cannot imagine what this Mother can do or endure."

"Can it think?"

"Not only think, but it can reason and compromise," said the Creator.

Finally, the angel bent over and ran her fingers across the cheek. "There's a leak," she pronounced. "I told you you were trying to put too much into this model. You can't ignore the stress factor."

The Lord moved in for a closer look and gently lifted the drop of moisture to his finger where it glistened and sparkled in the light.

"It's not a leak," He said. "It's a tear."

"A tear?" asked the angel. "What's it for?"

"It's for joy, sadness, disappointment, compassion, pain, loneliness, and pride."

"You are a genius," said the angel.

The Lord looked somber. "I didn't put it there."

About the Author

ERMA BOMBECK, who used to talk to herself a lot, is the author of a thrice-weekly humor column, "At Wit's End," for 900 newspapers throughout the world. It is read by an estimated 31 million people.

Erma's career began in Dayton, Ohio, where she was born, raised, and educated. As a copy girl for the *Dayton Journal Herald*, she wrote obituaries and the weather forecast (her first bit of fiction). After five years with the women's department, she retired to stay at home and raise three children. In 1965, her column on domesticity was syndicated.

A graduate of the University of Dayton, Erma is the author of seven books, including *At Wit's End, "Just Wait Till You Have Children of Your Own!"* (with Bill Keane), and *I Lost Everything in the Post-Natal Depression*.

She was named to the list of the Twenty-Five Most Influential Women in America by *The World Almanac* in 1979, 1980, 1981, 1982, 1984, and 1985.

Erma holds twelve honorary doctorates, is a member of the Society of Professional Journalists, and was appointed by President Carter to serve on the President's Advisory Committee for Women when the committee was formed in 1978.

For the last ten years she has been a regular on ABC's *Good Morning, America*.

Erma is married to Bill Bombeck. They have three children and make their home in Paradise Valley, Arizona.

Her hobby is dust.